**RED CHINA'S
FIGHTING HORDES**

中國紅軍

A realistic account of the Chinese Communist Army by a U.S. Army officer, who gained his intimate knowledge of this huge, incongruous force the hard way.

RED CHINA'S FIGHTING HORDES

By Lt. Col. Robert B. Rigg
United States Army

GREENWOOD PRESS, PUBLISHERS
WESTPORT, CONNECTICUT

Drawings are by the Author

Copyright 1951, by The Military Service Publishing Company

All rights reserved

Originally published in 1951
by The Military Service Publishing Company,
Harrisburg, Pennsylvania

Reprinted with the permission
of Stackpole Books

First Greenwood Reprinting 1971

Library of Congress Catalogue Card Number 70-138177

ISBN 0-8371-5634-3

Printed in the United States of America

*To my wife and to my mother,
who encouraged the creation
of this volume and lent
objectivity to its prose*

PREFACE

Somewhere in General Lin Piao's headquarters is a book belonging to me. I do not know whether this particular book has been translated into Chinese by Lin Piao's staff, but if it has, General Lin may be reading Volume III of *Lee's Lieutenants*. The Red general of Manchuria captured one of my prized books, but the score is even. I have "captured" Lin Piao's small book on *Short Attack* and have reproduced portions of it here. I believe this is the first time that any significant portions of the Red general's famed text have been published in English.

No single volume could completely describe Red China's army. My object here is to characterize the army, its weaknesses, its strengths, its men and commanders, and above all to record its state of military transition. I recognize that any text on a subject as gigantic and complex as this one will suffer from inadequacies.

The American observers who have been with the Chinese Communists in Yenan and other regions are many. Those US Army officers who dealt with the Chinese Communists during the trying peace efforts of General George C. Marshall, make up a group which, I believe, know the Communists exceedingly well. I hope that they will find a way to record some of their experiences and observations. My foundation for speaking with some authority on this subject lies in the circumstances of being shot at by the Chinese here described, marching within their ranks for several hundred miles, and, of course, being imprisoned and tried by them in 1947. In the campaigns of the China Civil War, I saw the Red Chinese at close range. This has given me some basis on which to gather and judge new source material for inclusion in this text. The Red Army I saw a few years ago has undergone some changes. I believe that the text to follow has kept up with these changes, and will indicate a few of those to come.

Robert B. Rigg

ACKNOWLEDGMENTS

One of the rarest finds, in source material hard to obtain, was a group of photographs of the Chinese general staffs. For these, and for most of the original Chinese and Japanese source material I am greatly indebted to Dr. Mary C. Wright, Curator, Chinese Collection of the Hoover Institute and Library, and to her husband, Professor Arthur F. Wright of Stanford University. Dr. Roy P. McNair was most helpful in directing me to Chinese source material and his criticism lent direction and emphasis to the final text. Colonel David D. Barrett and Colonel Morris B. DePass generously made similar contributions.

Lieutenant General Elwood R. Quesada found time to discuss points at issue on the Chinese Reds. His interrogations directed me to answer more fully the broader questions and issues.

Certain files of the History of Executive Headquarters were made available through the kindness of Charles F. Romanus, Office of Military History, Department of the Army. Vital up-to-date data were secured through the kind services of Dr. Arthur W. Hummel, Chief of the Division of Orientalia, Library of Congress.

Lieutenant General Sun Li-jen, Commander-in-Chief of the Nationalist Ground Forces and Supreme Commander of Taiwan Defense, has rendered this book more valuable by his 1951 letters of analysis to me. His other contributions began in 1946, when I was with his army in the China Civil War.

I was fortunate to benefit by one of the most thorough translations ever given Mao Tse-tung's works. Colonel Samuel B. Griffith, USMC, generously offered me his translation of Yu Chi Chan; and Major J. A. Pounds, III, editor and Publisher of the *Marine Corps Gazette*, granted copyright permission for publication of selected portions of the material.

Grateful acknowledgment is due Major General Robert H. Soule, O. Edmund Clubb, Lt. Col. Wing F. Jung, Lt. Col. Roland

M. Gleszer, Lt. Col. Edwin H. Garrison, Randolph V. Zander, Thomas N. Berdeen, Ralph A. Elliot, Lt. Col. John E. Beebe, Jr., Major John W. Collins, III, Captain Thomas R. Mitman, Henry R. Lieberman, and Captain Robert F. Phillips. Colonel Joseph I. Greene, Editor of the *Combat Forces Journal,* granted permission to use some of my material which the *Journal* had published. Mrs. Evelyn Fass, of the US Army Library in The Pentagon, rendered outstanding assistance in much of the research. Others can recognize their helpful contributions.

To all, I render a salute of sincere thanks.

RBR

CONTENTS

			Page
CHAPTER	1.	THE SWELLING HORDE	1
		Expendable Rabble	1
		The Army Creates a "Cause"	6
		The PLA Fears Fire Power and Bayonets	9
		The Army Is Not Modern	10
		China's Red Army Is Hard Up	12
CHAPTER	2.	THE HIERARCHY IN THE PALACE	19
		Sired by Brutality	19
		Commanders and Commissars	21
		Commander Chu Teh Demands Sacrifice	25
		General Lin Piao Is Bitter	27
		Liu Po-cheng Is Mobile and Elusive	31
		Militarist Su Yu Shows Promise	33
		Nieh Jung-chen Has Breadth	35
		Chou Pao-chung Typifies the Average	36
		"War lord" Chen Yi Is a Roughneck	38
		Peng Te-huai Believes in Manpower	40
		Gangster Ho Lung Is Brutal	43
		Huang Yi-feng Is a Nasty Commissar	44
		Chou En-lai Influences Strategy	45
		Mao Tse-tung Doesn't Fear A-Bombs	48
		The High Command Still Needs Education	55
		What Makes a Red General?	56
CHAPTER	3.	THE WEB AND TENTACLES OF ORGANIZATION	62
		Red Army Strength Today	62
		The Division Slice Is Low	64
		The Army Controls and Dominates the Nation	66
		The PLA Staff Is Seeking Final Foundation	71
		The Armies Vary in Size and Character	74
		Modernized Guerrilla Columns	77
		The First Field Army—Almost Last in Importance	79
		The Second Field Army Has a Half-Blind Commander	83

	Page
The Third Field Army Has an Unfulfilled Mission	86
The Fourth Field Army Is Changing Complexion	89
The Fifth Field Is the Mystery Army	94
Is the Mongol Army Worth Its Forage?	96
New Arms Enter the Army	98

CHAPTER 4. MEN OF THE OCHRE HORDES 104
    The Gentle Art of Sadism 104
    Red Soldiers, Run of the Mill 106
    Indoctrination—Always Indoctrination 113
    The Life Is Hard and the Pay Is Poor 116
    Background of the Red Soldier 124
    The Conscription of Volunteers 127
    Not All the Soldiers Are Given Land 129
    Women Also Serve, and Sometimes Fight 131
    What Makes the Red Soldier a Good Fighter? 133
    Propaganda Pays Off 135
    Vigor and Drive—While Winning 138
    The Soldier As He Is Today 139
    A New Soldier Generation Is in the Making 140

CHAPTER 5. AN ILLITERATE ARMY BEGINS FORMAL TRAINING 143
    Teaching the Soldier to Read and Write 143
    The Army Speaks Many Languages 147
    The Labor Pains of Military Training 149
    Military Training in the Lower Units 152
    Military Instructors 155
    Health and the Soldier 157
    The Soldiers Learn the Trade by Ear 158
    Guerrilla Training 159
    Military Academies Mold Men Politically ... 160
    The Communist Cultivation of "Beets" and "Radishes" 165

CHAPTER 6. MOB MOBILITY AND WINNING TACTICS 172
    Mobility Is Measured by the Foot 172
    Ambush! 176

		Page
	How Orders Are Transmitted	177
	Chinese Tactics Differ from Ours	178
	Basic Military Principles Are Few	179
	The Ten Military Principles	180
	The Ten Principles As Applied in Korea	182
	Tactics Are Flexible	185
	Mao Tse-tung's Military Concepts	186
	Armies Can Disappear	190
	Wait and See Tactics in Korea	195
	Human Waves and Strong Points	197
	How Lin Piao Views Command and Combat	201
	What Is the Soviet Influence?	207
CHAPTER 7.	GONGS, BUGLES, AND BANNERS	210
	The Trojan Horse Technique	210
	The Battles Are Noisy; the Small Tactics Tricky	213
	The People's Army Versus the People	217
	"The Quality of Mercy"	220
	Guerrillas May Rise Again in Numbers	221
	Red Psychological Warfare—Good or Bad?	228
	Prisoners Are Judged and Treated Unevenly	236
CHAPTER 8.	FOUNDATION OF VICTORY	241
	The PLA's "Plan to Liberate Asia"	241
	Manchuria Upset the Balance	244
	Loot and Pillage	245
	"Liberators" of Manchuria	248
	Into the Red China Maw Went Manchurians, Japanese, Koreans	249
	The Fight for Manchuria	252
	Blue Strategy Loses to Red Tactics	255
	The Realistic Fu Tso-yi	261
	The Weakness of Chiang Kai-shek	264
	Factors in the Nationalists' Defeat	265
	How the PLA Absorbed the Defeated Nationalists	272
	Sino-Korean Conflicts and Cooperation	278
CHAPTER 9.	SHOESTRING LOGISTICS	281
	Rifles and Rice; Mud and Sweat	281
	Keeping Manpower and Logistics in Balance	282

			Page
		The Peasant-Powered Army	285
		The Wounded Die Needlessly Because Medical Service Is Poor	290
		Fighters Who Farm	294
		Munitions Production Is Insignificant	296
		Bottlenecks Limit and Inhibit Military Massing	298
CHAPTER 10.		MAO TSE-TUNG'S CARPETS OF DEAD	302
		The Soviets Arrive	302
		The Phony Invasion of Tibet	305
		The Amphibious Technique Is Terrible	308
		How the Supreme Commander of Taiwan Evaluates the PLA	316
		The Future Pattern in Indo-China	318
		Air Force—the Reluctant Dragon	320
		Korea Shows Up Red Deficiencies	326
Appendix	I.	AN OUTLINE MAP OF CHINA	329
Appendix	II.	THE MORE PROMINENT GENERALS OF THE CHINESE RED ARMY	330
Appendix	III.	REPORT ON CHINESE COMMUNIST ACTIVITIES, 5 FEBRUARY 1946, BY AN UNRRA REPRESENTATIVE IN MANCHURIA	340
Appendix	IV.	BASIS FOR ESTABLISHMENT OF THE ARMED FORCES OF RED CHINA	343
Appendix	V.	CHINESE COMMUNIST GUERRILLA UNIT TABLES OF ORGANIZATION AND EQUIPMENT	344
INDEX			347

Chapter 1

THE SWELLING HORDE

Expendable Rabble

I can never forget that dead soldier's eye. It was a small symbol, insignificant perhaps, yet it drew focus to the body which, half submerged in the Grand Canal, rested on several other rotting corpses.

Here in the sunset the medieval wall of Tsining cast a long shadow over the canal which provided a moat around part of the city—a moat completely filled with the bodies of Chinese Communist soldiers. The glazed eye of one soldier looked at the city he and several thousand others had tried hard to capture. Across the moat bamboo ladders still clung to the high masonry of the huge wall, and the backs of the dead still evidenced the muddy footprints of those who had crossed to the ladders on the bodies of their comrades. The dead were not mere stepping stones, but a solid bridge of human flesh resting on an even greater number of Red soldiers. You could cross without wetting your feet. This was the wake of the Chinese Communist Army as I saw it in 1947. It is again laying new carpets of its own dead.

How long can it keep going at the expense of excessive casualties? Will it ever crumble as did the North Korean Army? What makes a Red Chinese soldier die with less hesitation than those of other nationalities? This oriental army poses many questions, the answers to which must be learned and studied if we are finally to halt its aggression, not alone in Korea but elsewhere.

This hostile force is on the verge of its greatest power. Its leaders have secret plans for other parts of Asia. This is an Asiatic army of many contrasts. No one, including its commander-in-chief, has seen its entirety. It is made up of some men who have served the colors of two other armies foreign to the cause of Communism.[1] Half the army's high leaders have not attended school beyond the first ten grades. Some of its old officers and multitudes of its men cannot read or write. Hundreds of thousands of Red Chinese soldiers are today working longer at labor in factories and on farms than they are in military training. Above all, it is an army that calls forth obedience unto death from men who only a few years ago surrendered easily in masses.

As their bullets smack the earth around you, the impression is gained that these men of the ochre hordes are poor rifle marksmen. But turn your field glasses slowly to the right and left, for it is there you must watch. The danger is not always forward. For a while you may feel secure in avoiding their bullets from the front, then suddenly you sense wherein this army is so strong. You are fired on from the rear! These uniformed Chinese move, and move fast, to ambush and to outflank. This is the army that has captured more men than it has ever killed or wounded.

The army has its sadistic side, of which you might have been victim had you been wounded and crowded body-deep into one of the United Nations' trucks trying to escape the Chinese near Chongjin Reservoir in the bitter cold of December 1950. You could not tell of your impressions of these Chinese, for they shot you as you lay groaning in a truck bottom. Some they did not shoot; the Chinese were short of ammunition, so they whacked open some gasoline drums and splashed the fuel over the compact, crowded masses of men who could not muster the energy to move away. Then the Chinese pitched hand grenades into the trucks

---

[1] As Chinese Nationalists and as Japanese puppets.

and danced and yelled like wild Indians.[2] Yet at this same hour, other Chinese soldiers were treating their American prisoners kindly.

It is a confusing army to view from behind its own lines. As you move back through their miles of marching men you wonder what gives such sure impetus to the companies and divisions. What real organizational structure, if any, holds these irregularly equipped and motley uniformed men together? Heavily loaded horse-carts vie for the road with modern trucks. A slaughtered pig is lashed to the outside of a T-34 tank. A dozen soldiers, with carrying poles on their shoulders, shuffle at the rear of an infantry company. One of them carries a big, blackened kettle. An overloaded horse cart, leaking a sickly yellow dust from square boxes, tries to get through the mud. The cart is pulled by eight horses, yet there are no reins—just a long whip that the dismounted driver cracks continually. Everything moves. Equipment rattles, but not with regularity common to modern armies. Ahead of you a soldier drops a canteen. Why does he not pick it up? As you pass by you see it is just a canvas sack of broken glass. Someone barks an order. You turn to see who it is, and then you sense one of the facets of this peculiar Chinese army. None of the officers wear any distinctive insignia. Every time you speak to an officer you have to inquire as to his rank; even then you get the unsatisfactory reply of "commander"—or, more often if you are a foreigner in these hostile ranks, "commissar!"

Where are the nerve centers of this army in the field? You have a most difficult time trying to spot the command posts. This is the army without formality or gestures. You come upon three serious looking officers sitting cross-legged before a soiled and wrinkled Japanese map that is spread on the ground. A tommy-gunner lurks nearby. He suspiciously scans the terrain and challenges, by eye or signal, those who approach. Dismounted mes-

---

[2] The tragedy of this ghastly carnage was told the author by Lt. Col. Robert D. Denchfield, who pieced together the circumstances under which his brother, Lt. Raymond C. Denchfield, was listed as MIA (missing in action) in Korea in December 1950. Survivors of the 31st and 32d Regiments (7th Division) stated that the Chinese brutality even extended to Chinese wounded who were bayoneted and shot.

senger traffic flows in and out of the hollow where the map is spread. Suddenly there is a written message from the rear and as the officer reads it you notice that the message is written on the back side of an old wall poster. A finger points to a symbol on the map. A word or two is exchanged and two of the officers look questionably at the third. The commissar nods. Dirt is brushed off the map and the document is folded and stuffed into a worn leather case. The three men rise. The restless thug with the tommy gun asks, *"Tso-ah?"* Assent is nodded. The battalion command post moves forward quietly and without fanfare.

You come to recognize a higher headquarters by the number of field telephone wires which, hastily strung, lead into a farmhouse. The army commander squats on some sacks of rice while a subordinate yells into a US field telephone, of which this army has thousands. (Someone is always coughing and spitting in these austere headquarters.) The paraphernalia of command post operation is simple, but functional. Tea and tea cups are the only items of "luxury." They are always in evidence. Over pale tea, battle decisions are made which will send thousands of men to death. These commanders know the measure of their men. No one doubts obedience. Political indoctrination has insured that.

Back in 1948 you might have encountered the famous Chinese Communist officer who now commands a field army[3]—an army almost twice as large as General Patton's in World War II. This officer has but one eye. At his CP he opened a tin box and took out what appeared to be two Chinese scrolls; but as the paper was unrolled it was seen to contain cobwebs of gray and black lines highlighted by symbols in red ink which marked the major towns. Roll by roll, a large map was hung on the wall. The one-eyed man in this command post was General Liu Po-cheng, commander of the Second Field Army. His, perhaps, is still the most mobile command post of all the field armies. He has fled too many enemy commanders not to know the value of a simple and mobile CP. Late in the China Civil war his CP could be packed up in

---

[3] Red China's army is divided into field armies, group-armies, armies, and divisions.

one hour and the maps, radios, and telephones loaded on a few horses or carried in two carts. General Liu Po-cheng's command post was rarely established in a town or village. Enemy fighters and bombers gave up trying to find it. Known as the "One-eyed Dragon," General Liu now commands a field army of 360,000 men, a force as mobile and elusive as his command post.

This is the army as one would see portions of it behind the front. You cannot judge this giant military force on its ragged and irregular interior lines alone. The view must be balanced by mention of other characteristics. There is a sense of the ridiculous in some of the army's efforts, yet at times it achieves remarkable efficiency. Its elements are often clumsy, yet some show adroitness. It trains and carefully nurses most of its soldiers to a good level of combat efficiency, then wastes thousands of them in useless sacrifice and slaughter; because, first, it can afford to, and second, a great portion of its officers are lacking in the tactical and strategic skill of modern war.

The Army of Communist China is formally titled the Chinese People's Liberation Army (PLA). It has a strength of 2,650,000, is organized into five field armies; it is supported by the people's militia, which is several million strong. This is a military force without typewriters or adding machines. The army must count and compute its numbers and supplies on the abacus. For all of its giant size, the PLA gets by with a very low minimum of paper work. It has to, for several reasons. First, the reports and records which an army must keep, are done mainly by hand and brush. Although some mimeograph machines are used, the stencils are hand-lettered. Second, the number of men who can read and write Chinese characters is rather small. This army, the PLA, exists with a minimum of administrative paperwork and a maximum of propaganda literature.

Led by fanatics and corrected and guided by commissars, the PLA is rising from an ill-armed rabble to a fairly well-organized and formidable military machine. Elements of this army have been engaged in almost continuous combat since 1 August 1927, when the army was born in blood. The PLA is the only army of modern years that has completely equipped itself from captured materiel. However hard it may be accurately to generalize about this army, it can be safely said that the PLA has a greater variety and conglomeration of weapons and equipment than any other military force in the world today. This is the un-uniform force that stands on the verge of great reorganization and purge. The PLA assumed its present form in 1949, and has since decked itself out with an air force and navy, plus some mechanization.

The PLA is laying claim to many firsts, but here are some facts which its propaganda machine does not blare out. The PLA is the poorest educated army of the world's great military powers. The soldiers of South China cannot speak a language understandable to those of the North. The majority of PLA troops cannot read or write. Many of them never will.

This is the army that is proud of its tough, marching feet; yet an army of human material that lost much of its vaunted mobility when it invaded South China—for its nameless masses contracted athlete's foot on a large scale. For all of its earlier threats to invade Taiwan (Formosa), the PLA never made public the 60,000 casualties the Third Field Army suffered from liver fluke, contracted during amphibious training in the dirty waters around Shanghai. For all its claims to military excellence, the PLA never defeated *in battle* the whole of the Nationalist Army.

This oriental army of Communism has other serious weaknesses. For example, within the ochre drab of its millions of men are tens of thousands who are not loyal to the cause of Chinese Communism. The commissars in the Imperial Palace of Peking know this and are already executing officers and men. The great purge is in progress. Such blood letting puts the Red into Communism. The Red Army of China is not yet the formidable force that some paint it—but the Soviets are busily strengthening this army.

The Army Creates a "Cause"

It is a characteristic of Asiatics, particularly the Chinese, to be at their military best when they are succeeding. Combat troops of any nationality can be intoxicated by success, but Asiatics show an especial tendency—when elevated to the ranks of policemen, prisoner guards, military commanders or successful troops—to be exceedingly brutal and arrogant. Conversely, Chinese military morale sags on a more precipitous curve than most Western nationalities (including the Soviet) when military campaigning shows hopelessness.

It is difficult and dangerous to generalize in simple terms about the 450,000,000[4] people of China. There are exceptions to all gen-

U. S. Army Photo.

THE RED CHINESE SOLDIER KNOWS WHEN TO SURRENDER.
A worried Chinese Communist is interrogated by men of the 19th Regiment, 24th Infantry Division, in Korea.

eralities, but it can be said that the average Chinese soldier knows *when* to surrender. There comes a time when he will "break." That time may be after a prolonged period of military failures, or after violent strategical or tactical surprise. The North Koreans

---

[4] The 1948 census listed 463,493,418 people but this figure is regarded by American authorities as too high. The Communists claim China has a population of 475,000,000.

are a case in point. They fought with vigor and violence up to the time they were outflanked by the Inchon landings; then they collapsed, to surrender in droves. The Chinese Communist soldiers also are capable of uplifting their hands in large masses. Should the cease fire negotiations fail and if the UN Forces in Korea keep up their destruction of PLA units on the scale of the first half of 1951, there is good chance that the late spring of 1952 could see mass surrenders of Chinese Red troops and the subsequent collapse of the Red armies in Korea. The effect of heavy casualties on Mao Tse-tung, Chu Teh, Lin Piao, and other Red leaders should not be overestimated, but the effect on PLA soldier morale bears watching.

On what is the Chinese soldier sustained? By tradition, the bearing of arms has long been one of the most looked-down-upon professions in China. This era has just passed. The lot of the Chinese soldier and his standing in the nation is improving. But in what war, in all of China's turbulent years of recent history, has the average soldier had a real interest, or felt that he was fighting for a cause? During the war lord era Chinese troops fought indifferently; the victor of one year was the prisoner of another. The soldiers were not, in large numbers, volunteers. Against the Japanese there was some semblance of a crusade, for there was an invader to combat. Here was where the Chinese Communists built their following. By drumming their cause, the Reds gave the soldier a feeling of a personal need to fight. Militarily, the Communists fed the individual soldier the intoxicant of minor successes. By raids and small scale action, the Red soldier lived in an atmosphere of monthly military achievement.

The Nationalist soldiers, on the other hand, were committed in heavy masses and too often were ill led and always poorly supported. The government soldiers met frustration, for while their units were ostensibly big and strong, they were weak technically and they were rarely spectacularly victorious. Furthermore, unlike his Red brother in arms, the government soldier was not given the propaganda treatment. No one bothered to associate the individual government soldier with a cause. In this alone the Communist have provided a lesson for Chinese military men to come; for in the words of Red General Peng Te-huai, "Fulfillment of any military plan depends primarily on the courage, self confidence, fighting power and esprit de corps of both officers and men. To heighten these qualities is the purpose of political work in our armies."

The Red Chinese soldier is sustained and encouraged by a variety of factors, one of which is presently dominant—hate! "Teach the soldiers to hate!" That is the first step in the political education of Chinese Red soldiers. Help the men recall the exploitation and oppression they have suffered in the old society. So reads an official military publication[5] of Peking which goes on ". . . this kind of political education enables them to develop a deep hatred for their enemies."

Although the Communists generate some hate among their troops, the soldiers would like heavier guns and greater all-round fire power to offset the Air Force napalm (incendiary) bombs, Turkish bayonets, and the heavy fire power of US units. These have put great fear into Chinese soldiers' minds.

The PLA Fears Fire Power and Bayonets

Chinese soldiers traditionally have feared bayonet steel, and the Chinese Reds have never before felt the horror of napalm. These troops can be panicked much easier than the more educated Western soldiers, for rumor has more substance in oriental ranks than in Western. The impact of tactical surprises can produce mass surrenders. Over and beyond the physical damage atomic bombs might have on Chinese field installations, the *fear* a few of these dread bombs would generate in the ranks is enough to precipitate the surrender of masses. The psychological effects would outweigh the destructive or purely military effects.

This army, which has achieved so many victories—like that in Tibet—on a basis of generating fear in enemy ranks, is itself vulnerable to the same technique. The Chinese People's Liberation

---

[5] *The Chinese People's Liberation Army*, published by the Foreign Language Press, Peking, 1950.

Army does not fear atomic bombs, because it has never felt or seen one. Its ignorance makes it brave.

The Army Is Not Modern

In 1950 this army was termed modern; yet this is the army that never used tanks until 1946, nor military aircraft until 1949. The PLA is not modern, except in size. It cannot be called modern merely because it possesses some jet aircraft, any more than China can be called modern for possessing the telephone and telegraph. The army is not modern because it has a few modern implements of combat, any more than China itself is modern because of its railroads and radios—while its homes lack plumbing and electricity. China has veneered itself with borrowed devices of the modern era, without ever developing mechanically within that era. Just so the Red Army has captured and borrowed tanks, motor vehicles, and airplanes, without ever having a real ordnance corps or a related industrial establishment.

The Chinese Red Army is simply entering its first period of modernization; for a few years to come it will, in combat, operate along the conventional lines of its immediate past.

Like the raggle taggle Red Army that emerged victorious from the Russian Civil War, the Communist Army of China seeks to be a *new* army. The PLA has emerged from its drab guerrilla cocoon of the anti-Japanese and Civil War days and is now flexing its wings. These sometimes look modern, and they show promise of being so, but the Red butterfly is clumsy. It still carries with it the remnants of its former life.

Mao Tse-tung and his army officers recognize the problems at hand. They are hard realists who have the reputation of biting off only the amount they can chew and digest. In 1947 they still visualized the China Civil War in terms of five more years of fighting. Then, sooner than they had anticipated, the Red militarists won the war. They had immediate problems with their giant army, which they sought to convert to a modern force. The very sorting of the hodge-podge of captured military equipment was a problem in itself, not to mention its allocation to troop units on an organized basis. The Chinese Communists, knowing that for a long period to come China could not manufacture the heavier items of military materiel, looked to the Soviet Union for tanks, artillery, and airplanes. Chinese soldiers would have to be trained to operate such items as Russian T-34 tanks and SU-76 self-propelled guns —items modern to the satellite armies of North Korea and elsewhere, but generally obsolete or surplus now in Soviet Russia's war machine.

Victory over Chiang Kai-shek brought multiple issues. There was the mainland's great land space to occupy, the invasions of Formosa and Tibet to prepare for, guerrilla uprisings to cope with, captured Nationalist troops to be reorganized and integrated into the PLA. The Communists had captured tanks they did not know how to operate or maintain. South China brought disease to the Red troops who had lived all their lives in the North. Training had to be more standardized, and military texts had to be printed. Differences in dialect confronted the army as it sought to induct men from the newly conquered regions. These and many other problems arose in numbers that called for plans, solutions, and decisions. The PLA's officers had their hands full, but their hearts were hopeful. They were building a *new* army from the already strong fiber of the old.

General Chu Teh, Commander-in-Chief of the PLA, recognized that the complexion of his army needed freshening with new men, and that the integrated Nationalist soldiers needed more political training. This move to feed better manpower into the PLA began in 1947-48 when, well up in its strength and increasingly victorious, it announced that it was selecting soldiers with greater attention to physical condition and political reliability. Above all, the soldiers had to be politically indoctrinated with great thoroughness. The manpower problem of the PLA was not a simple one. Chu Teh and his commissars knew the army contained many men who were very anxious to go home. But how many could safely be released? Junior officers were needed in numbers, and the system of military academies had to be expanded.

Then came the North Korean aggression in June 1950. The

Chinese waited, but shifted troops back to Manchuria. Confident that their's was the invincible army, they attacked the UN forces. Initially intoxicated by successes, they woke up, in 1951, to the fact that certain factors in the wars they had fought were missing in Korea. Landspace for maneuver was not there, and the support of a friendly people, on which the PLA has so long relied, was absent. Fire power, in a volume they had never before seen, killed Chinese masses in the PLA's first campaign on non-Chinese soil.

Thus, the Korean conflict, having failed to produce an early victory for the Chinese Reds, immediately slowed up modernization of the PLA and postponed the creation of a *new* army.

The Red hierarchy is up to its neck in the mud and blood of a war it cannot win. It cannot win because the PLA is not yet a modern army and the higher leaders don't know how to fight a modern war, especially one on a peninsula. With almost unlimited manpower for offense, the Red leaders miss the great land space which has helped them so greatly in the past. Korea is a new military experience for Red Chinese generals who, although they are excellent leaders of men, are being out-generalled.

China's Red Army Is Hard Up

The "Year of the Tiger" officially began on 17 February 1950. Exactly one month later there appeared in a Chinese Communist magazine a remarkable confession by a high military commissar. Under the title, "Report on the Tasks of the South China Armed Forces for 1950," [6] Commissar Tan Cheng let his officers, enlisted men, and the Chinese public know that all was not well with the great Chinese People's Liberation Army. Commissar Tan began by saying, "This is a financially difficult year. Steps must be taken to tide over this difficult period."

Chinese troops are accustomed to difficult years, but to the Red soldier viewing the Civil War as practically over and anticipating some measure of reward for his long and arduous service, these words of Commissar Tan fell on soldier ears with the impact of deep disappointment. "Soldier marriages are to be very limited in

---

[6] *New China Monthly,* 17 March 1950.

THE GROWTH OF THE RED ARMY OF COMMUNIST CHINA

(*Indicates Communist Title)

FIRST TITLE: "The Worker's and Peasant's Red Army*," 1927.
RETITLED: "Eighth Route Army," following Japan's attack in 1937.
TITLE ADDED: "New Fourth Army," for the extra force created in 1938.
RENAMED: "Chinese People's Liberation Army*," at the beginning of the China Civil War in 1946.
WARS FOUGHT: Civil War (Agrarian Revolutionary War*), 1927-37.
Anti-Japanese War*, 1937-45.
China Civil War (War of Liberation*), 1946-50.
Intervention in Korea, 1950-.
FAMOUS FACTS: Made military history with the "Long March," 1934-35.
The bulk of the PLA's generals lack formal education.
Army grew from a guerrilla body to a formal force.
Crossed Yangtze River in 1949 without modern bridging equipment.
GREATEST ASSETS: Unlimited manpower for offense.
Great land space for defense.
Marching ability and general endurance of troops.
GREATEST LIABILITIES: Logistically weak; possesses conglomeration of weapons.
Lacks an adequate air force and navy for its mass of infantry.
Still in process of reorganization and modernization.
GENERALSHIP: High officers are great leaders but lack skill at *modern* war.
Generals demand highest sacrifices; ignore losses.
MORALE: Good; but certain unit elements are subject to deterioration.
FLAG: Bright red with yellow star and three-symbol designation of "August One," the birth date of the army.
VICTORIOUS BACKGROUND: Survived to harass the Japanese. Enlarged on a guerrilla basis, to capture more Chinese Nationalist troops than it ever killed. Never faced modern fire power until Korea in 1951.

number," said Tan. This meant that marriages were out for the majority! "Furloughs are to be cut to the bare minimum." To cut home even sharper, Tan directed that Sunday, the Red soldier's only day of relaxation and freedom, be occupied with military duties. Furthermore, not only was the Chinese soldier to indulge in farming, so as to produce a large portion of his food, but also he was ordered by Commissar Tan to save a ration at regular intervals *by missing a meal or two!* These and other stringent measures of Communist austerity were applied to at least one quarter of the entire PLA, and possibly more. This is a harsh departure from the rewarding promises the Red militarists gave their men to encourage the winning of the China Civil War. Now the Chinese soldiers are having to die in a new war. They don't like it!

The Chinese commissars are now "division-slice" conscious. According to Commissar Tan, they are searching and purging the military ranks so as to produce an army that is cheaper to maintain. Here is part of what they are up to.

China is a land of bodyguards. The Red war lords use them extensively. I recall General Lin Piao's headquarters in Harbin, where carefully selected soldier-thugs guarded the moves and gestures of all generals. Lin Piao had several bodyguards, and in 1947 he even lent one of his personal protectors to escort and drive Major John W. Collins and me to our point of release from capture on the Sungari Front. This bodyguard was not only a walking arsenal, he also was a skilled marksman from among the harsh and brutal breed of handy gunmen China so well produces. General Chou Pao-chung is another who moved, even in combat, with the protection of private pistoleers. But the Chinese efficiency experts—the commissars—are now calling for a change. They are demanding that bodyguards be eliminated. The high officers do not like this, even though the commissars point out that such men are unnecessary now that the main KMT (Kuomintang) threat has been removed. The commissars are correcting the high officers' "bad habits," pointing to the overhead costs of bodyguard soldiers. But the commissars are not giving up their own bodyguards—yet.

Do Chinese Communist officers pad the payrolls with non-existent soldiers? Yes; this was recently done on a scale to warrant some concern, and the commissars are fighting the practice. According to Commissar Tan, it is now a regular practice for the commissars and higher officers to check physically the number of men in subordinate units against the written strength reports. The junior officers are said to be most guilty of padding the ranks, a sure sign that officer pay is inadequate.

These may seem to be small matters, but they are not. The army is large and the multiplication of individual concerns affects troop morale. Several hundred thousand soldiers are unhappy because they cannot get married. Millions are watching the contents of their rice bowls daily, and when they are told that they must sometimes skip a meal to save for the nation, elements of doubt and dissension revolve in their minds. Casualties have multiplied in Korea, but the Red medical service is in inverse ratio to the wounded. Among the nameless masses in the PLA there are smoldering thoughts which the commissars are working daily to suppress with propaganda and indoctrination.

But the higher officers have other worries. Their causes of concern extend geographically from Korea to Taiwan. Neither place has been militarily conquered, and in between those extremes there are some serious internal problems. Supply has been inefficient and it has become more expensive than the Red officers ever anticipated. Depots and stores are now being organized under more centralized control, and equipment is being doled out on a "need to use" basis, with only the units engaged in combat getting most of what they need. Inventories are being laboriously checked against stocks, and the excess materiel and trophies, of which many units were so proud, are now being taken away and stored or redistributed with guarded care. But this is only a sidelight on the concerns of the commanders. Korea is the primary worry, for the Reds are not winning, and the high command is at a loss for a solution to the problem. The Peking war lords are embarrassed because their strategy has stalemated; and their underlings, the army and division commanders, are worried because they feel that the Peking hierarchy may regard their implementation and execution of plans as poor and professionally unsuccessful. Field grade officers who see and feel the combat losses more intimately, have two primary worries: first, what is wrong with a strategy that, for all the expenditure of men, does not win; and second, how long, in the face of overwhelming losses, can they, as regimental and battalion commanders, live or be able to hold their units to the line of the PLA's traditional obedience?

It has surprised some observers to see a few of our soldiers released from their prisoner of war status in Korea. This is not any sudden generosity on the part of the Chinese Reds. The word has gone out that too many prisoners are financial burdens.[7] For the first time in its history the Chinese Communist Army is having serious financial troubles. The financial burden of a large army was being felt even before the Reds aggressively launched their swelling hordes into Korea. The higher officers and the commissars are examining all PLA ranks for excess overhead, and a determined effort is being made to slash off the fat! The bodyguards are only a small example. Orders went out in 1950 to get rid of men who were not good soldier material. This is a separate effort from the purge which has political motives. Today men are being purged daily—not always shot for laziness or inefficiency, but released from the service. This applies to the militia as well. The regular army and the militia, bloated in numerical strength, are being "strengthened" by doses of laxative applied by the commissars, who see the need for increased efficiency and lower dollar cost. Reorganization of the People's Liberation Army has just begun.

The worried men in China are not all in the Army. Mao Tsetung's regime includes a group of civilian bureaucrats who, from the caves of Yenan, once had a plan for every contingency. Now they are harried little men who fumble over the production and expenditure figures of military weapons—weapons which they used to put in the category of "capture these from the enemy." Now these tea-drinking idealists have to reckon with the dollar costs of such items as jet aircraft, tanks, and big shells. Arsenals, to them, had been piddling shops where under-paid and over-

---

[7] Report on the Tasks of the South China Armed Forces for 1950,

THE SWELLING HORDE

worked coolies and technicians ground out simple weapons on foot-powered lathes. Now the arsenals are modern, intricate, and expensive—for they lie in the USSR, and with each delivery of big war machines comes a bill from the Soviet Union. The cash for the transaction can sometimes wait, but the abacus must be fingered and the astronomical totals recorded, for the exchange of goods (if not the settlements of cash) that will come later. These Chinese production "experts" and Red bureaucrats are startled at the money cost of big military items they now use, and of which they need more. The military budget, which rose so sharply in 1950 with just the *occupation* of China's land mass, is draining the Communist shackled nation even more than before.

On about 1 June 1951 some twelve hundred Chinese business men listened to speakers in a Peking hall. The speakers came from a newly created committee. One might term it an emergency committee. "We do not have enough planes, guns and other weapons," the *Committee to Resist the US and Aid Korea* said. ". . . we must speedily supply them ["volunteers" in Korea] with more warplanes, guns, tanks, antiaircraft guns, antitank guns and other weapons." This meeting began a nation-wide drive for funds, to buy more military materiel for the Korean war effort.[8] Even school children are being asked for money. The Communists are passing the collection plate at clubs as well. This money is being used to "purchase fighter plane, submachine guns, and small food packages to ease the supply problem in Korea." So worried is the Chinese Red hierarchy that this effort has become an all out mobilization of the home front. "Labor emulation campaigns" to raise production have been in effect since 1950.

Liao Cheng-chih, a Communist with a finger in almost every Red pie, led off the campaign after his return from an inspection trip to Korea in May 1951. As chief of the "Comfort Mission," [9]

---

[8] "Red China Pleads for More Output," the New York *Times*, 2 June 1951.
[9] *Wei lao tuan* or "Comfort Mission" is the Chinese Communist counterpart of a USO troop. They are not new, but renewed emphasis is being placed on those missions which include actors, musicians, poets and actresses. Before Liao's mission went to Korea, in April, the Chinese Reds had raised a sum almost equivalent to three million dollars in US currency, to "comfort" the Chinese in Korea. Shanghai, reportedly, donated 65 percent of the total fund.

Liao said the Chinese troops needed more fire power, medical supplies of all kinds, and food put up in packages, so that the front line troops wouldn't go hungry so often.[10] The same week that Liao spoke, Chinese troops were surrendering in Korea, crying *"fahn, fahn!"* (rice, rice) at the first moment of contact; while back of the Red lines more than 400 "Chinese people's delegates" of a Comfort Mission visited Red soldiers in an attempt to boost their morale. When a Communist leader like Liao or a commissar publicly states that there is trouble, we can usually believe it, for they do not like to voice such pronouncements.

The Soviets are giving away nothing. Some quarters may hold that, if China supplies the flesh and blood for Korea, Russia will donate the materiel. To believe this is to show ignorance of history. Russia has always billed the Chinese, and the Red Chinese are no exceptions. Cash may not be called for; a barter of goods is the most common transaction. This is what has worried the Chinese in Peking into taking up collections from school children and urging the businessmen to work and contribute. The gouging of the people has just begun. The cost of planes and large-caliber guns will require Chinese coolies to donate free working time, and all of China's people are going to feel heavier taxation. The Peking war lords and bureaucrats are seeking ways to sugar a very bitter tea for the people.

---

[10] The Official Chinese Communist News Agency.

Chapter 2

THE HIERARCHY IN THE PALACE

Sired by Brutality

"Out of every five old Communists, two are crazy and two others have tuberculosis." This was the saying in Peking after the "liberation." It is just about the truth.

The coughing and spitting is always noisily noticeable in the army's various headquarters. The present military leaders are not healthy for their years. They are too often irritable and impatient and always are hard for a foreigner to understand. The same applies to the political leaders. Really to understand these men, one must recognize their state of health. One event in history undermined their physical being and has since influenced their outlook—the famous "Long March."

No fat and sadistic war lords of China's history will ever be able to compete with the grisly record of the militaristic Chinese Communists now enthroned and on the brink of a full expression of armed power.

These men are brutal. They are spreading their theories of brutality to countless masses of uniformed robots. The Soviet revolutionists only had to struggle four years to gain their dominance. The Chinese Reds have fought viciously for more than twenty years to reach the confines of the Imperial Palace in Peking—and only now they are beginning to show their true intent. When you have fought, murdered, and killed men for a fixed purpose, enduring conflict for more than twenty years, the world is foolish to expect that you will suddenly lay aside your weapons and your aggressiveness.

The Red war lords of China have just edged up to their point of power. Look at the murderous purges now underway in China. Today's generation of generals in China will have more life and death impact on the world than any Chinese of the past or near future. No future generation of Chinese Communists will likely be as bitter as today's men of yesterday's "Long March" and long struggle. There will be no real compromise with these jingoists, who individually are more anti-American than any group of Soviet generals. The Red generals of China are graveyard fillers.

It is important that we learn more about the Chinese militarists, not only because of their hostile and belligerent attitude, but also because they dominate the Red rule in China and greatly influence Chinese foreign policy. Take, for example, the Red ambassadors who now occupy posts in several nations of the world. Are they civilians? There is General Huang Chen, ambassador to Hungary; General Ni Chih-liang, ambassador to North Korea; General Peng Ming-chih, ambassador to Poland; General Tan Hsi-lin, ambassador to Czechoslovakia; General Wang Yu-ping, ambassador to Rumania; General Yuan Chung-hsien, ambassador to India; and General Wu Hsiu-chuan, the arrogant Red representative who came in 1950 to the United Nations' headquarters.

Very obviously the military dominate diplomacy; but look at the internal scene. General Chen Yi, while commander of a field army, is also the dictator of Shanghai and a great region around it. Liu Po-cheng, and other field army commanders, occupy similar positions in other regions of China. There are reasons why army officers figure so importantly in China's governmental structure. The Communist's long struggle for power was military, producing many military leaders. Until, and even after, 1945 the Chinese Communist Party (CCP) had comparatively little territory to govern; the weight was placed on producing military leaders who could win the armed conflict.

The Chinese Communist Party emerged in 1948 with about 3,000,000 members. Then the Communists won the armed struggle and the territorial demand for governors, mayors, *hsien* [1] chiefs, and other officials, was greater than the available trained supply. Army officers, the only large class with any ruling experience, had to fill the crying need for administrators. The CCP was so hard-pressed for civil officials that it quickly trained thousands of left-wing students and put them to work. However, the Party had to count on *reliable* men for the higher positions, and here was where the military Communists really ascended to civilian power. As one reliable source concluded in 1946, "the most capable group in the Chinese Communist Party is, as a whole, their officers." [2] It is a large burden suddenly to take over the great land mass of China and govern it with the firm and brutal hand so necessary to the preservation of Communist power. Army men are now in the saddle, and will be for some time to come. The hierarchy in the palaces of Peking and elsewhere are men who have been in combat most of their lives. Another war does not intimidate them, nor does the threat of atomic bombs. They feel that they have the answers.

Commanders and Commissars

What is the outlook of these men who command armed millions? What are their views on strategy? Who are the strategists, and who will implement their strategic plans? Of leadership there is much; of generalship in modern warfare, there is little. Good guerrilla leaders are not necessarily good army group commanders. The Reds have many of the former and few of the latter, men who are capable of successful command of combined arms. Infantry commanders abound and they are very capable; but what Chinese Red general knows anything about armor, large masses of artillery, antiaircraft groupings, airborne troops,

---

[1] Chinese equivalent of county.
[2] *History of the Peiping Executive Headquarters,* Fourth Quarter, 1946, Department of the Army, Office of Military History.

amphibious armies, air force, or navy? Before 1949 no Red general in China ever had under his command in combat more than 60 tanks at one time. For all their excellence at fighting, the

> ### THE "LONG MARCH" WAS A RETREAT
>
> To fully understand the Chinese Communists it is essential to know about the famous "Long March,"—the Chinese Reds' great strategical retreat. In this epic of hardship, physical endurance, and death, tens of thousands of Chinese Reds died or were killed along the 25,000 *li* (about 8,300 miles) march—one of the longest military treks in modern history. Many of those who survived this retreat had become diseased; all were bitter. The trek began in October 1934 after the Chinese Communist forces had been militarily bested and forced to flee the region of their combat operations. The Red Chinese held long-range views of revolution; to carry them out, they sought a region from which they could continue their campaigns of resistance. They chose the Shensi Province area as their future base, but from the moment of their retreat the primary matter was survival. The military ease with which the Red Chinese columns passed through some of the war lord regions of China resulted from a combination of military force, bribery, local diplomacy (as in the case of tribesmen) and the "let them through" attitude on the part of certain provincial authorities who saw that if they stopped the Reds the Communists would settle locally to become their permanent opponents. The route of the march followed the general course illustrated in Appendix I, but there were many side excursions and counter-marches along that general route which ended in October 1935 in Shensi where the Reds established their capital at Yenan. Out of approximately 300,000 Red troops in 1934, only about 20,000 reached Shensi at the end of the "Long March."

field army commanders never defeated a formidable foe of armed and armored modernity. Let us not rate these men too highly. They have infantry, and it is in formidable quantity; they have men to waste in human waves; but the PLA is still unbalanced—although the Soviets are endeavoring to correct this.

The commissars actually do not run the Chinese Red Army. Some observers express the opinion that the commissars do rule and heavily influence the PLA. That is wrong. Too much Soviet history is being absorbed by those who are writing on the Chinese Army, without proper study of the PLA's own rise to power. Many people will disagree here, but my point is supported by the following facts.

The Red Army of Russia was welded out of a heterogenous mass of soldiers, sailors, cossacks, partisans, workers, and a variety of minorities—political and ethnic in origin. The Red Army of the Soviets was put together in a short space of time, amid a chaos of confusion and disintegrating morale. There was considerable blood letting at the time the army of the Soviets took military shape; consequently there was in the Party's mind a definite need for thought control, discipline, and purge. The Soviet commissars cemented the bricks together in solid mass, eliminating the misfits and controlling the ones which tended to loosen.

China's Red Army, on the other hand, has grown over a much longer period of time—amid war and turmoil, but on a solid regional basis. Elimination has not been mainly accomplished by purge, as in the early days of the Soviet Army. The very length of the Chinese Communist Party's struggle served to eliminate the weak and wayward and, in addition, bind more closely those who continued to hold aloft the Red banner. Trust in military men grew with their accomplishments. The commissars were always present, but they were occupied more in indoctrinating converts than in challenging the military decisions of commanders.

There developed another feature which places the PLA in a more advanced phase of history than that in which the Soviet Army stood when it first controlled all of Russia. The Red Chinese Army officers did not always have a full quota of troops to command, so they occupied a variety of posts in the interims between battles. When they lacked commands they acted as commissars. What has developed in China is a group of army, group-army, and field army commanders who are *both commanders and commissars*. Many present day PLA officers began as commissars and are now primarily commanders. The members of the hierarchy, therefore, are not as concerned in watching each other (although there is some of it) as the Soviets were. The Soviets borrowed many Tsarist officers to start out with, held them in control by commissars, and then, when the Soviets felt they had gained their military feet, discarded the old Imperial officers. The Chinese Reds, on the contrary, have developed their highest military talent over a long period. Their high ranking officers know each other intimately and they are not relying on old Nationalist officers as instructors in their war colleges, as the Soviets did.

This is why I maintain that the PLA is not primarily run by pure commissars. It is true that some defecting Nationalist generals were accepted into Red ranks with their commands; these men are closely watched. The commissars rule with a heavy hand, not so much in matters of high command as in matters of junior officer and troop conversion and indoctrination. Mao Tse-tung controls Chu Teh like a puppet on a string, and Chu controls his generals—if Mao does not beat him to it. China is ruled by political-militarists of the worst war lord type. The sooner this is recognized the better we will understand the government that kills our own men.

The Red Communist generals cannot be called strategists because the PLA doesn't know military strategy. If we conceive of its leaders (with the exception of Mao-Tse-tung) as strategists we are making the sad mistake of over-rating enemy commanders. For all these years they have been concerned with tactics and operations on a level below the standard of what we term strategy. These men are not trained like the Germans, or even up to the level of the higher Soviet generals. The PLA has not even crystallized its own staff organization, much less launched into the higher military concepts. The field army commanders fall into the highest group, but only two of these men, Lin Piao and Liu Po-cheng, emerge on top of the army. Both are better than Chu Teh; but both have yet to range into the broader realm of Mao's strategical concepts.

There are not many general officers under discussion here, and China needs more. General Su Yu shows promise. Ho Lung failed, for reasons unknown, to make the very top grade. Chou Pao-chung is a man to watch, but he came late to high command. Politics and diplomacy have absorbed some of the old Red officers, who failed militarily but who are so politically reliable they cannot be discarded. Let us not dismiss Lin Piao, Liu Po-cheng, and a few others as poor *field army commanders,* but place them in the category of capable commanders, leaving the appellation of military strategist to one single man, Mao Tse-tung.

Before treating with Mao's thoughts and concepts on war it is well to examine the officers under Mao. The lines which follow are not biographies in the conventional sense; they are indexes to each of the more important military leaders in Red China today. The information is drawn from each man's own words and combat actions.

Commander Chu Teh Demands Sacrifice

Chu Teh is the pansy-faced opium smoker who reformed himself and is today the Commander-in-Chief of the PLA. Actually he is Mao Tse-tung's military stooge; he commands generals who exceed him in brains and military talent. To Mao belongs the army's so-called strategy of the World War II and Civil War years; to Chu belongs the credit for holding his scattered little army together, encouraging it, inspecting it, and building it slowly—since 1931 when he was elected its commander-in-chief.

Chu is a demander of obedience and human sacrifice.[3] He tells men it is their duty to offer up their lives freely. We should never misunderstand the many deaths China will suffer to win a war, with Chu at the head of the PLA.

From the ancient past of Sun Tzu and the classic of Chinese literature, Chu Teh has drawn and developed much of his military outlook. He had early interest in the theoretical aspects of combat. His thoughts on tactics and strategy have been shaped by

---

[3] Chu Teh, the *Heroism of the Eighth Route Army and the New Fourth Army.* (Date of publication unknown.)

his study of the European battlefields of World War I. His formal military education began at the Yunnan Military Academy; he was later given military polish in Europe, particularly in Germany. No doubt he developed there, his oriental contempt for positional warfare.

GENERAL CHU TEH, COMMANDER-IN-CHIEF OF THE RED CHINESE PEOPLE'S LIBERATION ARMY.

Chu also is Vice Chairman of the Revolutionary Military Council, Vice Chairman of the People's Government Council, and member of the Politburo, the Central Committee, and the Secretariat.

Chu began his career as an officer in the service of various war lords, to whom he "sold his saber" indiscriminately amid the turmoil of the war lord period.

Graduated from Yunnan Military Academy in 1911, he became a battalion commander on the French Indo-China frontier, where he learned guerrilla techniques. He became a brigade commander in 1919. In the 1920's he studied in Europe and was subsequently expelled from Germany.

Chu led the revolt against Chiang Kai-shek at Nanchang in 1927, but this and subsequent campaigns failed. He joined forces with Mao Tse-tung in May 1928 and three years later became commander of China's Communist army. He has fought in that capacity ever since.

The man is aging fast. He has had 40 years of practice at war, having first seen action in 1911 as an officer. There have been rumors that he will step down, or has done so; but until he is actually buried, the words from his wrinkled, owlish face will have influence on Red China's military policy, though his contribution to any strategy will be small.

How does Chu Teh visualize the war in Korea? He has not made any recent public utterances that throw light on his strategical thoughts, but he once said, "The type of warfare in which we must fight is to be decided by the type of arms we possess." Chu's troops are doing just that; they are fighting the war in Korea with the leftover weapons of the Civil War.

Early in China's war against Japan, Chu Teh said to Colonel Evans F. Carlson, "We can best offset Japanese superiority in modern organization and equipment by developing a form of resistance which will include the entire populace."[4] Chu emphasized that hatred of the enemy must be fully developed, and that the political commissars had the important mission to indoctrinate the people to resist. "Japan does not have enough soldiers to occupy all of our country." In this connection, Chu emphasized that the Chinese must develop an economic plan so as to provide "regions of self-sufficiency."

He holds firmly to the opinion that the officers should meet and have close contact with their troops just before battle. He refers, mainly, to the higher commanders, who should explain to their troops the reasons for coming campaigns and engagements. Chu counts heavily on military intelligence, so that he can move his forces to attack or disappear. Like many of his subordinates, he likes to choose his own terms and terrain for battle. The enemy's rear is ever the target Chu seeks. "Harass the enemy, give him no peace or rest in which to consolidate his gains." Chu Teh made a contribution here; he kept his army active. If it could not fight, at least it could keep up its reconnaissance and harassing movements. This old warrior has not manifested himself in written theories or volumes of written texts. Like Marshal Budyenny of the Soviet Army, he is the practical soldier whose moment is passing; but he will always be the army's mantlepiece of early Red military resistance. Chu Teh has lived into the atomic age, but it is doubtful that he has kept pace with it.

General Lin Piao Is Bitter

This man is impressive. He is cold, calculating, cruel, and embittered by his years of struggle. He looks and acts like a soldier.

---

[4] Evans F. Carlson, *Twin Stars of China*, Dodd, Mead & Co., New York, 1941.

Lin has the essentials of real leadership; he can command a crowd or move a mob by his voice alone. Beetle-browed and of sallow complexion, he drives himself to the limit of his endurance, with the result that he is chronically ill. Violently anti-foreign and especially anti-American, he could not be better picked than as a commander of forces employed against foreigners. Some say he is even anti-Russian, but this is open to considerable doubt. Regarded as the Chinese Communists' top military theore-

Wide World Photos.

GENERAL LIN PIAO, COMMANDER OF THE FOURTH FIELD ARMY.

A Communist for over 25 years, General Lin Piao conquered Manchuria and turned the tide of the Civil War in favor of the Communists. Lin is skilled in strategy and tactics and is author of a manual on the "Short Attack." He has spent several years in Russia, and bitterly hates Americans. Lin is leader of the "Internationalist" clique which seeks to dominate Asia. He is considered a likely successor to Chu Teh as commander of the PLA; his future will be strongly influenced by the outcome of the fighting in Korea.

tician, he is held in first place, by American officers of long experience in China, as the best Communist strategist. Lin is a man whom his enemies could well do without, and they, too, often build hopes on his death. Rumors constantly have him dying or wounded.

Once the military pupil of Chiang Kai-shek, Lin Piao showed early promise when he inflicted defeats on the Japanese at a time when other Chinese units were running before them. His 1937 victory over the Japanese at Pinghsingkwan (Pass) is still regarded as a military classic. A Party member since 1925, Lin is a Whampoa graduate (honor student in the 1925 class from which the late Tai Li was expelled) and a "Long Marcher." In 1936, he was President of Yenan's "Anti-Japanese Military and Political College." He took a small force to Manchuria immediately after World War II and built it up into an aggressive field army that turned the tide of the Civil War. Without realizing who the man was or what was his mission, the US Army Liaison Group is said to have let Lin board one of its planes from Yenan and transported him on the first leg of his journey to Manchuria in 1945.

Legends are growing about Lin. Like Rommel, he is coming to be regarded as "having the magic touch"; but the man is not invincible. He is not all dash and vigor.

In combat Lin can be very cautious. He likes to allow his enemy time to show his hand; it is then that Lin makes his final plans. He is a great user of reconnaissance and constantly seeks weak spots. It was his consistent application of reconnaissance that led him to discover how weak the Nationalists were in their defense organization in 1946-47. Until his combat reports thoroughly confirmed Nationalist weaknesses, Lin Piao actually was afraid the enemy would extend its drives against him, and for this contingency he methodically cross-ditched hundreds of miles of railways and roads north of the (Little) Sungari River.[5]

Lin Piao believes strongly in numerical superiority. He is such an advocate of "400 to 600 percent superiority"[6] that one sees here a weakness in this tactician of fame. Like Mao Tse-tung, General Lin Piao favors (for a real offensive) a strong attack in "one main direction," rather than a double envelopment. In his treatise on "Short Attack" he evidences favor of multiple short attacks along a front, to cut up the enemy. However, these attacks Lin visualizes as limited in depth of objective and for efforts short of the final blow which should travel in one giant wedge of main direction.

---

[5] Major Collins and I saw this in April 1947. So methodical was the effort that every 75 feet a trench crossed the road at right angles. Railways were similarly treated for scores of miles as we saw. The manpower and the man-hour effort expended in this operation was tremendous.

[6] These are the figures he most commonly expresses.

Lin will waste men; but when he does, it is for a definite purpose. He has written and also told his officers that in certain attacks the men should advance "shoulder to shoulder." Lin likes a superiority of five to one for offensive action, and he is dangerous when he has an ample supply of men. When he finds himself out-generaled, he withdraws "to discover the enemy's objectives." This is indicated not only in Lin's writings but in the tactics he has applied in his campaigns.

He does not favor calculated risks and, even when he does occasionally measure the odds and decide to take a risk, it is only after time-consuming preparation. Lin rarely rushes blindly into tactical action. He is calculatingly deliberate, but once the attack is launched, he is all "follow through," and blood and death deter him not a bit. The death patterns of Communist tactics in Korea give every evidence that Lin's teachings have had influence on Peng Te-huai and other officers.

Unlike some of the run-of-the-mill Red generals, he does not hesitate to launch costly attacks on cities, but his preference is first to surround them and wait out a period of siege. This Chinese officer attacks only when he is ready; when he is not, his army can be exasperatingly difficult to engage.

When this bitter and cruel man dies, it will probably be on the front lines. Like Rommel, he is a front line trouble-shooter. Wounded while fighting the Japanese in 1937, Lin Piao journeyed to the Soviet Union in 1938 for medical treatment and remained there until around 1942. No one knows exactly what Lin did during those years. It is probable that he took some military training. Lin was not casually picked in 1945 for the critical assignment in Soviet-occupied Manchuria. His strong point has been considered to be his Soviet liaison and orientation. Representing the "internationalist clique," he has run certain political risks. He was very independent in Manchuria between 1945 and 1948. If Lin introduces to Korea a newly trained Soviet-equipped group-army from Manchuria or replaces General Peng Te-huai, then he would be the foremost contender for power.

Either Lin Piao or Liu Po-cheng will probably succeed the aging

Chu Teh as the commander of the PLA. The selection of the heir apparent will rest in good part on the campaign in Korea. In short, Lin's fortunes depend on whether the "internationalist clique" or the "native group" will be vindicated by events in Korea.

GENERAL LIU PO-CHENG, COMMANDER OF THE SECOND FIELD ARMY.

General Liu Po-cheng is a member of the Revolutionary Military Council, the Central People's Council, and the Central Committee.

Moscow-trained, he is one of the Chinese Communists' best field commanders. He is known as the "One-eyed Dragon," and as the "Ever Victorious General."

Liu was an officer in Hsuing Ko-wu's Szechuan army in the 1911 revolution. By 1913 he was a brigade commander and it was at this time that he lost his eye. Often wounded, he has spent most of his military life in combat.

Liu Po-cheng Is Mobile and Elusive

Few generals pause to place in poetry their thoughts on tactics and strategy. The one-eyed Liu enjoys that distinction, and this verse of his reveals a portion of his basic concept:

> "When you keep men and lose land
> The land can be retaken.
> If you keep land and lose soldiers
> You lose both."

During the latter half of the China Civil War, Liu was criticized for the loss of some of the towns he had taken. His rebuttal was that "I traded seventeen empty cities for 60,000 of Chiang Kai-Shek's soldiers." The Nationalist generals on Formosa today rate Liu as Red China's Number One general; but what is more important, the Peking Red hierarchy regards Liu as their top best.

A realist who is terrain conscious, insofar as commanding heights are concerned, Liu Po-cheng places little value on holding military real-estate for the holding's sake. Late blooming, in the field of Red military poppies, Liu rose in public stature after 1946. In terms of campaign talent he shows great originality and should be ranked ahead of Lin Piao. Liu has originality; he is daring, but calculating.

Liu was the originator of the "take away" competition for American arms in the China Civil War. Liu set his units in competition with each other, using the catch phrase, "Which outfit can capture the most American arms?" Thereafter Liu's staff officers busied themselves at compiling trophy lists. He spurs his troops by such competitive measures.

Rarely if ever will this half-blind general use his best troops to defend a city. Rarely will he defend a city with real tenaciousness. Liu's command post is always in a village, or in a cluster of farm houses, but never in a large town or city. If the term "field soldier" were applied to only one general in the PLA, this man would rate the title.

Practitioner of mobile war, Liu is one of the most militarily elusive and wily field army commanders in China today. He is also one whose personal past is least known. His main imprint on the field of combat is visible in the China Civil War, not during World War II against the Japanese. Here is a man to be seriously reckoned with in combat. He has been surrounded many more times than written history records, yet he has escaped, not as an individual but as an army commander—with his troops intact, but dispersed. The "One-eyed Dragon" holds no fear of encirclement; his opponent should never brag until he has closed the bag.

A Party member since 1926, he was Moscow-schooled (1928-1931) at a Red Army military academy and subsequently became Chief of Staff to Chu Teh. Later he occupied the same position in the famous Eighth Route Army. He fought with the Red Russians in 1929 under General Galen against Chang Hsueh-liang, then war lord of Manchuria, and is a veteran of the Long March in 1934-35.

He is adept at devising his own strategy to meet changing military situations. He ably demonstrated this when, in 1947, under considerable Nationalist pressure, he led his six columns (armies) into the Tapieh Mountains and established a threatening base of operations that forced quite a re-adjustment in Nationalist strategy. To this day the answer has never been satisfactorily given as to just how he managed logistically to support his fast moving columns during this period, for about one year. He is obviously adept at "living off the land." In terms of the mobility of his campaigns, he might be called "China's Patton," but he has never handled any amount of armor. In the last great battle of the Civil War (at Hsuchou) he commanded five armies. His were the troops that, in 1950, tried to invade Tibet.[7] Liu gave material aid to Ho Chi-minh's Indo-Chinese Communist forces and he also supplied some technicians and advisors. One of the Chinese Red Army's boldest tacticians, he commands the sizable Second Field Army in South China. Individually he could show up in Korea any time. There, however, he will not find the region to his liking or talents, for Liu needs a land mass to maneuver over. Confine him to a peninsula and he may seem very ordinary, unless he can forge through the lines to foray in the rear.

Militarist Su Yu Shows Promise

Su Yu is the Reds' military darling of daring, who has a reputation for producing troops out of his cap. He has long served under General Chen Yi, and a measure of Chen's military reputation results from Su's efforts as a staff officer and commander as well.

General Su has more than the ordinary Chinese Red general's skill in handling artillery. He seems to like the heavy guns. From a given bolt of military manpower Su can cut, trim, fit, and sew together an excellent battle garment with a minimum of waste. Organizationally he achieves the maximum combat effectiveness

---

[7] A detailed description of the "invasion" of Tibet may be found in Chapter 10.

with a given number of men. Tactically he is a chance-taker, who has been lucky in his gambling. In the Battle of the Mengliangko in May 1947, Su was outflanked and hard pressed, yet during this combat in the mountains of Shantung he daringly used a portion of his force to screen his activities and intentions. Then he swung the remainder of his men into an attack against the Nationalist 74th Army. Amid this barren, waterless place of little cover, Su drove his troops to a victory that led his opponent, General Chang Ling, to pull the pin of a closely clutched hand grenade, which killed Chang and several of his staff.[8]

Certain of the Chinese Red militarists regard Su Yu as a more skillful field commander than Chen Yi. Lacking any formal military education, Su can skillfully handle large bodies of soldiers in combat. Su[9] commanded the forces which took the strongly fortified and pillbox-studded city of Tsinan (Chinan) in eight days during September 1948. The Reds had long hesitated to try to take fortified Tsinan, with its reported garrison of 100,000.

Whether Su persuaded the higher command to let him take it or not, is unknown. However, the attack marked the significant transition in Red tactics from mobile to positional assault, and undoubtedly the command selection for the attack was seriously weighed beforehand by the Red General Staff. Su was then, and is now, Deputy Commander of the Third Field Army.

An ardent exponent of the value of propaganda, General Su sent his battalions into the Tsinan battle with posters and paste pots. Within each captured city block Su's infantrymen had orders to paste up bulletins and posters. "Paste—shoot, shoot—paste," was the order of the day.

If one could conveniently label this officer with one title, it would be "trouble shooter." Where he shows up, the tasks will be tough. Some day he will try to plant his feet on the shores of Taiwan.

---

[8] Michael Keon, "Nationalist Failure in Shantung Pointer to War's Future," *The China Weekly Review*, 7 February 1948.
[9] Joined the Party about 1927, but did not make the Long March; instead he remained with Chen Yi in South China to conduct guerrilla operations. Their irregulars became the nucleus of the New 4th Army.

Nieh Jung-chen Has Breadth

He looks and acts like a gentleman. His calm, unaffected, and straightforward manner is impressive. An exponent of mobility, he likes to choose his own terms and terrain for battle. His combat record shows that he gives way to attack in order to swing around, outflank, and attack his enemy's rear. The Japanese made a study of Nieh's guerrilla tactics.

Nieh's foreign schooling tends to give him some breadth of

GENERAL NIEH JUNG-CHEN, VICE CHIEF OF STAFF OF THE PEOPLE'S REVOLUTIONARY MILITARY COUNCIL AND COMMANDER OF THE FIFTH FIELD ARMY.
In addition to being a member of the Central People's Government Council and of the Central Committee, Nieh also is mayor of Peking.
Nieh is one of the few well-educated officers in the Chinese Red Army. He has studied extensively in Europe and has attended the Soviet Eastern Laborers' University and a Red Army academy.

viewpoint. He was sent to France in 1920, under the worker-student plan, to study industries and chemical engineering at the *Université de Travail*. Later he was employed in the Renault Works. In Moscow, during the years 1924 to 1925, Nieh studied at the Eastern Laborer's University and at a Soviet military staff college. Nieh became secretary of the Political Department[10] at the Whampoa Military Academy in late 1925. He participated in the Northern Expedition and later, with his troops, he defected —to join the Communist army, where he was subsequently a political advisor to Lin Piao and later a "division" commander

---

[10] Chou En-lai was then chief of the department.

under Ho Lung. In 1927, following the Communist military failure in the attack on Canton, Nieh left China for the Soviet Union.

In the early 1930's Nieh returned to China, where he became Lin Piao's political commissar; and after the Long March he emerged as Lin's Deputy Commander. After 1937 Nieh based his troops in the Wutai Mountains of Shansi and began large-scale guerrilla operations against the Japanese. It was here that he built his military reputation on sudden attack and elusiveness. His record in the China Civil War was not as spectacular as that of

COMMUNIST GENERAL CHOU PAO-CHUNG, WITH THE AUTHOR, IN 1946.
General Chou's army had just captured the Manchurian city of Changchun.

some of his colleagues, but sometimes his opportunities for success were not as good. He now commands the "Palace Guard"—the troops stationed around Peking and presently forming the Fifth Field Army. Nieh has a future.

Chou Pao-chung Typifies the Average

Pock-marked on the surface of his skin, this man is battle-scarred outside and inside. Outwardly he is smiling and affable. His life has been so hard that he ranks as a peer among those whose military stock in trade is toughness. Bred of hardship, his will to win has been strengthened by lengthy guerrilla struggles against long odds. Hunted and hard pressed by the Japanese, he managed, near the close of World War II, to survive by eating grass. It is with modesty that he will give testimony to this crucial era of his personal and military survival. At the time he was Commander of the Manchurian People's Self-Defense Army[11] in Manchuria.

His formal education is meager; his mental prowess is not above average, but in the ways of war he is tactically wise and adroit. Chou's tough nature in the field is in contrast with his sentimental affection for friends and for those he would like to have like him. Chou is so devoted to the cause of Communism that his verbal expressions of thought are unconsciously, but rigidly, channelized by the Party line to a point where his rebuttal in any argument consists of standard Communist clichés. Despite this, he has demonstrated more than the usual Red Chinese talent to get along and cooperate, to some degree, with Americans. While he is as pure a nationalist as a Chinese Red can be, he has, at times, indicated a concealed favoritism toward America. He is one of the "internationalist clique," but he does not believe the Chinese should prostitute themselves to the Soviets. It is his belief that the Chinese can do without too much Soviet assistance.

First trained at the Yunnan Military Academy about 1924, Chou rose to military prominence when his army assaulted and captured the Manchurian capital, Changchun, in April 1946. A believer in mobility, he has great contempt for fixed defenses. One of his first moves, after he captured Changchun, was to tear down all pillboxes, even though there was the threat that Nationalist armies would soon break the stalemate of Ssupingkai and converge on his newly won city—an event which did occur a month later. This Chinese general would like to have airborne troops at his disposal. He feels he could employ them successfully—and he probably could in missions of harassment. For a ground force commander, he has been unusually active in air force matters.

---

[11] A Red guerrilla force that became a part of General Lin Piao's forces in 1945.

His enthusiasm is great. His emotions sometimes carry him away—as when he greeted me just after his gunners all but shot down my plane on landing at his defended airfield.[12] It was the only time I have been hugged and kissed by a Communist general!

"War Lord" Chen Yi Is a Roughneck

He looks and acts like a gangster, but feels that he has a flair for politics. Chunky Chen Yi stands in low esteem with both the

GENERAL CHEN YI, COMMANDER OF THE THIRD FIELD ARMY.
General Chen Yi is a member of the Revolutionary Military Council, the Central People's Government Council, and the Central Committee. He holds many other titles and is also the mayor of Shanghai.

He went to school in France, was expelled and returned to China about 1922, to become a political worker for a Szechuanese war lord. Later he became an instructor in the Whampao Military Academy.

While Chen did not make the Long March, he fought in many guerrilla campaigns and rose high in the Red Chinese military hierarchy. He has always chosen his subordinates with care and owes much of his success to the excellence of his subordinate commanders. Most of his campaigning has been in the Shantung-Kiangsu region.

Chinese Communists and the Nationalists, although he has managed to hold onto considerable responsibility. Some of Chen Yi's former subordinates and regional associates, such as Liu Po-cheng and Lin Piao, left him to become famous in their own right.

---

[12] I had returned to Changchun, in May 1946, to evacuate five American correspondents whom Chou was holding under house arrest. Two weeks earlier I had left the city in a patched-up liaison aircraft, with the understanding that I could bring a C-47 back into Chou's airfield. The planning and signals for this landing were elaborate (to fit Communist demands), but, as we were landing, the AA crews swung their guns on my plane. The pilot dropped altitude in a quick dive, to frighten the crews away from their weapons at the end of the runway. We almost crashed. Chou hugged me vigorously, happy that his men had not killed me.

Chen's deputy, Su Yu, also may do so. Chen Yi has received much of the credit that often was due others. He has hogged the spotlight from other leaders, usually his subordinates.

Opportunist and watchful, Chen Yi is looking out for himself first. He has hinted to Westerners that he might turn against Mao if he found money and arms from a non-Soviet source.[13] However, Chen Yi knows on which side his bread is presently buttered. His anti-Soviet attitude, if it has really existed, will be subordinated for some time to come. He might, in time, become a defectionist.

Like Nieh Jung-chen, he was a member of the worker-student group in France. He attended several schools there, including the University of Grenoble. For his political activities as a student, the French expelled him about 1921. He subsequently was an instructor at the Whampoa Military Academy, after serving a Szechuanese war lord. He never made the Long March but commanded guerrilla bands in South China. His were the troops around which the New 4th Army was built in 1937-38.

There are no known written texts that evidence Chen Yi's military talents. His record as a general shows that he is tactically aggressive but strategically cautious. Like many Red generals he has had to do without equipment for so long, that every campaign is closely weighed beforehand. He is not a particular risk-taker as such, but a conservative, well grounded general. Once he launches an offensive, however, one can be assured that he and his staff have carefully weighed beforehand every factor. Tactically, Chen favors night attacks—and infantry. He stresses the use of grenades and bayonets. He is inclined to treat his prisoners fairly.

If Chen Yi were given an atomic bomb, he would express the utmost confidence that he could use it better than any other Chinese general. He feels very capable of using any and all arms. This self-confidence with arms has influenced the Red command to give him the job of amphibious attack against Taiwan. Some indication of the way the man thinks is revealed by the fact that he has bought off more Nationalist generals than any other high

---

[13] "Trouble in Red China," by Rodney Gilbert, *Life*.

Red commander. The "silver bullet" concept is embedded in his brain.

Peng Te-huai Believes in Manpower

He looks like something that crawled out from under a log! Little affected or impressed by foreigners, Peng personifies the "pure" Chinese Red war lord. The man is a through and through rebel, even within his own family. He has turned his hand to every form of violence, including assassination. Chiang Kai-shek once

GENERAL PENG TE-HUAI, DEPUTY COMMANDER OF THE PEOPLE'S LIBERATION ARMY AND COMMANDER OF THE FIRST FIELD ARMY.

Commander of the "volunteers" in Korea in 1951, he is Vice-chairman of the Revolutionary Military Council, and a member of the Central People's Government Council and of the Central Committee.

Peng began his career as an ordinary soldier and later was graduated from the Hunan Military Academy. He commanded a brigade in the Kuomintang army of Ho Chen, in 1927, but in that same year he joined the Communist Party, in 1935-36 he was commander of Red military forces in the Northwest, but relinquished the command to General Chu Teh. He may yet take over Chu's title, but much will depend on how his fortunes in Korea are viewed by Mao Tse-tung.

posted a high reward for Peng's head. He is sometimes touted as being Chu Teh's military brains, but he does not seem to reveal any profound or original military thoughts. The only real "strategy" he has revealed in combat is his steady attempt to force the enemy to scatter troops. He holds the opinion that soldier morale and esprit de corps count more in the success of a campaign than the plan itself. He is great on the political education of soldiers. Peng is a harsh disciplinarian. Politico through and through, he has often repeated, "What we lack in weapons will be balanced by our men's knowledge of what they are fighting for." This still is his outlook, but it will have to change if China is to develop a modern army.

Peng's stepmother reportedly drove him away from home before he was ten years old and, as with other Chinese youths, an army carried Peng into its ranks. Somehow the youth gained his way into the Hunan Military Academy and emerged as an officer in a Kuomintang Army—from which he broke in 1927 to join the Party. He rose in rank with fair rapidity, and in 1930 he captured and momentarily held Changsha. His star rose for the next six years. He was the ranking army officer in the route-order Red army until Chu Teh superseded him as the major commander. Since 1937 he has been the Deputy Commander of the Communist Army. Because he is fourteen years younger than Chu Teh he is absorbing more and more of that old commander's duties. Peng Te-huai is one of the busiest generals of the PLA, for he also wears the cap of Commander of the First Field Army. The man is a strong supporter of Mao Tse-tung and belongs to the "native group." As such he will give Lin Piao and Liu Po-cheng competition for the role of next PLA commander-in-chief. While Peng is an acknowledged expert in the trade of war, he will compete with Lin's and Liu's military abilities on a basis of his political stature and intimate relation with Mao Tse-tung.

Peng Te-huai believes that, with her great manpower, China can outlast any enemy in a long war of attrition. As Deputy Commander-in-Chief of the PLA and commander of "volunteers" in Korea, he will carry through on this concept, to pour manpower masses into Korea—or into any other war.

This spitter of melon seeds is peppery in temperament, athletically inclined, hard working to the point of an ulcered stomach, and a very difficult person with whom to negotiate. He is perhaps the PLA's best logistician—at least he has good appreciation of logistical factors.

"Heavy as lead and sharp as steel," Peng entered the Korean conflict with a shiny military reputation that has since become tarnished with the failures of his 1951 spring offensives. He is good

Wide World Photos.

GENERAL HO LUNG.

The "old butcher" never made the grade as a war lord, but as a successful bandit he turned his talents to Communism, to become a high general.

Calloused and tough, he can swear with the roughest of his men. He has a reputation for caring well for his troops. Tuberculosis has sapped his health.

Militarily he is being eclipsed by smarter and better educated officers.

as a commander of large guerrilla forces, but in combat of modern nature his tactical skill is more that of a sledge hammer!

Gangster Ho Lung Is Brutal

The man is a butcher. He has ruthlessly murdered several missionaries. A great user of propaganda men in combat, Ho counts heavily on the local people for intelligence and labor. While he may now have lost it, Ho Lung has long had a contempt for armored forces. As might be expected, he is known for his skill in directing effective anti-tank defenses. His real forte is guerrilla warfare, in which he shows great ability to organize people for the assistance of his partisans. Pipe smoking, earthy and mustached, he greatly impressed fellow travelers and correspondents in the hey-days of Yenan; but he has not so favorably impressed US Army officers.

There are many legends about him, but few can be substantiated. His birth date, for example, has been variously reported, with the extremes varying as much as twenty years. The man began as a common Chinese bandit, sometime after he was fifteen years old. He has been shooting at people ever since, or directing other men to do so. Successful as a brigand, Ho Lung received a commission as an officer in a provincial army (Hunan) sometime in the mid-1920's. He and his rifle-toting ranks subsequently were incorporated in the Nationalist Army. He later rose to command the 20th Army of the Nationalist Revolutionary Army. Like so many of his present-day colleagues, he joined the Communist Party in 1927. He was in the profession and the Party for good, commanding an "army" from 1930 to 1937, when the Japanese attacked. After this his army was more properly redesignated a division and incorporated within the Eighth Route Army. Lacking education of any formal sort, he concentrated on combat against the Japanese. He and his men killed a good many, but in terms of real military talent Ho remained primarily a bandit with guerrilla skill.

Somewhere along the line Ho Lung missed his chance to become a top-flight field commander. However, if brutality is needed in any region, Ho will be called on for the job. He is one of the 22 members of the People's Revolutionary Military Council, which shows that the Communists reward their old-timers regardless of their mental or strategic ability. Ho Lung is out of place on a high military staff in this age, but perhaps the PLA's highest military body needs the balance of his brutality in the Council meetings. Ho Lung can hate or shoot anybody.

Huang Yi-feng Is a Nasty Commissar

Brutal and dangerous, Huang is a man Major Collins and I studied for many weeks. I have been before this man for eleven solid hours at a stretch, undergoing trial at which he was the presiding officer. The unconcealed hatreds which vented themselves across the courtroom in Harbin have had some chance to cool, and it is my honest attempt to portray this officer here, unbiased by an emotion which cannot help but linger.

General Huang is a prosecutor, and an intelligence officer. It will doubtless be his well-tailored frame that will dominate the scene in which any luckless Americans are up for trial by the Chinese Reds. Some twelve Marines were being embalmed for burial, and several others were having their wounds dressed, after the Red ambush of a Marine column between Tientsin and Peiping —when Huang arose in an Executive Headquarters session to try to twist the Anping Incident[14] into an American attack. One hardened American officer, Major Robert Ekval, called the turn on Huang during this stormy session, and Huang all but ordered General Marshall to have Ekval removed from Executive Headquarters. General Marshall backed up Ekval. Here occurred the first historical record of General Huang's violent and emotional anti-Americanism.

Huang's hatred of the United States was further revealed in 1947, when General Lin Piao and Moscovite Li Li-san placed him as a combination judge and prosecuting attorney before Collins and me. Despite his arrogance and self-assurance, Huang does not know Americans and their psychology as well as his superiors

---

[14] The Communists deliberately ambushed a US Marine column on 30 July 1946.

believe he does. Huang is wrongly chosen for the task of prosecuting Americans. His bluffs are blustering but hollow. His poker game of military interrogation may be backed by bayonets, but it lacks the skill and finesse of the Germans, whom Huang tries to imitate. I cite this man because he typifies the majority of the commissars in the PLA. Ruthless and intellectually dishonest, Huang and the many like him, can be more dangerous to the United States than the average Chinese army commander. Huang is one of the foremost leaders and prosecutors of the brutal and bloody purges now in progress.

Chou En-lai Influences Strategy

Somewhere within his career he was given the title of "General," but he makes no pretense of being a militarist. However, he is one of the five vice-chairmen of the Revolutionary Military Council, not to mention his larger roles of Premier, Foreign Minister, and member of the Politburo. In these various capacities he participated in the secret meetings that discussed and decided upon China's armed entry into Korea in 1950. (There are reports that the Chinese hierarchy was against this venture on the grounds that US fire power and air forces were too powerful. From other sources it is said that the vote which the Politburo took on the matter of entry into Korea was extremely close.)

Chou is very powerful in Politburo circles and lends direction to the over-all strategy. He is an old-line Communist, having led the organization of the Paris branch of the CCP in 1921, when he was a worker-student along with Li Li-san, Nieh Jung-chen, Chen Yi and others. With Chu Teh he also created the Berlin branch of the CCP, returning to China in 1924 to become a political instructor at the Whampoa Military Academy. Lin Piao and Chen Yi were Chou's students at Whampoa. Chou also served a term as secretary to Soviet General Bleucher, an advisor to the Academy. Chou was very popular with his cadet students, some of whom reportedly saved him from execution in 1927, when his Shanghai workers' revolution failed.

He has been prominent as a negotiator, begining in 1936 when

Wide World Photos.

GENERAL CHOU EN-LAI.

The "pale-faced general" who influences Red military strategy and exercises great power in international relations.

Chou is the Red Premier, Minister of Foreign Affairs, member of the Central Committee and member of the Politburo. He holds many other titles of lesser importance.

He has studied in France, the Soviet Union, and Germany. As political instructor at the old Whampoa Military Academy he taught Chen Yi, Lin Piao and other officers who later became Communists.

he was senior Red representative to the negotiations for the release of Generalissimo Chiang Kai-shek after the Sian incident.

Between 1937 and 1946 he participated in all negotiations between the Central Government and the Chinese Communist Party. Suave in manner, Chou persuaded the young Marshal Chang Hsueh-liang to join the Red cause in 1936. The marshal

Photo by Col. David D. Barrett.

GENERAL CHU TEH (LEFT) AND DICTATOR MAO TSE-TUNG EMERGED FROM THE CAVES OF YENAN, TO GOVERN FROM THE IMPERIAL PALACE IN PEKING.
Unlike their humble days shown here, Mao and Chu now wear snappy tailored uniforms. (Center—Colonel David D. Barrett, ace US military observer.)

brought an army with him to bolster the cause of Communism, which then was sagging.

The savagery with which Chou has turned on the United States shocked a few Americans who came to know the Communists in a limited way. Some believe that America may still have a semblance of a "friend" in Chou En-lai, and Chou's present savagery may be largely an act to convince his Soviet masters. This is very doubtful. The Chinese generals who fight us are taking direction from Chou En-lai's policies; he influences the strategy that keeps them in Korea. Any peace settlement will see Chou En-lai prominent in the negotiations. The humility with which he once impressed Americans will then be replaced by arrogance and toughness.

Mao Tse-tung Doesn't Fear A-Bombs

Here is the "Mr. Strategy" of Red China, the man who has a contemptuous disrespect for atomic bombs. "Even at Bikini," he has said, "atomic bombs didn't kill all the pigs." Mao doubts that A-bombs would be very effective against China. He is shifting Shanghai's industries inland and scattering them. He has no sentimental attachment to Peking. He has done without Mukden's arsenals before and the caves of Yenan still offer solid shelter for his government. Mao has ordered Red propagandists to play down the power and effect of US atomic weapons, and in addition he has made it a crime for any Chinese to talk about the true impact of such weapons. On 7 August 1951 Tseng Chung-jen was executed in Lokchang, South China, for "exaggerating the power of the A-bomb." Mao wants to keep his people ignorant; he fears panic, however.

Mao guides and directs the militarists. He has studied and written at length on military subjects. However, to find the meat of Mao's concepts, it is often necessary to strip his texts of a lot of Communist double talk. But the fact remains that Mao has a very definite grasp of military strategy and military operations. Like all dictators, he regards himself as "having a feeling" for the trends which escape other men.

"Our strategy is one against ten, while our tactics can be formulated as consisting of ten against one."[15] This was Mao Tse-tung's single-sentence analysis of the Red's approach to war in the 1930's, when Chinese Communists were opposed to the superior military power of the Japanese Army. *Today's Chinese strategy is ten against one; the Reds feel they can afford it.*

---

[15] *Strategic Problems*, by Mao Tse-tung.

Not all of Mao's concepts are original, however, for he has drawn on one of China's most ancient militarists, Sun Tzu. A leading American military student of Chinese warfare, Colonel Samuel B. Griffith, USMC, has this to say about Mao and Sun Tzu:

"The influence of the ancient military philosopher Sun Tzu on Mao's military thought will be apparent to those who have read the 'Book of War.' . . . Sun Tzu wrote that speed, surprise, and deception were the primary essentials of the attack, and his succinct advice: Sheng Tung, Chi Hsi (Distraction in the East, Strike in the West) is no less valid today than it was when he wrote it 2400 years ago. The tactics of Sun Tzu are in large measure the tactics of China's guerrillas today.[16]"

Sun's *Art of War*[17] has had lively and living effect on the Chinese Red approach to both war and peace. Note the following:

". . . a soldier's spirit is keenest in the morning; by noonday it has begun to flag, and in the evening his mind is bent only on returning to camp. A clever general, therefore, avoids an army when its spirit is keen, but attacks it when it is sluggish. . . . Peace proposals unaccompanied by a sworn covenant indicate a plot."

The impact of Sun Tzu goes beyond his influence on Mao and Mao's direction of the PLA; it extends down to the combat action and reaction of many generals, and even of some battalion commanders. It provides the spirit, if not the letter, of guidance.

Mao and his men from Yenan like to believe it was their *strategy* that led them to victory over the Nationalists in 1949. The PLA defeated Chiang Kai-shek's armies, not because of any real or superior strategy, but by employing the tactics of "ten against one"—coupled with a variety of other factors, such as Nationalist failures and inflation.

Strategy has many definitions. I offer no precise definition for Chinese strategy, for, in itself, it has not yet crystallized. There is much improvisation in Peking today. I prefer here to trace the military thoughts, varied though they be, of the man who has the most influence and impact on Red strategy. There is no

---
[16] Samuel B. Griffith in the preface to his translation of Mao Tse-tung's *"Yu Chi Chan,"* copyright by the Marine Corps Gazette.

STRATEGIST MAO FAVORS THESE PRINCIPLES

Sun Tzu's ART OF WAR [17] is the oldest military treatise in the world. It was written about 500 BC. His highly compressed comments are cryptic and to the point. After twenty-five centuries Sun's words provide the basic guide to the Chinese Communist approach to war. Here are some of his aphorisms which find favor with Mao Tse-tung:

All warfare is based on deception.

The art of war is of vital importance to the State.

. . . when we are near, we must make the enemy believe that we are away.

Hold out baits to entice the enemy. Feign disorder, and crush him.

If he (the enemy) is superior in strength, evade him. If your opponent is of choleric temper, seek to irritate him. Pretend to be weak, that he may grow arrogant.

If he is inactive, give him no rest. If his forces are united, separate them. Attack him where he is unprepared, appear where you are not expected.

If you lay seige to a town, you will exhaust your strength.

Bring war material with you from home, but forage on the enemy . . . A wise general makes a point of foraging on the enemy.

Captured soldiers should be kindly treated and kept.

In order to kill the enemy, men must be roused to anger.

. . . if our forces are ten to the enemy's one, surround him; if five to one, attack him; if twice as numerous, divide our army in two.

If equally matched, we can offer battle; if slightly inferior . . ., we can avoid the enemy . . .

By holding out baits, he keeps him on the march; then with a body of picked men he lies in wait for him.

Appear at points which the enemy must hasten to defend; march swiftly to places where you are not expected.

Force him to reveal himself so as to find out his vulnerable spots.

Keep your plans dark and impenetrable as night, and when you move, fall like a thunderbolt.

THE HIERARCHY IN THE PALACE   51

brief summary of Mao's military concepts; books have been written and books will be written explaining the man, his thoughts and his actions. However, below are given the more pertinent military views of Mao.

Mao believes in one-fisted strikes, not in the two-fisted offensives that can result in double envelopments. "In between offensives," he argues, "yield like a boxer; but once it is decided to attack, do so with great weight of numbers and in a single direction." Mao has greatly influenced his generals to be deliberate. He doesn't want generals who act rashly or recklessly. Timing must be correct; preparations deliberate. These are Mao's studied concepts; they have been evident in Korea—the great drives, with long intervals between offensives. He favors a war of maneuver and disdains positional warfare. In Korea he and his generals miss the land mass that permits strategic maneuverability. Long ago (1936) Mao dismissed guerilla methods and labeled them as a necessary interim measure. "Guerrilla fighting," he criticized, " . . . its irregularity . . . lack of concentration . . . lack of unity of discipline . . ." Mao is no longer thinking in terms of guerrillas. Mao criticized the Japanese militarists for their lack of main direction in the China campaign: "A drive is made here, and another there. Instead of throwing a large force in at the beginning, reinforcements have been brought in piecemeal." Mao is not afraid to order a retreat. "Fight only when victory is certain," he has said. "Run away when it is impossible. Every military man admits that you must sometimes run away. Only they do not run as much as we do. We march more than we fight. But every march is for the sake of a fight."

Mao and his hierarchy hold that retreats "should be executed so that tactically they will possess the same military value as advances."[18]

---

[17] Sun Tzu, *The Art of War*, translated by Lionel Giles, Introduction and Notes by Brig. General Thomas R. Phillips. The Military Service Publishing Co., Harrisburg, Pa., 1944.
[18] From a CCP document captured in 1946 by the Chinese Nationalists, the text of which is in the files of the *History of the Peiping Executive Headquarters*, Fourth Quarter, 1946, Department of the Army, Office of Military History.

Wide spaces have perhaps overinfluenced Mao's concept of strategy to a point where he finds himself hard pressed for a "strategic" solution in the field in Korea. "China is like a gallon jug," he once remarked to Evans F. Carlson,[19] "which Japan is trying to fill with a half-pint of liquid. When her troops move into one section, we move to another, and when they pursue us we move back again." In Korea Mao has a pint jug and he is trying to fill it with gallons of blood.

Part of Mao's over-all strategy within a given war is to measure the struggle in terms of "Are we winning the hard way or the easy?" He keeps his eye on the resources at hand, and if he sees that they are being expended too rapidly for the pace or length of the conflict, he slows up his commanders and patiently waits a while, to conserve and gather more energy and more resources. For instance, between 1946 and the first half of 1948, Mao felt that his army needed strengthening; so he carefully applied restraint; the army was not allowed to indulge very much in positional warfare. As if playing poker, he let several indifferent hands go by, to wait for some good ones in the later hours of the game. Here again he reflects Sun Tzu who proclaimed: " . . . if the campaign is protracted, the resources of the State will not be equal to the strain."

The idea that war should be carried into enemy territory is not original with the Chinese Reds, but the idea is firm in their minds. This was evidenced in point and in action during the Civil War. It is Mao's concept in Korea; he may apply it to Indo-China.

As we bring Mao's views more up-to-date, we find he has reached again into the ancient past to bring out[20] and strengthen an older concept. "Do unto others as they do unto you," is an aphorism Mao has coined from Chu Hsi, a philosopher of the Sung Dynasty. Mao is Machiavellian.

This is Mao Tse-tung's warning to his subordinates who would

---

[19] *Twin Stars of China*, Dodd, Mead & Co., N. Y., 1941, page 198.
[20] Mao Tse-tung, *People's Democratic Dictatorship*, Lawrence and Wisehart, Ltd., London, 1950.

carry over too far into a future conflict the tactics and practices of the last. Mao is very firm in arguing that one cannot always transfer the laws of one war to another; yet his generals have not learned this lesson too well:

"Different war situations determine different guiding laws of war, according to the difference in time, locality, and character. Speaking in terms of the time factor, war and the guiding laws of war are developmental."[21]

"Oppose mechanicalism in dealing with the problems of war," he repeats. "We must oppose it . . . for it is one of the basic concepts of the Marxist-Leninist military theory."

On the matter of war regions, Mao states:

"every country and race has its peculiarities, which also means the laws of war have their peculiarities and cannot be rigidly transplanted."

Mao dictates[22] to his militarists that, in viewing the history of a war, one must look for the general trends, and then project or exploit them in future conflicts.

About 1940, Mao Tse-tung set forth in his "New Democracy" the "united front" adopted by the Comintern in Moscow in 1935. The "People's Democratic Dictatorship" springboarded from that, and the Sino-Soviet treaty of alliance, on 14 February 1950, gave full expression to Mao's doctrine[23] of "leaning to one side"— the side of the Soviet Union.

In July 1949, Mao expressed China's international stand in these clear words:

"We still have imperialism standing beside us, and this enemy is very ferocious. . . . Our dictatorship must unite with all international revolutionary forces."

In September of the same year Mao added: "Our revolutionary work is not yet concluded." Thus, Mao announced China's stra-

---

[21] *The Marxist Military Line,* by Mao Tse-tung (1936), as resurveyed in *People's China,* 1950.
[22] Of incidental interest are Mao's thoughts on the methods of *studying* military science. He emphasizes that the best method "to study war, is from war." There is no Chinese monopoly on this concept (Mao stoops to admit that reading books also constitutes study).
[23] *People's Democratic Dictatorship,* 30 June 1949.

tegical role in Asia—to get rid of Western influence, unite with the USSR and assist other Asiatic Communist movements. The intention of Red China can be found in this line:

"Just as class struggle is the means of eliminating classes, so war is the means of eliminating wars."[24]

Mao's strategy is to persuade the United Nations, and particularly the United States, that war with China, in any sphere,

Photo by Colonel Edward T. Cowen.

MAO's SECRETARY - - - A COMMUNIST FANATIC.

The real Communist fanatic is typified in this smirking follower of the Marxist line. Yan Shang-kun's heavy-lidded eyes glitter like those of a snake—and his enthusiasm for his cause is as deadly.

Yang is shown here with Colonel Edward T. Cowen, United States Army. General Lin Piao is at the left, and Chou En-lai at the right.

Yang is Mao Tse-tung's secretary.

is hopeless. Already he has persuaded some people that no military force can defeat his army on the mainland of China. But Mao wants to make certain that no one will challenge any Red Chinese military moves in other portions of Asia. This Chinese dictator's ambitions are boundless.

---

[24] Mao Tse-tung, *The Marxist Military Line*, published in 1936; republished in *People's China*, Peking, 1950.

The High Command Still Needs Education

Chinese Communist texts on strategy, and on the Marxist-Leninist-Stalinist-Maoist military line, are fine guiding generalities for generals, but they are hollow in that they fail to get down to specific cases. The doctrines need firming.

PLA officers have not had the best material to study. It was not until about 1946 that the Chinese Reds massed their armies on a near level of strategical deployment, and not until 1948-49 did the PLA begin to move large armies within the framework of what we call strategy. The Red Army of China fought a *guerrilla war* against the Japanese; a *division war* against the Nationalists; and now they are fighting an *army war* against the UN Forces in Korea. The Red Chinese have yet to develop their own military manuals on the operation and employment of armies. They *can* move their field armies, but only a half-dozen officers, below Chu Teh, have ever commanded such giant forces. Mao's military men are tactically wise and experienced, but strategically the high Chinese officers have combat-studied two wars at too close range to have any real perspective or grasp of the larger aspects of modern conflicts. In short, all of them could profit by some formal schooling at war colleges. Furthermore, if one digs down below the level of the half dozen top Chinese generals, one is not likely to find men formally educated in the scope of modern warfare. China has many generals, but few really good ones for the size of her forces.

Are any of these many generals doing anything to raise their professional talents? Yes; they are being helped by the Soviets, but the Russians are not giving away all their top secrets on strategy, army groups, and high logistical and staff planning. The Soviets are feeding the Chinese on a diet of old manuals and texts, dating in concept from World War I. The Soviets apparently sense that the Chinese officers, while superb guerrilla commanders and victorious infantry leaders in China's peculiar Civil War, need to study the larger wars of other countries. Thus the Soviets are giving the Chinese a firm military foundation, adding a few up-to-date frills like armor and airborne, but in the main treating them for what they are—amateurs in modern war and modern logistics.

There is in use right now with the PLA an old Soviet Army manual that has the high-sounding title, "The General Principles of Army Group Tactics" (published in Chinese by Lin Piao's Manchurian Democratic Combined Army Headquarters in September 1947). Yet this document is dated back many years in its scope and treatment of military principles. It is pre-World War II; useful, yes, but hardly a compliment to the unschooled military officers of China who study it.

The PLA's high command should not be under-rated in the application of its own well-developed principles of combat, but it should not be vaulted into the professional realm occupied by the skilled high army officers of the United States, Great Britain, France, and the USSR.

The old leaders are in power now. Many are veterans of the Long March, an event in Chinese Red history which still has influence on these leaders. The privations of this gruelling test of endurance have affected the physical and mental health of the living leaders and put many in the grave before their time. The effect has been to undermine physically the men who cannot forget its torture. China's Red hierarchy consists of a group of bitter military men who have suffered, and who will not hesitate to demand death and suffering of the millions they control.

These men are devout in their fervor, narrow in attitude, hardened, and uncompromising. They are the world's most authentic Communists. The Soviets may bend them partially to Russian will and design—but in the end these Chinese militarists will prove to be Communists first, Chinese second, and Soviet puppets last.

What Makes a Red General?

I have often been asked what the average Red Chinese general is like—in background, education and Party connections. To furnish some answers, I have surveyed fifty-two of today's most prominent general officers in Red China. These officers make up the military

Photo by Col. David D. Barrett.

RED OFFICERS, LIKE GENERAL YEH CHIEN-YING, ARE POORLY EDUCATED, BUT ARE FANATICAL IN THEIR BELIEF IN COMMUNISM.

(Colonel David D. Barrett and other US Army officers inspect a battalion after World War II.)

hierarchy dominant in the Communist regime. They are the fifty-two men who are prominent, not only because of their past or present military roles but, also because of their present political importance in the Red regime. These men, for the most part, hold the most numerous and most importance posts occupied by military officers. A few, like the seven ex-Nationalist officers who are presently accepted officials, soon may be eliminated by purge or attrition. However, at this moment these are the highly placed army officers, from General Chu Teh on down,[25] who wield great influence and power in Red China.

Birthplace. The province of Hunan gave most of the Communist militarists to China. Manchuria contributed only two of the generals in the group. Of the 52 generals, these are their provinces of origin—

27.5 percent were born in Hunan;
23.0 percent were born in Szechuan and Kwangtung;
17.3 percent were born in Shensi, Shansi and Yunnan;
11.5 percent were born in Fukien, Hupei and Manchuria;
11.1 percent were born in Anhwei, Kwangsi, Hainan and Kiangsi;
9.6 percent, birth places unknown or uncertain.

Their Ages. The average general is a little over 49 years of age. The oldest is 70 years; the youngest 36; there is one of each of these extremes.

22 range between 41 and 49 years old.
17 range between 50 and 59 years old.
5 are from 60 to 70 years old.
1 is 36 years of age.
7—birthdates unknown.

The majority (33) are between 44 and 54 years.

Education. At least seven, and possibly one other, of these senior officers have attended Soviet schools of one sort or another. Five others have had education abroad—in Germany, France, Australia, and Japan. In all, 25 have had some form of formal military training, and 22 have had none. On five of the generals the

---

[25] Mao Tse-tung and Chou En-lai are omitted from the group, as are a few ex-militarists who have been a long time away from their original military fields.

records give no evidence of military schools, and they probably did not attend any. Of the seven ex-Nationalists, six attended military academies, two going to Japanese schools. None of the regular Communist officers (45 in number) attended any Japanese military schools. The Chinese and Japanese army schools attended are—

Whampoa Military Academy,	6 officers;
Paoting Military Academy,	4 officers;
Yunnan Military Academy,	3 officers;
Northeast Military Academy,	3 officers;
Hunan Military Academy,	2 officers;
Kwangsi Military Academy,	1 officer;
Hankow Military Academy,	1 officer;
Other Chinese Military Schools,	2 officers;
Japanese Military Cadet Academy,	1 officer;
Japanese Infantry School,	1 officer.

Except for eight or ten, there is absolutely nothing impressive about the educational background of these highly-placed Communist officers. General Chen Yi had no formal military training at all, but he studied chemistry at the University of Grenoble and was later an instructor at the Whampoa Military Academy. Chen Keng is a graduate of the Kwangtung Military School, the Whampoa Military Academy (1st class), and a school (probably military) in Moscow. Chu Teh received his education at the Yunnan Military Academy, and in Europe between 1922 and 1928. Liu Po-cheng is a graduate of an army officers' school in Chengtu. Nieh Jung-chen is without early military training of a formal nature, but is well educated, having attended the *Universite de Travail*, the University of Paris, the Soviet Eastern Laborer's University, and a (Soviet) Red Army academy.

MILITARY EDUCATION

Educational background:	*Officers attending:*
Chinese military academies	22
Soviet military academies	7
Japanese military academies	2
Military education unknown	5
No formal military education	22
Two or more military schools	6

If the seven ex-Nationalist officers are excluded, it becomes evident that, of the real Communist military group of 45, more than half have gained military (and subsequent political or diplomatic) prominence without the benefit of formal military education. Only one of this group is known to be a graduate of one of the Communists' own Red military academies, and that is Liu Jui-ching.

Political Status. All generals are Party members except the seven ex--Nationalists, whose Party membership status is unknown. The greater portion of the officers joined the Chinese Communist Party in 1926-7, the largest influx (14) being in the latter year. The joining dates of twelve are unknown. Only four are known to have joined the CCP after 1929. (The Chinese Communist Party was established in 1921.)

POLITICAL STATUS

Date of joining CCP:	Number joining:
1923	1
1925	2
1926	7
1927	14
1928	4
1929	2
1930	1
1937	2
1945	1
Date unknown	11
Not known to be member	7
Total officers surveyed	52

These 52 generals of the Red hierarchy have varied in origin from rich men's sons to peasant backgrounds. Of their number, only 19 endured the ordeal of the Communists' famous Long March. One other might have participated in it, and one other probably did not. Thirty-one, however, never knew that year of endurance and physical torture, but they have risen without being members of that clique, partly because so many others died as a result of the trek.

The highest military body in Red China, the People's Revolutionary Military Council, is made up of 22 of these 52 Red generals, and three-fifths of them are on the Central Committee of the Chinese Communist Party.

It is Communist Party membership that makes a Red general, but he has to have some military experience.

Chapter 3

THE WEB AND TENTACLES OF ORGANIZATION

Red Army Strength Today

No longer are temple bells melted down by the Red Army of China, nor does the army post its war maps on the dirty interiors of Yenan caves. This is the *new* army, a giant empire of military offices, depots, and garrisons in the largest cities of China.

From his drafty, but richly carpeted office in pleasant old Peking, General Chu Teh, can put on his spectacles and look up to a mighty wall map. The old man of Yenan has hoped, fought, and waited a good many years for this opportunity to decipher from a single map of China the 239 red pins that denote his combat divisions. There are other symbols on the map. Five miniature flags, each modeled after the red field army flags, denote the five major military groupings. These are—

    First Field Army, 240,000 troops of about 32 divisions;
    Second Field Army, 360,000 troops of about 47 divisions;
    Third Field Army, 540,000 troops of about 72 divisions;
    Fourth Field Army, 450,000 troops of about 60 divisions;
    Fifth Field Army,   60,000 troops of about   6 divisions.
  Field Force total: 1,650,000 troops or about 217 divisions
        —plus: 1,000,000 line-of-communication troops,
                comprising about 22 divisions

but mostly consisting of non-combat units.

A grand total of: 2,650,000 troops—239 divisions—in the PLA.

This combat core of Red China's armed strength on the ground is not as great as the Communist Chinese would have us believe. These figures represent a careful estimate based on the very best available sources. The estimate does not purport to be more than a general breakdown of PLA strength, but it is close to actuality. The strength of the average Chinese division is about 7,000 men. Some divisions are known to be larger; some are as low as 5,000; but with the Chinese adaptation of Soviet materiel and Soviet military concepts, the figure of 7,000 will be increased, to approximate the 10,000 to 11,000 figure of the average Soviet division.

Over the past few years the strength estimates and publicly announced figures on Red China's armed forces have grown to unreal proportions. It is very difficult to count heads in this army. The apparent lack of standard stables of organization for all units, up to and including the field armies, has made the problem of final estimates difficult. However, the following are the ranges of current strength—

An infantry regiment is supposed to contain 3,242 officers and men.

A division consists of three regiments; but, as these usually are not up to strength, the average division contains about 7,000.

Two or more divisions make an army (15,000 to 22,000).

Two or more armies make a group-army (30,000 to 80,000).

A field army normally ranges in strength from 130,000 to 600,000, and consists of several group-armies.

When the Chinese Reds held their National Conference of Militia Cadres in Peking in 1950,[1] it was announced that the militia of China amounted to more than 5,500,000 men. The final strength of China's armed forces should be judged in terms of both the PLA (regular army) and the militia, but recognition must be given the fact that the militia is not a real combat force, and

---

[1] *People's China*, 16 November 1950.

its armament is poor. The actual armed might that Red China can bring to bear against a foreign power consists of:

2,650,000 Regular field forces (PLA)[2]
10,000 Air Force personnel
60,000 Navy (not yet a striking force)

2,720,000 total strength of the armed forces in regular service

Like the potential military manpower of the nation, the number of men in China who have carried arms is great. The Communist figure of 5,500,000 militia is not in excess of the number of men which China has, who, at one time or another, have shouldered rifles. The Nationalist army left millions of ex-soldiers behind it when it sailed for Formosa. Counting the militia, Red China's final total of armed men (not armed power) runs around 8,220,000. The militia, however, is but a reserve of semi-trained manpower, unfamiliar and unequipped with modern weapons. The Reds find portions of the militia unreliable. In February 1951 the PLA executed over 5,000 militia-men in South China alone. We should not exaggerate Red China's armed strength by adding in all the militia.

The Division Slice Is Low

How effectively organized is the PLA's strength of 2,650,000? The PLA is said to have a division slice (army-wide) of slightly over 11,000 for a 7,000 man division. This is an approximate figure, but it is very close to reality. The figure is comparable with the low slice of a Soviet division. However, division slices can be overworked to the point of becoming misleading statistics. The US Army has remarkably high division slices[3] if one views the formula of combat in terms of figures only. Conversely, the Soviets and the Chinese have low division slices. But the slice should be considered always in relation to the size of the division. For example, a US infantry division is more than twice as large as an average Chinese division. Other essential points to remember are: (1) the Communists, and especially the Chinese, make ex-

---
[2] The published estimate of British War Office Intelligence is 2,500,000.
[3] Army-wide, theater-wide and on down.

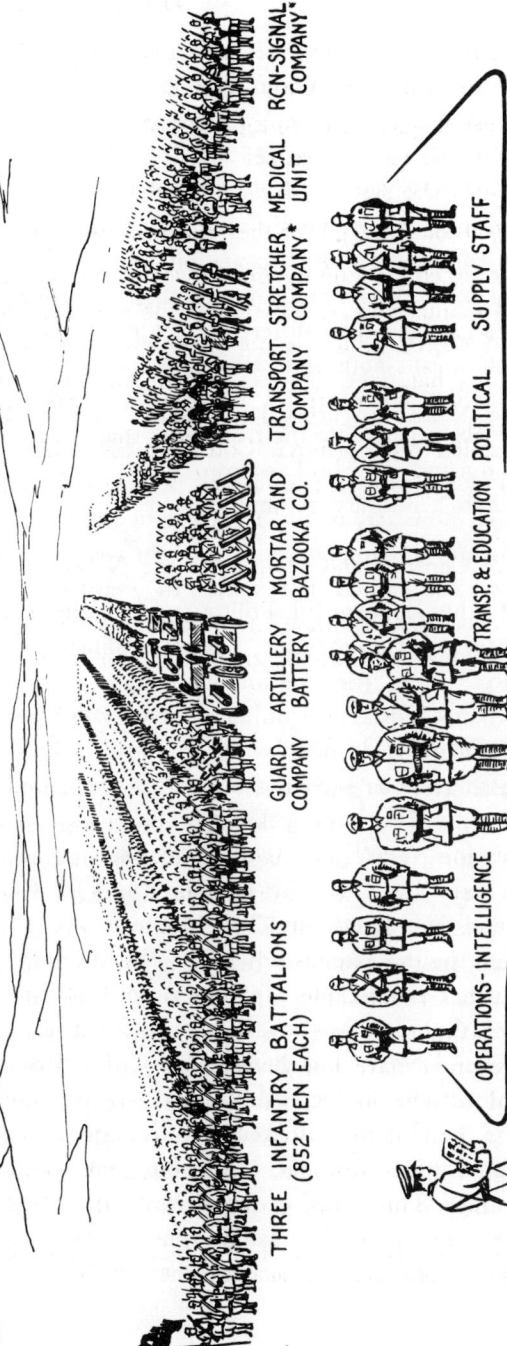

tensive use of civilian labor for line-of-communications and supply work, whereas the US Army does not; and (2) the degree of efficiency obtained by having effective supply, evacuation, and administrative services organized and trained within a combat unit, far outweighs the system of catch-as-catch-can that is inherent in the Communist armies. Our division slice may be larger, but our flexibility, communications, evacuation, care of the wounded, and other vital services are much better than in either the Soviet or the Chinese armies. The difference lies in the national approach. Human life means nothing to the hardened army officers of China and the USSR, where armies are more concerned about shoving the next replacements into the front lines than they are of removing the bleeding and bone-broken from them. But to us, human life is more than a military commodity.

The Army Controls and Dominates the Nation

Beneath the all-powerful Politburo rests the *People's Revolutionary Military Council,* the highest military-political planning body in Red China. (See the following chart.) It is in the Military Council that China's real military strategy is conceived—by the Council's twenty-two men, who are headed by the Chairman, Mao Tse-tung. Thus Mao not only runs the nation; he also controls the army. The interlocking of echelons, by the system of men "wearing two hats," is evident here in both Mao's dual positions and Chu Teh's, for the latter is Vice Chairman of the Council and Commander-in-Chief of the PLA.

The same system extends down into the lower military echelons. For instance, General Peng Te-huai is not only the Deputy Commander of the PLA but is also Commander of the First Field Army. General Nieh Jung-chen is Vice Chief of Staff of the PLA, and Commander of the Fifth Field Army. Within the field armies the interlocking also holds; often one of the deputy commanders of a field army also is a group-army commander within the field army. This is one of the elements of political control that guard the army from the inside. While trust may be cautiously placed in the old military leaders, the Communist Party takes a

THE WEB AND TENTACLES OF ORGANIZATION

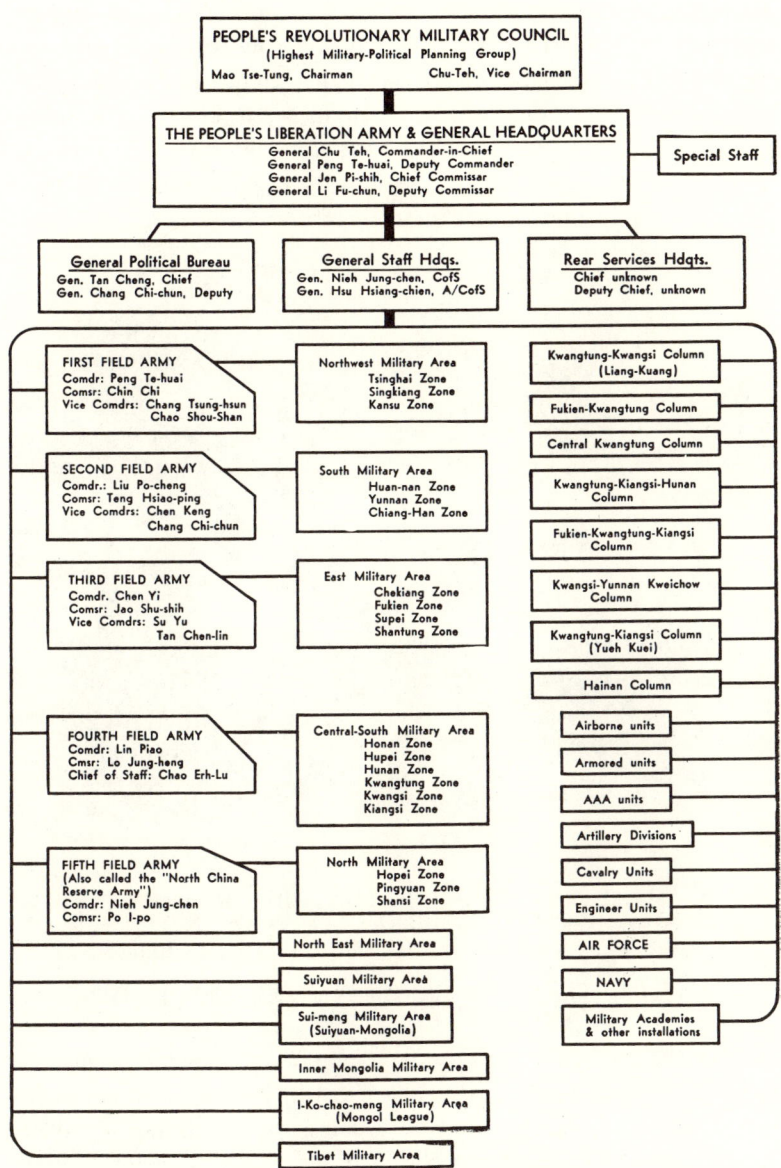

GENERAL ORGANIZATION OF THE CHINESE RED ARMY.

variety of measures to insure that there is no deviation by highly placed men. In this connection, it is noteworthy that there has been no rotation of generals within the higher command positions for years—the rotation that is normal in most large armies in other nations. The field army commanders have literally "grown up" with their commands and are likely to stay with them until they die—or possibly meet death in some future purge.

Official Red Chinese Photo.
from The Commemoration Volume (Chinese Text), 1949.

THE COMMANDER-IN-CHIEF, CHU TEH, AND THE GENERAL STAFF OF THE PEOPLE'S LIBERATION ARMY, IN 1949.
Back row: Wang Cheng, Chang Hsueh-ssu, Li T'ao, Li Kuo-ying, Yang Ch'eng-wu, Liu Shan-pen.
Front row: Lu Ch'eng-ts'ao, Nieh Jung-chen, Chu Teh, Fu Chung, Tai Ching-yuan, Yang Ch'i-ch'ing, K'ang K'e-ching.

Over the nation there is a web of civilian control emanating from the *State Administrative Council,* which rests in organization just below the Politiburo and on a par with the Military Council. Civilian control filters from the Administrative Council through judiciary, finance, trade, communications and related agencies to the six administrative regions of China. But on this level of final implementation, civilian control comes into losing competition with the two military organizations which are already meshed under one commander. These are (1) the *field armies,* the commanders of which are also (in most cases) commanders of (2) the *military areas* and are chairmen of the *Military and Administrative (Political) Committees* for each of the administrative regions.

So, while civilian control has extended down to the regions, the military commanders occupy the dominant positions and are backed with troops, to boot. The breakdown of these regions follows the same pattern, for there are subordinate military areas to match the provinces (each region consists of several provinces); and in many cases army officers are provincial governors as well as military area chiefs. Thus, there is a fixed web of civilian control; but the army extends tentacles which are, in the end, stronger than the civil web. See the chart titled, THE WEB AND TENTACLES OF CONTROL IN CHINA.

By law the armed forces of Red China consist of—
(1) the People's Liberation Army (made up of Army, Air Force, and Navy);
(2) the People's Public Security Forces (Militia and the Secret Police);
(3) the People's Police (regular police forces in cities and provinces).[4]

The entire Red governmental structure is balanced to keep power in a dictator's hands. The Army and the Public Security Forces fall under the command and direction of the Revolutionary Military Council, while the regular police are maintained as a counterbalance, under strict civilian control. The system of commissars extends its control down from the army high command to the infantry squad. Both the army's *Political Bureau* and the *Communist Party* have their representatives scattered throughout the armed services, so that the webs of political control are dual. The secret police, about which little is known, adds another measure of surveillance within the military forces. Thus, while the army

---
[4] Article 10 of The Common Program of the Chinese People's Political Consultative Conference, (20 September 1949), as published in a full-text translation by the American Consulate, Shanghai, China. See Appendix IV.

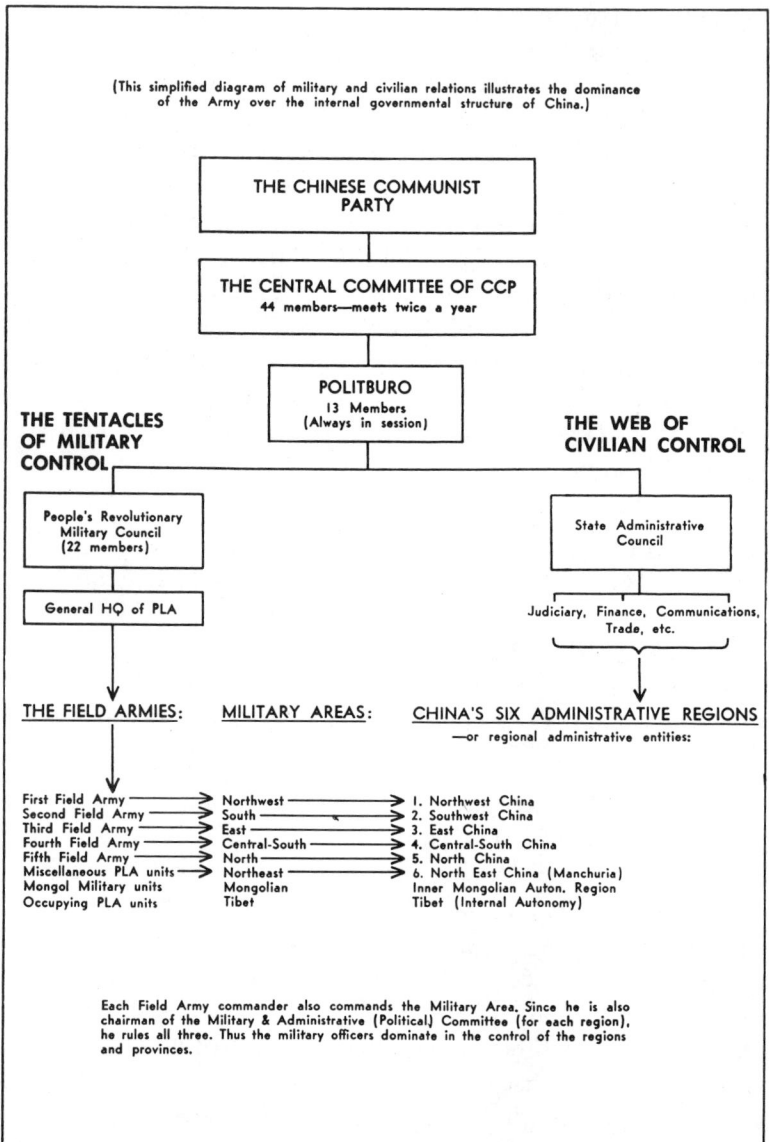

THE WEB AND TENTACLES OF CONTROL IN CHINA.

dominates in military and civil (regionary) control, in itself it is subject to watch from within and without. All of these control strings lead back to one man, Dictator Mao Tse-tung.

The PLA Staff Is Seeking Final Foundation

The "little devils" are still waiting on their masters. Perhaps the constant cups of tea increase the efficiency of the PLA's General Headquarters staff, but in any event it is a well-grounded habit to have the young orderlies scurrying about waiting on the men who have risen to great power. The boys are learning obedience, while the general staff enjoys "room service."

Within Peking's red-walled, yellow-tiled Forbidden City, the PLA's General Headquarters is growing rapidly, for it has discovered that to garrison and govern the China mainland is a task far greater than it ever anticipated. Office space is being measured to fit more personnel into the buildings. Desks for additional staff officers and Soviet advisors still are being moved in. Safes are being sought, for this headquarters is growing extremely secretive. The earlier, naive ideas on organizational simplicity for a higher headquarters have been abandoned in favor of a giant military bureaucracy. These Red Chinese have simply found that their austere Yenan concepts don't fit or work from Peking. For example, there is the matter of military communications, which is now complex and involved to a degree far surpassing the days of 1948. The very men who so criticized Chiang Kai-shek's government for its military bureaucracy and staffs are now knee-deep in staff officers and orderlies. These men are falling victim to the demands of giant responsibilities. And, since this headquarters machinery feels it must exert full control from its dictatorship level to the infantry squad, the resultant staff organization is consequently enlarging.

The PLA General Headquarters is divided into three main staffs, or bureaus: Political Affairs, the General Staff, and Rear Services. (See accompanying chart.)

Best organized and largest in its number of departments is the *General Political Bureau.* Here the *Propaganda Department* plans

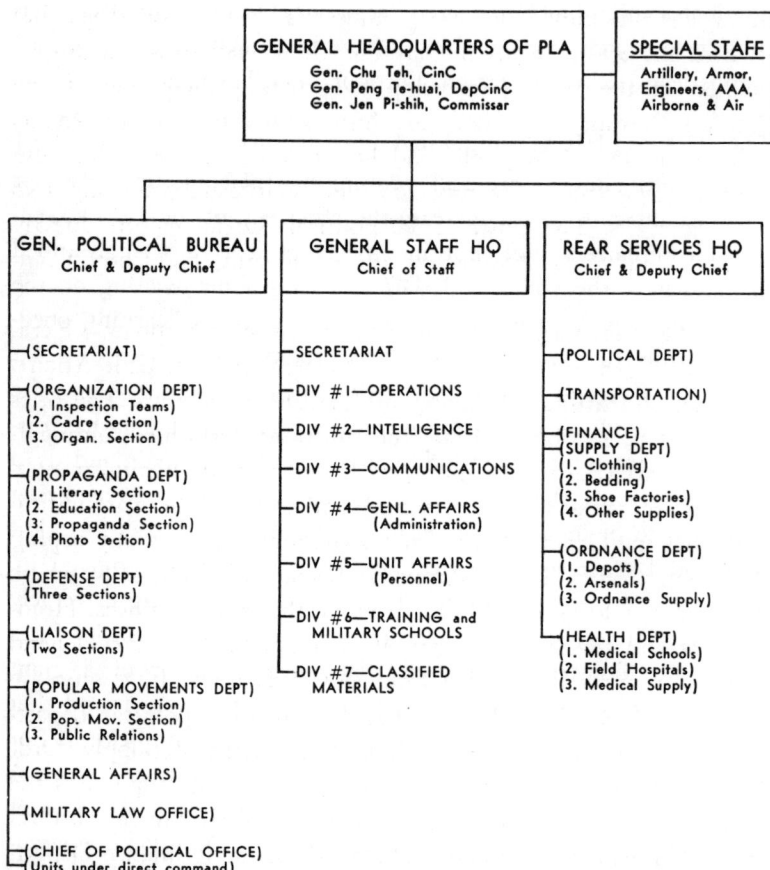

THE ORGANIZATION OF THE PLA'S HEADQUARTERS AND STAFF.

the army-wide campaigns that include self-criticism meetings, political indoctrination schedules, and education. The books which the army *can* read, and those which it *must* read, are selected by this staff. The *Popular Movement's Department* schedules and organizes the army's participation in farm and factory production. This department insures that the people see the army in the most favorable light. It endeavors to integrate the army into all possible civilian activities. This is one of the most important duties of the Peking military headquarters. The Political Bureau prepares multiple plans and issues many directives; but it also dispatches its own inspection teams to "spy out" how well these are implemented in the field. Censorship falls within the scope of the Political Bureau, for it not only insures that no military secrets leak out in the photographs and literature of the army, but also it makes sure that its commissars play their usual watching role over the ranks. The Chief of the Political Bureau reports directly to Chu Teh, Peng Te-huai, or to Jen Pi-shih, the Chief Commissar.

The *General Staff* is divided into seven staff sections: Operations, Intelligence, Communications, General Affairs, Unit Affairs, Training and Military Schools, and Classified Materials. The titles of these staff sections indicate the functions performed, although the General Affairs staff might be better labeled Administration. Unit Affairs is the G-1, or personnel staff section. There are indications that the General Staff is not smoothly or successfully coping with its problems. There is some confusion in Peking as to where the responsibilities should lie between the Rear Services Headquarters and the General Staff. It is noticeable that the General Staff is pretty well excluded from G-4 and supply functions.

The *Rear Services Headquarters* has its own political department in addition to its three main departments of Supply, Ordnance, and Health. The latter department not only supervises the medical schools and controls the field hospitals but is also responsible for medical supplies. The hands of the Ordnance Department staff are very full these days, for one of the biggest military headaches in Red China comes from the confusion of calibers of guns with which the PLA is equipped. Arsenal production comes under the supervision of this department, which also is in constant liaison with the Soviet Army on matters of new supply and standardization of arms. Actually, Soviet officers are actively assisting this portion of the Rear Services staff in its efforts toward weapons standardization and supply.

The PLA wears out shoes faster, perhaps, than any other army. This is not alone caused by the PLA's proclivity for marches, but results from the fact the shoes and sandals are lightly and cheaply made. The PLA has its own shoe factories, manned part-time by uniformed soldiers. Whenever these factories, or the staff plan, fail to provide the necessary footgear, the Supply Department puts several thousand women to work in their homes, to fill the deficiency. The Supply Department of the Rear Services Headquarters is the Quartermaster staff of the PLA and it directs and controls the activities of clothing and equipment supply.

Chiefs of armor, artillery, antiaircraft, engineers, and airborne troops are known to exist, but it is uncertain how much authority these officers exercise. They are believed to constitute a Special Staff. Soviet officers are very prominent here, as advisors with authority.

Since the Chinese Reds intervened in Korea, they have had to cope with a problem somewhat new in their experience—fuel and motor vehicles. It is believed that the Rear Services now include a Transportation and Fuel Supply department, separate from the Ordnance and the Supply departments. Undoubtedly, the Chinese have borrowed directly from the Soviet Army in staff organization and procedure. All of these staff organizations will change form in the years to come, for the Red militarists only recently have been vaulted to the "big picture" scale of operations. They know, and the Soviets can see, that much improvement is required in the General Staff and in the Rear Services. Like the army, the General Headquarters in Peking is undergoing changes. Organizationally it is in a state of great transition, with Russian advice directing it more toward the Soviet pattern. The entire General Headquarters staff is ill-organized and needs reshuffling into a more workable set-up.

The Armies Vary in Size and Character

The field army commanders answer directly to the PLA's General Headquarters in Peking. Large and unwieldy, in a sense, the field armies constitute the bulk of China's military strength—although there are some independent divisions, and units such as artillery, cavalry and armor, which are under Peking's direct control,

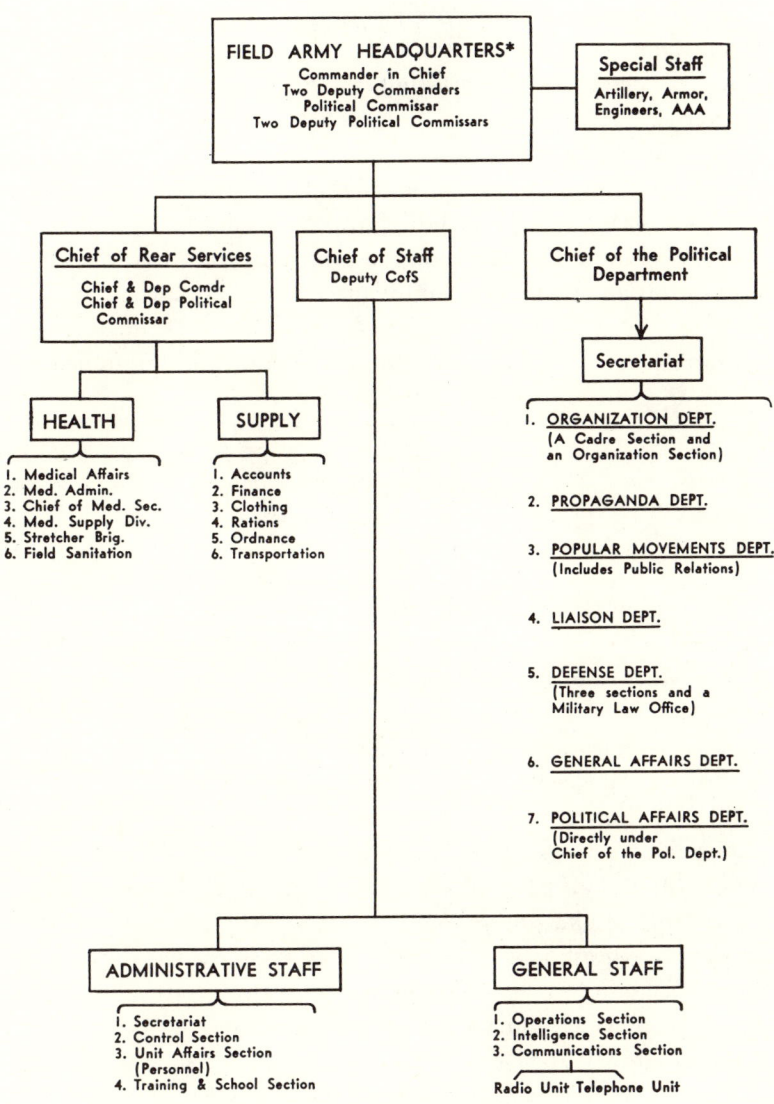

THE GENERAL ORGANIZATION OF A FIELD ARMY HEADQUARTERS.

The staffs of field armies are not yet too large, but as these huge armies take on a greater semblance of modernity, the staffs will grow. At present the political staff of a field army is as large as the general staff. The organization of a field army staff is shown in the accompanying chart.

Each field army is organized into two or more group-armies and each group-army is subdivided into armies of two to three divisions each. There are about 77 armies in the PLA. The divisions are triangular, consisting of three regiments each.

Under the direct command of the field army commander are his special troops, which include at least one each of the following:

>Special duty regiment
>Training regiment
>Transportation regiment
>Engineer battalion
>Reconnaissance battalion
>Communications battalion
>Antiaircraft battalion

There is no standard field army so far as organization is concerned. Each of these armies grew in accordance with the requirements which the war imposed upon it. Growth and organization were influenced by the characteristics of the region in which the field army operated. The wealth of their KMT opponents also influenced the development of each of these forces. The Fourth Field Army for example, was opposed by a large and well-equipped Nationalist force which, as it slowly crumbled, left inheritances of trained men and acres of arms and equipment. Thus Lin Piao's forces fattened like vultures on the carcass of General Tu Yu-ming's broken Northeast China Command. In contrast, the First Field Army, operating in the militarily poorer area of Northwest China, against foes which did not disintegrate so easily and quickly, had a slower growth than the Fourth. The Fourth also was aided by stocks of surrendered Japanese arms obtained through Soviet help in 1945.

Each of the field armies grew up in a particular region; and for a time each bore the name of the area in which it campaigned. As the Civil War drew to a close, these armies were far afield, so name changes were in order. Thus, Lin Piao's "Northeast PLA" became the "Fourth Field Army." The field armies, or almost the entire PLA combat force, originated north of the Yangtze River.

Official Red Chinese Photo.
THE SOUTH CHINA LIBERATION ARMY'S STAFF IN 1949.
Elements of this army and its staff officers are now incorporated in other field armies.
Back Row: Lo Fan-chun, Huang Yu, Mai Pai-shan, Feng Nai-chao.
Front Row: Cheng Man-yuan, Ku Ta-tsun, Chang Yun-i, Wu Chi-wei, Li Chin-chieh.

Modernized Guerrilla Columns

In South China, Red fifth columns sustained themselves for many years on a guerrilla basis until about 1948, when their numbers and arms began to grow. As the field armies swept southward in 1949-50, these *guerrilla columns* attacked more vigorously, gathered intelligence, and otherwise assisted the regular armies. All of these guerrilla bodies bore regional names, such as the Hainan Column, or the Fukien-Kwangtung Column; today these units exist in the PLA with their original titles but with more formal organization, arms and equipment. (They have the most awkward titles of any PLA units.) These units, ranging from 4,000 to 15,000 men in strength, are commanded by old-line Communists. The following columns are under the direct control of PLA's General Headquarters—

(1) Kwangtung-Kwangsi (or Liang-Kuang) Column, commanded by General Tseng Sheng.
(2) Fukien-Kwangtung Column, also known as the Min Yueh Border Double Column; Commander, Fang Fang.
(3) Central Kwangtung Column (or Yueh-chung) Column; Commander, Wu Yu-heng.
(4) Kwangtung-Kiangsi-Hunan (or Yueh Kan Hsiang Border) Column; Commander, Lin Ping; Vice Commander, Huang Sung-chien.
(5) Fukien-Kwangtung-Kiangsi (or Min Yueh Kan Border) Column; Commander, Liu Yung-sheng; Vice Commander and Chief of Staff, Tieh Chien.
(6) Kwangsi-Yunnan-Kweichow (or Kuei Tien Chien Border) Column; Commander, Chuang Tien; Vice Commander, Chu Chia-pi.
(7) Kwangtung-Kwangsi (or Yueh Kuei Border) Column; Commander, Liang Kuang.
(8) Hainan (or Chiung-yen) Column, commanded by General Feng Pai-chu.[5] Vice Commander, Ma Pai-shan.

The Kwangtung-Kwangsi Column of General Tseng has a unique history—and a future. In 1938 Tseng organized the nucleus of this guerrilla body under the title of the East River Column. It conducted effective operations against the Japanese in World War II. In 1946 the KMT and the CCP agreed to an evacuation of the East River Column and other Red guerrillas to Shantung. In July 1946 the US military forces in China implemented this evacuation by transporting the Communist guerrillas to the north. No sooner were these rough partisans back in Red territory in Shantung when General Chu Teh gave orders that they be oriented to future military plans and sent back to South China. Before the year 1946 was out some of these guerrillas were back in Kwangtung and renewing their subversive activities. Then on 1 August 1947 the remnants of the East River Column in Shantung provided the cadre for the official recreation of the

---

[5] These and other miscellaneous units are mainly identified from "A General View of the Chinese People's Liberation Army and the War Zones Which It Controls," Appendix No. 7 to a 1950 special book (Japanese text), by a bureau chief in the Japanese Ministry of Foreign Affairs. (Hoover Library Collection.)

THE WEB AND TENTACLES OF ORGANIZATION

Official Red Chinese Photo.

THE FIRST FIELD ARMY GENERAL STAFF IN 1949.
Back row: Ch'en Po, Wang Shih-t'ai, Ho Lung, Chao Shou-han, Lo Jui-ch'ing.
Front row: Tu Kuan-jen, Wang Chao, Sun Chih-yuan, Tso Hsieh-chung, Li Chen, Jen Pai-ke.

Kwangtung-Kwangsi Column. The Reds even announced that this outfit was going to fight its way back—which it did. In 1948 the column was placed under the Third Field Army, and its southern elements occupied much of Kwangtung Province before the arrival of the main Red forces in 1949. General Tseng is a man who has traveled extensively in southeast Asia; he and his column of modernized guerrillas may show up any place and cause serious trouble. So may the other columns, which have a cosmopolitan composition of personnel from several lands in south-east Asia.

The First Field Army—Almost Last in Importance

Smallest and least spectacular of the four *main* field armies, this was formerly the Northwest China PLA. It still has its original commander, General Peng Te-huai, although he wears the more honorable cap of Deputy Commander-in-Chief of the entire PLA. This is the "desert army," if China can be said to have one. Unlike the other field armies, this unit usually has not fought in large marshaled masses, but has conducted its campaign with more or less independent hard-hitting columns. Typical of this field army is the unit which crossed a part of the Gobi desert on foot in 1949, accomplishing a march of 1,500 kilometers in a little more than a month.[6] In its journey between Tunhwang, in northwest Kansu, and Khotan, near the Tibetan border, this Chinese column ran into severe winter conditions and the men force-marched for 18 days, shivering in their sheepskins for 13 nights of bivouac on the open desert. This element was without any tentage; one must admire the endurance of troops who can survive a crossing of the Gobi in winter, where many a hardy man has perished while traveling in the relative comfort of a caravan.

First in numerical designation, and first in that its commander is the senior field army commander, this army is not the one chosen by China for its first line of aggression (or defense). The First Field Army garrisons and guards the interior of Asia, where its most intimate contact with foreign armies is its string of lonely border posts that fringe the military garrisons of Outer Mongolia and the USSR. This is the land-locked, isolated Chinese field army whose comparatively small strength is now spread thinly over the barren, sandy wastelands of the Gobi's populated fringes, and across the ancient caravan routes to the rugged mountains of Sinkiang.

The First had its real beginnings in the combat backwater of the northwestern provinces of China, where the China Civil War was fought on a smaller scale than in the east and northeast. To the First fell the distinction of being the guardians of the cave-center of Yenan—the old Communist capital which fell to the Nationalists in 1947 after only a show of defense by this unit. The Communists took the loss of their revered capitol (it now has become virtually a national shrine) with a calmness and resignation that was in

---

[6] *North China Daily News*, 21 January 1950.

great contrast to the importance with which the rest of China, and the world at large, viewed it.

Much of the supplies and armament captured in the Civil War by other field armies has been redistributed to the First, but the First did not fall heir to the rich stocks of Japanese and American arms acquired by the others. This was the poor field army, at least until recently. It is still the least modern of the field armies and the most difficult to support logistically, primarily because it is widely dispersed in a region with very poor communication facilities.

Constructing roads, herding sheep, planting trees, erecting telegraph poles, and operating flour mills, this field army is helping to maintain itself. It is not, however, engaging in any large scale maneuvers, or training as actively for combat as the others.

The First is now a mixture of Asiatics, more so than it was at the close of the Civil War. Its recruiting base is such as to include more Moslems than any other of the field armies. Into its ranks it is drawing the Khirgiz, Kazakh, Sibo, Tartar, Mongol, Moslem, and Han people.

There are sizable remnants of former Nationalist military forces in the First. The "liberation" of Sinkiang was achieved without a shot being fired.[7] So well infiltrated with Red fifth columnists were the KMT forces in Western China that they turned over to the Communists with such a show of submission that they were allowed to become a regular part of the PLA. For example, General Tao Chih-yueh's former Nationalist Army is now the 22d Group-Army of the First Field Army. What was formerly called the "Sinkiang National People's Army," originally a guerrilla force, is now formally organized as the 5th Army.

The Soviets are presently establishing a military base in Sinkiang and the Chinese Reds do not have a large measure of control there. However, a considerable number of Soviet officers are aiding the Chinese in the reorganization and training of the Sinkiang elements of the First Field Army. General Peng Te-huai, who now commands this field army in name only, has as his two

---

[7] *China Weekly Review*, 28 January 1950.

deputy commanders, Generals Chao Shou-shan and Chang Tsung-hsun. The latter is the acting commander. The Chief of Staff is General Chen Hai-han and the chief political commissars are Generals Hsi Chung-hsun and Chin Chi. General Tao Chih-yueh has already been mentioned, as a group-army commander. In 1950 Generals Wang Chen, Hsu Kuan-ta and Yang Te-chih were the three group-army commanders.[8]

The *Northwest Military Area,* commanded by the "Old Butcher" Ho Lung, is subordinate to the First Field Army which garrisons most of the region. This places old Ho Lung under a former subordinate of his, General Chang Tsung-hsun. Certain line-of-communication (or district) troops are under Ho Lung. His military area is divided and commanded as follows[9]—

Tsinghai—Commander, Ho Ping-yen; Political Commissar; Wang Shang-hsieh.

Kansu—Commander, unknown; Deputy Commander, Hsu Kuo-chen.

The Sinkiang region is directly under General Wang Chen who is a unit commander as well.

Should the Chinese Communists need to commit to combat an entire field army in a hurry, it will not be this one; but if they desire to strengthen any combat force with excellent cavalry, it will probably be taken from the First. The Communists have reported[10] that they have 100,000 troops in Sinkiang. This is about one half the strength of the First Field Army, which is estimated to number 240,000 men, officers, and political commissars. There were reports in 1951 (mostly from Chinese Nationalists) that elements of the First Field Army were withdrawn from Sinkiang, and replaced by Soviet Army units. Several Moslem units of this field army moved to Manchuria in February 1951, and other elements cooperated with General Liu Po-cheng's forces in the 1951 occupation of Tibet.

---

[8] According to the Chinese Problem Research Dept., Democratic Review, 1 November 1950 (published in Hong Kong), and other sources.

[9] Appendix No. 7 to a Japanese Ministry Foreign Affairs publication (in Japanese), 1950.

[10] *People's China,* 16 February 1950.

Official Red Chinese Photo.

THE "ONE-EYED DRAGON," GENERAL LIU PO-CHENG AND HIS GENERAL STAFF OF THE SECOND FIELD ARMY, 1949.
Back row: Chang Nan-sheng, Ma Hing, Pu K'e.
Middle row: Tsêng K'e, Ch'ien Hain-chung, Liao Yun-chou, Wei Hsiao-t'eng.
Front row: T'eng Tai-yuan, T'sai Shu-fan, Liu Po-cheng, Kao Shu-hsun, Yang Li-san.

The Second Field Army Has a Half-Blind Commander

"Waders of the Yangtze," "Liberators of Tibet," the sloe-eyed men of this field army have probably worn out more sandals and shoes than any other comparable force; for General Liu Po-cheng, if he has done nothing else, has worried his enemies and tired his men by marching and countermarching.

This field army is foot-mobile—and elusive, even to aircraft. It has a commander who knows when and how to stop and fight, yet senses the moment to run. It is a force that is proud of its retreats—retreats which confuse the enemy. The men of this force are mainly from Central China. This is the former "Central Plains Liberation Army." Outstanding in its combat record is its participation in the campaign around Hsuchou, Northern Kiangsu, where it demonstrated its traditional maneuverability. It has its proportion of ex-Nationalist soldiers, but they are fairly evenly distributed through all ranks.

The Second Field Army was the "unknown Army" in 1946 and 1947 when the force and its commander were just coming into prominence on a strategic level in the Civil War. So limited was information about Liu Po-cheng and his veterans, that foreign correspondents were willing to pay $100 US for a single photograph of the one-eyed commander. There was then an aura of mystery about this force. It was known to have once been part of Chen Yi's forces, but its true organization and character became known only after 1947, when it swept down from Shantung to upset Nationalist stomachs—and strategy.

This field army seemed to grow and thrive on hardship and movement. It gathered grain and recruited men as it passed quickly through villages. It had no motor vehicles until 1948. Its men knew how to scramble over high city walls, however, and in city fighting they showed skill in avoiding the streets and in tunneling through walls from house to house. This army's rear services were usually strung out considerably, but somehow were efficient. Liu Po-cheng moved so fast that he rarely had his rear service staff with him at his command post. "Their job *is* in the rear," he often remarked. Actually his logistical staff and supply elements were usually busy "closing out a rear area"—a polite military phrase for "looting the land we leave of all we can get." When resources of the rear had "dried up," Liu pushed forward to new fields of rice and other grain.

Unlike Lin Piao, Liu Po-cheng had no land to divide up and thus entice recruits into his army. Men stuck with Liu and others flocked to him because he was a winner. It amused these rough troopers to hear the Nationalists announce that Liu was dead; once in 1948 his death was even "confirmed" and the body allegedly found. Nationalist sentries on outpost at night feared elements of this army when it was known to be ranging about. One night, twelve of Liu's soldiers, with only one machine gun, captured a fair-sized town garrisoned by about a hundred Government troops by the simple expedient of firing into the north and south gates, then calmly walking into the town the next morning! The twelve men are typical of most of the 360,000 who make up this field army.

General Liu is a scholarly soldier. He likes to have his staff study when there is time. Two hours a day is regarded as a reasonable minimum study period. The works of Marx and Lenin are pawned off by Liu as good appetizers before breakfast.

General Liu formerly had only 200 men in his headquarters, not counting "sentries and orderlies," a headquarters that was appropriately modest in strength and mobile. Today, Liu's command group numbers less than 300.

The present known deputy commander is General Chen Keng, a man of considerable tactical skill. Both Generals Li Ta and Wang Chi-ming have been reported as the Chief of Staff. General Teng Hsiao-ping is the field army's political commissar; General Liu Yu-kang was listed, in 1948, as the Chief of the field army's Political Department. Somewhere on the staff, or in one of the subordinate commands, fits General Hsieh Fu-chih.

In 1950 the known group-army commanders were: Generals Yang Yung, Chen Hsi-lien, and Chou Shih-ti.[11]

Like the other field armies, the Second occupies and dominates a military area: Liu Po-cheng is the commander of the *South Military Area* which is divided as follows[12]—

Huan-nan (Southern Anhwei), commander unknown.
Yunnan, commanded by Chen Keng.
Chiang-Han (confluence of the Yangtze and Han Rivers, near Hankow), commanded by Li Jen-lin.

It is on this fragmentary knowledge that one must rest a description of this force—a force which exceeds in size (360,000) and in combat experience some of the national armies of the world. The character of this army lies mainly in its colorful commander, who shares the hard lot of his men in combat. His orders, however hard to carry out, are well obeyed. This is the only army in

---

[11] *Democratic Review*, 1 November 1950.
[12] Appendix 7 to a Japanese Ministry of Foreign Affairs Publication (in Japanese), 1950.

Official Red Chinese Photo.

THE THIRD FIELD ARMY'S GENERAL STAFF IN 1949.
Back row: Wei Lai-kuo, Lai Shao-ch'i, Hsieh-k'un, T'ang Kuo-tung, Li Lan-t'ing, Li Yun-chang, He Chi-li.
Front row: Wang Ch'ien-an, Cheng Shih-ch'u, Su Yu, Chiang Wei-ch'ing, Tu Chung-fu.

modern history whose elements have suffered, in the high winds and deep snows, in order to penetrate into the remote fastness of isolated Tibet.

The Third Field Army Has an Unfulfilled Mission

Formerly called the East China PLA, this is presently the largest of the field armies, with a strength of about 540,000 men, officers, and political commissars. This is the army which took inventory of the 70,000-odd flush toilets in Shanghai,[13] the army whose men could not operate the tanks they captured or understand toilet bowls. However, the country bumpkins of Chen Yi's Third Field Army are more sophisticated now, for they garrison Shanghai, Nanking, Hsuchou, and other cities. These simple farmers and farmers' sons are the proud liberators of Shanghai's prostitutes and Hsuchou's political prisoners. They can be re-

---

[13] *North China Daily News*, 25 February 1950.

garded as among China's very best soldiers. The commissars hope that the cities will not spoil them.

The climate of Shantung, where this field army originated, is fairly pleasant, comparable to that of Illinois. When this army moved south in 1949, however, it ran into trouble in the more tropical climates. Its ranks were thinned for a time[14] by malaria and black water fever; and the tough feet of these northerners were softened and made spongy by the fungus of athlete's foot. To such a serious extent did illness prevail in this force, that in February 1950 General Chen Yi ordered an "army health drive."[15] As to the number of sickness cases, there are no exact figures; but the information available indicates Chen Yi and his staff were decidedly worried for a time.

Despite Communist claims of a great health drive and thousands of inoculations, the Reds admit to a total of only "80 medical doctors and experts"—a very small number of medical personnel for a field army as large and widely spread as the Third. Between the lines of the press accounts of this health drive one gathers that the medical teams probably spent more time trying to teach Chen Yi's troops how to get rid of lice than they did in giving inoculations. If the Chinese Red soldier successfully rids himself of fleas and lice, he has achieved epochal progress in sanitation and health preservation!

The record of this force is impressive for its tenacity, which is the product of fine leadership. In 1946 the army was small, reportedly[16] only about 70,000 men; but though of small size it was of good combat quality.

In 1949 this army (then the East China PLA) stood in the way of a Kuomintang advance to the north. It represented the major obstacle to the Nationalists between Nanking and Tientsin. A weaker force than the East China PLA might have given ground under the pressure which the Generalissimo's troops applied; but

---

[14] This army also had 60,000 casualties from liver fluke contracted in amphibious training in the dirty waters near Shanghai.
[15] *North China Daily News,* 25 March 1950.
[16] General Su Yu "Liberation of Taiwan in Sight," *People's China,* 16 February 1950.

Generals Chen Yi and Su Yu held their force together against heavy odds, while they blocked, feinted, and maneuvered to bar the corridor to Tientsin. Steadily these Red commanders built up their ranks and flung out guerrilla cadres to harass Kiangsu on the Nationalists' right flank.

All Chinese Red armies are skilled in destroying railroads, but this army was not content to rip up the rails and carry away the ties. It burned the timbers, melted the steel, and, by dint of mass regimentation of the people, reduced miles of railway embankments to flat terrain and planted them with crops. Even air observers complained that they could see no trace of the railway lines destroyed by Chen Yi's men.

General Chen Yi had a limited amount of square mileage from which to recruit troops, and his losses between 1945 and 1949 were high, so he looked to his enemy since the "trained recruits were at the front." He culled his bags of prisoners for younger men, particularly technicians and those who had relatives in his domain. With these he steadily swelled his ranks. By 1947 he began to expend his men more freely, and by 1949 he was regularly committing his army to positional warfare in which he did some maneuvering. With the help of General Liu Po-cheng's forces, Chen Yi's field army fought the climactic Hsuchou[17] campaign, after which the occupation of South China was mostly a matter of marching. To this field army and the Second must go the credit for fighting the hardest campaigns and battles of China's Civil War, or the "War of Liberation" as the Communists call it.

General Chen Yi is fortunate in having Su Yu as a deputy commander and has not hesitated, at times, to let General Su Yu assume almost independent command of a portion of the Third Field Army. The other Deputy Commanders are General Tan Chen-lin and General Chang Ting-cheng. General Chen Shih-chu is Chief of Staff, while shrewd little Jao Shu-shih, formerly well liked by some Americans, is the number one Political Commissar.

---

[17] The Hsuchou Battle is also called "Huaihai"—a combination of Huaiyin (a town in Northern Kiangsu east of Hsuchou) and Haichou, eastern terminus of the Lunghai Railway.

Of the known subordinate commanders, General Chen Jui-ting commands the Third (Mechanized) Army in Nanking, and General Li Yun-chang may still be with Chen Yi as an army commander, although he is now listed as a cabinet minister.

In 1950 the Third had four group-armies commanded by Generals Wang Chien-an, Sung Shih-lun, Yeh Fei, and Chen Shih-chu.[18] Two of these generals were also regional commanders.

The *East Military Area* within which this field army is disposed, is also commanded by General Chen Yi. The subordinate districts of this regional command are[19]—

Chekiang, commanded by Wang Chien-an;
Fukien, commanded by Yeh Fei;
Su-pei (North Kiangsu), commanded by Chang Chen-tung;
Shantung, commanded by Hsu Shih-yu.

This part of China's Red Army contains a considerable number of mechanized units, hence it is ostensibly more modern than the First Field Army. It has undergone extensive amphibious training. It is China's amphibious army; it is scheduled to attack Taiwan some time in the future.

The Fourth Field Army Is Changing Complexion

With war and time the complexion of an army changes. It is useless to record that an army has this or that health and color one year; for combat, training schedules, discipline, replacements—any one of these can reshape the army for better or worse in a short time. This part of the Chinese army is no exception; but, for the record, here is its character and personality in 1951.

Manchurian peasants and the unskilled workers of Mukden, Harbin, and other cities comprise most of its enlisted numbers. However, the cement that binds together this force of none too enthusiastic Manchurians is the core of old "New Fourth Army" men, mostly from Shantung. This cadre consists of simon-pure, politically tested Communists, almost everyone of whom marched

---

[18] *Democratic Review*, 1 November 1950.
[19] Appendix 7 to a Japanese Ministry of Foreign Affairs publication (in Japanese), 1950.

Official Red Chinese Photo.

THE FOURTH FIELD ARMY'S GENERAL STAFF IN 1949.
Back row: Huang Ta-hsuan, Hu Ch'i-ts'ai, Tsêng Tsê-chêng, Liu Pai-yu.
Middle row: Su Ching, Han Hsien-ch'u, Ting Chih-hui, Liu Mei-ts'un.
Front row: Li T'ien-yu, Chung Ch'ih-ping, Lo-Jung-huan, Chang Chen.

on foot to Manchuria after VJ-day. Made up of proud men, particularly proud of the traditions of the New Fourth Army (also their present numerical designation), this hard core has done well. Promotions have come fast for them since 1945. They know they tipped the scales in favor of Red military victory during the Civil War. It was *their* army which never lost its aggressiveness, even during and after the "truce period." It was *their* army which completely defeated a demoralized Nationalist group army, then swept down from Manchuria to fall on General Fu Tso-yi, whose back was turned on the Northeast because he was so occupied with fighting Communist hordes from the south.

But this field army is not composed altogether of die-hard Red opportunists. It has picked up and politically retrained Nationalist remnants all the way from Manchuria to South China. Some of the field army's personnel of today were once Japanese puppet troops. Gun-wise Japanese from the old saber-rattling Kwantung Army were earlier found in these ranks. They may appear in the future in an "International Volunteer Corps." The Red 50th Army is the old Nationalist 60th Army lock, stock, and barrel. But the Reds like to test in combat the loyalty of those who have defected from the KMT armies; so the 50th was one of the first units committed to hard fighting in Korea. Of its original number less than 20 percent remain alive today. Chinese from Hainan Island are in the ranks as individuals. The Fourth Field Army once had full control of the Hainan Column, a unit of professional fifth columnists.

This is the cosmopolitan field army. It has long spoken Russian to Soviet Army men and received training from them. In some messes, only Mongolian is spoken, for the Fourth Field Army contains Inner Mongolian cavalry units. When this field army entered the war in Korea in 1950, one might say it was repaying an old debt; for in the autumn of 1946 a large element of hard-pressed troops of Lin Piao's field army escaped Nationalist annihilation when the North Koreans permitted them to cross over their border at the airfield city of Antung. They later crossed back into Manchuria at a more northern point within Red territory.

But the Fourth has more intimate relations with North Korea; it has had Korean units within its fighting hordes since 1945. I saw these Koreans in Chinese uniforms as early as 1946, when the Nationalists captured some of them. A year later I saw some of them in Harbin and confirmed my impression by asking a Chinese Communist commissar if they were Korean. He unhesitatingly replied, "Yes, they do garrison duty here; they fight well, also."[20]

The relations between Lin Piao's forces in Manchuria and the Koreans and Soviets north of Parallel Thirty-Eight have been cozy and intimate since 1946. The Korean elements of this force were reported [21] as 50,000 to 70,000 men in 1950; but in terms of

---

[20] In late 1947 some of the units of the Nationalist "Training Forces" (prison camps) in Mukden were composed entirely of Koreans. Most of them, however, had been born in Manchuria.

[21] East Europe and Soviet Russia, 1950, and other reports.

units they have all been repatriated and placed under North Korean command.

Unlike the other field armies, which slowly grew from their more solid "Anti-Japanese bases," this army started from only a few thousand men, who handily walked into Japanese military depots, doled out Kwantung Army arms and then further equipped themselves with captured American weapons between 1946 and 1949. This became the most modern and well equipped of the field armies up to 1950. There was a plentitude of supplies and equipment in this force. It knew the comfort and pleasure of big cities, the usefulness of steel works, motor vehicles, and arsenals, but it was never spoiled by them. The men grew to like Manchurian horse carts so well that they had a contempt for motorization. After all, hadn't they seen General Tu Yu-ming's motorized masses fail before them?

We must not, however, hold up this field army as a superior force, as we mistakenly did the Japanese Kwantung Army. The latter, bled of men and units, so changed in its combat complexion that, by 1945, when the Soviets entered the war in the Far East, the army had largely lost its former toughness of fiber. The strength of the Fourth Field Army is being sapped in Korea. The day will likely come when the Fourth will be reduced to the lowest type of war lord army which, when finally too hard pressed, gives up in easy surrender. This army can retain its former combat quality only by draining the cream of "volunteers" from the other field armies, thereby weakening them also.

The strength of this army has been variously estimated as from 600,000 to 780,000. Due to losses sustained in Korea,[22] it is probably now about 450,000; but it is doubtful that even General Lin Piao knows the exact strength of his command. It is a characteristic of Chinese military commanders to lack precise estimates of their strength on a given date.

As to the regional composition of this army, it is safe to as-

---

[22] This field army is believed to have sustained the most losses of any field army, although other forces have contributed "volunteers" to the war in Korea and suffered a share.

sume that Manchurians make up a good half, if not two-thirds, of the army's total strength. Here is a potential weakness. The Manchurian peasant soldiers are stout and stoical, capable of enduring the extreme cold and hardships of their climate; yet the Manchurians are not enthusiastic soldiers. They, and their fathers before them, have heard the marching feet of many foreign soldiers. The Manchurians are obedient to power, and as soldiers they need strong and determined leaders. These they have. But let the proportion or quality of leaders lessen and these men will have little heart in fighting for anything but the defense of their own farm acres.

General Lin Piao has a field army today because yesterday he had land to divide. General Lin often had to use forceful recruiting methods of the "rope together and lead away" variety, until he attained the position where he could offer land to recruits.

In Lin, the Fourth Field Army has a real leader. His best deputy commander, General Chou Pao-chung, is also a fine leader; he is of stern stuff and appeals strongly to the Manchurians.[23] General Hsiao Ching-kuang is the other deputy commander. General Chao Erh-lu is Chief of Staff.[24] In the eyes of Peiping at least, Chief Commissar Lo Jung-huan has done his job in a manner to make the field army strong. General Teng Tzu-hui is director of the Political Department, and has helped weld the army together by propaganda programs. Commissar Chen Yun is in the same category. Ex-Nationalist General Tseng Tse-cheng, who commanded the 50th Army, is now believed to be a staff officer, in a position where he can be watched.

The General Staff of this army is perhaps more logistics minded than that of any other field army. Where the forces of Chen Yi, Peng Te-huai, Nieh Jung-chen, and Liu Po-cheng had only to tear up railway tracks and burn ties, Lin Piao's staff directed the

---

[23] Chou Pao-chung has been out of the limelight recently and may have been given a higher post. Like most of the high Red army officers, his services are at a premium and he occupies some civil posts in addition to his military assignment.
[24] Hsiao Keh was earlier reported as chief of staff but is believed to have been killed in Korea.

operation of significant amounts of railway mileage and rolling stock during the Civil War.

Of the subordinate commanders there is Manchurian-born General Lin Chen-tsao, who is credited with being a capable army commander. General Teng Hua has a good combat record. The Commander of the 49th Army is General Chao Li-huai.

In 1950 the Fourth reportedly had six group-armies commanded by Generals Teng-Hua, Wang Ching-hsiu, Yang Cheng-wu, Wan Yi, Peng Ming-chih, and Hsiao Ching-kuan.[25]

The *Central-South Military Area* is the region normally dominated by this field army. The subordinate zones of this area are:[26]

Honan, commander, Chen Tsai-tao;
Hupei, commander, Lin Hsien-nien;
Hunan, commander, Hsaio Ching-kuang;
Kwangsi, commander, Chang Yun-i;
Kiangsi, commander, Chen Chi-han;
Kwangtung, commander, Yeh Chien-ying.

The Fourth Field Army *has been* a most formidable force, but combat losses have thinned its ranks. It is still a well-officered force, obedient to some of the most enthusiastic army officers in the PLA. Since 1949, this field army has been generously equipped with motor vehicles by the Soviets. Elements of this army, if they ever punch through the United Nation's line, will roll—and roll fast. This is the force that has contributed most liberally to the holocaust of Korea.

The Fifth Field Is the Mystery Army

A new field army is forming around General Nieh Jung-chen's "Palace Guard," or the North China Reserve Army. There is, however, considerable mystery as to exactly what military shape this new force is assuming. After the Communist occupation of Peking, General Nieh became the Peking garrison commander, somewhat of a come-down perhaps for Nieh who had commanded larger forces. Thus Nieh missed the opportunities of adding final combat luster to his name in the sweep of the Red armies

---

[25] According to the Chinese Problem Research Dept. of the *Democratic Review*, 1 November 1950, published in Hong Kong.
[26] Appendix 7 to a Japanese Ministry of Foreign Affairs publication, 1950.

THE WEB AND TENTACLES OF ORGANIZATION 95

to the South. But the PLA's high command, of which he is a member, decided that, large though they were, the field armies would not be sufficient in themselves to provide the maximum military security. A national or GHQ reserve was needed, and Nieh was chosen to prepare plans for the creation of such a reserve.

Initially the task was one of converting some of Fu Tso-yi's old units into Communist-indoctrinated and organized troops, and gathering up some Red units and cadres from the established PLA armies. From out of the technically trained ranks of surrendered Nationalist armies, artillerists, tankmen, and other soldiers were organized into new units. A few artillery divisions and tank regiments emerged. The Soviets helped give shape to these organizations. Cavalry elements, heretofore scattered (in both the KMT and PLA armies), were lumped together and retrained in formations larger than regiments. The PLA gradually created a mobile reserve, but it was not large in 1950 when portions of it were transferred to Korea and Manchuria.

As it stands today, the force under Nieh is estimated at about 60,000 officers and men, organized into at least six special divisions. Around this specialized nucleus the PLA is still building up a new field army that may emerge as Red China's most modern combat striking force.

However, not all of General Nieh's command consists of GHQ forces. He is responsible for the *North Military Area* which is divided into three subzones or districts—

Hopei, commander, Sun Yi;
Pingyuan (the new province in the Yellow River plan), commander, Liu Chih-yuan;
Shansi, commander, Cheng Tzu-hua.

Thus Nieh has vital line-of-communication (or district) troops under his command, including antiaircraft defense units for the security of the large North China city of Tientsin, and for Peking, the capital of Red China.

The Communists have not publicly announced it yet, but the Fifth Field Army, however small, is in being as the PLA's reserve.

A Sixth Field Army was to have been created in Southeast

China, probably under General Yeh Chien-ying; but confirmation of its organization is still lacking.

Is the Mongol Army Worth Its Forage?

"The grandfather of all headaches is the Mongol." This Chinese expression of contempt for a minority which once conquered them, was rendered by a Chinese Nationalist General who fought Lin Piao's Mongols in the 1947 Battle of Ssupingkai.[27] According to him, the Mongols were extremely tough and constituted a formidable foe.

Are the Red-maneuvered Mongols of China the screaming, fighting hordes that swept across Asia under Genghis Khan? Is this cavalry of the consistent combat quality that typifies the Russian Cossacks? I would say "no," for several reasons. China's Mongols are desperately poor and their horseflesh is lean and undernourished. I visited a few portions of Inner Mongolia in 1948 and was struck by two things: bitter poverty and Mongol opportunism. The Inner Mongolians of China were badly weakened in 1945-46, when the Soviet Army took away thousands of their horses and other livestock. Starvation and disease were so rampant in Inner Mongolia in 1947 that the US Government organized and sent to the region a special relief mission with food. In the areas where I visited, it was said by local authorities that 80 percent of the population were infected by syphilis or gonorrhea. The men and the horseflesh were anything but prepared for combat. Their lot may be improving, however, for the Communists have done better than the Nationalists in at least having a policy and program ostensibly intended to help this minority group.

Politically, from 1945 to 1948, the Mongols played both ends against the middle in a shrewd game of opportunism that sought the utmost from the Soviets, the Chinese Reds, and the Chinese Nationalists, with the predominate idea of gaining the most for the least commitment. In 1947 I talked with some of General Lin Piao's lesser staff officers, who conceded that the Mongols in Manchuria were too often getting things their own way. Inner

---

[27] There were two large battles at Ssupingkai; one in 1946, another in 1947.

Mongolia, which stretches into Manchuria, was anything but unified, even those portions of the region under Chinese Red control.

Lin Piao did get some troops from this minority; but in the period of 1945 and 1946, so far as I could observe during the Manchurian campaigns, they never did participate in any of the really hard fought battles. There was their one good show at Ssupingkai in 1947, but Chinese Red troops were in the majority here. From the Communist standpoint, the Mongols are not politically too reliable.

The Mongols need to be reestablished on a firm agricultural basis, with ample herds and full stomachs, before their morale will be high enough to carry them through combat with anything like the fierceness and determination of their hard-riding ancestors. The Red press so far has printed nothing to indicate unusual military prowess on the part of this minority.

The Mongol army exists, however; and it appears that small elements of it are in Korea. General Yun Tse (alias Wu Lan-fu) is commander of the Inner Mongolian People's Defense Army, the central headquarters of which was established on 26 November 1947.[28] Yun Tse had much bickering with the Chinese Reds in the years which followed World War II, but the Communists in Manchuria have ensconced him in the dual positions of Army Commander and President of the Inner Mongolian Autonomous Region. The strength of Yun Tse's little army is uncertain, but it probably does not exceed two cavalry divisions of about 7,000 men each, plus some infantry. The total strength of all his forces probably does not exceed 20,000 men. The PLA probably will employ elements of the "army" on reconnaissance missions whenever they are committed to combat. On a map, Inner Mongolia appears geographically impressive, but the population of the region is very small. So is the Mongol military contribution to the PLA.

Certain of the Chinese Communist military regions (extending into Mongolia) are directly under the PLA's General Headquarters.

---

[28] *New China News Agency,* 18 December 1947.

This serves militarily to break up the Mongols, who are by no means all under General Yun Tse. These are the military regions that come directly under PLA headquarters—

Suiyuan; commanded by General Fu Tso-Yi, with General Po I-po as the political representative to watch General Fu.[29]

Sui-meng (Suiyuan-Mongolia); commanded by General Yao Che, with Kao Ko-min as the political representative.

Nie-meng (Inner Mongolian); commanded by Yun Tse; deputy commanders, Wang Tsai-tien and Na-chin-shuang-ho-erh.

I-ko-chao-meng (Ike-cho Mongol League); commanded by Wang Yueh-feng; political representative, Ma Yen-Kang.[30]

General Yun Tse's Mongols are those mainly in the region of Manchuria. Both for political reasons and by circumstance of communications, Inner Mongolia has had to be divided up militarily. The Mongols of Red China could be forged into effective, hard hitting cavalrymen; but at present it is doubtful if they are worth much more than the cost of their animal forage. Better cavalry, although distant from any point of combat use, will be found in the remote region of Sinkiang.

New Arms Enter the Army

The extent to which the PLA will indulge in motorization and mechanization will depend on Soviet "generosity." So far as motorization is concerned, the USSR is providing the PLA with trucks. The PLA also has gathered together its captured American vehicles and is using most of them in Korea. The sightings of vehicles by our aircraft have shown great motor columns in constant use, especially for supply and evacuation purposes; but the number of tanks in Chinese hands has been negligible in Korea.

Right now, the militarists of Communist China are building up an armored force, which is being given the status of a *corps elite*. But armor is in its very infancy in China and there is a great

---

[29] Fu Tso-Yi, when he was a Nationalist commander, dealt very harshly with the Mongols of this region.

[30] These are as outlined in Appendix 7 to a Japanese Ministry of Foreign Affairs publication of 1950.

MADE-IN-AMERICA ARTILLERY PIECES LIKE THIS (WITH IMPROVISED WHEELS) ARE NOW BEING FIRED BY CHINESE REDS, WHO TOOK THEM FROM US-TRAINED CHINESE NATIONALISTS.

muddle about what to do with the 622 old tanks they do have.[31] These tracked vehicles are mainly Japanese and American, and they are worn out. Even when the Nationalists had this very same equipment, I remember inspecting tank units in which 50 percent of the vehicles were deadlined. Turrets had to be hand-cranked for rotation. Engines overheated in no time; and the radios were mostly long dead from lack of care or parts. At the Nationalist tank center in Hsuchou in 1947, American sergeant instructors said that the best tank companies couldn't enter combat with any chance of success because the tanks continually broke down. Much of the armor in China today is simply good for a parade show, to impress the peasants. China needs new Soviet tanks, and time to train crews and maintenance personnel; then more time to train units in armored tactics.

For three years to come, no foe of China need have serious fear of devastating or skillful onslaughts by Chinese armor, for it can be licked wherever it appears. Furthermore, it is certain to be wasted whenever it is used in combat.

Armor in the PLA had its humble and timid beginnings in April 1947, in the Third Field Army, although some platoons of tanks were used in combat in Manchuria as early as 1946. I saw some of these employed in the Battle of Changchun, in April 1946, when the tanks were entirely manned by Japanese.

The present pride and joy of the PLA is the Third (Mechanized) Group Army, last reported in Nanking under Chen Yi's Third Field Army. General Chen Jui-ting commands this army and talks loud and long about it, claiming steady increases in his armored and artillery strength.[32] This modern mechanized army consists of two armored divisions, an artillery division, a motorized regiment, an AAA battalion and two or three infantry regiments. This may be the largest single component of armor in the PLA, but separate battalions are known to exist, one or more to each field army.

---

[31] "The PLA's Battle Record," *People's China*, 16 August 1950.
[32] Accounts of this army, and one of Chen Jui-ting's speeches in Nanking, are contained in *People's China* and other Chinese periodicals for 1950.

Photo by Eastfoto.

OLD ARMOR IN NEW HANDS.
This tank unit of the Red Chinese Army is equipped with old Japanese tanks captured from the Nationalists. It is shown parading in Peking in 1950.

Paratroop training is being given to an unknown number of thousands within Red China. Additional numbers may be receiving such instruction in the Soviet Union. (Selected officers of the PLA are being trained by the Soviets in a variety of military fields.) In the next five years China may train as many as 100,000 parachutists, but this does not mean that she can launch a sizable airborne attack due to many limiting factors which restrict the complete modernization of the PLA. It may have the paratroops, but does it have the cargo aircraft and the trained staff officers and technicians to implement airborne warfare? Paratroop training and jump-troops will become the show-pieces of Red militarism in China, but it will be years before the airborne arm can be regarded as a serious threat in combat. The army has too many other things to catch up on before it can embark on large scale airborne projects. The present day leaders feel they can win wars without all the modern frills, but they want just enough in the way of *elite* troops to place them in the public show-case for *"face."*

A Nationalist parachute battalion surrendered to the Communists a few years ago. These troops were fairly well trained, and some of their numbers are now in the uniform of the PLA. Perhaps the greatest immediate use to which the PLA's few paratroops could be placed would be in a specialized operation, like an attack against Taiwan.

Destructively, Chinese Red engineers rank among the best in the world. They can demolish like locusts. Constructively, they are hard working and accustomed to recruiting and making the most use of civilian labor. However, they are only beginning to learn the use of heavy equipment, such as pontoon bridges. They lack heavy tractors and other modern equipment. They can be expected to become prominent in mine-warfare, however.

Artillery is getting a big boost. The Chinese like artillery and are not bad artillerists. They possess a hodge-podge of guns and howitzers, the still usable leftovers from the Japanese and the Nationalist armies. The former American artillery weapons are in good condition. They were never fired to excess in the Civil War, for lack of sufficient quantity of shells—and because the Nationalists were often afraid to place them near the front for fear they would be captured! Self-propelled weapons, like the old SU-76, will come from the Soviets. The Chinese Reds never fired an SP gun in combat before 1950.

For a while, the bulk of the heavy artillery will be held under control of PLA General Headquarters or within General Nieh Jung-chen's jurisdiction. It is now organized into brigades and divisions. Each field army has its regiments of artillery, but the weapons vary in design and caliber. In general, the 75-mm and 76-mm pieces dominate on a division level, with 122-mm and 155-mm pieces under higher command. Until the close of the Civil War, there was no standard artillery organization used consistently throughout the various Red armies. Each force organized its artillery according to the number of weapons it had captured and for which it had ammunition stocks. The high command is still busy re-allocating weapons and working out tables of organization and equipment. From its own standpoint, the PLA needs better organized and trained artillery units, and more of them. The army is still very weak in artillery, with an undue preponderance of infantry. The Soviet officers will take care of this situation soon; but the Chinese themselves will have to train their artillery units to a modern standard of efficiency.

The PLA claims to have captured 54,430 heavy and light artillery pieces between 1946 and June 1950.[33] If one-half of these are assumed to be usable, then the PLA could have 6,800 batteries of four guns each, or over 2,200 battalions. This, however, is theorizing. The fact is that the PLA has thousands of artillery pieces for which it cannot manufacture the ammunition.

In terms of the future, Soviet artillery weapons and technique will dominate this arm of the PLA, for it is only from the USSR that China can obtain quantities of shells.

One of the best artillery schools in the PLA was run by Lin Piao in Manchuria. The school exists today and is named after General Chu Jui, the artillery commander of the NEPLA who was killed in action in 1948.

The number of antiaircraft battalions is being increased, with Soviet assistance. This is a relatively new arm for the PLA, although its soldiers have never hesitated to fire into the air with anything they had, and sometimes they downed hostile aircraft with a combination of rifle and machine gun fire. The antiaircraft units are more common to city defenses than to field army installations. Little is known about the radar and other equipment of these units, but the Chinese are manning Soviet antiaircraft guns of several calibers.

Little by little, the PLA is adding newer arms and strengthening its combat forces. It still has a long way to go, but there is great military activity in the *Northeast Military Area* (commanded by Kao Kang) which is a special one directly under PLA headquarters. Here Soviet guns, tanks, and trucks are pouring in and the training activity is intense. This was what General Peng Te-huai referred to in August 1951 when he promised his "volunteers" new weapons, more artillery, and a better airforce.

---

[33] "The PLA's Battle Record," *People's China*, 16 August 1950.

Chapter 4

MEN OF THE OCHRE HORDES

The Gentle Art of Sadism

The man's naked back drips blood from a series of deep slashes into which a Chinese stuffs cotton saturated with a familiar-smelling liquid. One might suspect that crude medical treatment is being given, but for three things—the stripped man is being firmly held by others, the cotton is soaked in kerosene, and the victim is screaming and twisting. He screams even louder and rolls on the ground when the cotton is ignited.

The entertainment, from the Chinese Communist viewpoint, is being furnished by those victims who, crazed by the pain, run instead of throwing themselves into the dirt. Such victims of Red torture are called "Dragon Lanterns."[1]

This is one of several conventional tortures used by the Chinese Reds. I lack documentation on how many times this particular torture has been applied, but I know the practice is not uncommon against spies and saboteurs who are caught by the Red military.

There are other such Chinese Red devices. Take, for example, the "urination corps." This practice has been resorted to often, in Red

---

[1] *The History of the Peiping Executive Headquarters,* Fourth Quarter, 1 Oct.-31 Dec. 1946, US Department of the Army, Office of Military History.

areas, during sessions of the people's courts. The army has been known to form platoons, and even companies, of its soldiers to urinate on victims. One of the most recent accounts came from Dr. Ernest M. Lippa, who described the humiliating incident where two American girls from a Mennonite Mission near Kaifeng "were dragged into the street and a whole company of soldiers soiled them with urine."[2]

There is a sadism and brutality inherent in many Asiatics that is not commonly found within men of the better educated areas of the world. Bloody brutality by Red Chinese soldiers should be expected. This does not mean that the majority stands for, or practices, such brutalities as the *"Tapestry Chair"* and the *"Dragon Lantern"* but enough torturers do exist to produce atrocities. Is it small wonder, then, that we sometimes find our wounded being bayoneted and grenaded in Korea?

Many a Red Chinese has been a party to the horse cart torture that drags a victim, head down, along a road until the unfortunate's face and head are only a shredded, pulpy mass. The "Tapestry Chair," a big basket of thorns, glass, and rusty metal, tortured human bodies in the "liberation areas" of North China after World War II. Such cases have been documented.[3] Nothing is more gruesome than to see human heads severed from their bodies. The Chinese Communists, in some regions, not content just to kill, have hung their victims severed heads on trees, as warning fruit that obedience to Red Law is mandatory![4] Red China's army contains a good many men who, as civilians or soldiers, have indulged in these and related practices. One should never be surprised at atrocities committed by the PLA.

Some Chinese troops take dope. I have seen a few uniformed soldiers in Lin Piao's army who very obviously were doped; although I never actually saw them taking it. In a front line area on 1 March 1947, Jack Collins and I were the butt end of some bayonet

---

[2] Ernest M. Lippa, M.D., "I Was a Surgeon for the Chinese Reds," *The Saturday Evening Post,* 28 April 1951.
[3] Files of the History of the Executive Headquarters, Department of the Army, Office of Military History.
[4] Ibid. Communist Methods of Enforcing Law and Order—photographs taken near Hailung, July 1946.

prodding by a few such troopers. We had been captured about six hours before. We were in a farm compound in which animals were milling about, when our guards let in a curious bunch of soldiers who tried to push us into the rear ends of some of the mules. Some Reds laughed and some swore. The oaths were strong. I didn't understand most of them, but I recall something about being addressed as, "You bloodsucking big-nose!" and "You capitalist turd." These rascals were nasty, but we resisted their pushing around until the doped ones stepped out of the mob and began to prick us with their bayonets. There was some real eye-to-eye staring. The faces of these men wore stupified glazes.

You'll find them loaded with liquor sometimes; but the drunks are a small minority, and the military punishment for drunkenness is severe. I do not believe, however, that any significant numbers can be charged with dope addiction or drunkenness. The commissars and their informers are too watchful to permit these practices to gain much impetus. The soldiers just don't get the money to afford such indulgences.

Red Soldiers, Run of the Mill

The army is large; its human elements diverse; but almost all the men in Red military service have one thing in common—they have seen bloodshed on a large scale. The men are hardened to nearby death and bleeding. If they haven't seen it within the army and in combat, they have viewed carnage of some sort amid the conflicts that swept over China from 1937 to 1950. They are a combat calloused lot—but they also have their more human side. These men are unhappy in millions, problem-ridden, worried over personal issues, just as other humans are. But this is largely hidden, as it has been with generations of Chinese soldiers. The foreigner rarely sees or feels the undercurrents, even if he is with the army.

How many thoughts, loves and hatreds are there in those long columns, yellow as the dust they raise? The many, many men, submerged in massed formations, appear to have lost all individuality. But how many, whose feet obey the orders and direction, are truly loyal to the cause they serve? A young soldier laughs, an

HE ONCE SERVED IN A JAPANESE PUPPET ARMY, BUT WAS SOLDIERING IN THE NATIONALIST ARMY WHEN PICTURED HERE.

Now he is probably a Communist soldier, because his unit defected to the Chinese Reds in the Civil War.

elderly one makes a sharp remark to a nearby farmer. A serious one eases out of the column to look back at its progress. He, at least, is completely devoted to his work; he is truly loyal, as you can see in his demeanor and by the way he packs his Mauser. The young one is seeing new sights—he is far from home. It is an adventure for him. The flavor will last for a while. His parents are no longer starving beggars. He has *seen* his father's land; that is what he is fighting for. It is tangible. The older one has fought before; under other colors. He knows he is watched for his obedience. He is landless with family connections severed. He joined the army because he knew the trade and the Party knew he was out of work. He looks at the youngster shifting his rifle to another thin shoulder. The old one could dampen that youthful enthusiasm by telling him of the regimes he has seen come and pass. But the young one would not believe. Besides, talk is dangerous.

The commanders know their men pretty well; the commissars know them even better. The units are mixed, containing individuals of strange and varied backgrounds. The companies were nearly "pure" at the end of the Anti-Japanese War in 1945; only the trusted ones had survived. But expansion followed until, by 1948, it was necessary to assign the loyal ones, as leaven, more evenly through the units, to insure the loyalty and obedience of all.

The Reds found that complete conversion of men was hard to achieve. Many former KMT soldiers had had a bellyfull of the army and wanted to go home; but the Communist Party could not unleash these thousands into potential unemployed masses, which might turn to arms as bandits and guerrillas. As the Red army swept into new regions and received the surrender of disintegrating Nationalist divisions, the soldiers of the enemy army became a serious problem. Even Nationalist units which surrendered en mass were not to be in the least trusted by the Party, although, in fear, the PW's mouthed the most loyal oaths. The majority of KMT officers obviously had to be purged from the units, but it was deemed temporarily expedient to let units of men stay together. Cadres of real Reds were inserted into these units. The old Chinese army of Communism had to deplete its ranks to provide cadres to retrain, reindoctrinate and insure the loyalty of these new units. Thus, the old Red army spread thin its Communist core to provide the controlling nucleus of the *new* army of China.

The Chinese Red Army of today is a mixture both of men who are politically reliable, and those who are unreliable to the cause of Mao Tse-tung; but the mixture is well governed and controlled. On the surface, the Party's hold is strong, but a long, severe test of war could see portions of the Chinese Communist Army crumble as readily as did the Nationalist Army of Chiang Kai-shek.

Most of these PLA soldiers are different from the relatively sophisticated soldier of Chiang Kai-shek. In the environment of cities they are still ill at ease and somewhat lost. They washed their rice in the toilet bowls of Nanking in 1949. Others, in Shanghai, were amused at spring locks and running hot water. These conquerors flushed the porcelain toilets in the skyscrapers simply because it was amusing to watch the results. Elevators they had never seen. When they first occupied the big cities of China they slept, initially, on the sidewalks. They were not "worldly wise" like the Nationalist soldiers, who knew that a sidewalk fronted a building within which there could usually be found comfortable bedding. But these men are at home in the mountainous or rice-paddied countryside, and it is in those places that their lives are designed to be spent, for war is their business. They can endure the toil, hardship, necessitudes of campaign and combat with greater ease than can most other nationalities.

Each man has his problems. The young ones would like to get married, but the army keeps saying to them that they are the "new professionals" whose life will be devoted to soldiering. So the commissars let only a few men marry. An old soldier sees some mistakes about which he would like to voice some honest criticism. However, he is afraid of the results. The squad leader, like most others of his rank, is a Party man, and he urges the old soldier to take more interest in the "self-criticism" meetings. But young or old, fears often enter their minds and the questions or statements so near their lips are swallowed for another day.

Death or wounds are the only certain discharges from military service, for there is no organized system of release. Age helps a little, for the veterans who grow feeble. Some of the older men were getting discharges before the PLA entered the war in Korea. They needed money, so the army referred them to civil authorities who helped them out under terms of Article 25, of the Common Program. Such men fall into the category of "revolutionary servicemen," suffering from privation, or ready to retire. The commissars make great stock of the government's care of these poor men. The soldiers view discharges with skepticism. They know that the take-home pay is small.

Some are "Combat Heroes" and wear the first-class order of the medal, Military Hero. You must acknowledge they are tough men. Quick movements, sharp eyes and ready replies characterize them. There are already a thousand or so of them. The army spreads these men through the units, for their sinewy bodies and courage are needed everywhere. The commissars hold them up as examples. The soldiers like to place them in categories of how many men each one has killed. The snipers have the most accurate counts. Everyone acknowledges there is a bit too much bragging on the part of the snipers.

The Combat Heroes are an officially decorated and recognized group of elite soldiers, although the Communists claim that such men are first elected to or nominated for the title by their own units. Company commanders have a special book in which they record, at regular intervals, the outstanding combat achievements of individual soldiers. Later on the best actions are recorded in "orders of the day" and are read at troop formations. Red commanders regularly give verbal and written recognition to outstanding feats. It is from these records that the "Combat Heroes" are chosen. On 25 September 1950 the army had its first national conclave[5] of these troopers, and 360 reportedly attended a series of flag-waving, speech-making meetings. These men rank above the "Labor Heroes," who wear the "Model Worker's Medal."

"Model Troops" comprise another but lower category of the growing military caste system. They earn their titles in peace as

---

[5] *People's China*, 16 October 1950.

Military Hero's Decoration.

Model Worker's Medal.

Citation Badge of the Red Star (issued by the Revolutionary Military Council).

Military School Political Committee Member's Badge.

Badge for Delegate to the First National Congress.

Commemoration Badge of the Chinese Communist Republic.

DECORATIONS OF COMMUNIST CHINA.

well as in combat. Both Combat Heroes and Model Troops form the small corps of elite soldiers, but so far they have not been formally organized into any special units. However, the Reds did place many Model Troops in provisional platoons and made them the spearheads of some amphibious landings on small islands in 1950. The term, "model anti-US fighter," is in vogue in Korea today. It is not yet an officially and formally conferred title.

Most of these Chinese have fought so long that each individual tends his rifle with affectionate care, for he knows his survival will probably depend upon his weapon. In the Civil War this was very noticeable. Out of almost every slung rifle muzzle protruded the red patch of cloth that kept the barrel clean. Some units went so far as to supply little brass caps for the tips of the rifles. But this degree of care did not always extend to the larger pieces of equipment. At first, trucks were foreign to them. Vehicles had a way of exasperating these simple men. Chinese soldiers were not, and are not yet, motor-wise and mechanically minded. Trucks froze up often in Manchuria, so the men built bonfires on the ground under the hood to thaw them out. Later they poured *Kaoliang* wine into the radiators for anti-freeze.

The Chinese soldier is not a simpleton, but he does some very stupid things sometimes. This one is typical: On the cold night of 5 December 1950, elements of the 1st Marine Division were fighting out of encirclement and trying hard to avoid becoming frostbite casualties. To their surprise, considering that they were encircled, the Marines found 200 Chinese soldiers walking up to them and surrendering. The Chinese were "tired of war," and had been cold and unfed for five days. Surrender was a smart thing to do. However, one of the soldiers was barefooted and had feet frozen solid, like refrigerated meat. When asked why he let himself get in such a condition, he replied, "Because I knew that after my feet froze I would no longer feel any pain!"[6]

"Army life in the PLA can never be dull or boring for the soldier, as is the case in a reactionary army where the rank and file so often

---

[6] "200 Chinese Surrender to Encircled Marines," New York *Herald-Tribune*, 7 December 1950.

get 'browned off' and turn to women and wine for solace in their boredom . . ."

So reads an official description of the PLA which paints life in its army as the ideal existence—except that it makes no mention of the mass death and multiple hardships which characterize that military body. One of the myths the Communists have worked so hard to build up and support is that the PLA's multi-million force is a breed of "monks" who never so much as cast a glance at a feminine figure. To paint this lusty army of millions of men as devoid of passion and its resultant action is nice for the foreigners who might believe the fairy tale; but there are millions of women in China who, if canvassed by a poll, could admit that the PLA is no more sexless than Chinese armies of the past—except that the soldiers have such a measure of discipline that they do not indulge in mass rape or organized orgy that might make headlines. The simple fact is that PLA soldiers do not receive the monthly cash to allow them to buy up cases of wine for a given price. But, as the PLA belongs to the people and springs from the people, nothing is too good for PLA soldiers. The people are not yet required to turn over regimented groups of virgins to PLA units. The Chinese Reds have given great propaganda space to their liberation of prostitutes; but this Red regime—which has broken the traditional family bonds and made children into informers on their parents—this regime is not strengthening moral conduct, to say the least.

Indoctrination—Always Indoctrination

There is no escape from indoctrination. It follows the soldier when he marches away and is there to greet him at his destination. If the training march is long, the commissars see to the establishment of "political education stations" along the route. These stations run off mimeographed or hand-printed "march column newspapers" combining soldier chit-chat and local news with political remembrances and slogans. Soldiers are invited to make contributions to these mosquito papers—which are not entirely dull, for from the ranks comes originality. However, the Party men like to keep the items in line with Communism's serious

Photo by Col. David D. Barrett.

MEETINGS AND LECTURES, ENDLESSLY, MOLD THE MEN POLITICALLY.
Red soldiers of China listen to commissars who tell them why they fight.

purpose and the soldier items usually have a moral or a message like this simple poem, "Love Thy Feet," which was composed by a trooper on the march in 1949:

> Very useful is a pair of feet;
> Without us you can't do a damn thing.
> I am glad to learn we're marching again,
> For here comes a chance of rendering service.
>
> In case you get blisters,
> Gently pierce and dry them, applying kerosene.
> For heaven's sake, don't peel blisters;
> Bathe them when you camp down
> And don't forget to give them credit at summing up time.

"Rifle-barrel poems" are used to brighten up marches and take minds off weary feet. Anyone who can write and feels inclined to be poetic can get paper and pencil from commissars and political workers with which to pen a poem and paste it on his rifle barrel or on a field piece. The Reds also make use of combat pictorials and trench handbills—some nicely printed, others made on the spot by hand, but always designed to keep slogans before the soldiers.

Red minds work overtime to devise items which will occupy soldier attention. "March radio stations" are one of their propaganda products. The "station" consists of a banner between two poles, and on the banner is written the name of a soldier who has performed some outstanding deed. When the unit halts the "station" is set up and he "broadcasts" his views on a subject, or tells how he won nomination to unit fame. This all sounds very simple and childish, but it is not out of place in Chinese ranks. The soldiers are often more interesting in their speeches than the political workers. For example, Wei Lai-kuo, the super-sniper of the Third Field Army, is often called upon to tell how he killed so many enemy soldiers. He lacks just four stories of having a full year's supply. Wei hasn't notched his rifle, but according to the Communists 361 men are buried because of his bullets.

To do the daily work without complaining or shirking, is not enough; the Communist Party, through its political organs and army commissars, demands that the soldiers think rightly. The Party's machinery of "supervisory personnel" continually watches the troops for what may be "incompatible thoughts." Much is made of the device of public confession. Self-criticism meetings are conducted for the benefit of those who want to demonstrate their interest and loyalty by the process of letting down their hair. A soldier who is known to smoke American cigarettes or admits that he cares for US movies, is invited to one of these meetings. Why do they confess? The politicos put them on the spot by direct questions, and the suggestion to confess follows. It is easier to admit to minor faults and gain big "face" with the politicos than it is to challenge the system and lose one's head.

What is the motivation of the ex-Nationalists who are now in the PLA? More than 70 percent of some of the batches of Chinese prisoners captured by UN forces in Korea have been soldiers who formerly served in Chinese Nationalist armies. Why do these men fight? Why do they not surrender more readily? First, they are under strict political and military control by officers, non-commissioned officers, commissars, and party workers—from the regiment down to the squad. Within the squad there is at least one Party man whose duty it is to watch the other men. Fear is a factor among the soldiers. The penalty is death for any who refuse to serve. A bullet in the back of the neck awaits any who carry surrender leaflets.

The Life Is Hard and the Pay Is Poor

The pay is better than it used to be, when there was none (sic). During most of the Civil War, Red soldiers were given no cash. I often talked over this fact with Communist officers in 1946-47. They explained that the soldiers who smoked were regularly issued tobacco and those who didn't were given a compensating allowance of confections or sweetmeats. Regimental and other funds were used to buy certain luxuries which were issued in the name of the Party. The commissars said that the army endeavored to keep its troops well fed. This it did; at least the Red soldiers were not as poorly fed as were some of the Nationalist troops, who stole chickens to supplement their scanty rations. Cigarettes I saw regularly issued to the soldiers (even to me as a prisoner in 1947). None of the soldiers ever seemed hard-up for a "tailor made" smoke[7] as were some of the Soviet soldiers I had seen earlier in Manchuria and Iran. The private's monthly pay today is about 16000.00 Jen Min Piao (or JMP, as it is called), or the rough equivalent of about forty-one cents in US cash. The only thing that can be said of this amount is that it *is* pay. NCO's, barbers,[8] and technicians in the higher grades get a little more. The system is such that the troops get their entertainment free, and some extras which make them feel "cared for." They are taught, of course, that they serve for a cause, not for money; and that only "capitalistic soldiers" are in the profession for cash.

The Chinese soldier's day begins early, as in almost all armies.

---

[7] Curiously enough, the brand of cheap cigarettes which Lin Piao's field army issued so generously in 1947, was manufactured in Nationalist Shanghai. Each pack had twenty matches wrapped with it.

[8] Communist troops always have barbers along with them, who fight when they are not clipping hair.

But here in the PLA, the soldier's lot is harder than in most armies, except perhaps in the Soviet. A bugle blows, and while there may be only one clock in the regiment, the soldiers don't have to be told it is about 5:00 a.m. In most Chinese units, there is a two-and-one-half-hour study period the first thing in the morning. This means lectures and readings by one member, for the majority cannot read. There are songs which are chorused in unison—army songs, guerrilla songs, and the new people's songs, all with their slogans. This is a singing army. Many of the soldiers come to believe in these slogan songs after a period of time. New soldiers have to sing the "Three Rules and the Eight Remarks" until they know these lines by heart—

Our Rules Are:

>All actions are subject to command.
>Do not steal from the people.
>Be neither selfish nor unjust.

We Are to Remember These Remarks:

>Replace the door when you leave the house.
>Roll up the bedding on which you have slept.
>Always be courteous.
>Be honest in your transactions.
>Return what you borrow.
>Replace what you break.
>Do not bathe or urinate in the presence of women.
>Do not, without authority, search the pocketbooks of those you arrest.

Slogans keynote the verbal and mental drills of this army. Nowhere in the world, even in the Soviet Army, do slogans have such a role in the indoctrination and training of troops.

Breakfast, a mixture of vegetables and rice, sometimes with a soup poured in, occurs around 7:30 a.m. The work day begins at eight and lasts until about five in the afternoon, unless there are special activities or night exercises. The day is not unlike that of any other soldier, except that these soldiers may be harvesting grain or rice, building dikes, constructing roads, repairing bridges, digging canals or working part-time in factories. Depending on the season, the region and the requirements, the work will vary from routine training, to maneuvers; but always there is the requirement that the army perform physical labor for the people. Of marching there is plenty. Schedules are not rigid and when the officers don't know what else to fill the program with, a march will strengthen soldier legs and impress the people. The soldier's evenings will vary, but the commissars try to keep them regimented at meetings.

Two meals a day has long been the practiced rule, but there are indications, in some regions, that the soldiers are getting three. When there are only two meals a day, the second one is given about 4:00 p.m. and work continues afterward. Where there are three, 5:00 p.m. is the hour for supper. The meals are simple; a typical one is steamed wheat bread (or rice), two vegetables and tea. It behooves a soldier to follow the Communist dictum, not only of planting a garden or a unit garden but also of caring for it well, because the only palatable abundance of food will spring from these projects. There is enthusiasm for these garden and crop projects, but not the kind the Communists proclaim. It is the enthusiasm of men who seek fuller stomachs. By formal directive, each PLA soldier not in combat is required to produce one quarter of his food or its equivalent each year.[9]

The Red soldier's rice bowl is not always as full as he would like to have it, but the PLA has done much better than past Chinese armies to make a full rice bowl a symbol of the Communist army. For generations soldiers of China have been cheated in the chow lines, not only by corrupt quartermasters but also by high commanders. The Reds studied the effects of such past corruption and inefficiency and long ago concluded that theirs was to be a fairly well-fed army, even if it had to be underpaid.

One mustn't be so naive as to suppose that corruption and "squeeze" don't occur within PLA ranks. The commissars are on guard to fight these traditional malpractices all the time. So far they have kept these ills to a minimum so that we might describe the corruption as local and small-scale at this date. (Anything big is "legalized" in the name of the Party or the Army.) But

---

[9] *The China Weekly Review*, 1 April 1950.

MEN OF THE OCHRE HORDES

the Party and the PLA recognize the fact that among Chinese of any political color, personal greed is bound to show up sooner or later; so they are alert. The PLA uses the device of *soldier mess committees* in line companies to insure that mess funds are properly spent. Thus, no one NCO or officer can misspend the

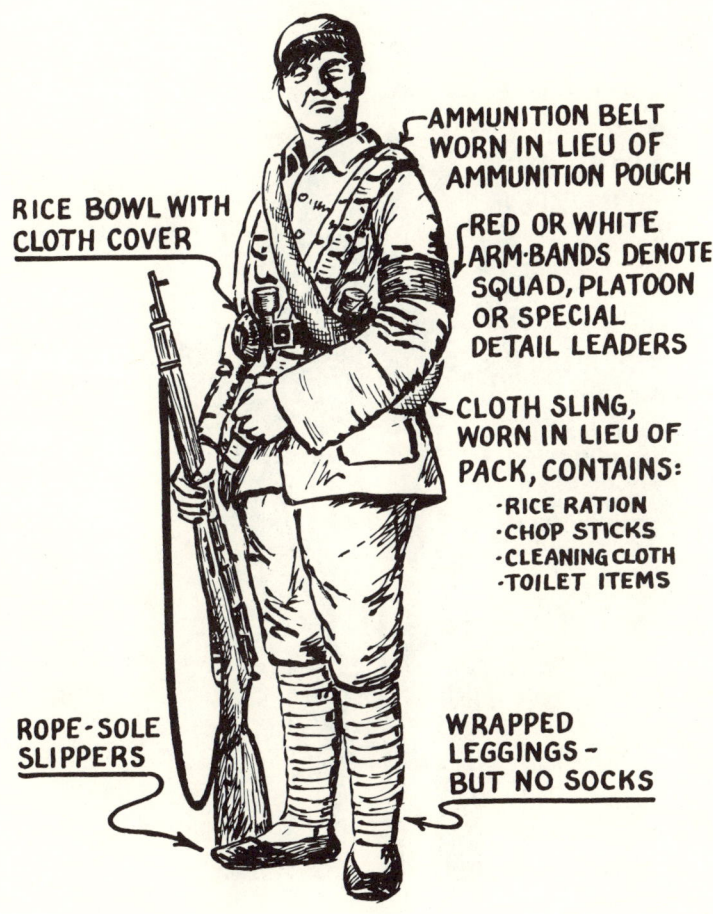

UNIFORM AND EQUIPMENT OF THE CHINESE RED SOLDIER—RIFLEMAN, IN SUMMER UNIFORM.

company mess funds, for these committees are obliged to post their accounts to the unit at fixed intervals. These so-called *economic committees* are composed of men elected from each squad and platoon of the company.[10] Thus the mass is represented,

[10] *The Chinese People's Liberation Army,* published by the Foreign Language Press, Peking 1950.

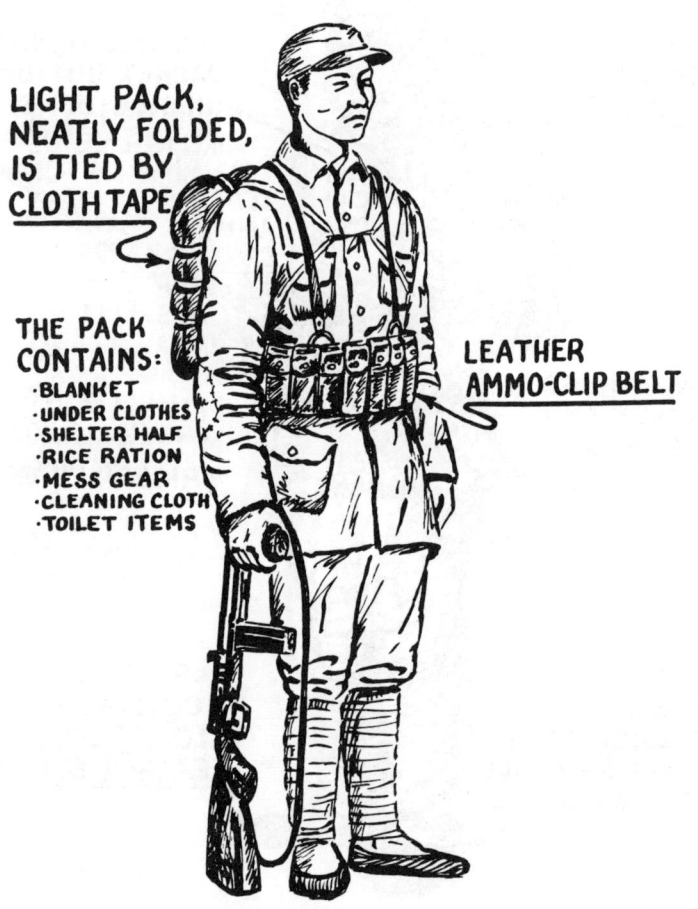

UNIFORM AND EQUIPMENT OF THE CHINESE RED SOLDIER—
TOMMY GUNNER, IN SUMMER UNIFORM.

MEN OF THE OCHRE HORDES

and by this technique the rice bowls are filled with the maximum that allotted funds will permit.

Chinese soldiers of the past, especially in the war lord armies, were disciplined by a variety of measures and subjected to "officer"

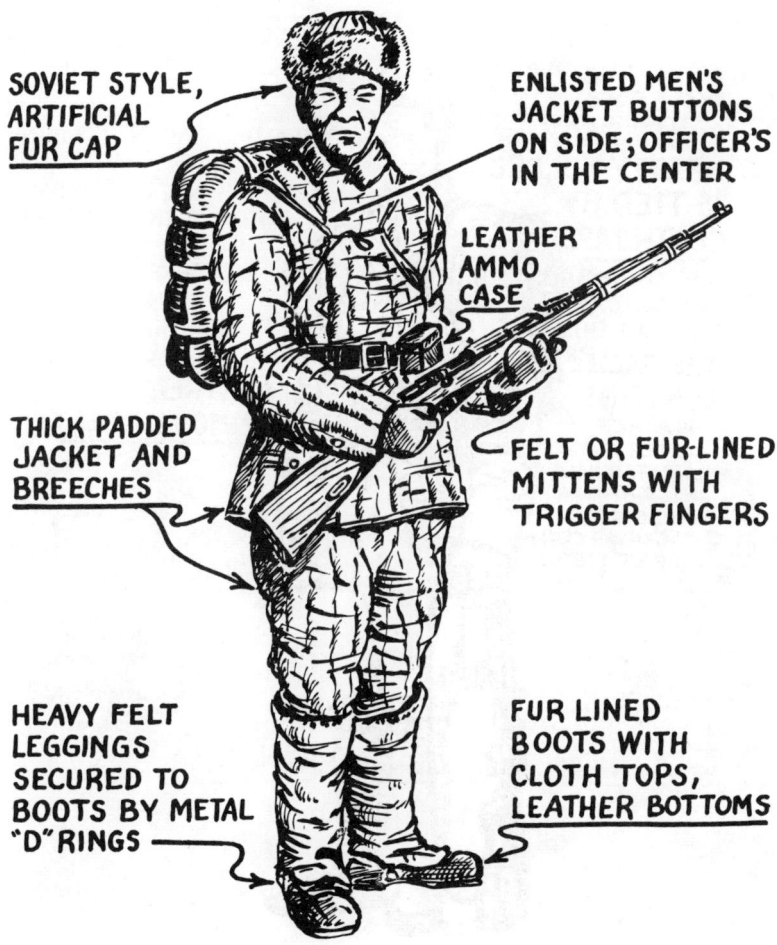

UNIFORM AND EQUIPMENT OF THE CHINESE RED SOLDIER—
RIFLEMAN, IN WINTER UNIFORM.

treatment ranging from indifference to cruelty. Today's Red officers, most of whom have risen from the ranks, are generally consistent in the fair treatment of their men. This is according to regulation and orders which state that officers are not allowed to strike their men. As anyone can recognize, fair treatment pays

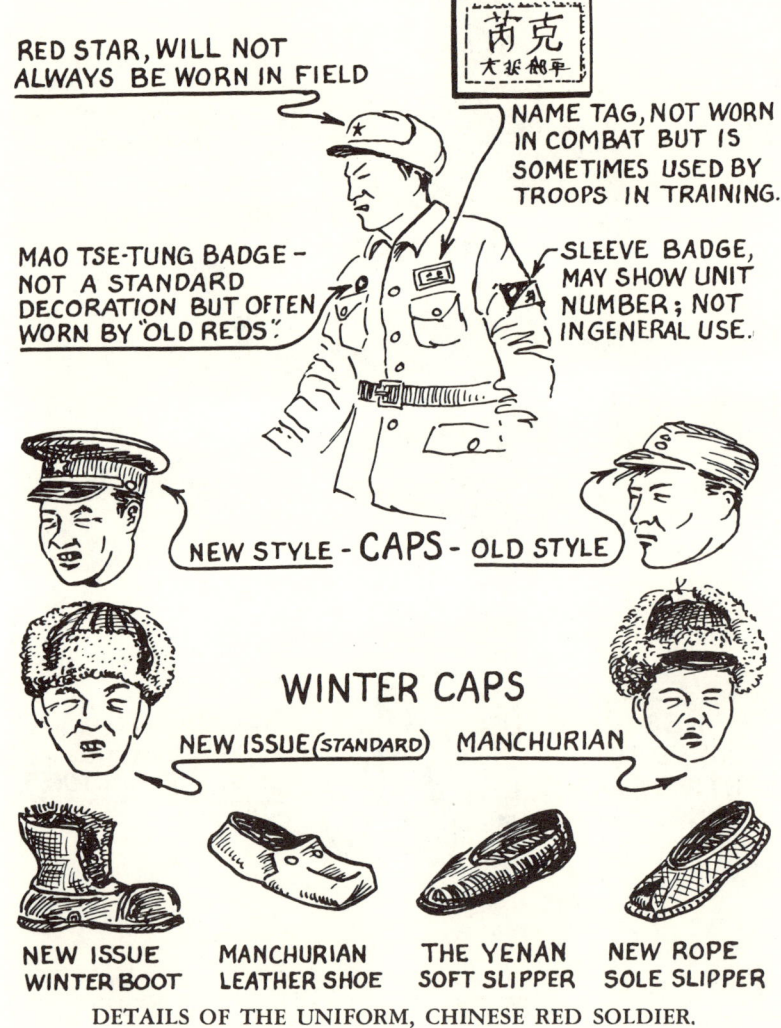

DETAILS OF THE UNIFORM, CHINESE RED SOLDIER.

SOLDIER LIFE IN THE CHINESE RED ARMY

MONTHLY PAY: Private: 41 cents (actually 16,000 JMP (Communist) dollars), plus a vegetable allowance of 3 cents a month.

    NCO or junior officer: 52 cents
    Battalion commander: 84 cents
    Regimental commander: $1.18 (US)
    Division commander: $1.30 (US)

Staff officers are paid according to rank, but get a "feast allowance" (for entertainment) in addition.

RATIONS: In his usual two meals a day the soldier eats:
    31.2 ounces of rice (Northern soldiers get millet instead)
    1.4 ounces of meat
    10.0 ounces of vegetables
    Unlimited water, but little real tea.

MESSING: The average enlisted man eats in the "Little Stove," or third class mess.
    Invalids and combat-distinguished enlisted men eat in the second class mess.
    Officers eat in a "Big Stove" or first class mess. They get better quality food than the enlisted men.

UNIFORMS: Soldiers get one for summer, one for winter—both worn until the patches wear out. Replacement is irregular. Officers get reissues easier. New style uniforms have been issued only to a small number of troops. The Red Air Force has new uniforms throughout.

PERIOD OF SERVICE: No announced plan. Death or wounds are the only certain discharges from service.

DISCIPLINE: Very strict. The soldier is watched even for his opinions. Reckless driving of a vehicle can merit death.

PRIVILEGES: Very few. The average private cannot get married. A soldier is fortunate if he gets a furlough once every two years.

MEDICAL CARE: Poor. The wounded are lucky if a doctor even sees them. Battlefield evacuation is by civilians.

TRAINING: Daily political indoctrination. Little marksmanship, much marching. Soldiers spent part time at labor.

AGE GROUPS: In general, 18 to 35 years, with emphasis on the youngest.

CONSCRIPTION: Each family is required to furnish one male. Schools may be allotted quotas. Unemployed intellectuals may be arbitrarily conscripted. No consistent plan exists.

dividends. In the PLA the officers make great demands on their troops and when one says, "You hold here till you die," obedience usually results.

What can the soldier do if he doesn't like a particular situation or circumstance? Theoretically, he has the right to criticize, but this is narrowed down to three aspects—

(1) He may criticize anyone who disobeys orders or violates discipline;

(2) He may only criticize at certain meetings;

(3) His criticism will not have much impact unless he is a Party member.

The PLA has Revolutionary Soldier Committees but, unlike those of the early Soviet Army, their power is more limited, and such meetings are rigidly supervised. They are, in fact, more representative of the Party than of the soldier. Only at certain meetings are non-Party members allowed to attend.[11]

Old Marshal Yen Hsi-shan, who lived for years on his military island surrounded by Communists, remarked once that the chief weakness and mistake of the Communists is that they think only of the Party and not of the people. They train the people with the objective of dying for the Party.

The Party is first in the army. The officer or soldier who wants to get ahead in life joins the Party.

Background of the Red Soldier

What are the backgrounds of the men now in PLA ranks? How many of the old Communists survive in the ranks? Not all the soldiers who fought in World War II received promotions, but the majority did. Thus the old Communist soldiers became noncommissioned officers and officers; many, of course, were killed in the Civil War. It is doubtful if more than 15 percent of the enlisted men have seen continuous service since 1942. This is about the composition of the PLA today—

    15 percent veterans of World War II;
    25 percent veterans of the entire Civil War;
    30 percent ex-Nationalist troops;
    30 percent inducted into service since about 1948.

The 30 percent ex-Nationalists can be termed critical in two ways: First, they are the least reliable element, considered as a group; and, secondly, a portion of them have talents as tank

---

[11] *The Chinese People's Liberation Army,* published by the Foreign Language Press, Peking, 1950.

drivers, artillerymen, motor mechanics, and such, this makes them essential technicians in the PLA. In the Civil War, the Reds always screened their prisoner groups to select these men.

The lengths to which Red officers would go to get much needed technicians into their service can be illustrated by the case of Major Koo Fen-Wei, who had been a bazooka instructor in the American-trained New Sixth Army. He was captured in the Battle of Chinchow in 1949; and his captors learned of his special talents with a weapon they were anxious to use. But Major Koo couldn't be persuaded to join up, so he was tortured. The Reds broke his teeth and slashed his face; but Koo resisted to the bitter end of their brutality and eventually got his broken body to Taiwan where he is today.[12]

Another group, small in over-all numbers but probably significant in present loyalty, is made up of wounded ex-Nationalist troops. On many battlefields the Reds inherited the terrain upon which lay the bleeding and the groaning. It was a humane policy, and a smart investment, to care for these broken bodies. Treatment was not extensive. The hardy survived, the weak died; but those who remained felt an obligation to their Red saviors, who made the most of the situation to convert them. As Communist General Liang of Chen Yi's army said, "Take care of them if wounded, and an impression is made." These men were easy to convert, for as Mao Tse-tung has remarked, "Chiang's soldiers are very good soldiers. They only need a little political training."

Where does this Red soldier come from? If we only glance at the total figures on urban versus rural populations in China we can safely say 80 to 90 percent of the soldiers come from the farm. However, if we use the official Communist "slide rule"[13] for rural people, we would have to classify the soldier, in origin, as coming from one of the following classes:

(1) Rich peasant

---

[12] *Modern China*, published by Prof. Chen Shih-chuan, Taipeh, Taiwan, October 1950.
[13] "Decisions Concerning the Differentiation of Class Status in the Countryside" as adopted by the Chinese Government Administrative Council, 4 August 1950.

(2) Poor peasant
(3) Middle peasant
(4) Worker
(5) Well-to-do middle peasant
(6) Reactionary rich peasant
(7) Poor odd-jobber
(8) Intellectual (officially, not a class)
(9) Bankrupt landlord
(10) Idler
(11) Worker from rich peasant or landlord family
(12) Landlord or rich peasant, who is concurrently a merchant or industrialist

Fortunately, we can leave the figuring of these statistics to the Reds who have dreamed them up. The average Chinese Red soldier is a peasant accustomed to little comfort, much back-breaking work, plain and meager food, the minimum of clothing and the maximum of toil. One does not need to amplify his background to see that these are the reasons why he makes such a good man in uniform. General "Vinegar-Joe" Stilwell and others have said there is no better soldier material than the Chinese if he is fed fairly and decently cared for. The Chinese Reds have no magic formula; they simply give their soldiers their normal requirements of food and clothing. There is no pampering. The soldier stock is of such origin that it is inherently obedient to power, responsive to discipline, and unaccustomed to asking for much more than is daily required to exist moderately. It is not my purpose here to create any single typical soldier beyond what has already been described. The Communist Army of China contains a multiple of individual types, whose endurance and reaction under ultimate stress will project them into realms of heroic resistance or mass surrenders. The army as a whole is firm in its structure; but like a giant hillside of enduring rock, it can crumble apart piecemeal or, given the conditions, tumble and disintegrate like an avalanche.

The men of the ochre hordes have marched far and felt just as homesick and lonesome within their own vast territory as the soldiers of other nations whom the seas have separated from their homelands. The Northerners find the South as strange and different, almost, as a foreign nation; for often their language is not understood. To the Southerners, the situation can be the same. Men desert this army mainly to get home.

The Conscription of Volunteers

How does a man actually become a volunteer soldier without volunteering? The Communists play a neat trick here. It is a subtle bit of persuasion and manipulation. The Communists confess that they recruit men under what they term "social pressure." The PLA sends a commissar and a few officers to a *hsien* (county) and they proclaim in public that, "the army needs men. This hsien will fill a quota of 230." Meetings are held with the area elders, civic leaders, and others. The burden, as always, is placed on the people. Fathers persuade their sons to "volunteer" or neighbors may shame a large family of males into volunteering another son or brother. Entertainments, mass meetings, and similar devices are resorted to by the recruiting officers.

The public is made to feel a definite need to contribute men to the army. Under organized "social pressure" a few volunteers are secured. Others, more reluctant, are tricked into the service, since the Communists use the people as an instrument of pressure. The recruits are often given festive "send offs"; but the people, not the army, usually pay for these affairs. Paper flowers and rosettes are pinned on the recruits, who are momentarily feted and given special seats at shows and *Yangko* dances. Regardless of how the men are obtained, the army officers, in making up the rosters, list the recruits as *volunteers*. Thus each soldier is officially listed as a volunteer, and the army is clever enough to treat him as such.

This form of recruiting differs greatly from the older and physically more forceful methods formerly employed in China. It is a slower method, for it may require several weeks, as against the few hours of the "rope and tie" system of the warlord area. The PLA, when not under the stress of campaign, undertakes its recruiting with a good deal of patience, which pays good dividends.

Land converts bandits and conscripts peasants. Here was the army's most persuasive device for swelling its ranks. By the land division program, the army can call on a family to contribute one or two sons for the regular service and the remaining males may be asked to enter the militia. Few families are hesitant about contributing "volunteers" when they receive land; few can afford to resist the army's call for men. But the land is pretty well distributed by now.

Bands of bandits roved and raided in Manchuria following the surrender of the Japanese. Red Governor Lin Feng admitted to the presence of 20,000 of these *Hunhuzes* (Red beards), which General Lin Piao's army had to fight at various times. It has always been difficult to eradicate bandits in China, and this has been especially true of Manchuria. When he found he could not exterminate them and fight a civil war at the same time, Lin Piao resorted to the traditional Chinese method of winning friends and influencing people. He "bought out" some of the bandits by giving them land. This device is being applied today on a very limited scale with some anti-Communist bands of guerrillas.

Land as it is now given, in very small plots, goes to soldiers who are war veterans. It is a device to reward, rather than one to entice.

However, even today the Communists physically round up men needed for the army. Men and boys who cannot account for themselves in some form of work or occupation are herded together into labor gangs, from which the army draws the best specimens. During the Civil War the records show that Red military "press gangs" often entered villages in KMT controlled areas and forcibly rounded up recruits.

It was always a significant part of the conscription policy of the CCP (Chinese Communist Party) to recruit from the counties forward of their own or in the path of advancing Nationalist armies. By their own admission, the Communists never wanted to disrupt the economy of their own rear areas by conscripting additional men there.

Several hundred wounded Chinese prisoners of war owe much thanks to a US regimental surgeon of the division that has probably killed more Chinese than any other in Korea. He is Major Joel N. McNair of the 9th Regiment, 2d Division. On many days he has tended more Chinese wounded than American. Major McNair knows the Chinese well. He was born in China and speaks the language fluently. I have no record of how many hundred Chinese soldiers Major McNair has talked to, as he stopped the flow of their bloody wounds, but he has given me a summarization of what many of the soldiers say. This is the average story.

"I was working in a millet field in Shantung (or elsewhere) when the Communist cadres came toward me. I did not run, but I knew something unpleasant was coming. They led me away. A few days later I was in a railway station with other reluctant recruits. We were taken to a training area and given 40 days military instruction. Next thing we knew we were en route to Korea. I arrived in this war zone ten days ago. Now I am a prisoner."

For some, the period from farm labor to a prison camp at Pusan was only 48 days! When the Chinese Reds first attacked United Nations troops they were using a higher proportion of their best soldiers. Later they fed in poorer trained personnel and a high percentage of ex-Nationalists—their most unreliable elements. Small wonder, then, that they attack with these men in "human waves." The Reds tried, however, to save portions of their best soldier material.

Not All the Soldiers Are Given Land

Land brought soldiers into the army, especially after World War II. Lin Piao's field army was helped the most of any field army by the program of land division, but it took Lin Piao about a year before his divided land began turning in recruits.

In 1945 Lin's troops were just arriving in Manchuria. En route there, his columns grabbed men from every town they could. I recall talking to people in Chinchow, just north of the Great

Wall, who said it was the fastest recruiting campaign they had ever seen. The *Balu-jen,* or Eighth Army men, as the Reds were then called, were scurrying northward with General Tu Yu-ming's 52d Army[14] on their tail. The Reds had only a few days left to stay in Chinchow, so they conducted "street campaigns" in which they physically rounded up able-bodied men. Those who could not give documentation, or evidence of labor-livelihood, were herded into Red compounds under guard. They left Chinchow as "volunteers"—protesting somewhat, but under the duress of armed guards.

The following spring Lin Piao's forces were busily sacking factories, along with the Soviets, and fighting a delaying action against General Tu's forces. The Red military was hard pressed and the Nationalists kept up their advance despite Soviet obstructionism, which I witnessed in Mukden, Changchun, and other places. At Ssupingkai, Lin Piao gathered the bulk of his forces and fought a vicious toe-to-toe battle in April and May 1946. Nationalist artillery (and aircraft, in limited degree) got the best of Lin's forces, and, while not sorely beaten, they nevertheless withdrew and were in full flight across the Sungari when the Americans imposed a truce on the fighting in Manchuria. Until then, Lin Piao hadn't had any real amount of time, in which to consolidate his portion of Manchuria and convert it and the land to Communist will. The truce gave him the opportunity, and here was where the Fourth Field Army grew to mature stature.

The army itself got to work and assisted the Red government in dividing up the land. This role placed Communist army units where they could be seen by the people. This is always an important point with the Reds. The army must be seen. Lin Piao's little army was disciplined to good conduct; the people were impressed. Lin had all summer, fall, and a portion of the winter to evolve the change. The region was most suitable, for the land holdings were large and the people many. Actually, there was

---

[14] This army, commanded by General Chao Kung-wu, was only one army of General Tu Yu-ming's army group, later called the "Northeast China Command."

no shortage of land, and many poor farmers did well on small acreage. Today Lin Piao regards this interval and this particular land reform program as one of the most significant contributions to his military success; for it gave him, or allowed him, to take men into military service and build up his army.[15]

The technique was simple and offered opportunity for Red persuasion. The acreage was divided; the Communists simply said to the family, "Now we need two of your sons to fight for this land." Off the sons went, for the farmer could not actually say that the Reds had been ungenerous or *too* demanding. Thousands and thousands of soldiers came to the army through this device—and are still held in the army by it.

But there are men in the PLA who were never given any farm plots, nor were their families. The Communists would have us believe there was, and is, land for everyone. There is not.[16] The Nationalist soldiers who surrendered individually and in units during the Civil War did not, as a group, get in on the land division program. The Reds offered them the "privilege of serving"—again the aspect of making men feel they were being given *something,* even if only an opportunity. These men occupy many thousands of jobs within the army today. They are kept in the service, for they must "prove themselves," as the Reds say. The ranks of the PLA are swelled with men the Reds *could* release but are afraid to. China has too many guerrilla bands already. Besides, the army is a vehicle to educate men to the Marxist-Maoist line. Not all of these ex-KMT soldiers swallow the Red bait; but the Communists work hard to smother any of the smouldering thoughts or resentments.

Women Also Serve, and Sometimes Fight

The army has its women—rough bosomy creatures in pants. They are a happy-go-lucky lot whose very presence in a combat area raises male morale. They all seem to look alike; perhaps

---

[15] *The China Weekly Review,* 7 January 150, and other sources.
[16] Land is distributed at the rate of one-half acre per capita, which is hardly enough to support the farmer himself, much less meet the heavy taxes now being levied.

because of their uniformly bobbed hair and the low way in which they wear their caps. Their jobs vary. Some hundreds have actually participated in combat as gun-shooting soldiers, but their regular roles are those of medical technicians, nurses, unit propagandists, cultural workers, and in lower units, even political commissars.

Their main roles are with the cultural and medical services. In 1949 the Reds said that 30 to 40 percent of the Third Field Army's medical staff consisted of women.[17] These females all double in the field as walking blood banks; they freely give transfusions of their own blood to wounded men. They are a hardy, rugged lot, for in campaign and combat they lead the muddy and dirty existence of other troops and take many of the same risks.

For cultural activities, which parallel our special services, the women are organized into "companies" of 20 or less and tour the field units, putting on plays, singing ballads, playing music, and otherwise entertaining. These companies beat the propaganda drum loud and long, for all plays and ballads are designed to put over a political lesson. One of the most popular of the present plays, put on for the army, deals with the life and woes of a group of Peking prostitutes. Written and acted by several prostitutes whom the PLA "liberated," the play is a hammy portrayal of "their life under the KMT rule."[18]

The Red Air Force has taken and put into new uniforms several thousand women, who now help staff the communications, work at airfields and otherwise perform valuable service as technicians. These women, in their smart new-style uniforms and black peaked caps, divide their time between long hours of work and added hours of study and schooling. For one thing, they are being taught the Russian language; for, as China's Red Air Force grows larger, this language will assume even greater importance than it presently has. Air Force Women's Service detachments

---

[17] "Armywomen Marching with Armymen to Cross Yangtze," *North China News Agency*, 9 April 1949.
[18] *The China Weekly Review*, 8 April 1950.

have among their number translators and interpreters, who work on the preparation of Chinese texts taken from Soviet Air Force manuals, and on stock record catalogs, technical instructions, and similar publications. As interpreters who can speak Russian they are in big demand. Other women are learning to operate radios and radar, for here is a whole new growing empire in Red China's military structure. Air Intelligence keeps many women busy translating American and other foreign magazines on technical and military subjects.

The "shooting-est" females in Red Chinese uniforms are the militia-women—armed amazons who do police and sentry duty around depots and certain critical installations.

The morals of the Communist women soldiers are a subject of much debate. I have seen the flirtations within the ranks and the strolls of uniformed couples to the fringes of camp at dusk, but I never knew how far these relations were carried. Officially the Reds try to enforce good moral conduct; unofficially, they must wink at certain realities. Among the Communist women, some are sexless political automatons, party-pure, determinedly devoted to the cause and studiously virgin. Others are bubbling with life and vigor, so much so that they have a form of sex appeal that bursts out of their drab, heavily padded uniforms, to the delight and amusement of the rough and ready soldiers. With these particular women, moral conduct is not viewed in terms of obedience to Party orders, but in terms of, "Don't get caught." These uniformed women are not deliberately wanton. Rugged, best describes them. The number of women in military service is nearly 60,000, and the number is growing, especially in the Air Force.

What Makes the Red Soldier a Good Fighter?

Why do men and women continue to serve a cause in which many thousands of them do not believe? The answer is simple: Control that makes it difficult to escape, and fear of punishment for escaping. Secret police, local police, militia, the army, the Party, all webbing throughout China, to the extent that a homecoming or a journey after desertion invites death. The old tradition that a Chinese soldier gets only the final discharge of death or wounds, is still being perpetuated.

How are these men in the ranks controlled? Discipline directs their ways; political indoctrination polices the wayward; and rewards, although small, encourage the masses to follow somewhat blindly the power of the Party. When the Fourth Field Army converged on the pleasant old city of Peking, it purged its ranks of the ill-disciplined, so as to eliminate them from the numbers who later had the glory of parading and sightseeing.

But discipline takes grimmer forms. Rope is wound and crossed over the already raw flesh of a pair of wrists. The military code calls for the hands to be bound behind the back. This scene is old to China, and it is regular in pattern. The bound figure kneels on the earth of a compound, where the idle and the curious watch the transition from life to death. The Mauser's muzzle is held about one foot from the back of the kneeling figure's neck. Aim may be careful or careless, but the result is always certain. This is punishment for disobedience to orders, desertion (in most cases), and a variety of lesser infractions. Take, for example, the case of a Red Chinese soldier who killed a pedestrian in Shanghai. He was quickly executed by the Woosung Garrison Headquarters in February 1950 for reckless driving.[19] Other executions are on record for much lesser offenses. The PLA has the harshest of punishments for infractions of its rules and regulations. The men, consequently, hesitate to disobey or desert.

What about the quality of the men now in the army? Manchurians, Northerners, and men from North Central China still dominate the PLA's mass; the South Chinese are still a regional minority, as are those of the other geographical areas. This will gradually change to a more even regional distribution. The Northerners make excellent soldiers; some believe they are better than the Southerners.

The training is tough and the training day is long. Only Sundays theoretically, have been free from specific military activity.

---

[19] *North China Daily News*, Shanghai, 15 February 1951.

It is the hard training they receive that molds the Red Chinese into good fighters. The men of China's uniformed hordes do not have very much ammunition with which to practice target shooting. Furthermore, they have a great variety of rifles. The net result is that they are not very good individual marksmen.

The noncommissioned officers are tough little men, with loud voices and an exaggerated sense of their importance in the scheme of things. Almost without exception they are Communist Party members. Almost every NCO has participated in combat, to some degree. They are close to their men; a good portion of them have been elected to their positions by the soldiers. Swaggering and hand waving, they make every soldier's business *their* business. They are excellent leaders and few soldiers choose to argue with them. They pack a lot of authority and are well backed up. This makes an army.

Propaganda Pays Off

There is a lot of paper work in the PLA, but it is not the administrative type. Posters, handbills, books, magazines, broadcasts—and always the proclamations, written and verbal. The army does a lot of bragging. Propaganda is paying off in two ways in the conduct of the soldiers. To us it may seem silly that the Communists keep harping on the fact that the PLA "never takes so much as a thread or a needle from the people without returning it." But this scheme has helped establish the general concept among the Chinese people that this army is their friend. The second way this propaganda is paying off is that the soldiers are coming to believe in themselves as superior to all other generations of Chinese soldiery. This point is drummed home incessantly. The result is—pride in self-restraint, in little matters, which makes for bigger "face." The soldier is given more respect by the people, and this heightens his morale. He treats the people well, except when under orders to raid or shoot, and the people, therefore, treat the soldiers well, as individuals. These are little chain reactions that build up soldier spirit into unit *esprit de corps*.

However, this army is not made up of docile peasants who

always reek with politeness and concern for other human beings. Their own lives are held so cheaply that they regard others' the same way. Although they may have learned to treat their own people with a measure of respect, new for Chinese soldiers, they have lost none of the brutality that typifies so many elements of Asia. The men are like trained dogs. Point out an enemy and they will attack and viciously tear him apart. Call these soldiers back and show them the people who are not their enemies and

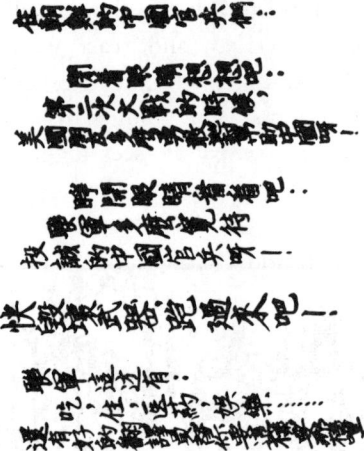

U. S. Army Photo.

SAFE CONDUCT PASS—KOREA, 1951.

The legend on this pass reads as follows:

    Close your eyes and think—
    During World War II
    How courageously the American friends
    Helped China.

    Open your eyes and look.
    Ask your brothers, who know Americans,
    How well the UN Forces treat Chinese officers and men
    Who have ceased resistance.

    Destroy your weapons and come over!
    The UN Forces will provide you with:
    Food, shelter, medical treatment, and recreation.

    Furthermore, you will have good interpreters,
    To ask this and that for you.

Note: Directly under the title are instructions—in both English and Korean—on the good treatment to be provided.

they will be friendly. The Chinese Red soldier has now undergone several years of violent anti-American indoctrination. This vicious hate campaign has taken effect among a large number. Its effect among those who do believe it, is such as to sweep the remainder (who do not believe, or are in doubt) along with the current. When it comes to fighting us, there have been no polls taken; the soldiers simply have obeyed orders. When first shot at, they know they must shoot back. When they have been shot at often and hard, they recall the hatred in which they have been schooled, and react with added vigor and resistance. Red China's soldiers make excellent troops with which to slaughter Americans. The soldier may not know the issues at stake, but once in combat he sees tangibles like shells coming at him; men of white skin and no slant eyes. The enemy is from a distant land, while he, the Chinese, is close to home. But always there rings

U. S. Army Photo.

SAFE CONDUCT PASS, KOREA 1951 (REVERSE).
Upper right: Reproduction of Safe Conduct Pass.
Lower right: Destroy or bury your weapons. Come over the open roads only.
Upper left: Hold your hands high over your head. Bring your wounded brothers with you.
Lower left: The UN Forces guarantee good treatment to all Chinese prisoners of war.

in his ears: "The officers and commissars have said the Americans would attack us, and now they have. I must shoot them."

These soldiers have little education; they believe most of what they are told. As prisoners, they will come over to believing our side, if they are indoctrinated; but do not make the mistake of crediting the Chinese soldier with—

(1) Any education that will permit him accurately to judge international issues; or,

(2) Any martyr-like resistance against the military leaders already entrenched in power.

The thing that makes the Chinese soldier outstanding is his enduring obedience to orders. One could take 60 percent of the PLA today and, with new leaders, reorganize it under an entirely different political and military system, then commit it to battle in Korea and get practically the same results as the Reds have achieved.

Vigor and Drive—While Winning

But the Red crust will crumble and military structures will dissolve in a foreign-soil war of long test. This can happen in Korea. The men in the PLA are no different from those of the North Korean Army of 1950. Their enthusiasm for the conflict can be compared with that of the Red Korean soldiers, who fought well while they were winning but who surrendered in droves when the military tide turned against them. One factor separates the comparison, however; and that is—China has more men to throw into the maw of war; therefore, the breaking of the crust will not come as soon as it did with the Red Korean Army we defeated in 1950.

I have carefully studied these soldiers during many hours on the march with them, while waiting in their various headquarters, while eating with them, and when under guard of their guns. I have also seen them fight at times when I could count more of their dead before me than I could number the living. In combat they were impressive beyond a doubt. Their vigor and drive led them directly and quickly against machine gun strong points that would have caused longer hesitation in other soldiers. Their ability to take losses and to rush forward over their own piles of dead was appalling. Their direction from officers was hardly visible or verbal, yet there always seemed to be a momentum that the Nationalists could muster only on the defensive. I have heard of the Reds driving civilians or refugees before them in actual attack, but I have never seen it. I do, however, credit them with resorting to such practices.

Of their cruelty, especially against a foreign enemy, I have no doubt. I believe the very presence of a foreign opponent or superior fire power will heighten their battle brutality. On the other hand they do not become the die-hard escapists from prison camps that some other nationalities breed. Some of these soldiers have had so much campaigning and combat that it is to them a perfectly normal existence. That factor must be reckoned with.

The Soldier As He Is Today

Summed up, the soldiers of present-day Red China as a group can probably outmarch those of any other nation, including the majority of our own. Like the Japanese, they can get along on less food than can US soldiers. Their attitude toward death is not necessarily one of indifference, but they obey orders that other troops would challenge. PLA men are products of a stiffer and more brutal system of discipline than are our own. Their health is below the standards we apply to our military service. Their training is below American standards of completion, but this is compensated for by the fact the greater part of these Chinese soldiers have been in actual combat for years. Their stealth is superior.

The morale of Chinese troops in combat on foreign soil will probably sink below that of the troops opposing them. Belief in the cause for which they fight and die varies according to the degree and effect of political indoctrination. This is hard to measure in over-all percentages. There is a weak element, but many of this element have already been fed into our guns. Those who remain are held together by a hard structure of men who believe, if not in their nation's political philosophy, at least in their army.

Initiative in the Chinese private is dull and indifferent compared to that of the US soldier, but the Chinese is adept at improvisation.

Education-wise, the average Chinese soldier is just now attending third grade. Because his patience and endurance is good, he will, in time, learn to read and write a little. His marksmanship is not good; he likes a tommy gun, as does the Soviet soldier. The technical ability of the majority of Chinese is such that they cannot efficiently adapt themselves to the larger and more modern weapons in a short time. The Chinese soldier began as a farmer or peasant's son. Hard physical labor has been a part of his life and always will be. Therefore, the discomforts of campaign affect him less than they do the more urban Westerner. The Chinese will momentarily endure more hardship perhaps, than his Western opponent; but he will die or get killed sooner. Into his place is gradually coming a newer soldier. This one is a student now; he will believe his masters even more readily.

A New Soldier Generation Is in the Making

Some writers maintain that a noncommissioned officer will lose his rank if his family falls into disfavor. This is a little oversimplified. It can happen and perhaps does occur, but the noncommissioned officer, or any soldier, can retain his rank providing he renounces his family for their deeds. Here is where the Communists are breaking the old family ties which are so much a part of China's tradition. Note, further, that in the 1951 purges it was the young people who appeared to be most listened to by the commissars and secret police. A complete generation of informers is being nursed and strengthened by the Reds, and this generation will bite deep and bloodily into its own family flesh.

The army is building on this new generation. Whereas, earlier, it sought *any* soldiers or men who would half-willingly shoulder a rifle in its cause, now the army is bringing into its ranks the most politically reliable. Beginning back in 1947, the military and political hierarchy agreed upon a plan of more careful selection of recruits. This plan is in its interim stage. In 1951 the PLA announced that for that year it would conscript 250,000 students and young workers as cadres for modernizing the military services. Five more years and it will have stocked the army with new youths, who have had full Red political indoctrination. The system is to organize the youth and train it politically before it is

U. S. Army Photo.

IN FIVE MORE YEARS THE RED CHINESE ARMY WILL BE STOCKED WITH NEW YOUTHS.
Captured Chinese are questioned by South Korean and American officers north of the Han River, March, 1951.

ripe for the army. The Communists have 470,000 youngsters organized into the *Pioneer Youth Corps*. Uniformed in white shirts and scarlet ties, they already have marched and hurrahed with red silk banners and "peace" torches in a strength of 15,000 in one city.[20]

Then there is the *New Democratic Youth League* which also follows the pattern of the Soviet *Komsomol*. This organization has a reported strength of 1,800,000 members.

---

[20] *People's China*, 16 May and 16 October, 1950.

The young boys of these organizations are being told one story, one political theme; and they are growing to military age amid a period of bloody purge. They are made to feel that, young as they are, they have the power to spy and inform on others. Some have already committed family members to prison, and even death. As in Russia, the hands of the youth are being bloodied, so that they are put in a position of *having* to serve and support the Communist government or the local people will tear them bodily apart. The youth of China is being prostituted by Peking's Red masters to the point where the young cannot escape military slavery. This is the generation that will provide tomorrow's Red soldiers.

Chapter 5

AN ILLITERATE ARMY BEGINS FORMAL TRAINING

Teaching the Soldier to Read and Write

Many printed leaflets fluttered to the snowy ground in Korea during that winter. At night, shadowy Chinese figures would surreptitiously pick them up and tuck them into hiding places until daylight. The curiosity of these men was heightened when they saw the familiar characters of their language printed on the leaflets. But what did the printed characters mean?

In the winter of 1950-51 in Korea, our army shot and baled out tons of safe-conduct or surrender passes, only to find that these documents were not succeeding in their purpose as they did in Europe. Later in the conflict, the reason became more apparent. The Chinese Reds form the world's largest army of illiterates and semi-illiterates. But even when they could read, Chinese soldiers were afraid to pick up the squares of paper in Korea. Thus, the tank-mounted loud speaker became the more useful device for inducing surrender.

Surrender is an individual thing. To confide in surrender, a soldier not only must know his comrades well, he must have also sure knowledge that their morale has reached the low ebb of his own before he chances talk of desertion. A surrender leaflet is a dangerous possession for the Red Chinese soldier, whose conduct is closely watched. It is useless for the Chinese soldier who cannot read, for too often he is afraid to ask his literate friend or officer to read it to him.

It should not be thought that the Red Army of China is entirely of poor quality because it has a high percentage of illiterates in its ranks. The nation itself suffers in this respect. Of its 450-million population, 75,095,000 were children below school age (1945-46), with 373,905,000 above school age. Of the latter group, only 198,695,066 were listed as literates.[1] Thus the army is drawn from a population only 53.1 percent literate.[2] This problem has long been recognized by the Communist leaders, who are now launching a "large scale attack" on illiteracy. The army is reported to be a huge school. Actually it is not, but it has made a beginning.

A preparatory survey of the illiteracy problem was first made, in December 1949, among the troops in Manchuria. This survey revealed that a "considerable number of troops and *commanding personnel* . . . have not, or have only just, reached an elementary school standard of education . . . the fighters . . . (being) mostly poor peasants or hired farm laborers . . ."[3]

The Red Army, that had for years busied itself with regular and guerrilla combat, has partly settled down to educate its masses. The new program started informally when several divisions, which were relieved of campaign duties, began in July 1949 to devote five hours a week to the elementals of reading and writing. By November 1949, the school time was raised to twelve hours weekly. Preliminary examinations in the spring of 1950 reportedly showed that in five months the average soldier had mastered 370 characters. In one artillery regiment an average of 600 characters was attained.[3] The educational program gained its *formal* start in September 1950, within the Northeast Command and its first stage was scheduled to end in late 1951.

At present, where it can be implemented, the educational project within the army calls for 31 hours of general education

---

[1] *The China Handbook*, Rockport Press, Inc., New York, 1950, page 639.
[2] This is one of the highest percentages given; other sources show literacy well below 50 percent.
[3] *People's China*, Peking, August 1950.

a week, or 70.2 percent of the weekly *study* period, the remainder of the time being devoted to military and political subjects.

In August 1950 the Communists estimated that by the autumn of 1952 "every soldier" will have received a full elementary education. The Chinese decision to enter the war in Korea has obviously blocked a good portion of this program which, as planned in 1950, foresaw a full secondary education in the next five years for "all commanding personnel." [3]

In Southwest China the "cultural offensive" got under way in 1951, with the illiterate men coached in 1950, so as to get some basic knowledge and learn a few hundred characters.[3] Envisaged here is a three-year plan, wherein "a million troops" are scheduled to devote a few hours each day to study and instruction. Secondary education is being given those men possessing primary schooling. However, those men who have already completed secondary training will not, generally, go higher, but will sit in attendance to military and political instructors at related army schools. It should be noted that, when these hardened rough soldiers take their primary education, they are participating in the equivalent of the six-year courses *normally given to children* between the ages of 6 to 12 years. Education on the so-called secondary level normally includes middle, normal and vocational schools. The average middle school in China used to require student attendance for three years in the junior division, plus three more in the senior.

Until this ambitious progam is completed, every eight or 12 soldiers who cannot read must take up the time of an officer or noncommissioned officer who can; for the present system requires Chinese Red troops to be indoctrinated daily, not only in the over-all Communist line—but also in current events. It is natural that the Reds conceive that the soldiers must be brought to a level of education where they can ferret out their own news from such Communist slanted publications as the "Fighter's Companion." The Communists want soldiers who can read newspapers and NCO's and officers who can read orders intelligently. There are reams of propaganda to be absorbed, also!

The question arises as to what the soldier will get under this education program. He will be taught, in these abbreviated courses, to read and to write[4] some; but he will not be overburdened with mathematics, nor will he labor in physics or chemistry. Hygiene will be stressed, for the Communists want to eliminate, if they can, the filth and fleas that abound in China. Instruction in history will begin with heavy emphasis on the *Long March* and the *Long Struggle*; then it will swing to the evil doings of the capitalists in the Orient and elsewhere. Geography will be local in scope; the land masses of China, Russia, and India will more than give soldier-students a full dose of this subject. Geographically, Southeast Asia will be treated as the land of oppressed peoples; Japan the home of the hated invaders. America, the soldiers will be taught, is the realm of the "Paper Tiger."[5]

This makes two non-military programs in which the Army is now required to participate, education and national labor. The army is working long and hard; so much so that, in some regions, language learning is being combined with either military work or actual labor. Instead of classrooms, some units, which are busily engaged in civilian production, study their simple lessons in the fields, on the roads, or on the levees and dikes which they are repairing. The Communists have devised a system in which two characters (words) are written on multiple slips of paper, and these are stuck on nearby objects, so that soldiers may learn as they work.[6] The characters are also chalk-written on sticks of wood, which are stuck into the baskets of dirt or produce. Large cloth banners may be erected between two poles in the fields, to keep before soldier eyes the two characters which the trooper is required to learn each day. Walls and buildings which are near labor details of soldiers are also painted with words. This system

---

[4] In connection with this educational program, the Reds are making much propaganda hay over the purchase of 7,000 fountain pens by one division in North China and the fact that one model student mastered 2,000 Chinese characters in seven months.

[5] To the Chinese a "paper tiger" means outwardly fearsome but really empty and harmless.

[6] *The China Weekly Review*, 27 May 1950.

is simple, but is typical of the Communist approach to a problem. The army must learn, but it must also labor.

What will be the effect of all this energy directed towards educating many millions of soldiers? Most of them won't be given too much to absorb, but they will learn certain characters which have significance in military parlance. There is an element of propaganda in the program. The government will make much to-do over the benefits of such training. The troops will feel they are, at least, learning *one thing* in the army that will benefit them in civilian life—if they ever do get out of service. The secondary schooling will probably do the most good, for it will advance those NCO's and officers who already have a basis of education. These men will learn to read and write China's difficult language to an extent beneficial to the army—and this the army needs badly.

In his 1950 critique of the South China armed forces, Commissar Tan Cheng expressed the essence of a great truth when he said, ". . . the great percentage of illiteracy of the soldiers should be eliminated. . . . It is impossible to utilize modern equipments, to learn to conduct modern warfare, or to learn how skillfully to command soldiers in combat if the soldiers are uneducated. The knowledge of military science and the social sciences will be made the principal contents of basic education." [7]

The Army Speaks Many Languages

In the United States, the southerner understands the speech of the northerner. In the USSR the Ukrainian is not misunderstood by the Great Russian. The Asiatic elements of the Soviet Union may speak their own language, but they have to know, in some degree, the Russian tongue. Large, and long un-united by either communications or government, China has grown linguistically, for centuries, as a conglomeration of dialects. The average Manchurian cannot understand a Shanghailander; the Cantonese finds difficulty in understanding the purity of Mandarin speech; the

---

[7] Tan Cheng, "Report of Tasks of the South China Armed Forces During 1950," *New China Monthly*, 17 March 1950.

Mongolian, being of a minority, knows a little Chinese, but he often is laughed at by his rulers when he speaks it. The men from Sinkiang speak Turki, Russian and other languages, but generally they know no Chinese. United on the map, and held together by the ruthless rule of fanatics, China linguistically is a dis-united nation, and the Communists are decades away from a solution of the problem. One of the announced tasks of the Chinese Communist Government—a problem now undergoing determined study—is the reform of the Chinese language. The staff problem has been put to committees of experts: they are to work out a "Unified dialect for China on the basis of . . . the North China dialect" (i.e., Mandarin).[8] The problem is a national one, but right now the differences in dialect are a definite handicap to the modernization of the army. The men of one region must be instructed and trained by those knowing their dialect. These men can be transferred to armies and units other than their regional ones, but there are many impractical aspects to this. In the more advanced technical and specialized training, the soldiers from the south, southwest, and west will be out of step in language with the armies in more centralized establishments of the north and east. What will be the results in the army? First, the northerners, because they speak Mandarin or near-Mandarin, will dominate and furnish the bulk of the army's higher leaders. Second, the non-Mandarin speaking will probably supply men mostly for the infantry, labor service, and such. Third, there will be units regional in character because of a common dialect; and, if the Chinese Reds lean at all in the direction of the Soviets on this issue, they will not greatly favor the organization of units on such a basis.

Thus, in training millions of men, the Chinese Reds not only have the problem of teaching soldiers to read and write, they also are faced with the problem of teaching them to speak a common language. Herein lies the serious but not insurmountable obstacle to the modernization of the Red People's Liberation Army.

---

[8] *The China Weekly Review*, J. B. Powell, 22 October 1949.

The Labor Pains of Military Training

However, the army has fought long without education. How does it stand in military training? This army is smug about feeling it is well trained. It launched into its attack on us in Korea on the assumption that it knew all about fighting a big war and was trained for one. But it isn't. However, its masses, so regularly and deliberately committed to bloody death, compensate for certain training deficiencies.

When the Nationalist armies either had been defeated or had fled to Taiwan, the Communist field armies paused to gather up their scattered forces, organize their regional bases, redistribute the equipment, and improve the organization of their units. The armies were winded and needed a rest. They had made hasty distribution of captured arms, but their standard units were still irregular in strength, organization, and armament. Armies and other units had grown in disproportion to each other, and the military patterns and standards fitted no common template.

Victory on the mainland was practically an accomplished fact when Mao Tse-tung, and Chu Teh, after visiting the depots of captured stocks, issued orders to the field armies that they were to get ready for reorganization. Everyone agreed. The army deserved some standardization, for its elements had emerged out of the Civil War as organizational products of their own regional environment and experience. This was why the field armies varied so much in strength. So the armies eagerly awaited shipments of the new style uniforms and the newly printed texts that were to standardize appearance and training in the PLA. Then the armies received orders to put their soldiers immediately to work in the fields and factories. The nation was fighting inflation and the Communists, for the first time, were burdened with an army that had no profitable mission. So its manpower was diverted from military training to common labor. The Communists needed farm and factory products. Roads and railways were in disrepair or destroyed. Communications, so vital and so few, were urgently needed by the Red regime. So, in the interval between the Civil War and the Chinese entry into the Korean war, military training was, on the whole, subordinated to compliance with the *Common Program*[9] of rebuilding and feeding the nation. Special units like those newly created of armor and artillery were exempt from this labor. Elements of Chen Yi's army were allowed to concentrate on amphibious training. These were exceptions.

The big demand used to be for guerrilla gunmen and for "specialists" who could handle Japanese and later, US mortars and machine guns. That is changed now. The army now lacks mechanics—airplane and motor vehicle—truck drivers, tank gunners, artillerymen, radio operators, navigators, and pilots. These and other technical slots are being filled by a variety of personnel, ranging from inducted students, who are being trained for such jobs, to ex-Nationalist soldiers who for a period will hold their positions. The manpower is available. It can be culled from the best fitted, but the army is having its problems in the personnel aspects of modernization. Here the training program is more nearly centralized, but not completely so. The human material for good mechanics, for example, is in short supply. While industrialization in China has only begun, it has its priority in selection of the machine-skilled. Thus for the army, the problem of modernization narrows down to how fast and how well technical and specialist personnel can be trained.

For all of its industrial progress, the USSR was unable to give its army much in the way of mechanics and technicians before World War II. China is even more backward in the fields of motorization, industrialization, and military aircraft. China was reported[10] to have had about 10,000 trained technicians and about 400,000 skilled factory workers at the close of the Civil War. How reliable these figures are I do not know, but they do index the low ratio of machine-skilled personnel to the over-all population of 450,000,000 people. The Red Army of China seeks to become modern, but it is starting out under the handicap of having to train thousands of men for jobs which the Western armies manage,

---

[9] Common Program, 29 September 1949, adopted by the PPCC, was a program of political principles used by the Red government in lieu of a constitution.

[10] Harrison Forman, *Blunder in Asia*, Didier, New York 21, N. Y., 1950.

in better part, to fill with soldiers experienced from civil trades.

The Soviets are helping with the technical training program now getting under way in the PLA. However, these "big brothers," as the Communists say they call them, don't all speak Chinese, and very few Chinese troops can understand Russian. However, help is being given here, but mainly in the fields of radar and aviation. The Chinese Air Force is receiving priorities in selection of personnel. The army, in the main, is having to stand on its own feet and slowly train its soldiers in the jobs of handling motors, machines, radios, and big guns. Meanwhile the army is giving rough treatment and poor care to its battered vehicles. But they will run for a while even with poor care. They will be wired and held together—the Chinese are extremely adept at improvisation, and at nursing clanking vehicles. But it takes lengthy instruction and constant discipline to make Chinese soldiers look under trucks and tighten the bolts before they drop off.

A Chinese soldier doesn't have to be able to read in order to be taught how to drive a tank. The mechanics can rely on a clerk to read the spare-parts catalog and make up requisitions. The armor noncommissioned officer may not be able to read the field manuals, but his officer can impart much tactical information to him through charts and diagrams. The Reds are finding a way. The tanks and the bigger guns have crews which can drive and shoot. There are some men who can repair damaged machines and instruments. New men, without any degree of education, are being trained for jobs they never dreamed of holding. But the essential point is that all of the technical training takes *longer* in the PLA than it does in Western armies. The end product is not individually as good. If the PLA maintains the pace of its present program of training specialists and technicians, it can superficially advance in a short time to where it has sizeable modern components. But the army is sacrificing quality for mass and speed in this program to vault the army from its antique past to a semblance of modernity.

The war in Korea has slowed up the PLA's technical advance; its training, except for the newer specialized units, is generally hasty and given over to attaining the minimum levels that characterized it in the Civil War days. This means that the training emphasis is mainly on infantry with the desired modernization postponed. While certain Chinese troops are undergoing armor training, probably they will not undergo advanced training in armor-infantry cooperation and techniques before being committed to action. The commanders, who have never handled any amounts of armor and artillery, cannot successfully learn the advanced techniques and higher tactics in a short space of time. Quite probably the Soviets realize this and are restraining the Chinese from trying to utilize too much modern equipment. In 1950-51 the Chinese Reds fought the Korean war with the tactics and techniques of the Civil War. The main emphasis in today's training is on infantry, with secondary emphasis on field artillery. The Air Force, under the most direct Soviet tutelage, is training and growing separately from the army.

Military Training in the Lower Units

Soldier training is decentralized down to the lower units. There are no large training centers for recruits and replacements. The latter are recruited locally and trained by units in the particular region. The Communist leaders want army units to be leavened, at all times, with the proper balance of new men interspersed with the old. No new group must be given guns overnight, even though they may be only raw recruits, for the Communists are alert to the possibilities of small or large garrison revolts. The rail and motor transportation facilities of China are such as to preclude very much centralization of replacement training.

In military training, the infantry companies are broken up into small groups—the recruits or less experienced men undergoing training in the basics of soldiering; the older men undergoing various stages of advanced instruction. Training schedules vary from company to company but can be said to fit loosely into the master schedules put out by the armies.

The emphasis, for the majority of troops, is on the use of rifles, bayonets, and grenades, with marching and discipline paramount. The men must know how to march long, march rapidly, and march well. This means practice, and it is rugged. Little time is yet devoted to regular parade ground drill. Red troops drill by marching in the country, not in a drill area. Officers measure and discipline their men by long marches of relative uniformity, rather than by the precision of parade ground steps and salutes. This is the PLA's heritage. Its columns always look route-order and sloppy to the critical foreign eye, yet the value of this type of field training cannot be underestimated. There is an effort to give as much realism to combat training as possible, but the officers do not make a fetish of combat courses. Their primary measure of the man is, "Can he endure the marching?" and "Does he keep his weapon clean?"

Considering that the rifle is the primary weapon of the Chinese Red Army, the Chinese soldier is a poorly trained marksman. This is mainly the result of ammunition shortages. With its millions of men and limited arsenal production, the PLA cannot yet allot any sizable number of rounds to each individual for target practice. The old concept, when the Reds had fewer troops under arms and less ammunition, was, "If you have ammunition and want to practice; shoot at enemy troops." The essence of this concept prevailed, by necessity, even through the Civil War. It was a naive concept, but necessary in the minds of Red officers, who had to husband their ammunition stocks very carefully and were often so short that they either had to capture shells or withdraw from immediate battle. Today there are hundreds of organized target ranges which, by our standards, are poorly equipped and not steadily used.

Aside from the general shortage of ammunition for training, there is always the problem of the variety of gun calibers. Some riflemen will receive training and limited target practice with a particular weapon because, locally, that is the only one for which there is stocked any amount of ammunition. However, the soldier may go into combat with the Gimo Rifle after he has had target practice with a Springfield. It is extremely doubtful that the average new Chinese soldier has the opportunity to fire more than 50 rounds of rifle ammunition before entering combat.

There remains, however, the fact that a large portion of the present day army has fired in combat weapons of one sort or another. But that doesn't prove that they have greatly improved their marksmanship. Present day military training in China can be said to produce poor individual marksmen; but the officers are not overworried, for they know that they will have a sufficiently large number of weapons firing at an enemy to make him duck for cover. In this connection, I recall Jack Collins' joking remark, as we actually fell into Chinese hands after having been shot at by about 30 men. We had jumped into a ditch when the shooting started, and crawled out when the Reds ran up to us. Relieved at not being hit, Jack said, "Hell; they don't aim, they just fire in directions." The prime target of our captors was our jeep, which fled amid a hail of bullets from within 60 yards of a Red firing line. (The driver and our interpreter abandoned us, very suddenly and contrary to our instructions.) The jeep had to travel 500 yards to get in defilade. It received only four hits, and luckily the frightened occupants were unharmed.

With thousands of American soldiers facing Communist bullets in Korea, I hesitate to generalize on the basis of my limited experience, more than to say this about Chinese shooting: I don't think their aim is very accurate at long ranges. It was my observation that they prefer to open fire at ranges below 400 yards. However, hits by Chinese bullets, aimed or not, can kill at many ranges.

Grenades the soldier must handle well, for his belt will always be loaded with these small "potato-mashers." If he can toss one 20 yards his throwing is acceptable; if he can throw it 35 yards he is in for a commendation. The soldiers are put into a lively competition with each other in subjects on which ability or skill can be measured in physical terms. Grenade throwing is a great competitive sport in the PLA, including unit competition. Obstacle courses are not uncommon, but again the march is the yardstick measure of the man.

The PLA has a proclivity for the use of land mines and may resort to an even more extensive use of these weapons in the future. The arsenals of China are not tooled for turning out large guns in any quantity, but they can be equipped for the mass manufacture of land mines and booby traps. The old Red army could make mines out of anything—from chamber pots to rocks—and it blew off thousands of Japanese arms and legs by mine warfare; but today's army isn't generally in the business of *making* mines. It does, however, show the old tendency to favor mines with the pull or cord type of detonation. The PLA hasn't shown much originality in land mine warfare in Korea. The idea of a man sitting in a foxhole and pulling a rope to set off an explosion seems still as prevalent as it was in the Civil War.

Red mines are still sown on a hit-or-miss basis with little thought or organized control by the higher echelons. Lower units, not the higher commands, appear to control the use of planted explosives. The technique and the results, at least by our standards, are rather promiscuous and irregular.

The mines in use vary from ready-made jobs to hastily constructed Bangalore torpedoes made of powder-packed cast iron pipes. The Chinese often use a wooden box (10"x10"x4") filled with nitro-starch. They also use standard Soviet mines, including:

PMZ-40 Dual Purpose Mine, a circular mass of 8 pounds of explosive and 10 pounds of metal;

YaM-5 Anti-tank Mine, sudden death packaged in wood and set for pressure detonation;

TM-38 Anti-Vehicular Mine, a sheet-metal wrapped box of Trotyl explosive, complete with carrying handle;

PMD Mines of the anti-personnel, mortar, block and bottle types—the latter guaranteeing bloody wounds from glass fragments as well as wood.

Military Instructors

The noncommissioned officers and junior officers with combat experience are not all good instructors. They were good leaders, most of them elected or selected for their jobs, but their military lives had been spent mostly as leaders. When peace followed the Civil War, the new burden of full-time instruction was placed on these men, some of whom couldn't read; and many of whom were found to be deficient as instructors. But the armies couldn't throw these fighting men out or demote them, so commanders cast about for a solution and evolved a system of demonstration teams. These teams resulted in soldiers instructing soldiers. A "small instructors system" was begun, in the summer of 1948, by General Lin Piao's field army in Manchuria.[11] The Communists thought it very original. Actually it gave the better skilled common soldiers a chance to demonstrate their techniques before audiences that included some of their own commissioned and noncommissioned officers. This system calls for demonstration groups who carefully rehearse, then put on their show.

The subjects covered range from attack of strong points to use of weapons. This type of training has strong impact, for it is given by men who have actually stormed strong points or used the weapons in combat. Rarely are any texts referred to in preparation of this training, for the "small instructors" know their subjects from practical experience. Much of the squad training is conducted informally and without prearranged plan. The squad leader is allowed to pick his subject in order to strengthen his unit on weak points. Within the squad the Reds have the *mutual help system* of instruction, which is also informal and is aimed at improving individual weak points. In the US Army this would be called the "coach and pupil system." Chinese recruits are instructed that it is their duty to ask questions at all times. An older, more experienced soldier is "assigned" to one or several recruits to help them gain knowledge of the trade.

Ex-Nationalist noncoms and technicians are rather prominent in instructor roles, especially in tanks, artillery, bazookas, motor vehicles, and related items of American heavier equipment with which they have had experience. The English-reading ones are also busy translating US field and technical manuals into Chinese texts for use in military training. These ex-Nationalists also speak before units on US tactics. They are the so-called experts on

---

[11] "Army New Style of Training Said Morale Booster," *New China News Agency*, N. Shensi, 16 September 1948.

"Know your enemy"; but it is doubtful that the men in the enlisted grades impart much knowledge of real value to the Red troops on American military tactics. The Communists have a few ex-Nationalist officers who have attended US Army and Air Force service schools, including the Command and General Staff College at Fort Leavenworth. Some of these officers, while not in command positions with the PLA, are in advisory staff positions. For the sake of their own skins they are doing a good job of interpreting American military ways, tactics, and technique. After a period of a few years these officers will be purged, in one form or another, but for the present they have a degree of influence on Communist military training.

Health and the Soldier

The soldier is well schooled, by formal instruction and field practice, to take care of himself. The commanders and the commissars now insist that the soldier drink only boiled water. This is relatively an innovation in a Chinese army. Care of the feet is not ordinarily the problem it is in western armies, where the footgear is thick-soled and heavy. The light sandals and slippers of the PLA troops do not rub or grind the feet. The question in the PLA is more one of developing callouses than of caring for blisters. In North China and Manchuria the winter footgear is heavier and the Communist soldiers, like any others in such climes, must wear heavy shoes. The officers have had trouble with the frostbitten feet of their men, who still need more training on the care of feet. Personal hygiene is being stressed more than ever before.

Until 1948 the Red troops, while they ranged far and wide tactically, had not generally been transferred far from their native localities. Since that time, however, PLA units have swept south and southwest, to undergo a variety of changes in climatic and health conditions. Red Army units which enjoyed such good health in the North, had large sick lists in 1949 and 1950 when in South China. The PLA, lacking in adequate medical facilities, didn't have the wherewithal to stem this sickness initially, and the army was given a shock it had not anticipated. So now the soldier receives an emphasized bit of instruction in how to care for himself. However, this army hasn't yet rid itself of lice and fleas, though it is trying hard to do so.

The Soldiers Learn the Trade by Ear

"It is a beautiful chart, but what in-the-turtle's-bottom does it say alongside the diagrams?" The young soldier is impressed as the officers set up a nicely painted chart. "Listen, you dung-heap, you can be glad they're teaching you the modern, easy way with pictures. When I joined this army I never knew what a trajectory was until I got on the plunging end of one!" But the battle-hardened old soldier cannot read either, and his squatting companion rubs this in with some of the appropriate gutter language which Chinese soldiers can aptly apply.

The chart shows a variety of arches and angles which portray the theory of fire and how it applies to human targets. The instructor coughs, spits, then begins his lecture, pointing with a stick to the lines he discusses. The scene is familiar to soldiers the world over—the hot sun, and the warm earth with its sitting troops. Like those in other armies, Chinese troops know that once the instructor begins to project his hard-studied lecture, he will not stop for at least an hour. But clock watching is not as prevalent in this particular group as it is with the non-orientals. The wrists are, for the most part, bare of watches.

The Red Chinese soldiers spend many of their hours at the usual chores of military housekeeping and at the unusual civilian tasks of a "People's" army, but their military training also proceeds with regularity and studied emphasis. It would be useless to present all the details, for much of the training given Red Chinese troops follows the patterns in other armies. But, there are some peculiarities in Chinese training which I can cite.

The soldiers, as a whole, are taught by the conventional system of demonstration, application, and practice; but many million man-hours of soldier eye-strain are saved because the troops don't have to read books or charts. Some can, but it is encumbent on the instructors to recite the texts and the labels so they can be absorbed by ear. The PLA is finding that modern charts and visual aids are short steps in comparison with older techniques. The army is making wide use of these, borrowing heavily from American training methods—but not admitting it.

Field manuals are still somewhat varied and very scarce. There are translations of various US Army ones, but before use these have to be purged and doctored to fit Communist theories. The US manuals most in use are those which pertain to weapons. Soviet manuals on tactics are much in evidence, but here, too, the Chinese believe in applying their own experience and ideas first and foremost. So there is a mixture of foreign translated material and the more "pure" Communist documents, which contain many borrowed axioms and instructions, but which are varnished with Chinese Communist phraseology. All literature which the officers and NCO instructors use has to be approved by higher authority beforehand, but there is still a lack of total training uniformity in this large and scattered army. The PLA has not yet had time to unify all its various training practices and procedures. The result is that in each field army, and in the various subordinate armies and units, differences of methods, ideas, originality, and standards prevail.

Guerrilla Training

The multiple series of small anti-guerrilla campaigns now under way are giving good practical training to several hundred thousand men, including recruits. This merging of training and actual combat has long been a special feature of China's Communist army.[12] This was how the army developed its muscle from 1937 to 1948. Old General Yen Hsi-shan's Nationalist "island" of fixed defenses was a favored training ground for new troops after World War II. Neither side was aggressive here; the Communists had Yen's forces under siege, but Yen's arms and equipment were so old and unmodern that the Communists weren't over-enthusiastic about trying to capture this materiel. However, the Central Shensi

---

[12] *New China News Agency*, N. Shensi, 16 September 1948.

Liberation Army did regularly test and train its small units by harassing attacks against specific objectives of Yen Hsi-shan's "island."[13] These were ideal for platoon and company training, at combat costs that were not excessive. In terms of present punitive activity against guerrillas, Red China has one of the world's best military training grounds. Here, the Chinese Communists are learning a role new to them—anti-guerrilla campaigning. It is a taste of their own bitter tea.

Military Academies Mold Men Politically

Ask the average Red Chinese company grade officer where he received his formal education and the usual answer you'll receive is, "at the front." He may give you the name of a school you've never heard of—for the Communists ran many, but the courses were only weeks long, and then mainly political in scope.

Informed sources estimate that 70 percent of the junior officers in the PLA are essentially without any formal education, and are completely lacking in formal military education. But they are good officers. Combat-wise and campaign-hardened, they know how to lead their men in maneuver and combat. Project them 15 years into the future and they will be good regimental commanders; but would they be the material for higher staffs and commands of modernly equipped forces? The Communists don't think so, although they expect that a few will emerge.

To bring this particular cross section of officers up to par in the future, when the army will be more modernly equipped and organized, the Chinese Reds are giving special attention to a talented few and are culling the ranks for the politically reliable. These will be given training in China, and some in the USSR—training which will fit them for promotion to higher responsibilities. This is an interim measure to correct present deficiencies; but the PLA's high command is looking ahead. A new generation of generals is beginning, and these young men are being sent to formal military-political academies in Shanghai, Nanking, Peking, Harbin, and other cities. For the first time in its short history,

---

[13] *New China News Agency*, N. Shensi, 18 September 1948.

the PLA is launching into the organized production of young officers who may never be taught how to keep their fingernails clean but will know, when they graduate, the cliches and axioms of Mao—and of Marx, Lenin, and Stalin.

The production line is geared and going. Entrance to the military-political academies is by competitive examination, and those young men who have already memorized a part of the rote of Communism's creed will be given favorable consideration. Those who cannot now answer the political questions with accuracy might well wipe off their slabs of ink and dry their brushes. Initial selection is based more on political reliability than on mental ability. The enlisted ranks are favored as a source of students and are encouraged to compete; the loyalty of these Red "heroes" can be measured in the foot miles of campaigns completed and the wounds received.

In combat, the losses of junior officers is very high. To keep the PLA supplied with this commissioned cannon-fodder, not one, not six, but more than a dozen military-political academies are necessary. Most of these academies originally grew up with the field armies, which, until 1949, governed them. General Lin Piao was president of the Northeast Military and Political Academy, for a while located in Harbin. He had another one in Chiamassu and is believed now to have one in either Mukden or Changchun. General Liu Po-cheng was president[14] of one, but the title was more honorary than active. The cave city of Yenan had an academy for years, but it is now in Peking and has a student body of nearly 4,000. The East China Military-Political Academy, in Nanking, graduated 9,000 young men in 1950 and assigned them to the Army, Navy and Air Force.[15]

Other academies are: the Central China Military Academy, 6th Branch, at Canton; Southwest Military and Political College; and the Hupei Revolutionary College. The course at the Central Academy is 18 months long. Students are mostly from the regular

[14] *North China Daily News Agency,* 12 September 1948.
[15] *New China News Agency,* 26 December 1950.

army, but are cadets while in school. They graduate to become lieutenants. These schools are an important part of China's military future.

What sort of junior officers will these academies graduate? The word "political" has not been casually inserted in the title of the new academies. These institutions are actually more political than military in curriculum. Their object is to produce politically *reliable* leaders first; military talented ones second. The pink-cheeked young men who now receive their diplomas will be devoted to the cause that educates them. The academy commissars will watch over the future cadets, for their political interest and enthusiasm. The reports of the commissars will have more influence over the decision to graduate a cadet than will the cadet's own military grades.

The courses are rugged, the cadet life austere, and the bunks hard. The old Red militarists remember, with disgust, how some of the cadets in their days at the Whampoa Military Academy came to the parade ground in rickshaws. There will be none of this in the Red schools. The present-day instructors, with their memories of the horrors of the Long March, will teach marching and politics well, if nothing else. The desire for "a comfortable life" is officially listed by the academies as an "incorrect thought" to be removed by discussion, investigation and self-criticism.[16]

What are these new cadets taught? How long are they schooled? Unlike the military academies of Western nations, which give courses ranging up to four years, China's academies are presently requiring cadet attendance for only one to two years. Red officer schools of the past graduated junior officers in semi-formal courses at the end of eight months.[17] Today, within the short span of a year and a half, Chinese cadets are taught three main essentials—politics, discipline, and the basics of military science. Discipline receives great stress and is second in emphasis only to political training. By our standards the cadets are emerg-

---

[16] Tan Cheng, 1950.
[17] *North China News Agency*, 15 September 1948.

ing weak in military science, but they are well grounded in the lowest elementals of the subject.

Politically, the cadets "get the works." The PLA has a mighty mechanism established to shape its troops, officers, and cadets. Since the latter are required to do nothing but attend school, they are on the receiving end of the most thorough political indoctrination given any Chinese in or out of uniform. It is here that the PLA's vicious political apparatus takes the most careful and direct aim, then lets go.

Even though they have already seen it, each batch of cadets begins his political course by sitting through China's first color film, "The Victory of the Chinese People," a semi-documentary motion picture[18] that glorifies the Chinese Red Army. The PLA is not known to have any training films as yet, but the government is turning out political propaganda motion pictures as fast as the cameras can grind, and the military-political academies get to view them almost immediately. The political course starts by showing immediately what has been accomplished. It then vomits up the vilest propaganda to show the former Chinese government in a wicked light, demonstrating the whys of reform. The future tasks of the Red nation are explained next, and here the military is fully read into the national role. Next the theme turns to the "capitalist nations which threaten China." The aggressive PLA is labeled as the savior of the people, and so forth. The appeal is to the *emotions* of the young cadets, and the manner in which the propaganda keys are played is such as to build and to heighten hatred. Many people do not properly understand why the vaccine of political indoctrination takes so well. The political ideology is not launched into at the very beginning. These cadets and the millions of other Chinese guinea pigs are made ready for the political needle by careful exploitation of the *emotions*. The young men are made to see objectives in the form of ogres which threaten them. Chinese political indoctrination is well conceived and skill-

---

[18] Begun in 1949, the picture is the joint product of the Soviet Documentary Studio and the Peking Film Studio. Four film groups followed PLA elements, to catch them in action as the Civil War drew to a close.

fully administered—but by psychological degrees. It is convincing to the uneducated masses and especially to the young who lack the background both of experience and of knowledge.

If the campaign-hardened faculties of these academies achieve no other objective than to mold the cadets politically, they are satisfied. These officers, many lacking in any extensive formal education, are not going to let their students rest too long in the classrooms of military science alone. The idea still prevails (because they did it) that officers learn most about war from war. To confine cadets for four years in academies is at present considered a poor idea. Get them out with the troops and let them learn proper officer-enlisted men relationships as the PLA views them. Besides, young officers are presently needed.

It is probable that, with the passage of a few years, the courses at these academies will lengthen. Formal schooling, like much else the PLA is now doing, is a relatively new field for the older officers who grew up the hard way.

Foreign languages are given superficial treatment in the academies. Both Russian and English are taught, with emphasis on the former. There is nothing unusual about this emphasis on the Russian language; the program is even being carried out, for a fraction of the public, by the technique of giving lessons over the radio.[19] Giant new Chinese-Russian dictionaries, of three volumes and 300,000 words[20] each, are being distributed throughout China and to the military-political academies.

In military science, the academies are leaning heavily on the lessons learned from the PLA's own experience, with some emphasis being given to Soviet techniques. Tactically and campaign-wise the recent Civil War gets the most play, with the Battle of Huaihai taught as the great campaign classic of large forces. While certain US Army tactics and technique are borrowed, they are written into the texts as if they were Chinese originals. The general effectiveness of the US Army is studiously played down, but

---

[19] *People's China,* 16 April 1950.

[20] This work is not Chinese, but is a Soviet-published document, prepared over several years by the Academy of Oriental Science at Leningrad.

secretly the Red high command is studying translations of our manuals and doctrine.

One of the projects receiving the highest priority right now is the establishment of military medical colleges. Several already have been established and are turning out "doctors" at the fastest possible rate. Again the militarists are having to take short-term measures to compensate for interim deficiencies. What the military needs, and needs quickly, are military doctors who can wrap bandages, apply splints, cauterize wounds, cut away dead flesh, and amputate limbs. The refinements of medicine and surgery will have to wait for another generation of soldiers.

Red China's military academies cannot be said to have high over-all standards by our yardstick. Yet for China they will perhaps produce a harder, tougher and more determined lot of young officers than ever consistently came out of the old Whampoa Academy—which produced such a clannish group. In giving the present-day cadets a course shorter than is normal in most other armies, the PLA may be said to be investing more in producing crops of lieutenants than in developing future generals. Actually, it is mainly seeking lieutenants because of present necessities. The older officers believe that war will best train men to become the higher officers of the future. So they take this view: Give these young men the political polish they need; experience will develop them militarily.

The Communist Cultivation of "Beets" and "Radishes"

"The PLA is one of the toughest and most highly politically-indoctrinated forces the world has ever seen. There have probably been few forces in history in which the officers have been in closer relationship with their men, or have tried harder to look out for their interests and really lead them in battle." This is the evaluation of an army officer who has lived most of his professional life in China and who has spent long periods with the Chinese Reds. Colonel David D. Barrett[21] is one of the United States' few real

---

[21] The lengths to which the Peking regime will go to attack Americans is illustrated by its violent and lying charge in August 1951 that Barrett was involved in a plot to assassinate Mao Tse-tung.

experts on China and Chinese militarism. I value his analysis highly and believe that he gets at the factual core of the matter.

The big question about China's Red Army has been, and is, "How does it manufacture the automatons that march so willingly to mass slaughter?" The Communist answer is "political indoctrination and discipline"; the Western answers to the question are many. We seem unwilling to believe that political indoctrination is so strong and so effective. On that point we must change our minds. Recent history and present events are set neatly before us. The conclusion that political indoctrination has effective impact— is inescapable. But, like radiation, political indoctrination will stick to some objects longer than to others and will also dissipate itself unless additional doses are administered. The Communists don't give their troops a single indoctrination lecture and then march them off, with the naive assumption that this does the trick. No, they pound home the political and ideological themes until many of the troops know the Communist line by heart. Indoctrination and political training are daily measures in the PLA, no matter how simple or repetitious the message. Repeat and repeat—by rhyme, rhythm, and redundancy—the Marxist-Mao-ist line. Military training time often is sacrificed to non-military labor, but political training periods are rarely ever sacrificed to other jobs or interests. The early morning and late evening hours are periods for the daily ritual of indoctrination. The first morning hours in the army are "sacred" to the commissars and other political preachers, who consistently lead their flocks before the Red altars—with their ever-present pictures of Mao and Stalin.

Formally, in large halls where these faces stare down at the troops, or informally, where the smaller photographs appear in a book held by one who can read out loud, the troops get their daily dosage of indoctrination. Soldier minds may wander on some days, but because of the regularity of the training, the soldiers cannot long escape a good measure of "Why we fight," "Who our enemies are," "What we are doing," "What we will do," and so forth.

Like so much that the leaders do, this training is conducted along simple lines and the political pills are sugar-coated with such devices as group singing and plays. When he gets up in the morning, the soldier knows he will have to do something. To sit and listen to someone read a dull political book still is more comfortable than the labor of the later hours. So they gather in little or large groups, squatting on the earth, smoking, breaking twigs, drawing in the sand. The monotone of an uncultivated voice makes some men doze, but some one else jabs them to alertness. No officer or commissar stands by just to plant his boots in some soldier's ribs. It is a gathering in which all may not *want* to take part, but one in which are all made to *feel* a part. The chronic wool-gatherers are watched by their NCO's and officers. The kitchen smells remind all that "after this is over there is food"—and those who demonstrate no interest in the lecture are reminded by the kitchen odors that the cooks are always in need of details. So the laggards pay the measure of attention that befits those who want to keep out of trouble.

Not all of the sessions are boring. There is fresh news and the Chinese, like others in the world, are interested in news. As in all Communist newspapers, few individuals, but many organizations are cited, for one reason or another. The soldier never expects that *his* name will appear, but he wonders if his army or its leaders will be mentioned. He begins to feel a part of something bigger than just himself—an organization. If he were a coolie he would be just a particle in an unnamed mass, but here he *belongs*—to *something formal and organized!*

The propaganda varies in theme. It is not all abstract. The Communists cleverly build up cases which play on the emotions. Someone is to be hated; some nation is to be pictured as a threatening power, so that the soldiers and the people will not question why there is so large an army. Spies, guerrillas, the "wily, bloodsucking rich, the brutal landlords"—the soldier is made to feel that he protects himself and his family from many threats. Always threats! People are plotting; nations are plotting! "We must watch," says the commissar, "our nation must be prepared.

We have been enslaved—now we are free." And so it goes like rain on a roof, dulling their simple minds to all but the rain. "The roof is leaking—the storm threatens to grow worse—we must protect ourselves—we, in uniform, protect the people!"

This ceaseless drumming is so studied and regular that it diverts the mind while clouding the truth. It is like the prisoner who is allowed but one newspaper a day. Does he read it? Or does he turn it down for a document he really wants? No, after a time he will read it for reading's sake. Poor or inaccurate news is better than no news at all. He may even come to believe parts of it. After all, is he in a position to verify on the real facts?

But do the Chinese soldiers believe all they are taught? No, they do not, but they become convinced by many of the slanted sides of one argument, simply because they haven't heard the truthful rebuttal.

Do they seek the truth? Do they question the wisdom of their Communist warlords? They would *like* to know the answers to many questions, but to *seek* the truth actively is physically dangerous. The Red system has them enmeshed to the point where any question challenging the propaganda stories is regarded as heresy. It is simply easier and safer to obey. After all, the soldiers of China have served brutal masters before. The fatalist philosphy of *Mei-yo-fatze* runs deep.

The Red leaders have been militarily successful; the Nationalists were not. The Red side won with nothing; therefore many soldiers take the view that the leaders have *something* that is different enough to be followed—for a while at least. The bottom could be knocked out of much Communist propaganda if it were not for the fact that the Reds won a war—the China Civil War. The fact of victory does lend so much support to the concealed lies in other issues, that many Chinese soldiers are convinced that the whole Red propaganda fabric is pure.

What does the Chinese soldier believe regarding Korea? There is much indoctrination on Korea. This propaganda I have seen in Chinese documents of various sorts. It boils down to the clever breeding of one thing—hatred. It is well supported by photographs

AN ILLITERATE ARMY BEGINS FORMAL TRAINING 169

of bleeding, bandaged, and dead Manchurian farmers, purportedly the human victims of air strafing by UN planes. This propaganda is exhaustive in its details of time, place, and even in the number of cows, pigs, and chickens that were "casualties." These cases are cleverly treated to relate blood and suffering to the matters most dear to any human—the family, the home, possessions, and property. These cases are described as so numerous, and are given such high case numbers, that there is indication the Communists have used fake photos and false facts, and have multiplied and magnified a few farm yards into many acres of reported mass suffering.

This is where the propaganda campaign in Korea jumps off with a violent start, to stir the emotions of the masses. Just as the presses are bringing one death to play on the sympathy of millions, the Red propaganda campaign, pulled taut by the arm of the Red hierarchy, has now released from its bowstring the mighty arrow of "attack on our soil." The Communists say "We told you so; there was threat when you did not believe it. Now march to your duty—there is the enemy threatening our borders!"

The Chinese soldier does not know the tricks of photography, the fact that an entire motion picture can be shot on a few acres of ground and yet seem to encompass miles of terrain! He sees the "slick" magazines; he can't read or write, but those who make the magazines and speeches can read and write; therefore, by his low educational background and limited knowledge *they* must know more about the issues than he does. Yes, he believes; he believes on little evidence because he is not educated, and if he is educated he is being schooled to view things by present rules—his thinking processes dulled and channelized. But, while beliefs can be deep, they can also be temporary. They can be changed overnight by exposure to facts, especially facts resulting from action, not words.

Kneeling and weeping, crying out and holding their clasped hands aloft, Chinese soldiers have met capture by UN troops *believing* they would be massacred to the man, upon surrender. We know this fact, which is the direct result of Red indoctrination, designed to deter them from easy surrender. But minutes, hours, perhaps a few days, have destroyed for good that belief in the minds of those captured.

I have written this book primarily to tell and teach, but here I strongly recommend—on one subject. We have treated our Chinese prisoners with our traditional care and fairness. *After*

U. S. Army Photo.

DOCILE CHINESE REDS
Ragged and resigned, four Chinese Communist captives await questioning at the command post of the 24th Regiment, 25th Infantry Division, near the front lines in Korea in 1951.

good indoctrination on the United Nations' side of the issue, turn these prisoners back to the Red Chinese. They don't amount to many numerically, but their return could have huge impact, favorable to us, on the hate campaign that is generating at such high speed in Red China. This would destroy many Communist-nurtured beliefs among the people and swing to our side those who hang now on the doubtful edge of belief in Communist "facts." By this *action* we would take much of the effective poison out of the Red propaganda.

The PLA is presently a mixture of those who believe in the Red cause, those who are caught in it and reluctantly believe; and a fair portion of the army which would be definitely unreliable in the event of a showdown. Measured as a whole, the men in the army are held together by a variety of controls and devices, of which political indoctrination is a significant but not necessarily a lasting one. If measures are taken to destroy the propaganda myths, or if war losses are sustained at the 1951 ratio over a long period, the army will start to crack apart. However, given a few more years in which to instill one political and propaganda theme, and given any significant military successes, the army of Red China is going to become increasingly harder to defeat. The army as it now stands has its soldiers who are beet-red all through; but also it has many whom the people accurately call "radishes"—red outside and white inside. The next generation of soldiers will be well cultivated "beets."

GROWTH OF THE CHINESE COMMUNIST PARTY

1921		The Chinese Communist Party is established
1924-27	59,000*	(Era of KMT-CCP coalition)
1927	10,000*	(KMT and CCP split up)
1934	300,000*	(Long March begins)
1937	40,000*	(Japanese attack China)
1945	1,210,000*	(World War II ends)
June 1946	about 1,800,000	(Civil War formally begins)
December 1947	2,700,000**	(Truce effort fails)
December 1949	4,500,000*	(Civil War nears end)
June 1950	5,000,000*	(Red Regime firmly established)
June 1951	3,500,000	(Purges reduce the Party)

The figure of 5,000,000 for 1950 is regarded as excessive.

* Figures, issued on the 29th Anniversary of the CCP (1 July 1950), on the growth of its strength.

** Mao Tse-tung in his December speech, 1947.

Chapter 6

MOB MOBILITY AND WINNING TACTICS

Mobility Is Measured by the Foot

Half frozen with ice, the river looks cold and raw. It isn't deep but it doesn't have a bridge. This, you say, will give halt to the long Red column that has been marching so fast and so tiringly long. You no sooner pick out a nearby rock on which to sit than a noncom yells, *"Tzo, tzo!"* You get tired of hearing them yell that, for it means, "Go!" At the river's edge there is no halt. This is winter, but it is also a ford. Someone hauls out a potato-masher grenade, unscrews the bottom cap and yanks the string. The explosion breaks the shore ice. Other grenades are tossed; but the army column paused hardly long enough to telescope more than a battalion when the lead men splash into the water on foot. The column follows in trace—and a thousand or more men curse the cold water, but march through it. Momentum has not been lost.

When you march with this army, you get the feeling that *you are going some place,* not just obeying orders to cover miles. There is an urgency to these columns. No individual is obedient to the trace of another, yet like ants they never get much out of line. The form and force of these winding columns are strong. The pace is lively; no one seems to question why. The horses seem to influence the men to keep pace with their greater speed. Everyone seems to gauge speed on the animals.

This is the army of the 8,000-mile march, the epic route of torture and death. Some who march with you were on that historic trek and will remind you of its pace, tortures, and length. So you sense it—this marching, this ability to keep going when the heart is already pounding and the breath comes short. This, you say, is what makes the **army of Red China** great. Its tactics are mixed and varied, but its marching is consistent—and by its marching it manufactures its tactics.

The tactics can be poor, and they often are; but the mobility of these masses is excellent. It is this mobility that has counted for so much and is still their main stock in trade. Sometimes there are no real, preconceived tactics—just movement and mobility which, in themselves, have precipitated Red battalions into accidental action at weak enemy points.

Mobility is still measured by foot miles and not motor distances; for while this army uses trucks to supply its units, its infantry is not motorized.

Why can these troops march so fast and travel so long on foot? The simple answer is that they are hardened to it by much practice—and they are not overburdened with equipment. Their personal gear is simple and their packs are light. They carry, possibly, the lightest weight of any soldier of any major power.

The Reds have their marching technique down to a fine SOP (standing operating procedure) that results in column fluidity; yet the technique is such that good control is maintained. The infantry columns may wait for seemingly confused periods in assembly or bivouac areas, but once the order is given to *"tzo,"* columns know where they are going, what route to take, and what to do when they get to their destinations. What about pauses en route? Do these army columns ever make the wrong turn or get confused at a crossroad? PLA forces are not immune to common mistakes, and often they are handicapped by poor maps. Company, and even battalion, commanders often lack maps. Furthermore, company grade officers and NCO's generally are not good at map reading. Chinese maps are anything but easy to read. They lack clarity and are too often poorly printed. Nor are they the most accurate. The Communists of China still rely largely on old Japanese army maps. While junior officers and NCO's may not pore over maps, they do have a good sense of direction and observe the terrain carefully. They don't get lost easily, at least within their own country, for they rely to a considerable degree on civilian guides and local information. Thus the army units preserve a good sense of direction, especially on the march.

Division and army commands superimpose their directional control on subordinate units by using staff officers and control points. Notices are posted at intervals (or control officers and guides may verbally impart the information), to specify the points of rest, direction, and messing and bivouac areas for the marching columns. As a result of this control, marches are made with smooth rhythm and the minimum of confusion. It is in infantry marches that Chinese staff planning is at its best. As for motor convoy control, the Reds have yet to reach the standard of excellence and precision prevailing in western armies.

Sandwiches are not carried in the Chinese army. These soldiers believe a meal isn't a meal unless it is hot. Where at all possible, officers try to provide hot meals for their men on the march. It is not unusual to see an iron kettle and provisions on the two ends of a man-borne carrying pole. The kitchen and provisions for an infantry company can be carried by six to ten men, who will also prepare and serve the meals—of rice, tea, vegetables, and sometimes meat. Units are allowed to provision themselves en route; but they are also issued certain basic stocks, such as rice or flour. Kitchens are simple, in terms of equipment; they are mobile, like the companies they serve.

Moving into a bivouac is performed much more smoothly than one would imagine. The preplanning is good, the staff officers and commanders experienced. PLA divisions disperse and camouflage their elements very effectively in bivouac. A division may be a big symbol on a map, but it usually looks awfully small in field bivouac. Lacking air superiority, the Reds do their utmost to avoid making profitable air targets. Behind the lines the infantry marches are made mostly at night, for the units have learned that they cannot afford to present big daytime targets to hostile aircraft. Units move out of an area at a time which will allow them to reach their destinations at dawn, when they disperse into villages, groups of farmhouses or, if the weather is not subzero, into scattered but camouflaged bivouacs on the terrain itself. PLA units present miles of profitable road targets at night, but few large marching columns in broad daylight.

Order of battle maps are deceptive; as a result of good intelligence, they can show accurately the disposition of Red Chinese units. But don't stare into that map too long; PLA units move and move fast. Nationalist General Sun Li-jen[1] who, with his New First Army, fought the cream of Lin Piao's troops in Manchuria (1946-47), has this to say:

"Communist armies can march fifty miles, with full equipment, between dusk and dawn and be ready to fight. I know. I used to tell myself the enemy was 70 miles away and could not possibly attack. And the next morning they were right in front of me." [2]

While 50 miles a day is not unusual, 20 to 30 miles a night always should be expected of PLA units.

Battalions move very fast; but how about armies? Several of General Lin Piao's armies left the area of Yihsien, a town south of Mukden, on 22 November 1948, and 22 days later, on the night of 14 December, these same units struck at Fengtai, south of Peking.[3] This was a winter march of about 600 miles. Chinese

---

[1] Commander of Chinese Ground Forces on Taiwan and formerly commander of the New First Army in Manchuria.
[2] "Yanks 'Too Mechanized' to Fight Chinese Reds," by Jim G. Lucas, Scripps-Howard staff writer (Interview at Fengshan, Formosa), 15 November 1950.
[3] Alan Winnington (New China News correspondent), "To Peiping March the Manchurian Troops," *New China News Agency,* 20 December 1948.

armies do cover ground rapidly, and they do not require extensive road nets, either.

Ambush!

You are alone in the dark on a lonely outpost, or riding a jeep on a road of death, when you first learn of the favorite tactics of this oriental army—ambush! Hundreds of American soldiers could describe Chinese Communist ambush tactics better than I, but they are dead! My own capture on the Sungari front, on 1 March 1947, came from a clever Red ambush. I was led into it because two Communist riflemen wore the Nationalist uniforms of the blue-overcoated infantry regiment I had just left.

What makes the Chinese ambush tactics so deadly? Two things: their marching and their patience. They will plod many miles cross-country, and over rough terrain that you think is securing a flank, to get into a position to ambush! Then they will slowly wriggle and scrape their bellies for hours, to lodge in final positions from which to fire fusilades of sudden death.

This is the guerrilla in them—and in this army which is still effectively borrowing from its past experience. But it is no longer waiting for platoon or squad targets. It is after road-bound motor convoys, tanks, and infantry units on the march. Tactically, this is often the army of no fixed fronts, the force which breaks formal contact to establish informal ambush. Reduce the tactical equation of the PLA down to its lowest common denominator and one of its primary factors will be *ambush*.

The Communist Army of China first used ambush on a large scale against US forces on 30 July 1946, between Tientsin and Peiping, when it deliberately laid in wait for a 1st Marine Division convoy. The initial result was eight US Marines killed and others wounded. In the Civil War fighting between 1945 and the end of 1947, the Reds relied primarily on ambush tactics.

In Korea, the Chinese have nastily ambushed many units of the United Nations forces. The "Massacre Valley" ambush of elements of the 2d US Infantry Division north of Hoengsong, in February 1951, was one of the bloodiest and deadliest. It was not the first.

Against the 1st Marine Division and the 7th US Infantry Division, the Chinese Reds laid multiple ambushes to hamper the December 1950 withdrawal of these units from North Korea. Watch out for these Chinese when they withdraw and invite you forward. Death lies ahead for those who are not careful!

"When he (enemy) keeps aloof and tries to provoke a battle, he is anxious for the other side to advance."

—Sun Tzu [4]

It is the Chinese Communists' seventh Military Principle[5] which says: "Strive to destroy the enemy while he is in movement."

How Orders Are Transmitted

Orders must come before tactics begin. Chinese orders, for the most part, are verbal to units from divisions on down. This would seem to lend great flexibility to the lower combat elements. No excessive paper work, no time-consuming writing and paragraphing. It sounds fine to Western officers who, perhaps, have seen the over use of written words and voluminous annexes. But one point must be remembered: The PLA does not have the excellence of communications or the quantity and quality of radio equipment that is common to Western army units. Furthermore, the Chinese have big organizations and there are many battalions to be finally instructed, ordered, and redirected in combat. The net result is that control and coordination over a wide frontage is clumsy, slow, and lacking in flexibility. Red battalions often act and react on the initiative of their own commanders, but as a coordinated group of teams they lack excellence. Much of the communicating is done by messengers.

For large and coordinated attacks, it is a Communist practice to brief as many of the subordinates as possible on the pertinent details of the operation. Time and combat circumstance will modify this procedure some, but it can be said that the Reds try to read a good portion of their troops into the picture.

---

[4] Sun Tzu, *The Art of War,* Military Service Publishing Co., Harrisburg, Pa., 1944.
[5] From Mao Tse-tung's "Present Situation and Our Tasks" 25 December 1947, as reported by the *New China News Agency,* N. Shensi, 1 January 1948.

The army moves well and exerts fine control over its routine marching; but in final combat, where it needs the maximum of control, it is very deficient.

Chinese Tactics Differ from Ours

The fire power of a Chinese unit is based essentially on its multiple riflemen, who shoot rifle and machine gun bullets in a forward direction. In Korea these units face a fire power that attacks mainly by explosion. The Chinese Red Army, primarily, is a rifle and machine gun army; while ours is a force that counts most on mortars, artillery, tank guns, rockets, bazookas, and bombs. Herein lie differences in staying power and tactics. The Chinese have their small mortars, which they use often and effectively. They have their artillery; but in essence the PLA builds around its man-carried weapons.

On this basis, we find Chinese small-unit tactics predicated on both infiltration and mass attacks by infantrymen, where the rifleman carries the combat burden. Conversely, we build our squad tactics around 3.5 rocket launchers, 75-mm recoilless rifles, cannon, and other squads. The Chinese are still multiplying single men by rifles and machine guns, to achieve a combat objective; whereas we multiply the shot and shell poundage by the explosive quantity per man.

Tactically, the Chinese are still living in the era of World War I, and their arms and equipment are so proportioned, with the resulting fire power nearly the same as in 1918. I think that Fletcher Pratt in his article, *"The Man Who Pulls the Trigger,"*[6] has well analyzed the Red Chinese and US differences in these words:

" . . . a modern company of infantry (has) more fire power than was possessed by a battery of field artillery in World War I.

"With the (US) front line containing so many weapons that produce burst effect, the slightest concentration of manpower can and does bring down the kind of fire capable of wiping out a whole group. The Communist tactics in Korea—infiltration, night movements and attacks—are simply methods of avoiding burst and trying to reach a situation where hand weapons will be effective.

---

[6] The Atlantic Monthly.

"The major tactic of the Reds in Korea consisted of this: Throw in another 10,000 men; enough of them will survive to infiltrate and break the line."

Colonel Louis B. Ely[7] remarked to me, when he returned from Korea in the winter of 1950-51, that our BAR (Browning Automatic Rifle) men would pile up as many as 20 enemy dead before a single gun, when the twenty-first enemy soldier would get in behind the BAR man and shoot or bayonet him in his foxhole. "How," asked Colonel Ely, "can you stop these onrushing hordes when they are so willing to pay these tremendous prices in battle casualties?"

This question was often asked during the Communist offensive that drove us back below the 38th parallel in 1950-51. However, at that time we were fighting the Chinese on their own terms—rifle to rifle, machine gun versus machine gun, and mortar against mortar. Some bigger artillery weapons were used; but in those months ours was a rearguard action, where battalions, not corps, mainly fought the Reds. Thus we fought more on small arms terms than on the combined weight of *all* heavier weapons, including corps artillery. We were not defending, we were delaying; and to the layman we looked bad. But in the spring of 1951, when we did line up and bring our combined fire power to bear, the enemy got a tactical jolt and took much greater losses.

In foot speeds and distances, PLA units still have an advantage over us; but in terms of real fire power per man we are fortunately superior.

Strategically, we must never let Red over-all numbers awe us. Tactically, we must never try to fight the Chinese with platoon weapons alone.

Basic Military Principles Are Few

New military concepts are being developed in the PLA, which has in the past borrowed tactically from the Soviet and other armies. We can find that some of our own tactics are being applied to Chinese amphibious training. We could study Soviet

---

[7] Author of *The Red Army Today,* Military Service Publishing Co., Harrisburg, Pa., 1951.

tactics and discover that the Chinese have lifted much from Russian combat concepts; but an analysis of the PLA's tactics should be based upon what the Chinese consider as their own 10 Basic Military Principles.

Why are there only 10, not 20? Napoleon had 115 Maxims, and we have volumes of field manuals on our tactical concepts and principles. The reason the Chinese Reds have reduced theirs to 10 simple rules is that they require the 10 to be memorizd by all officers and by as many NCO's as can absorb them. These 10 principles are purposely short, because the Communist hierarchy wants them learned and applied. And they are indeed applied, not all at once but in a sequence, to fit the conditions and the enemy.

Not all of these principles are tactical; the sixth, for instance is not. Some, like the first five, can have strategical as well as tactical application. It can be said that all 10 were effectively applied by the Chinese Reds in the Civil War. Although designed for that particular conflict, they are sound in principle. They deserve careful attention, for they are their guiding principles.

The Ten Military Principles

(1) First strike at scattered and isolated enemies, and later strike at the concentrated, powerful enemies.

This was the essence of the PLA's strategy when it was fighting to gain military ascendency. It is applied today in ambush and small unit tactics.

(2) First take the small and middle-sized towns, cities and the broad countryside, and later take the big cities.

An amplification of the first principle. It is more applicable to China than to Korea.

(3) We take the annihilation of the enemy's fighting strength, and not the holding or taking of cities and places, as the major objective. The holding or taking of cities and places is the result of the annihilation of the enemy's combat strength, and this often has to be repeated many times before the enemy is contained.

The one Red principle to remember. In Korea the Chinese appear to have this one objective. They are not concerned over cities.

(4) In every battle, concentrate absolutely superior forces (double, triple, quadruple, and sometimes even five or six times those of the enemy) to encircle the enemy on all sides and strive for his annihilation. Strike the enemy in annihilating combat; concentrate full striking forces on the enemy's front or side, so as to annihilate part of the enemy's strength; then swiftly transfer forces to smash other enemy groups. Avoid battles of attrition, in which the gains are not sufficient to compensate for the losses, or in which gains merely balance the losses. Thus, we are inferior taken as a whole numerically; but we have an absolute superiority in every sector, in every specific campaign, guaranteeing victory in each. As time goes by, we shall become superior, taken as a whole, until all of the enemy is destroyed.

What cannot be done by skill must be done by mass numbers. It is a well practiced principle, insofar as the first part is concerned. While the last sentences were written at a time (in the China Civil War) when the Reds lacked over-all superiority, they do bespeak the PLA's practice of achieving local superiority before an attack.

(5) Fight no unprepared engagements. Fight no engagements in which there is no assurance of victory. Strive to prepare and assure victory in every engagement, based on the relations of our conditions and those of the enemy.

Here is a principle that is more and more adhered to. When the Reds do launch a big attack or offensive, they usually have made careful plans and are confident of their chances of winning.

(6) Promote the valiant combat characteristics of not fearing sacrifice, fatigue or continuous action; of fighting several engagements in succession within a short period of time without respite.

In short, train the men to be tough, enduring and indifferent to hard campaigning.

(7) Strive to destroy the enemy while he is in movement. At the same time lay emphasis on the tactics of attacking positions and wresting (away) enemy strong points and cities.

The PLA makes a special point of seeking motorized and mechanized units on the march. This principle (of ambush) is the strongest rooted of any in the PLA.

(8) With regard to the question of assaults on cities, resolutely wrest from the enemy all strong points and cities which are weakly defended. At favorable opportunities wrest all of those hostile points which are defended to a medium degree. Wait until conditions mature to wrest all enemy strong points which are powerfully defended.

It was by patient observance of this strategy, and its related tactics, that the Chinese Reds let the communication lines ripen with strongly held cities, until the demoralized and isolated Nationalist garrisons became easier plucking. The sound and patient observance of this maxim *won* the Civil War.

(9) Replenish ourselves by the capture of all of the enemy's arms and most of his personnel. The source of the men and matériel of our army is mainly at the front.

This is not nearly as applicable or as widely practiced now as it was in 1945-1948. Personnel-wise, the PLA cannot expect to convert foreign prisoners of war into Communist troops; but they may try.

(10) Be skilled at using the intervals between two campaigns for resting, regrouping and training troops. The period of rest and regrouping should, in general, not be too long. Insofar as possible do not let the enemy have breathing space.

Well observed; but, in Korea the Chinese Reds have indulged in some long intervals between serious combat actions. These long intervals probably are due to supply difficulties and a hesitancy to attack except when and where their chances of winning are good.

These are simple principles and they can easily be memorized. As a result, they are highly practical. Woven through these 10 principles are three basic concepts which stand out——

(1) Don't hurry; be certain;
(2) Capitalize on enemy weaknesses;
(3) Insure everything; mass everything and attack with superiority and violence.

The Ten Principles, As Applied in Korea

For all of its great mass and its international aggressiveness, the Chinese Red Army reveals a cautiousness and strategic timidity in those ten rules. There is a tendency here to let the enemy play his hand first. As revealed in Korea, the PLA has repeatedly avoided contact until forced into local battles. It has often broken contact, with skill, to do some reshuffling behind its own lines and invite the UN forces forward. The PLA is not really *certain* in Korea. It knows its mission, but in terms of over-all operations it is fumbling for strategic and higher tactical solutions. It has met solid strength and superior fire power in a force of lesser numerical strength and it is finding obsolete and impractical some of its older concepts.

The conflict in Korea is a different war for the Chinese Reds who are facing realities to which their doctrine has been blind. The old originality which gave Communist tactics such bloody flavor is absent, because they were brought up on small-scale warfare conducted over a large area. Now they are involved in a big conflict, on a small land mass that is not only a peninsula but a foreign one as well. The *people,* on whom the Chinese relied so religiously (or pressed into service) in the past, are of small help in Korea. Most of the Red Chinese generals grew up leaning on the crutch of many people over large regions. In Korea, the crutch is gone, for no longer can these generals range and forage, far and wide, to force the enemy to chase them. These generals must move up or down only, and toe to toe. They do not encircle us strategically as they like so well to do Here is where the army commanders of the PLA have lost their power of battlefield dictation. Put our forces into China, however, and we would restore these generals to the warfare they know and conduct so deathly well.

Few American generals know the Chinese Reds as well as does Major General Robert H. Soule, who was Military Attache to China from 1946 to 1950, and who then, with an interval of only a month or two, took the US 3d Infantry Division into combat in Korea. He has seen the PLA from battlefront to rear areas and back again. His analysis of their tactics is worthy of attention.

"Even though the Chinese have vastly superior manpower in Korea

". . . whereas they were outnumbered by their former foes . . . the Japanese and the Chinese Nationalists, . . . they are still sticking close to the principles they have always used in warfare. (They) always attempt to mass their forces so that they outnumber the enemy five and six to one. Even when the opposition had superior over-all numbers, the Reds probed for a weak point and then threw overwhelming masses at that point. If they were stopped, they proceeded to withdraw in order to regroup their forces." [8]

In Korea, General Soule has noted the Chinese propensity for attacking enemy forces which are on the move. "They accomplish this by infiltrating forces behind the line; and thus they cut lines of supply and communication. When this is accomplished, the unit has to move. That's the time when the Reds want to hit. If they lose men who try to infiltrate they simply send more on the same mission." [8]

General Soule emphasizes the importance of not leaving a lot of Reds about in the terrain when moving forward. This, he points out, was the Japanese mistake—holding just the lines of communication.

One cannot help but see where the military leaders of the PLA draw heavily on the ancient axioms of Sun Tzu for the spirit if not the letter of their tactics. "One cartload of the enemy's provisions is equivalent to 20 of one's own. . ." [9] This, in essence, is the Ninth Military Principle of the PLA. It was the keystone of Communist success in the Civil War, for out of their foraging on a large scale for arms and equipment they built their army. The practical importance of this principle has subsided slightly now, however.

Old Sun Tzu's principles are those of the PLA today. Take this one: "Military tactics are like unto water, for water in its natural course runs away from high places and hastens downwards. So in war, the way to avoid what is strong is to strike what is weak. . . . Therefore, just as water retains no constant shape, so in warfare there are no constant conditions." [9]

---

[8] Interview, in Korea, by Jim Becker, Associated Press correspondent, March 1951.
[9] Sun Tzu, *The Art of War*, Military Service Publishing Co., Harrisburg, Pa., 1944.

Tactics Are Flexible

Red officers, as a result of considerable combat experience (and not very much formal study) modify their tactics to fit the terrain and situation, rather than hew rigidly to conventional solutions. No single book could describe all the tactics these officers apply. They direct their troops with a remarkable fluidity of action and, like water, their hordes bear against the barriers, flowing through the points of least resistance.

Here is a major difference between the Chinese and the Soviets. The latter are more rigid, more deliberate, and more controlled from above. Given more initiative on lower levels, the Chinese are tactically more flexible; but they are beginning to incline toward the sluggish pattern of the Soviets.

Tactically, the Chinese have reached a transition point where they still retain and practice their old techniques, yet are borrowing from the Soviets and seeking to do things in a more modern manner. Chinese officers sometimes don't know whether to borrow tactically from their guerrilla past or to temporize with their Soviet future. Mixtures of tactics are resulting in many mistakes being made in combat. At the expense of repetition, I say again that the Korean conflict is a new type of war for the PLA. This army needs space. It likes space. But it doesn't have it. However, if the PLA ever successfully turns a major flank or makes a deep penetration in Korea, its numbers will avalanche into space.

Essential to any tactics is the art of camouflage. In camouflaging themselves and their field installations the Chinese Reds are most skillful. This has been proved in the China Civil War and in the Korean conflict. One American officer, Lt. Willard Latham, who flew 60 observation missions for the US 1st Cavalry Division, said[10] that the Chinese forces move deceptively and employ baffling camouflage techniques. One of their most common methods of wintertime camouflage, he said, is to spread sheets of cloth over vehicles and artillery pieces. He confirmed the known Communist practice of moving in small groups (20-25) in the daytime, with

---
[10] "Camouflaged Chinese Units Hard to Spot, Says Officer," *Army Times*, 10 February 1951.

units as large as 200 occasionally marching in a body. The excellence and consistency of the Chinese camouflage benefits them greatly in their tactics.

The PLA does not have effective cavalry. It employs a little, in piddling amounts; but the army seems to lack the grasp of the arm that the Soviets so well maintain. Cavalry tactics and effectiveness can be dismissed as ordinary reconnaissance.

Chinese infantry tactics are enhanced by the ability of the soldiers to successfully endure for long intervals without food; by their ability to make long marches on foot, to climb hills and mountains, and to dig in well when they arrive. Small units achieve much, tactically, by their skill at infiltration. This is where the Reds are at their best.

Defensively, the PLA has yet to show any unique qualities. This army has not been much on the defensive in recent years. It is doubtful if it could muster the strong staying qualities of the Soviet Army, and it certainly lacks the artillery and antitank guns the Soviets found so necessary against an organized enemy. The Chinese, however, are showing a tendency to use land mines extensively; but they often neglect to cover their mine fields with fire. The Chinese Red Army can integrate its defense works to a fair degree, and can prepare skillful ambushes, but it is still more inclined toward mobile defenses than toward big systems of fixed defensive works. It does lack armor for mobile reserves in defense. Its probable future tactics, in any lengthy and extended defense will be to leave a certain number of regiments or divisions in multiple island bases, from which they will sweep out and attack moving columns, then return to their hidden bases. PLA units have enough men to do this, at the same time saving out larger forces for "strategic" counterattacks. In short, the PLA, if forced to defend, probably will resort to its old guerrilla pattern of operating from bases—except that the units will be much larger than in World War II days.

Mao Tse-tung's Military Concepts

For years, one of the standard textbooks of the PLA and its

military schools has been "Strategic Problems of China's Revolutionary War." This was written in 1936 by Mao Tse-tung and, while it has a certain dated character its soundness of concept will prevail in the future, with some modern embellishments. To reproduce Mao's entire original text would be to burden a reader with the earlier gropings of the Reds for tactical and strategical solutions to combat problems. However, these selected excerpts are worthy of present day attention if one desires a view of the pure Chinese Red combat concepts.

On Command and Fear: "We cannot let a single commander . . . act rashly and recklessly. . . . There are many instances of set-backs caused by fear of the enemy. Underestimation of the enemy resulted in the defeats of many of our guerrilla detachments and in the Red Army's failure to break up encirclement campaigns (of the enemy) on a number of occasions."

On Strategic Withdrawal: "All of us know that, in a boxing contest, the wise boxer yields a step, while his stupid opponent displays all his might and skill at the very first moment, like an avalanche. The result usually is that the yielding one downs the avalanche.

"The object of strategic withdrawal is to preserve the forces and prepare for counter attack.

"The preparation for a counteroffensive requires the selection and creation of a number of conditions favorable to us but unfavorable to the enemy. To alter . . . relative strength . . . we should generally secure at least two of (these) conditions . . . so that we can shift to the offensive. These conditions are— .

(1) A people who actively assist the Red Army;
(2) Terrain favorable to the operation;
(3) Complete concentration of (our) main forces;
(4) Discovery of weak spots of the enemy;
(5) An enemy fatigued and demoralized;
(6) An enemy made to commit mistakes.

The last three can be created.

"A retreating army can choose favorable terrain . . . and impose it upon the attacking army. This is a favorable condition in fighting in the interior line.

"It requires reconnaissance to find out which column is strongest . . . which is weakest. This often takes a long time to get the desired result and is one of the reasons why strategic withdrawal is necessary.

"If the number and combat power of the enemy is greatly superior to ours, it is only by drawing him deeply into our area and forcing him to undergo . . . hardship that the relative strength . . . may be altered. As the chief of staff of a certain brigade in Chiang Kai-shek's army . . . remarked, 'the fat have been worn thin and the thin worn dead.'

"We must know that, however wise a military commander may be, he cannot help but commit some . . . errors. There is the possibility of taking advantage of (this) enemy flaw. We can artificially cause the enemy to make such mistakes, such as 'feint,' advocated by Sun Tzu (feint in the East but strike in the West)."

Strategic Counteroffensive: "To win victory in a strategic defensive is basically dependent on one thing—concentration of forces. According to my (Mao's) opinion, whether there is a force of ten thousand, or a million, or ten million, there should be only one main direction of operation at a time, instead of two. I do not object to two or more operational directions, but there ought to be only one main direction at a given time."

War of Maneuver: "War of maneuver of positional warfare? Our answer is war of maneuver. It is only by today's fluid way of living that we can secure a relatively stable life tomorrow, and finally settle down." (Here Mao cites the "Long March" as a case in point.) "Fight only when victory is certain, run away when (it) is impossible. . . . When the enemy . . . is large it is inadvisable to fight. Second, although the enemy . . . is not large, yet if (he) is adjacent to neighboring forces, it is inadvisable to fight. Third . . . it is inadvisable to fight an enemy . . . which is not isolated but is entrenched in a very strong position. Fourth, an engagement which cannot bring favorable results shall not be continued. Under any of these conditions, we are prepared to run away, which is permissible as well as imperative.

"To say that it is basically a war of maneuver does not deny all positional warfare. It should be granted that the stubborn defense of bases of containing forces in a strategic defensive (and the attack against) . . . an isolated, unsupported enemy in a strategic offensive, both involve positional warfare."

On Guerrillas: "There are two aspects of guerrillaism. One, its irregularity and lack of concentration; (two, its lack of) unity of discipline and simpleness—all of which were infantile attributes of the (Chinese) Red Army. (These) were necessary at the time. But they must be eliminated."

War of Quick Decision: "A protracted war and a campaign or battle of quick decision are two aspects of the same thing. They are principles of equal importance in the war of the Chinese (Reds) and can be applied in an anti-imperialist national war.

"The preponderance of the strength of the ruling class and the gradual growth of revolutionary forces, together condition a protracted war. Impatience in this respect is harmful and the advocacy of a quick decision . . . is incorrect.

"But there should be no expectation of overnight success. It is good morale to vow 'to eliminate the enemy before breakfast,' but a concrete plan on such a basis is inadvisable.

"On this basis, the formulation of a strategic plan of a protracted war is one of the important principles in directing our war.

"The principle underlying a campaign, or a battle, is contrary to the above; it is a quick decision instead of protraction. Desire alone cannot bring about a successful quick decision. In addition there must be many concrete conditions, which chiefly are—

Thorough preparedness;
Correct timing;
Concentration of a preponderance of force;
Tactics of encirclement;
Favorable positions;
And attack on a moving enemy; or on a stationary one in a weak position.

Unless these conditions are properly met it is impossible to bring a campaign or a battle to a quick decision."

War of Annihilation: "A 'contest of attrition' is untimely for (us). While such a game of 'matching pearls' is nothing between two Dragon Gods of the Seas, it is ridiculous between one beggar and one Dragon God. A basic directive for the (Chinese) Red Army, which possesses nothing but obtains all from the enemy, is a war of annihilation. It is only through the annihilation of the enemy's effectives that it is possible to cope with the annihilative encirclement campaigns and to expand Red areas. It is for the annihilation of the enemy that casualties are inflicted on him; otherwise enemy casualties would be meaningless. We incur attrition in inflicting casualties on the enemy, while in annihilating him we secure replenishments. This is the application of the rules of trade in warfare."

On Logistics: "The establishment of a war industry in the (Chinese Red) area must not encourage dependency . . . (on such). We have a claim on the output of the arsenals of London and Hanyang, to be delivered by the enemy's transport corps. This is not a joke, but the truth.

"Another colossal war of world-wide attrition is impeding."

A Summarization: "We are against guerrillaism of the Red Army, yet we must admit the army's guerrilla character. We are opposed to protracted compaigns and a strategy of quick decision, while we believe in a strategy of protracted war and campaigns of quick decision. Since we are opposed to fixed operational fronts and positional warfare, we believe in unified operational fronts and a war of maneuver. We are against simply routing the enemy, and we believe in a war of annihilation. We are against 'two-fist-ism' in strategic directions and are for one-fist-ism. We are against the institution of a big rear and believe in a small rear."

Armies Can Disappear

If the Chinese Red Army had suddenly mounted up on a fleet of pearl-handled rickshaws, the Nationalists wouldn't have been more surprised than they were in the trench-ridden ground at the Manchurian town of Ssupingkai on 19 May 1946. For several weeks five Nationalist armies[11] had slugged it out with a comparable combat grouping of Lin Piao's troops, under Generals Kao Kang, Chou Pao-chung, Hsiao Hua, Teng Hua and Liu Chuan-tien. I watched the initial development of this battle when I was flying over the front lines in an L-5[12] locating the newest points of attack, for General Marshall's truce teams.[13] For several miles the ground was pockmarked with shell holes, and both sides were digging in like mad. This was in early April 1946.

Later in the month we managed to fly out of Red-held Changchun. Since our small aircraft had been damaged (we were wired into the seats with baling wire, our plane having been looted of safety belts), and since we were flying on a mixture of Jap "gas" that looked like cough syrup, our plane couldn't get above 1000 feet. So, in this flight to Mukden, we decided to swing away from the battlefield of Ssupingkai. But, to our surprise, we found that we had misgauged the extent of the battle, which, since we had

---

[11] These were the Thirteenth, the Fifty-second, the Seventy-first, the New First, and the New Sixth.

[12] Piloted by Sergeant Clayton Pond, whom I later managed to have decorated for his achievements while we were over and on various fronts under Communist fire.

[13] These were under Colonel George P. Tourtillott, Colonel Rothwell H. Brown, and others, under the direction of Brigadier General Henry A. Byroade.

seen it last, had spread out for miles. By this time the trenches were extensive and the ground was churned.

There were later battles at Ssupingkai, in 1947, but this was the largest in terms of troops involved. This initial battle was a slugfest of positional warfare for weeks; then, on the morning of 19 May 1946, Nationalist soldiers adjusted their eyes to the light of dawn and carefully peeked over their trenches. No rifle or machine gun fire spat out from the Red side. An ominous silence prevailed and conferences were called in the Nationalist dugouts. With caution bred from weeks of keeping low in their trenches, the Nationalist soldiers were not very fast in their movement forward. They reached the shattered town of Ssupingkai at about 7:30 a. m. A few Chinese and Japanese civilians crept out of their cellars to tell them that Lin Piao's entire army group had closed out of the city at about 1:30 that morning. This placed the rear Red elements about six hours' march away.

Nationalist forces got under way late that morning.[14] General Tu Yu-ming, the army group (NECC) commander, was very embarrassed by the fact that 65,000[15] of Lin Piao's personally led troops had escaped without the slightest notice. While he fumed and held off the press down in Mukden, fighter and bomber planes warmed up and took off for the roads and region between Ssupingkai and Changchun. They scouted this spring-scented farming ground, made some ineffective strafing passes at small Red units, but never found the bulk of the "missing" Red army group. Not only had this large enemy force evacuated a close-range battlefield without being discovered until it was hours away, but the Red forces had "disappeared" on the terrain itself.

The Nationalists did not get close to the main Red bodies until after 1 June, when the Communists made a halt along several crossings of the Sungari River. Where and how had the Communists disappeared by daylight of 19 May? Why didn't the

---

[14] Many units were occupied with the task of kicking the Japanese out of their homes.

[15] Nationalist estimates of the forces opposing them here were much higher. I believe this one is the most accurate counts that can be made.

Nationalist armies catch up with them before the Sungari[16] was reached?

There are many detailed answers, but the essential reason the Chinese government aircraft never discovered the main Red body was the Red army's dispersion into small groups and its skillful bivouacking in hundreds of Manchurian farmhouses by day. Furthermore, the Reds marched much faster than their opponents did and thus kept out of ground reach.

This was about the biggest tactical surprise ever perpetrated on the Nationalists in Manchuria.[17] Although the Nationalists had modern aircraft, they were always hard pressed to discover Communist troop concentrations thereafter. For guerrillas, dispersal and disappearance are obviously easy; but for regular units of larger size it must be conceded that the Chinese Communists are most skillful at tactical disappearance.

Many other Nationalist commanders were mystified by the Red tactics of disappearance. Often, when Nationalist forces closed in on what they thought were masses of encircled Reds, they found the terrain empty of the enemy. The Japanese had similar experience, but they could better expect these encircled vacuums for they were fighting guerrillas.

Where and how do the Red units vanish? Much depends on the degree of encirclement, and much more on the terrain. No military encirclement is as tight as it may look on a map. The Chinese Reds aren't looking at maps when they seek to "evaporate." They are looking at the terrain and physically testing the enemy's strength with active reconnaissance. If only one weak spot is found, the Reds will attack it with all their might—after a feinting attack to mislead the enemy in another direction.

---

[16] At Lafa, a point north of Kirin, the Communists halted to virtually annihilate the Nationalist 88th Division about 4-5 June 1946. Then a truce was imposed on the fighting in Manchuria (6th June) by Executive Headquarters.

[17] An interesting postscript to the battle of Ssupingkai was General Lin Piao's apparent dejection when interviewed a few weeks later by several US news correspondents. Sallow and sad-looking, Lin said he never again would fight a battle of fixed position until he had real troop strength. He kept this vow, built up his army in the truce era that followed, and only in 1947 did he cautiously begin to risk big battles.

The Chinese usually succeed in this maneuver, for while the enemy has to keep a tight hold over a large circular frontage, the Reds can concentrate all their strength in a wedge. It is even more mystifying when they simply evaporate without attack. This means the Chinese have found *several* holes in the encirclement. What happens next depends upon the size of the Red force. If it is only a battalion or regiment the order will go out, "Disperse as individuals or small groups, make your own way out, and assemble X days later at point Y." If it is an army, the "evaporation" will be by squads and platoons, which will filter through all possible weak points. In terms of technique, some of the Chinese Reds are apt to discard part or all of their uniforms, taking civilian clothes from the local people. Refugee groups, therefore, should be suspect near any areas of encirclement.

When are they prone to escape by the infiltration process? Usually when the enemy has an overwhelming force against them. In June 1946, a reported force of 60,000 Reds of the Central Plains Army led several hundred thousand Nationalist soldiers on a merry chase in North Hupeh. Encircled by their enemy, the Chinese Reds were seemingly "in the bag." The truce teams sought to intercede at this point, and sent airplanes over the region to find the Red forces they wanted to contact. The planes couldn't spot a uniformed body of Red troops, yet they searched for more than a week.

This is what happened. General Wang Chen had a portion of these Communist elements and ordered his men to "take to the hills" as best they could. Two months later he saw his scattered remnants assemble in Shensi. Earlier, however, to avoid a complete compromise of direction, the encircled Reds had split and moved in two main directions. Wang Chen's units went toward Yenan in Shensi, and the remainder went east toward Kiangsu on the China coast. Split like an atom, the Red force was rendered ineffective in one particular area only to join up with other Reds in two other regions. Officially the Nanking government had "annihilated" the Communists; or at least that was their claim.

Actually the government had reduced a threat in one area only to have threats emerge later in two other regions.

When the Chinese Reds are forced into a bad military position, such as an encirclement, they take every possible advantage of the terrain. They also take to the mountains, if there are any. Generals Su Yu, Ho Lung, Liu Po-cheng and Lin Piao, have all resorted to this technique when hard pressed. It is also an understandable pattern used by a great many lower-ranking officers—a result of guerrilla experience.

When the Reds run to the hills, watch out; for they will probably try to lure you into a trap. This technique has been practiced with regularity since the Chinese Reds began to make war. In the famous Battle of Laiyuan, General Wang Chen used mountains this way. Lin Piao and Ho Lung, at the narrow pass of Pinghsingwan, in October 1937, feigned weakness, then demonstrated strength to trap a Japanese brigade. Years later, Su Yu retired to the barren mountains of Mengliangko to tempt and defeat a large enemy. In 1947, Liu Po-cheng based himself in the Tapieh Mountains and openly dared government troops to come and get him.

In Korea, the Chinese have been able effectively to break contact with the main masses of the opposing armies. This is the Red technique of saving their own men from enemy artillery fire and cutting down casualties. The Chinese may foolhardily waste masses of their men, but usually for a specific purpose. However, on many occasions, they are skillful in avoiding waste. They remember their 10 Military Principles. "The strategy of vanishing," as one war correspondent[18] terms it, often has been confusing to UN troops in Korea.

Why do the Reds fail to give battle when UN forces search them out? Why, when they have greatly superior numbers, are they not consistently more aggressive, over a period of time and along a length of frontage? There are several reasons, all directly related to the PLA's Military Principles:

"Fight no unprepared engagements . . ."

---

[18] George Barrett, of the New York *Times*.

"Avoid battles of attrition . . ."

Wait and See Tactics in Korea

The Chinese Reds are hesitant to really fight except on their own terms of terrain, time, and relative strength. They always seek to have superiority of numbers; when they don't have it in a given sector they don't wish to fight. They know our mission in Korea is to grind them up, and they are keeping out of the jaws of the grinder. In this they are tactically sound.

UN battalions and divisions don't worry about holding towns or cities. The Chinese Reds have been so used to attacking and harassing garrison and line of communication troops that they are often tactically at a loss as to how to deal effectively with aggressive field units which are fighting them at their own game.

Tactically, we have the Chinese in repeated states of uncertainty, so they reach into their bag of old tricks and come up with ambushes and sudden withdrawals. Their control, from army to battalion, is bad because they don't have the communications or the signal system that will permit them to coordinate combat units in a hurry. They are very mobile on foot, but they have learned that once they get into a firefight with us, everything from tactical aviation downwards will be slapped at them. Red infantry is *good,* but it takes more than just infantry fire power to counter our superiority in weapons. Here is where this enemy army shows its great weakness. It simply is not modern.

So the Red armies tactically bide their time, bidding for a few local points, parrying our thrusts, threatening some areas but patiently building up for a big battle or offensive to be conducted, if they can so arrange it, on their own terms. When they attack, it is with the full weight of numbers and a disregard for casualties. In-between times they play hard to get, saving again for the major effort. The UN strategy of keeping the Reds tactically off balance is the surest and most successful way to fight the Chinese Communists—for in their recent past, they simply haven't been used to such aggressiveness. To the person who would ask, "Why haven't the Reds pushed us out of Korea?" the answer is that we have applied part of the PLA's own tenth rule: ". . . do not let the enemy have breathing space."

Chinese tactics initially appeared to be excellent, when they swept into Korea in the winter of 1950-51. Our military posture was poor. We were moving forward in columns, and had to march back in columns; so we were attacked "while in movement." The Chinese couldn't have picked a better time to attack us. But were their tactics so superior? They were not. Had they been, the 1st Marine Division, the 7th US Infantry Division, and other UN units would now be buried in their own vehicular wreckage. Chinese Communists did heavy and ghastly damage, but they didn't have the tactical ability to stop the 1st Marine Division and the 7th Infantry Division from reaching the Hamhung-Hungnam area. While the newspapers headlined, "Rout," the Chinese couldn't and didn't make it one. But they tried their best. When the showdown came, General Soule's 3d Infantry Division ringed the Hamhung beachhead. Where was all of the much-vaunted Chinese tactical ability and strength with which to break it apart? The Chinese hadn't had even a final successful roadblock to their credit up to that time; then, with the war going their way, they failed to mass their might and overwhelm our beachhead. Why? Because, for all of its great strength, the PLA is not modern, organizationally, tactically, or logistically. One may chew at, and chew up, an enemy by guerrilla tactics; one can inflict heavy losses on an enemy by virtue of superior numbers; but these alone do not necessarily inflict final defeat on a modern and well-organized military force.

Tactically, the PLA forces in Korea are applying old concepts to a war new in type to them. They figured out how to seal Nationalist troops up in cities; they were patient enough to wait years for Nationalist morale to decay; they gnawed at the fringes of their enemy, surrounded him regionally, captured his arms and troops piecemeal, and marched the feet off their own Red soldiers. But they never before faced modern fire power as it is known to them today. The Chinese militarists need either a large land mass in which to envelop their enemy and apply their

MOB MOBILITY AND WINNING TACTICS 197

Ten Military Principles; or, if they stay in Korea, they need to develop a new set of military axioms. The old 10 are not unsound, but they are peculiar to a war that is now history and to an army that is modern only in the sense that it is overly large. The tactics of "vanishing" and "evaporating" belong rightly to guerrillas, not to field armies supplied by thousands of trucks and vulnerable to hostile air power.

Photo by the Author.

THE PSYCHOLOGY OF THE NATIONALISTS IS INDICATED BY THIS PILLBOX WHICH THEY BUILT AT A RAILWAY STATION.
It was this static defense attitude that cost them heavily in the Civil War.

Human Waves and Strong Points

As the Chinese Communists forced their Japanese, and later their Nationalist, enemies to resort to pillbox and blockhouse posts, so they learned, in turn, how to cope successfully with these fixed points of resistance. China and Manchuria are still studded with thousands of these concrete blockhouses, whose embrasures range from two-story height to ground level.

If a fortified point is of formidable strength and supported by integrated systems of wire, trenches and pillboxes, the regular Chinese military units may build a model of it for study. Attack rehearsals have not been as prominent a feature of PLA military practice as they are in more modern armies; but the Chinese compensate for this, in part, by a careful study of the objective. They seek its weak points and if they do not find any, within the category of structure or organization, they are patient enough to sit and wait for some human weakness to appear.

They may even create human weaknesses in the enemy. For example, this ruse was often employed against the Japanese to "ripen" the objective. At a safe distance the Reds would surround the objective with a few riflemen and many civilians, "armed" with firecrackers. The usual practice was to do this at night and thus force the enemy defenders into their pillboxes or blockhouses. Just enough bullets would be fired to frighten the enemy; and firecrackers contributed to the enemy's confusion. The Japanese were not long in sensing the fact such an attack was but a demonstration. The Reds would repeat these "attacks" and the Japs would become less and less concerned until, one night, the attack would be forceful and real.

It is often the Red practice to maneuver with a small body of men and draw the enemy out of his fortifications, either into ambush or open battle. Here again, Red Chinese officers reveal the tendency of the entire corps to fight on ground of their choosing.

Against the Chinese Nationalists, the Reds, both regulars and guerrillas, harassed the garrisons of the strong points at night so that the occupants lost sleep. Sniping kept the pillbox and "concrete cell" occupants awake in the daytime. By fire and maneuver Red units interrupted reliefs of the more isolated posts. Gradually the Communists wore down their sedentary enemies; then, at an opportune moment, they would close in, capitalizing on weaknesses they had studied. The large-scale occupancy of fixed defenses was one of the biggest mistakes the Nationalists made in the China Civil War.

The "human waves" method is a technique, not a tactic. It is the technique of "last resort" or, if it can be termed a tactic at all, it is the "tactic of mass" which, by all known military standards, ranks at the very bottom of military science. But if one's art, armor, air, and artillery have failed, *it* is the trick to pull out of the bag—providing one can afford to cover the price tag in multiple masses of human flesh. The Chinese Communists have no hestitation in spilling their "human" purses for certain military objectives.

The "human wave" technique is usually successful on a tactical level. It is the technique we must watch, but never copy. The determination of outnumbered men and the precision and power of superior weapons are American deterrents to the success of Chinese "human waves." Wherever Chinese Communist troops fight there will be the application of "human waves." This does not mean that the technique is applied daily in combat. Chinese troop units also favor the technique of mass infiltration.

If one could expect the application of "human waves" on one's more vital combat holdings, the technique would not be so dangerous, for a measure of preparation could ordinarily be made. But one can never truly gauge where the "human wave" assaults may take place.

I saw a "dike" across the Grand Canal, made of human bodies, produced by a "human wave" attack on the Shantung city of Tsining (Chining) in July 1947. It was an attack militarily foolish. No one has ever satisfactorily explained why the Chinese Reds tried to take this objective at a time when they were being pursued, yet the Reds assaulted Tsining's medieval walls for one week. Tsining is surrounded by two wide and deep moats. The Grand Canal is a part of one these moats. The city's ancient walls are 50 to 60 feet high and equally thick at the base. Red artillery shells simply pock-marked this mass of stone. The city gates were well defended by the Nationalists, so the Reds elected to undertake crossing the moats and scaling the massive walls on bamboo ladders. This movement was not made easier by the Nationalist artillery and infantry defense.

Red human waves swept forward across several hundred yards of flat, pond-dotted terrain to reach the Grand Canal moat, where a group of frail houses stood. The Communist troops paid a heavy toll to get the remnants of several regiments into this shelter, to concentrate and reorganize. The Chinese Nationalists by this time were defending Tsining from trenches dug in the wall tops, and their artillery was firing from within its spacious city. The Communists had 50 to 100 yards to go to reach the moat. So decimated were their ranks that it took about two days to build up enough strength in the housing area outside the wall for the assault on the water and stone barrier. In this interim, Nationalist artillery delivered a hail of shells on the houses, which were leveled with surprising speed. Fires broke out and soon united; the small buildings became roaring furnaces, with Red troops "dug in" outside them.

With the support of a regiment of field artillery, the Communists concentrated their main attack upon the southeast corner of Tsining's wall. Battalion after battalion rose up out of the burning and exploding shambles near the wall and rushed forward to dive into the moat and swim. Wave after wave of ochre-uniformed soldiers swept up and exploded into the moat. The defenders fired downward at point blank ranges; the Red sea of milling and splashing humanity was so dense there was little need for the defenders to do more than fire in a downward direction. The bodies of Red soldiers piled up at the outer edge of the moat, but the Reds came recklessly on, leaping forward on the corpses of their own comrades. A veritable bridge of human bodies, split bamboo poles, and ladders grew across this moat. The assault grew more determined as the Reds viewed their losses. Even the wounded crawled across the human bridge to get to the relative safety of the wall base, for by this time Nationalist mortars were dropping shells just over the wall. The bamboo ladders were swung up—they had been carefully measured to be slightly shorter than the height of the wall not to give the topside defenders a hand-hold with which to push them back.

Once the Red soldiers began scaling the ladders, the Nationalist troops on that part of the wall—grew panicky and withdrew about 75 yards from the point of assault. When the Reds leaped up onto the high wall they dived into empty trenches. Thus, for an hour or so, there was combat up and down the trenches near the southeast corner. Some ladders were hauled up and dropped inside the wall. More Communists went up over the wall and down into the city. For a while the Reds dominated the city corner; but after a day the Nationalists managed to kill or capture the few who got into the city. This heartened the wall-top defenders, who gave their full attention to further attempts of the Reds to scale the wall in traditional medieval fashion.

It is to the credit of the Communists'[19] great daring, bravery, and determination, that they succeeded in getting *any* men over that massive wall into Tsining. This was their greatest effort. Judging by the way they smashed in the city's South Gate, they might better have concentrated their main assault there. The attack on the city was suddenly given up and a quick withdrawal was made, as other Nationalist forces were en route to beseiged Tsining. The attack was not only a complete failure, it was also a tactical mistake. On the other hand, the Nationalists made their greatest mistake in failing to pursue the battered Reds. It was not until several days after the city battle was over that the Nationalist garrison sent reconnaissance patrols outside Tsining—to find that the enemy had completely disappeared. The very impact and shock of the Communist human wave attack had shaken all ideas of aggressive action out of the Government troops.

How Lin Piao Views Command and Combat

Heretofore unpublished in English, the following "Principles of Combat" were written by General Lin Piao in 1946[20] and were subsequently used by officers and instructors in his command. To date, little has been known, outside of China, about Lin Piao's tactical thoughts and concepts. Lin's principles of *"Short Attack"* serve here to give us some measure of the man who won over Manchuria and whose troops were the first Chinese to attack us in Korea. Most interesting are Lin Piao's comments on the lack of support from the Manchurian people. One of the

---

[19] These were the troops of Generals Liu Po-cheng and Chen Yi.
[20] The Chinese text of this work was published in a military manual in Harbin, Manchuria, on 30 September 1946.

dominant themes in his *"Short Attack"* is the need for numerical superiority. He even introduces his text in a paragraph titled, "Assembling Superior Strength," in which he says—

The present strength and equipment of the enemy (Nationalists) precludes our doing more than carrying out extermination tactics; and even for this we must assemble superior forces. In this we are handicapped by lack of manpower, technicians and organization. To have a superior force for war one must have a superiority of 400 to 500 percent. To undertake a successful offensive there must be a superiority of 500 to 600 percent.

Reduced to briefer format,[21] but without injury to Lin Piao's original outline and general concepts, here are his "Short Attack" principles:

Methods of Battles. The so-called one-point or short attack (i-tien) tactic is like sticking a long sharp-pointed knife into the enemy's weak spot. But this is not enough. There must be double or multiple attacks. This type of action may not result in cutting off the enemy.

Important Battle Situations and Instructions. In the face of a superior force we have to give way to discover the enemy's objective . . . string (him) out . . . and deceive him. Retreat may be to flanks. After a retreat, ambuscades can be set along the . . . route. Only the highest officers may issue orders. No independent action may be undertaken.

Initial action may have one or several phases, but it can only destroy a section of the enemy. Continuous strikes must be carried out until the enemy breaks. He may seek relief . . . or run. Our forces can then act accordingly. Cutting up a section of an army may result in a general breakdown. If (so) . . . our forces can boldly surround superior forces . . . (and) must not await orders but initiate independent action immediately.

Initial and follow-up actions will result in a number of victories but large masses of enemy troops . . . 50,000 to 60,000 will still be left. If the enemy leaves (our) area, we may end the campaign or follow. If action in enemy territory is decided on, it must be carefully planned.

If, while in action against one objective the enemy's reinforcements arrive, the decision must be made to—

(1) Finish the original action before attacking the reinforcements;
(2) Leave to attack the reinforcements;
(3) Or attempt both actions simultaneously.

---

[21] Items in parentheses are the author's words, shortening or paraphrasing Lin Piao.

If there are sufficient troops, the last course may be undertaken. Envelop the reinforcements, by direct assault or ambuscade. The main thing is to prevent a junction of the two enemy forces. . . .

Raids and assaults are two good ways of reducing strong points. To be successful, the cooperation of the masses is necessary or enemy intelligence will learn of the plan. Our plans must take into account that, if a raid fails, a heavy attack must be made. However, our mobile forces do not engage in positional . . . or seige warfare. This can be done by guerrillas.

When the enemy is well entrenched . . . our commanders should quickly recognize the time to change from raiding tactics to heavy attack. For this . . . artillery and engineers are needed. Technical equipment is only an aid to, never a substitute for, bravery. If it appears that the enemy cannot quickly be exterminated . . . approach his strong point on three sides leaving what appears to be a loophole of escape . . . fall upon him on four sides when he endeavors to escape. When a frontal attack has been made and a breakthrough secured . . . destroy the key points of the enemy's defense, after which the remaining points may be breached.

Principles of Command. First, decide whether to initiate an action . . . If a commander believes he has a chance of success . . . he should proceed even though . . . the bulk of his staff may advise against it.

Action is necessary to maintain morale of a military force . . . the effect is two-headed, it invigorates his forces and discourages the enemy. Final victory cannot be won by hit-and-run tactics . . . (but) . . . must be won in main engagements and he who recognizes (such) an opportunity . . . should proceed, if necessary, without orders from above, or even in the face of contrary orders from a higher commander out of touch with the situation.

On the other hand, a commander who initiates action without proper knowledge of the real situation, or in spite of being certain of defeat, risks breaking . . . the morale of his troops. . . .

Once an action is begun, it should be carried through regardless of difficulties. If the going is hard . . . think of the enemy's losses and his fear. A commander should not ignore the possibility of (enemy reinforcements) . . . but he should not be overly worried about such. . . . To persist and win through reveals a commander's strong will to win . . . (but) when circumstances so change a situation as to make it hopeless, a reversal of the order reveals a commanders versatility.

A commander should base his strategy on a superiority of 5 to 1 for attack. He should choose one attack route, seek out his enemy's weak point and attack it with a dagger-like thrust, throwing his strength into the enemy's weakness. Having (thus) achieved victory at one point, he can take advantage of the enemy's confusion to expand the action.

Commanders should make front line reconnaissance for themselves and do it with dispatch. A commander must be sure his reserves are (close) before he initiates a general action and he must know that he has numerical superiority so he can deploy (his) reserves to carry out flanking action or meet enemy reserves.

(To prevent the enemy from escaping when a one-point thrust is used, Lin Piao advocates the placing of strong points or advance forces, in the path of his withdrawal. This is Lin's substitute for "having to execute a costly new flanking and enveloping movement." This has several times been evident in Korea.)

Whether (attacking) at one point or . . . several, the greatest strength should be against the enemy's weakest front . . . and at this point (achieve) a superiority of 3 or 4 to 1.

No soldier or organization is worth having that does not dare to carry forward a bayonet-grenade attack.

Basic Methods of Achieving Victory. Promote military spirit among the troops by advisors . . . political commissars . . . slogans. . . .

Before an action, the company and platoon officers should reconnoiter; platoons should get as close as possible to the enemy.

In attack there can be no . . . vacillation or indecision even though a bayonet charge be involved.

Calculated Risk Engagements. (These) should not be undertaken at random . . . and only if there is a 70 percent . . . prospect of victory. (With this), courage and brilliant command can overcome a 30 percent risk. Preparation must be thorough . . . action tenacious in the face of odds. . . . Extermination of the enemy (is) complete victory . . . routing the enemy, or a stalemate with heavy enemy losses (is) . . . a completed mission.

(In the following paragraph Lin Piao makes the historic admission that the people, in 1946, were not behind the Communist military effort.)

This is not our main type of strategy. This is a special-purpose and not a general-purpose type of warfare. (It) is being employed in the Northeast (Manchuria) because there is not yet the wide base (1946) of popular support for the movement that there was . . . in North China. In the Northeast, the people are not yet prepared to maintain the secrecy for us that they do inside the Great Wall. Thus it is necessary to employ (these) wearing-down tactics while organizational activities are carried on behind the lines.

Mobile Warfare. Rapid strides with large forces . . . is an excellent form of warfare to which our leaders are accustomed. In this warfare the secret lies in discovering . . . enemy weak points and attacking them with superior forces (of 5 or 6 to 1). It calls for . . . rapid disengagement and retreat when persistence in attack appears unprofitable, or to avoid an advancing enemy. A well-planned withdrawal . . . creates in an opponent over-whelming confidence in his superiority, a factor which makes him easy prey to sudden attack.

When one's terrain is unfavorable or the enemy . . . superior and solid, the enemy may be decoyed into an unfavorable area and led to spread his forces so that his weak points show; . . . (then attack him).

In this . . . warfare, an action (is) profitable when it results in capture of enemy materiel, and large numbers of prisoners . . . Battle should not be joined when the enemy is superior in strength . . . one should wait for favorable conditions.

Utmost secrecy regarding troop movements (is important).

Troops must be inured to hardship for this campaigning or it cannot succeed. Adverse living and weather conditions must not be permitted to weaken . . . determination. . . .

Voluntary withdrawal . . . to maintain freedom of action, should not be considered as defeat . . .

Shock troops, cover troops, and reserve troops are indispensable. . . . Shock troops . . . wear down the enemy. Cover troops stabilize the situation . . . and protect the shock troops. Reserve troops . . . cut off enemy retreats and reinforcements. . . .

Short Attack; Two-Pronged Battle Tactics. . . . In fighting a mobile enemy, one should strike only one flank or only one sector. Rather than making scattered, random threats in all directions, an enemy weak point should be selected for attack. One must have numerical superiority . . . at the point of attack . . .

It is necessary to insure that shock troops . . . are not only sufficient, but are so disposed that every thrust of a bayonet will draw blood. They should be deployed in deep column formation instead of wide frontal . . . .

Ordinarily two-thirds of a unit is deployed as shock troops and the other third as a spearhead; but . . . this may be revised to (a proportion) of eight-ninths to one-ninth. In making an encirclement, care should be taken to maintain strength at all points of the circle.

In this form of warfare we pit our main force against a segment of the enemy and chop him up by segments. In the attack, our troops must fight shoulder to shoulder, without permitting an opening in the line, until the enemy is overcome. (This is Lin Piao's emphasis on *human waves.*)

Multiple-Point Attacks. In attacking an enemy on the march . . . engage him in frontal attack while the main forces attack his flank. Cut him in two; a strong force should attack the center and another strong force the rear. In attacking an enemy . . . on the defensive, a small force may make a frontal attack while the main force makes a single or double flank attack, or (attacks) the rear. Whether the forces involved are . . . divisions . . . or squads . . . this plan of attack from different directions can be carried out with good results.

A frontal attack alone has the disadvantage that the enemy may retreat and cannot be cut up, or that he can bring up reserves without fear and drive the attackers out of points they may have occupied.

Multiple-point attack prevents enemy retreat, creates psychological problems for him and permits capture of arms and prisoners. When lack of numerical superiority prevents attacks against more than two points, then a flank attack should be considered of primary importance and a frontal attack . . . secondary.

The one-point (short attack) and multiple-point tactics require careful planning, ample intelligence work, and plenty of time to gather and deploy forces. They are not rushed into blindly.

Night Attacks. Take plenty of time . . . know thoroughly the lay of the land and the conditions of the enemy. Simultaneous attacks in several places at once should not be attempted. The main attack should be made in force at one point to make a breakthrough. Diversionary attacks at other places should employ only small forces. When attacking a village, scaling ladders and demolition charges should be carried for convenience in breaking through and scaling walls. In street fighting, advances should be made through buildings rather than in the streets.

It is noticeable here that Lin Piao adheres to Mao Tse-tung's general concept of a strong attack in one main direction, a weighted fist, supported of course by scratching and probing fingers along other parts of the line, for purposes of diversion. Double envelopment is not stressed by either Lin Piao or Mao Tse-tung. The general Communist reliance on heavy superiority of numbers evidences not only their deficiencies in fire power, but also a lack of tactical skill.

What Is the Soviet Influence?

Soviet officers and Russian military textbooks are slowly making the PLA more dangerous, for they are teaching the Chinese how to mass their troops more efficiently. This doesn't mean the Soviets have any mastery of logistics. They do not, and the Chinese have even less; but the Soviets have broad combat experience with large army groups, experience that will be of eventual value to the Red Asiatics. Therein lies the most dangerous tactical and strategic influence of the Soviets on the Chinese.

The Soviets have much to teach; the Chinese much to learn. Yet all of this is not going to take effect over night and have immediate impact on the battlefield. The one thing common to the two armies is mass.

Where the Chinese formerly went by a combination of past experience (guerrilla-influenced) and instinct, they have now absorbed some of the more formal Soviet rules for tactical groupings. Instead of saying, "Liu, you take your unit there and Chou, you remain here," the Chinese lower commanders have learned to designate their tactical groupings as assault troops, secondary attack troops, and reserves. Each is assigned its mission under those headings. Zones and boundaries are being designated with more precision. Main attacks are being narrowed down to prescribed frontages and are being supported by deep echelonment. Secondary attacks are widened to fit the studied concepts of the Soviets. The use of more maps, more top control, and better communications is being emphasized. Better staff procedure, more warning orders, and more liaison officers are points the Soviets teach in order to bring the PLA units under more formal guidance. But in Korea, Chinese units still get badly scrambled and pile up on one another.

"Don't wait for complete information on the enemy," preach the Soviets, who say in addition, "To delay action in an emergency, because of incomplete information, shows a lack of energetic leadership."[22] The Soviets want a little more over-all boldness out of their Chinese proteges.

---

[22] A Soviet text, *General Principles of Army Group Tactics*, which has been in use (in Chinese) in the PLA since 1947.

"Without justifiable reasons the decision should never be changed," say the Soviets. "In an emergency . . . the decision (can) be changed. Then the commander should make a new decision without losing ground."[22] The Soviets lend formality to military technique by emphasizing that all commanders must be taught the combat decision process of—

(1) Understanding the mission thoroughly;
(2) Determining the objective;
(3) Estimating the situation;
(4) Then making the battle decision.

In modern communication equipment and practices the PLA has been weak, and still is; but the Soviets are improving Chinese technique and tactics by assistance and instruction. Here is a fertile field for communications instructors. The PLA is weak in radio, but it has reached the field telephone stage. Much of the control, however, is still by runners who hand-carry messages.

However, the Soviets aren't going to teach the Chinese much about reconnaissance on the ground. The Chinese already are very aggressive at this.

It is in the field of artillery that the Soviets, with all their tradition and experience as good artillerists, are strengthening the PLA—with marked effect. The Chinese now have artillery regiments and divisions like those of the Soviet Army. They don't, however, have as much artillery in proportion to their infantry as the Soviets do, but they like to use artillery as much as the Russians do. The day soon will arrive when the PLA will have greater and more effective artillery support—organized, trained, and applied according to the Soviet concepts of massed guns.

Armor-wise, the Chinese have a lot to learn. Every one of the PLA's parade tanks must be replaced by a new one. It has been believed that the Soviets would furnish the Chinese with a number of medium tanks, if they haven't already done so. Quite probably the Soviets have pondered the poor showing the North Koreans made with armor and have concluded that the Chinese Reds wouldn't do much better. The Soviets are aware of the deficiencies of China's infantry-heavy army and doubtless have concluded that it is better to bring the Chinese Reds up to strength in artillery, motor transport, and other basic essentials, than it is to load them with armor and thus foster a lopsided growth. It can be said that the Soviets have had no perceptible influence *to date* on Chinese armor.

On the objectives of combat the Soviets and the Chinese have little disagreement, for the Soviets hold that the primary objective is "the destruction of the enemy's armed forces and his supplies,"[23] but as to how this is to be done there may be differences of opinion—on strategy, tactics, and technique. On these subjects, there may be some conflict between Chinese and Soviet concepts. It is probable that the Soviets expressed impatience with the Chinese over the inconclusive results in Korea. The Chinese are slower, because of the nature of their past experience and the lack of modern field forces. Neither Communist side weeps over wasted losses in manpower, but the Chinese, who are paying the daily death prices in casualties, are going to want to conduct the war along their own lines. Both the Soviets and the Chinese are Red to the core, but they are of different nationalities, with distinctive characteristics and pride of race.

Summed up, the greatest Soviet influences on Chinese tactics are the lending of formality, form and better control of units, in the application of their traditional tactics; teaching the Chinese to achieve better artillery support; and, in general, strengthening Chinese tactics by the indirect aids of a more modern logistical "know how" and increased communication effectiveness, which has resulted in more adept handling of large troop masses.

[23] General Principles of Army Group Tactics.

Chapter 7

GONGS, BUGLES, AND BANNERS

The Trojan Horse Technique

Lieutenant Colonel M. P. A. den Ouden met a miserable death just outside his command post in Korea in February 1951. What made his Netherlands soldiers so bitter was the fact that his death resulted from his own kind generosity. Others can die in a similar way, for Chinese soldiers have a bag of brutal tricks in combat. They delight in killing by treachery. That was how they shot the unsuspecting Colonel den Ouden and his men.

Some 40 soldiers needed ammunition in a hurry and asked for it at the Netherlands battalion CP (command post). They were Asiatics, and looked like South Koreans. Their uniforms and helmets were American, their spokesman talked convincingly and said they were Korean allies. So Colonel den Ouden ordered ammunition issued them. Tucking away their issued shells, the Asiatics eased casually away from the command post. But not too far. The Netherlands soldiers turned to other tasks. Suddenly the CP area was cracking with gunfire and Netherlands soldiers were the targets! One minute he had been alive, and the next Colonel den Ouden lay on the ground dead, his bloody uniform showing where he had been shot with his own ammunition. The killing continued, but finally the Chinese ambushers were driven away.

This daring act of treachery is typical of Chinese soldier methods. Low-cost warfare they call it; many enemy casualties for few of your own. They know so many combat tricks, from their guerrilla background, that you can never be too suspicious. Use of enemy uniforms must be expected, at intervals. Such treachery was used in December 1950 by a whole company of Reds in an unsuccessful attack on the UN perimeter at Hungnam. This practice is of long standing in the PLA. It began when the Chinese were fighting the Japanese. The Chinese Reds clothed entire companies in Japanese or puppet uniforms, then boldly marched the units through enemy territory—for reconnaissance, for interception of messengers and puppet merchants, and for capturing prisoners. The technique is as daring as it is dangerous. When the Chinese took Japanese prisoners they relieved them of their uniforms, dressed them in Chinese clothes, then marched them along in their disguised column, giving it an even greater resemblance to an invader column. Marching for miles, such enemy-uniformed Chinese companies picked up valuable intelligence.

There were ramifications to this technique of disguise. Sometimes the Chinese Reds, still in Japanese uniforms, turned in Chinese prisoners to the Japanese, who were manning strong defenses. This placed the Chinese close or even inside the enemy strong points, and massacres like that at the Netherlands CP sometimes resulted. Many a Japanese garrison was deceived by this ruse, which will undoubtedly be repeated elsewhere.

There is something else to watch for in this "Trojan Horse" technique. A disguised Chinese column may be supported by small guerrilla groups, which move as refugees or travel in a surreptitious fashion some distance away. In such cases, there are prearranged signals between the disguised body of soldiers and the partisans who maneuver to support it. Sudden, gut-spilling death awaits those who do not take precautions against this Chinese ruse.

Their clothing may not be the uniform of their enemy. Chinese guerrillas, and even regulars, have been known to put on women's clothing. There have been cases in which soldiers, so disguised, have resorted to distant "flirtations" and to crude and vulgar forms of expressing "sex appeal" in order to bait or entice enemy troops out of fixed positions.

In January 1951, as the UN forces slowly abandoned the city of Seoul, enemy troops "clad in white Korean clothes began to appear as refugees and marched into the city with their guns hidden,"[1] an old Chinese trick, but this one didn't work for the military precision of the civilian-clad soldiers "gave them away tc US rear guard units." One can expect any number of disguises by Red guerrillas, regular reconnaissance units, or infiltration columns which weave themselves in among refugee groups.

If they don't come at you with some bit of treachery up their sleeves, these Chinese soldiers, or guerrillas, may invite you to violent death. It is our tradition to pick up our battlefield dead and bury them. Here is a characteristic the Chinese Reds may work on; so it pays to be careful. If a convoy has been ambushed, or one's own dead on a battlefield momentarily abandoned, such areas should be re-entered with care. Skillfully camouflaged Chinese soldiers, or guerrillas, may be waiting to add more stench and corpses to the combat area. Sometimes, when fighting the Japanese in World War II, Red Chinese units would collect Japanese dead in carts and pile the corpses in conspicuous places. Knowing that the Japanese usually sought out their dead for the ritual of cremation, the Chinese waited in ambush near these "decoys of dead."

Because it was small, the Chinese Communist Army resorted to a great variety of ruses during its growth to power. The tricks have not been forgotten. They are so many and so varied they could fill a separate book. However, some of these unorthodox methods and techniques merit description here.

---

[1] Gene Symonds, "Tricky Flag-Raising Crew Lost as First Reds Got Into Seoul," *United Press Dispatch*, 6 January 1951.

The Battles Are Noisy; the Small Tactics Tricky

"It was eerie and I was scared," said Marine Sergeant Donald L. McGunical. "The first night we ran into the Chinese on the way up to Chongjin Reservoir, about November 4 or so, the contraptions blew, and we knew they were headed our way." Sergeant McGunical was hearing the cheap and blaring Chinese bugles for the first time—and they were being blown for a purpose. "They'd launch in at us, furiously blowing the things; then, all of a sudden, the blasts would fizzle . . . got the bugler . . . but just as suddenly, someone else would take it up." Sergeant McGunical was no stranger to combat, yet he reacted to the Chinese "bugle and gong" technique as the Chinese hoped he would.

There were many other such battles. On New Year's Eve 1950, the bugles blared from Chinese positions, and the Chinese Reds began their bid for South Korea. But the UN troops were no longer frightened by noises. They held.

Elsewhere in Asia other soldiers had reacted differently—and the world's most remote nation began its slow tumble into the Communist orbit. The lonely fortress of Chamdo was garrisoned by 3,000 Tibetan troops on the night it prepared its defenses against an attack by General Liu Po-cheng's soldiers, 18 October 1950. The poorly armed defenders of Tibet anticipated a conventional attack, but in the early morning of 19 October, a crescendo of explosions and "bright stars" shocked the garrison. The garrison looked up into the sky to see a pyrotechnic display of bursting star-shells and rockets. Rumor produced further panic and the garrison commander, General Nga Ben, mounted and rode off. The abandoned Tibetan garrison was not long in following its fleeing general. Reportedly, not a shot had been fired by either side.[2] Liu Po-cheng's troops marched into Chamdo. This is why the Chinese Reds like battle ruses—they sometimes work, and they always add some to the enemy's fear and confusion.

The bugles are blown for other purposes than to frighten, however. Communication facilities in PLA military units are poor.

---

[2] Based on a report given by *Time* magazine. There is some indication, however, that battle casualties were sustained somewhere in the vicinity of Chamdo.

There are no "walkie-talkie" radio sets with present day infantry companies of the PLA, so they rely on time-honored bugles and whistles for signals. They have a series of bugle calls to attack, to withdraw, and so forth.[3]

I have often questioned whether the Chinese soldiers understand and react to the notes of all of these various calls, but their use is standard practice for control purposes, as well as to frighten.

We are not yet seeing in Korea many of the small unit and guerrilla deceptions which Communist soldiers have applied in the past. Even if seen, these little strategems would not involve very large units on either side, but they are significant in understanding the Red Chinese.

"Sparrow tactics" or resistance by "twos and fews," are resorted to by guerrillas and regulars who cannot operate successfully in large groups. The object of this form of warfare is to retain a measure of initiative, inflict losses of opportunity, and frighten enemy patrols and guards. It is guerrilla war at its lowest tactical level, and usually signifies that the Chinese are too weak to employ more effective tactics. Sparrow tactics are so named because the guerrillas scatter, singly, in pairs or threes, to roam, hide, and wait in ambush in order to pick off enemy stragglers, messengers, vehicles, and sentries. It is organized assassination.

"Jointed Worm Tactics" are a combination of ambush and hide and seek, with local informants misleading the enemy by saying "They went that-a-way." If the enemy unit follows such directions, it will be skillfully led into ambushes. The Chinese action starts with an ambush or road block which, if unsuccessful, finds the Chinese fleeing hurriedly and inviting pursuit. The Chinese head for villages and, to throw off the scent, secretly drop off at each place a few of their men who will be absorbed in the local population. Villagers will be instructed by these Chinese to mislead the pursuing enemy by giving false directions. If the pursuing unit is not careful it will end up "chasing the wind," as the Chinese call it. Upon return through the area, the unit will be ambushed by re-assembled elements of the "jointed worm." To

---

[3] General Robert H. Soule (CG of the 3d Division), in Korea, March 1951.

be successful, these tactics require local civilians who are friendly to the Red Chinese cause. Both regular and guerrilla units favor these tactics, which can be deadly to the enemy patrol or reconnaissance unit which does not evaluate civilian-given information with care. The return from such an empty pursuit should be by a different route, or tommy-gun slugs in the belly can be expected. These are well-studied textbook tactics, well applied by small red units.

"Tunnel Tactics." Red Chinese patrols and partisan bands can dissolve and disappear in several ways. Going under ground is a long established and well developed stratagem. It began in the war of resistance against the Japanese. Cellars are not normal to the houses in most villages of China. When fighting the Japanese, the Reds had underground shelters dug in such places for the momentary "escape" of their guerrillas and soldiers. The Japanese were not long in discovering these, so the Reds dug tunnels connecting various houses. Later, at its "scientific" best, *villages* were connected, not by straight tunnels but by ones which twisted horizontally, varied in depth below ground, and were insured against enemy detection and surprise by secret entrances, false mazes of tunnels, mined entrances, and armed guards. The daytime disappearance of small Red units can be accounted for if there is evidence that the Chinese have resorted to tunneling.

These tactics baffled the Nationalists on many occasions in the Civil War. In the great battle around Hsuchou, in 1949, Red regulars used tunnels offensively to penetrate fixed Nationalist defenses. Surprised by the grimy, sweating soldiers who emerged out of the ground from tunnels, Nationalist troops in small groups were so badly shot up that others were demoralized and surrendered readily when thus surprised. Siege tunnels were dug toward Nationalist strongholds in Central Hopei and other places. It is not well to estimate the tunnel network or linear yardage by the size of identified units in the area. The Reds employ many civilians to labor with spades and baskets, while the officers map and plot the networks—which result in the most baffling, and extensive mazes imaginable.

Occupied villages should be well searched for hidden subterranean entrances. A command post operated too long at any point is vulnerable to attack from secret tunnels dug into it.

Tunnels may be abandoned by Red regulars or guerrillas, but they may then become the hiding places for arms caches. In late October 1950, an American salvage team of the IX Corps discovered an amazing plan to supply North Korean guerrillas. A huge arms cache was unearthed near Waegwan. There the Reds had carefully buried an entire field artillery battery, including trucks and ammunition. Only the aiming quadrants were missing from the cannon. Unearthed were ten howitzers, ten antiaircraft guns, four anti-tank guns, two self-propelled guns, ten trucks, and a quantity of shells.

Attack the Tail. This is the Communist Army's favorite tactic (small and large unit) when it is attacked and does not choose to engage in combat on the enemy's terms. As the enemy attacks a region held by the Communists, they withdraw from the area; but in so doing the Chinese Reds move right or left to the enemy's flanks and then toward the enemy's rear, where they attack. The objective is to cause the enemy to withdraw from the position he occupied offensively, and to inflict casualties. This tactic is also used when the Chinese are outnumbered. It is their application of the principle of substitution of movement for fire.

Rice Patrols. Nationalist officers at army headquarters would scratch their heads and look at the operations maps. "Why are they attacking there?" they would ask; "there is no pattern, no sense to the Red web of strategy." There were strange attacks and forays for which there seemed no militarily logical reason until you thought of food. This Red Army often fights for the possession of food stocks. It has, in fact, predicated entire campaigns on food-supply objectives. The Reds say, "The food doubles its value when you capture it from the enemy because you gain and he loses." This often explains the why's of a particular combat action that otherwise seems so lacking in tactical objectives.

What size units participate in such campaigns? They may be armies whose logistical support has been weakened, or they may be small units seeking enough rice or flour on which to survive. The campaign is not always from necessity, but usually it is. The Chinese Reds, in the past, have been so militarily poor that just the capture of enemy stocks is to them a significant victory. They often fail to realize that an opponent may feel little relative loss as a result of the Red capture of a particular depot. The Chinese measure these objectives more from the standpoint of their own poverty than from the viewpoint of "does this really have much loss-impact on the enemy?" For that reason the Chinese may spend considerable casualties on a supply objective, which a non-Chinese opposing force would destroy without hesitation or regret if circumstances warranted. In the Chinese Army there is no shortage of men, but there is often a dearth of military supplies.

The People's Army Versus the People

When the Chinese Reds invest a town or city it is usually with a purpose and, if necessary, they will slap down a heavy price in human bodies. The misery does not end here, it only begins—for the townspeople. While the documentary source for what follows is somewhat dated (1946), the control procedure still generally applies. This Red order, issued to a combat unit, is typical—

> When a combat unit enters any town, the commanding officer of the unit will assume emergency control as follows:
> (1) The garrison commander will protect the town.
> (2) He will divide the town into areas and place it under full military control.
> (3) War criminals and traitors will be registered and arrested.
> (4) Control will be established over all military installations, warehouses, factories and schools.
> (5) Trains, vessels, vehicles, railway stations and ports, post offices, telegraph, radio and telephone installations will be placed under military control.
> (6) Guards will be placed over all airbases, warehouses and stores of military matériel.
> (7) Traitors will be wiped out; the city and civilians protected.
> (8) No one will be permitted to hide weapons.
> (9) There will be military control over food, coal, charcoal and electric power.

There is no wanton looting when the PLA takes over a city. The soldiers are not allowed *individually* to plunder the area. Looting is organized and formalized in the name of the PLA. The army "liberates" what it wants—and it has no compunctions about taking from civilians.

I recall the case of a ragged *droshky* driver in Red-captured Changchun in 1946. As usual, the Commies were waving the banners of "freedom for the oppressed people." The equalizers of people went to work as soon as the firing (but not the sniping) stopped. The *droshky* driver was asked by some Red commissars how much rent he was paying for his hovel. The driver gave a figure of about $5.00 (US) a month and the commissars held him up to the crowd as a poor worker who was being exploited. The Reds ordered the driver's landlord to cut the rent in half. The crowd was impressed. The Red occupation was still only a few days old when another Communist military functionary came to the same *droshky* driver.

"How much are your horse and *droshky* worth?"

After considerable doubt as to how honest to be, the driver replied with the realistic figure of about $53.00 in US currency.

"That makes you a man of means," said the Red functionary. "You have tangible wealth. We are levying a special tax of 40 percent of the value of one's capital goods on all persons who have wealth."

The poor driver was stunned. He had been taxed before, but never in these terms. Like all in his trade, he made a poor living and had no savings. It had taken him years to get money enough to buy his buggy and horse.

"I cannot raise such a sum of money," replied the driver, who wished he had given a much lower price tag to his animal and buggy.

"You will be given one week to get the tax."

"And if I don't raise it?"

"Then our only course is to take the horse. All people of means have to contribute something to the Northeast Democratic People's Army."

The driver lost his horse to the Reds a week later.

This incident typifies the inconsistent demands of the Chinese Communist forces when they take over cities. However, this is only the beginning. The first step is always to get control of every important installation. Second, a Red Army may, and usually does, impose its own tax on the wealthy—which is a dignified phrase for robbery at bayonet point. The wealthy homes are sacked of all visible items of value. You are "wealthy" if you have anything of even small luxury, or anything like a horse which the army wants. The droves of refugees which consistently fled before the Reds were not wealthy people[4] to begin with. Why had they become refugees? Primarily because the Commies would forever regard them as the wealthy. There were millions of such men who fled, and fled again. By the time the Red forces did envelop them, these men, once proud members of a solid middle class, were reduced to beggars, and were a liability to the Communist Party. By its own clumsy bungling (which Mao Tse-tung has often criticized), the Red bureaucracy has added to its troubles and responsibilities.

But the occupation of a city is never complete until paragraphs Three and Seven of the order are carried out. This begins with unwarranted arrests, proceeds through the rituals of people's courts and police inquisitions, and ends with swarms of flies buzzing over the broken and beaten bodies of the dead. The army is a party to almost all such procedures.

"We make use of the rabble," a Red leader admitted in 1946,[5] "for the purpose of overthrowing the privileged classes. After having served this purpose, these worthless elements are also expelled from our own organization."

---

[4] While my wife and I were with the Collins' in Nanking we gave Monte Carlo parties to raise money to feed some of these refugees. We fed a batch of several thousand one Sunday, and inquired into the background of this particular starving group. They were anything but beggars to start with. It hurts their pride to take charity, but their women had small babies dying for lack of milk. The men had been small shopkeepers, merchants (but not rich ones), farmers, artisans, and men very obviously of the middle but not the wealthy class.

[5] *The History of Peiping Executive Headquarters,* Fourth Quarter (1 October to 31 December) 1946, Department of Army, Office of Military History, pages 25-26.

"The Quality of Mercy!"

The most brutal book yet unwritten is a documentary record of the people's courts conducted in China. Even yet, Americans have no true grasp of the horror and holocaust of these multiple scenes of limb-tearing, hand-cutting, and body-beating. I have talked to missionaries who have been victims of these public orgies, or have seen them when the victims were Chinese. The process of accusation, mob inspiration, and final death were all of the same pattern. Only the mode and method of murder varied. Sometimes it was by stoning. In Shantung, within the military command of Chen Yi, soldiers in one instance shot the victims in the back of the head as they were eased down off the platform of inquisition. Dr. Ernest M. Lippa[6] recently has given one of the most vivid of the first-hand accounts published. I believe his is a very accurate description of this organized mob violence.

The Communists like to claim that not they, but the *people*, do the dirty business. That is "hogwash." At every so-called court the Reds have their professional agitators. These men, the commissars, and other Party functionaries direct the meeting to its final function of violent execution. Does the army participate? Often it does so, but always indirectly, for the army is charged with responsibility for maintaining order. Mob violence is not order. As evidenced in Peking, the military hierarchy is taking part in these scenes. General Wang Pei-huan spoke before a crowd of 5,500, in March 1951, demanding the execution of 25 persons accused of being "arch counter-revolutionary criminals." His agitating, along with Mayor Peng Chen's, generated the mob hysteria which led to shouts of, "Shoot the despots!" "Shoot the leaders of secret religious societies!" "Avenge the people!"

Red China's army must be viewed in terms of all its tactics, such as the brutal exploitation of noncombatants.

Small children, dirty and unkempt; old women, tear-stained and staggering; unshaven men who turn their heads to look back over anxious shoulders—thousands of them, in columns as far as

---

[6] "I was a Surgeon for the Chinese Reds," *The Saturday Evening Post*, 28 April 1951.

the eye can see—have been fleeing before Chinese Communist armies since 1946. Homeless and hungry, these refugees have saddened the hearts of everyone who has seen them. From these pathetic and frightened masses emerges one outstanding fact supported by several years of human action and documentation: The majority of fleeing refugees have marched *away* from the PLA, not toward it.

Not content, however, to let the masses run, the Chinese Reds have used refugees to military advantage in three ways. One, the Reds—both Chinese and North Korean—have infiltrated their own gunmen and guerrillas behind our lines by use of refugee columns. Two, the Communists have driven their own regular units right behind refugees, so as to get them forward without being fired upon. The third military advantage, though one of circumstance and not necessarily of Communist design, is that we, not they, must assume the burden of feeding and caring for these transient masses. As William L. Worden[7] describes it—

> The refugee is a weapon admirably designed to harry the enemy, to disrupt his communications, to permit infiltration of his lines, to confuse his civil government, and generally to impede his army. The refugee is a self-starting expendable sort of a weapon, which can be put into operation by a rumor, a threat, or a few shootings. Only one requirement is necessary to use him. You must be brutal enough or desperate enough.

The People's Liberation Army of China is both.

Guerrillas May Rise Again in Numbers

The country-side looks quiet under the stars. The road has been unobstructed for miles. Your tension eases after a little travel over the quiet terrain, so you light a cigarette. The presence of other vehicles in the convoy gives you reassurance. There are guns and men aboard in case something happens. Suddenly it does—the windshield shatters in your face, brakes grind, shots and shouts ring out, the column telescopes, for the lead vehicle has struck a mine. Men tumble from their vehicles, some already dead. Over the din of gunshots the wounded can be heard groaning.

---

[7] "The Cruelest Weapon in Korea," *The Saturday Evening Post*, 10 February 1951.

The hail of organized fire is but weakly answered by the disorganized shooting from those who survived and made the ditch. The "enemy of no fronts" has been met and engaged, but the official communique will probably not list your action, for it was too small. Your Purple Heart had no relation to the "big battle" that received so much play in the papers. They didn't even give a name to your battle, except to state that it was a "skirmish against irregular forces in the rear areas."

Irregular forces. Ten years ago the PLA was a conglomeration of irregular forces, which tactically harassed but did not strategically threaten. The guerrilla origins of that army are evident today, and they could quickly manifest themselves on a large scale, given the circumstances. What situations could produce an upsurge of Chinese guerrilla activity against an enemy of China? There are several.

(1) If the PLA, or any of its large elements, should be defeated in the battlefield of conventional combat, certain remnants of such forces would turn to guerrilla warfare, if only to escape.

(2) If atomic bombs and other weapons were to destroy Red China's few industrial centers and otherwise knock the logistical props from under the PLA, the inner core of this army would simply drop back ten years in its history and reassume its traditional guerrilla role, *providing* there is an enemy land force nearby for it to attack.

(3) If you drive the regular Chinese forces out of a region, like North Korea, you are bound to inherit partisan bands, in the land occupied, unless the country is combed thoroughly as the advance is made.

(4) Chinese guerrillas can grow up in one's rear areas by the process of infiltration but if the people of the region are at all cooperative with one's own forces, the Chinese cannot establish bases essential for guerrilla operations. It was the support of the people which made them so effective against the Japanese and the Chinese Nationalists.

There are three significant things to remember in connection with the Chinese guerrillas—

(1) If the PLA loses in a war of conventional combat, it will reorganize along guerrilla lines and revert to this type of resistance.

(2) The larger the land mass, the more effective Chinese guerrillas will be. Korea is not a good base (by Chinese concepts) for such resistance.

(3) On soil not their own, the Chinese Reds will fail in achieving their traditional guerrilla excellence—unless they have a period of undisturbed occupation in which to organize the people.

To invade Red China with ground forces and attempt to occupy large regions of that land mass is to invite a whole generation of conflict in a tough war of attrition. This is what the Red hierarchy would like to see, for then they could apply their traditional combination of regular and irregular resistance. To accept this invitation would be to fight the PLA on its own terms. This is well recognized. As the Communists put it, "This (Red) army is powerful because it is divided into two parts, its main army and its local army. The former can carry out . . . operational tasks not limited to any locality."[8] By this combination of forces of Chinese can apply their tactics of "exhausting the enemy." Chinese patience is a weapon. Exhaust the enemy. Wear him down. Wait for him to move first. They are never in a great hurry to win a war. The Communist leaders are a patient lot and they like to hold their enemies on the watchful-waiting edge of armed conflict.

> "A Communist war which lasts ten years may be surprising to other countries, but for us this is only the preface. Historical experience is written in blood and iron."—*Mao Tse-tung*.

The PLA is trying to modernize its gigantic infantry. The bulk of its forces in Korea have been fighting along conventional military lines, but there is also reason to examine the PLA's guerrilla past because the army has a guerrilla future, whether its regular forces are defeated or not. The PLA's partisan warfare future does not lie primarily in Korea, but in Burma, Indo-China, and Southeast Asia, where Communists not only are following the guerrilla strategy and tactics of the Chinese Reds, but where some of them are receiving guidance and material assistance from the Peking

---

[8] Yenan radio broadcast, 13 October 1946.

Government. Chinese Reds have provided the pattern of revolt for all Communist groups of Asia. Governments now seated in Asiatic countries adjacent to China may some day find themselves upset and ousted because of their failure to study and combat these Chinese principles of guerrilla warfare.

Some of the minor tactics and ruses which are inherent in Chinese guerrilla warfare have already been described. These and others should be known and studied, but also important is a general knowledge of the over-all Chinese concepts. It is often difficult to hang on a guerrilla war the label of "strategical direction." However, this form of war and resistance, as conceived and applied by the Red hierarchy, has a definite element of strategy in it. Here are the actual Chinese Communist concepts on guerrilla warfare, some of which we may see applied in the future:

"Select the tactic of seeming to come from the east but attacking from the west; avoid the solid, attack the hollow; attack; withdraw, deliver a lightning blow, seek a lightning decision."[9]

All partisan strategy must be based primarily on alertness, mobility, and attack. It must be adjusted to the enemy situation, the terrain, the lines of communication, the relative strengths, the weather, and the situation of the people. The key to the Chinese approach lies in the last word—*people*. "The major task is to arouse and organize the masses. This includes training guerrilla units and local armed forces." This consolidation, says Mao Tse-tung, is essential to maintain during a long war. "Without consolidation, one will have no strength for further expansion. In guerrilla warfare, if one only thinks about expansion but forgets about consolidation, he will not be able to stand up under enemy attack.... The correct policy is expand on *bases* of consolidation."[10]

Where can successful guerrilla warfare be most advantageously waged? Mao has studiously stated that small countries offer little possibility for successful guerrilla resistance because they lack land space.[10] "In a large territory an enemy is usually lacking in a suffi-

---

[9] Mao Tse-tung, *Yu Chi Chan (Guerilla Warfare)*, published in China, 1937, (translated by Colonel Samuel B. Griffith, USMC), copyright by the *Marine Corps Gazette*.

[10] Mao Tse-tung, *The Strategic Problems of Guerrilla Warfare against Japan*, published in China, 1938.

cient number of troops to occupy it all in force; therefore he is vulnerable to guerrilla attacks." Bases form the "rear areas" for partisan warfare. There are three kinds of guerrilla bases: Mountains; plains; and lakes, rivers, and inlets. The mountains are the most suitable. Guerrilla war and its strategy are inseparable from the conflict and strategy of regular armies. There must be a clear understanding of the relation between the two. At certain periods guerrilla units should be expanded in area of conflict and size of forces; at other periods they should consolidate. All such decisions should be based on the circumstances.

What are the circumstances and conditions? Mao and his generals have worked out a set of guiding principles which have strategical and tactical merit.[11]

> When the enemy is on the strategic offensive he is fighting on exterior lines; we are thus on the strategic defensive, fighting on interior lines. *This is the enemy's first form of encirclement.*
>
> However, we have numerical superiority since the enemy advances toward us along separate routes from his exterior lines. Consequently we adopt a policy of taking the offensive in our battles and campaigns and we operate on exterior lines. We thus encircle each separate enemy unit which advances on us. *This is our first form of encirclement.*
>
> Perceiving that guerrilla bases are in an enemy's area, each (according to Mao) is encircled by the enemy on three or four sides.
> *This is the enemy's second form of encirclement.*
>
> However, if we analyze our various (regular army) bases and their inter-relation, plus the relation of multiple guerrilla bases to the regular army's front lines, then we are encircling portions of the enemy. *This is our second form of encirclement.*
>
> Since we and the enemy confront each other with *two types* of encirclement it is very much like a game of *wei chi*.[12]
>
> If internationally we can build up an anti-foreign front in the Pacific, making China a strategic unit and also making the Soviet Union and satellites into other strategic units, we shall have one more encirclement than the enemy. We shall then be fighting along exterior lines in the Pacific. (In 1938

---

[11] Mao Tse-tung, "On Establishing Guerrilla Bases" *People's China*, 1 August 1950.
[12] A kind of chess based on principles of encirclement and counter-encirclement.

Mao Tse-tung concluded this point had no practical significance against Japan, but added, "yet one cannot say there is no such prospect; the world is changing . . .")

Mao Tse-tung has outlined the steps necessary in the realization of a sound guerrilla policy—

(1) Arouse and organize the people.
(2) Achieve internal political unity.
(3) Establish guerrilla bases.
(4) Equip and arm the forces.
(5) Recover one's own national strength.
(6) Destroy the enemy's national strength.
(7) Regain lost territory.

He stresses that every part of the effort must be *organized*. The steps should be taken, he says, in the order given. It is a Communist sin to arm guerrillas before they have been politically indoctrinated, or before their bases have been established. The organization and size of the resistance units will be determined by the people. In a general war of resistance (large scale guerrilla war), the people in an area should organize themselves into two groups, one *self-defense,* the other *combat*. All males from 16 to 45 are considered eligible for these two categories of partisans. Even guerrilla war must be financed, so the Chinese Communist slogan is, "Those with money give money." As regards discipline, the Red axiom states that, "It should increase with the size of the unit." [13]

Guerrillas, Mao Tse-tung has written, "should be as cautious as virgins and as quick as rabbits . . . (They) are like innumerable gnats which, by biting a giant in front and rear, eventually exhaust him."

Much of what the Chinese Communists did guerrilla-wise against the Japanese has been overplayed and exaggerated by the Yenan "public relations bureau" and the foreign correspondents, who further projected the Red statistics to the Western world. Communist claims were out of proportion to their accomplishments for the Reds devoted a part of their military

---

[13] Mao Tse-tung, *Yu Chi Chan,*

effort, in World War II, toward their brothers in Nationalist uniforms. The Communists suffered heavy losses from the Japanese Army—which they never did drive out of China, even though they forced it to remain in cities and along communication lines. These points had military significance and were held despite recurring interruptions from Red guerrillas against the Japanese.

However, concerning the Chinese Communist guerrillas of World War II, it may be said that—

(1) They were strategically well conceived and directed;

(2) Tactically they demonstrated originality and conducted operations with keen skill, resulting in local successes;

(3) Organizationally, the Chinese Reds made the utmost of meager resources;

(4) The guerrilla leaders had great patience, the soldiers great endurance.

However, they did not win the war in China, nor did they inflict any lasting defeats on the Japanese; but they killed many men.

There are potential Red guerrilla bands in Asia, which are as yet unarmed and unorganized because they lack materiel and experienced leaders. The Chinese Communists have already indicated their intention to provide both. They have scheduled the killing of more men.

But the Red hierarchy is now forced to take a different view of guerrilla war. Originally the Yenan warlords worked out a fine set of guerrilla principles and tactics, borrowing heavily from the partisan experiences of other nationalities.

The Chinese did not invent guerrilla tactics, although they may claim to have done so. However, if they are really inventive, the Reds can now go to work on a new and different set of tactics. Mao Tse-tung, whose writing has been so prolific on the subject of war, confesses that his government is plagued by 400,000 anti-Red guerrillas. He probably is exaggerating the strength figures to make the problem appear big, but for all of his wisdom and available military forces, he has not begun to eliminate armed unrest in his Communist paradise.

Photo by Col. David D. Barrett.

THE CHINESE REDS LACK INSIGHT INTO THE MENTAL CHARACTERISTICS AND HABITS OF WESTERNERS.

The author and Major John W. Collins III, immediately following their release from the Communist lines, arrive at the distant end of the bridge over the Sungari River. They are met by Major General Robert H. Soule, then Military Attache (left), and by Colonel Edward T. Cowen and Mr. O. Edmund Clubb, Consul General in Changchun (right).

Red Psychological Warfare—Good or Bad?

The Korean conflict is the first war in which we may expect that our enemy will seek to change the political ideas of our men who are in their hands as prisoners.

Red officers may win Chinese friends but they don't know how to influence Westerners. The psychological warfare methods employed by the Red Chinese against a foreign foe are not nearly as good as their psychological approach to the Chinese people. The Communists induced wholesale surrender and defection in the Civil War, but their simple techniques apply only to that form of conflict; they are no good today. They have already failed to induce any desertion or easy surrenders by psychological warfare techniques and devices, such as surrender passes. However, the Peking hierarchy believes it has some well-tried formulas which will convert their American prisoners to the Red cause. Hundreds of saddened families in several of the United Nations are now wondering about the fate of their brave men who are now in Chinese prison camps. Will the Communists who "sold" so many foreigners in the Yenan days, be able to convert, in some degree, the prisoners they now hold? The Soviets did it to large German and Japanese prisoner groups. Why can't the Chinese succeed with some they now have under guard?

Perhaps because of their long isolation in the rural areas, or more probably by virtue of their narrow education, the Chinese Reds lack insight into western mental characteristics and habits. The closest official contact which the Chinese Red hierarchy has had with Westerners occurred during the era of General George C. Marshall's peace effort in 1946-47. The Red Chinese leaders, both military and civilian, were placed in the Executive Headquarters and on the various truce teams. Americans learned much about them but recorded little for official histories. The gaps of misunderstanding were many; the verbal conflicts frequent; but differences in the politics of the three sides—American, Chinese Nationalist and Chinese Communist—were not alone the barrier to understanding and agreement; the Reds utterly failed to understand their American colleagues, on even the smallest issues. They often grew angry and insulting. This was expected, but the Communists also demonstrated poor psychology in their timing. Their's was a consistent failure to understand American reaction. The conflicts multiplied, and when they reached levels higher than the truce teams, there was still the inflexibility of Red minds to contend with. No common ground seemed to exist as a basis of negotiation. Communist Chinese ways are devious underneath an outward crudeness. In negotiations it is essential to look for the hidden motives which may be long range in character. Red "face" is of the moment; they can break a promise later and feel no loss of "face." In the Civil War and in Korea, Chinese truce negotiations were devices to gain time.

The Communists were naive to the point where it approached the humorous. They were suspicious to the point of exasperation. They sulked, and rarely displayed a sense of humor. Their utter seriousness of political purpose blinded them and confused the negotiations. At one moment they would react like children; the next, like hardened fanatics. Discounting all of their nasty accusations, which surprised no one, they blocked many of their own efforts through their sheer stupidity and ignorance of Americans. Socially they were always ill at ease, so some friendly gestures were made, in an effort to help them along. The response was cold. I was not a participant in these affairs on the high level at Nanking, but I observed many Communist officers and generals in Peking, Mukden, and Changchun, during these trying and fruitless negotiations. Later, when captured, I was imprisoned, and put on trial by some of the very generals who had visited my home socially in Changchun and drunk my wine, I saw the Communist officer in a different light. It is not my intent to enlarge upon these differences, which were obvious in the trial of Major Collins and myself. My only point is that, during our trial,[14] the Communists made extreme efforts to produce an international incident of our capture; to place us in jeopardy with our own government,[15] and to falsify the entire circumstances of capture—but with such poor and naive psychology as to contradict their own ulterior objectives. Their processes of interrogation were crude, sometimes laughable, and their verbal approach was even worse.

In such a trial, the Communists always publicize the information in a false, distorted form, and one wonders why they resort to any attempt to break a prisoner.

US Marine officers who negotiated with Chen Yi's officer-

---

[14] We were 34 days in solitary confinement (2 months in prison) in Harbin, during which time we were separately placed on trial before a special military tribunal. These sessions never lasted less than six hours and went as high as 11, during which time we were not allowed out of one chair. Physical torture was threatened; never used. The Communists tried desperately to get us to confess to a variety of phony charges; they were unsuccessful! However, we barely escaped a people's court from which death sentences are more than common.

[15] They sought classified information, tried to get us to confess to a variety of charges (including espionage) and endeavored to trick us into statements usable as propaganda.

thugs in Shantung over the release of American prisoners, told the same story. The Communists simply do not understand Americans. I believe that the Chinese Reds are even harder to negotiate with than the Soviets. Any American officers who ever had to deal with the Chinese on a peace settlement should strengthen their patience, yet be prepared to be tough. It will be an unpleasant task at best. The sessions will be long and tiring.

We have never had an army whose elements have been susceptible to "surrender passes" thrown out on the front lines by a foreign enemy. However, one would think that the Chinese Reds could improve the crude passes used in Korea, and could make them more readable and more interesting to Americans! The Chinese are hopeless at psychological warfare against Americans, but they are also very conceited.

The UN soldiers who are prisoners in China are getting courses of indoctrination. These unfortunate men are being exploited for two Communist purposes—propaganda and future influence on American politics. The Red scheming and efforts toward these ends are clever; some are even subtle. There is trickery involved, too. Chinese broadcasts have indicated that the UN soldiers were not briefed on what to expect. Perhaps there was no time for this, but it is worthy of future consideration.

The first use the Chinese Reds make of prisoners is to elicit statements from them which can be projected as propaganda. Sick of combat, depressed by capture, tired and hungry, a prisoner may be ripe for an interrogator who questions, "Do you really want to fight us?"

"No, but . . ."

The "No" is all that the propagandist interrogator will use when he prepares a statement saying, "Lieutenant Brown, of US Army unit so-and-so, has freely stated that he does not believe the United States should be attacking the Chinese people."

The interrogations are not all formal. A casual reply to a slant-eyed interpreter, or an overheard remark, is all the Chinese need to inflate their propaganda balloons. When hard up, they will dream up false phraseology and tack on a known name as the source of the statement. You have only to read some of the statements put out by the Chinese and Korean Reds to realize that they never fell from American lips.

Americans are fortunately accustomed to free expression of thought; but militarily they, sometimes, talk too easily. The Chinese Communists know this, and arrange clever pitfalls. The commissars can harass a silent prisoner, by long talks or violent accusations, to a point where the prisoner's temper will unleash replies of defense. Once they get the prisoner talking, the next device is to lead him subtly down the path to a point at which he is off-guard. The prisoner is made to think he is winning the argument. A commissar will bait him thus, and then throw in a question that the prisoner may not fear answering, even though it goes slightly against his own case. So the prisoner briefly concedes a minor point, in order to focus the argument on a bigger, more important issue. But the commissar's work for the day is done right there. Out of all the argument and wordage, he has been seeking one statement which, if stripped of all the other wordage, will make a "confession." The propaganda "rewrite" men will put the prisoner's mistake into shape for broadcast and publication. Soldier gripes can become pro-Communist propaganda on short notice. If an argument with a Chinese Communist led somewhere other than into their propaganda mill it might be worth something. However, one's words are always used for purposes for which one never intended them.

It was a Red technique in the Civil War to broadcast purported "confessions and statements" by Nationalist officers which would do them personal and professional damage upon return to their own territory. Some of these admissions the officers had made under duress; others were pure fabrication. Recalcitrant prisoners should anticipate Red execution of this technique.

The Red attempt at conversion, at the beginning, will usually be smooth. It will be prefaced by fair treatment of the particular prisoners being addressed. The most disciplined and incorruptible Chinese guards will be used over the prisoners, so that a good impression of the PLA will be registered. The prisoners will be fed decently, not necessarily on fish and rice, but on potatoes, soup, and meat. The interpreters will be little men who will ease in and out, telling the prisoners how they learned English, perhaps how they served under the Nationalists and how happy they are under the "new conditions." Watch out for these sly rascals. They are the puppets of the commissars. The objective will be to instill in a prisoner the feeling that "These guys aren't so bad."

Contact increases, familiarity grows, and conversation widens. Fear has been eliminated. It is simply a matter of waiting. The quarters and living facilities will be crude; the Communists will explain that "it cannot be otherwise for prisoners of war, even though we do not want to fight you." The stage is set. The Reds have repeated their stock cliche: "We are not at war with the American *people,* we are only against the imperialists who rule." Captor patience will wear longer than prisoner patience. When the internees ask for reading matter, they will get *Thunder out of China, Red Star over China, Twin Stars of China* and related literature. Then, into any reading will be inserted the present-day Communist literature, in English. It will not be readily accepted by the prisoners, but time weighs heavily; one must read something. Atrocities, well built-up and seemingly documented, may cause the pages to be flipped over or discarded in disgust but other portions will be read.

From this point the Red indoctrination effort will get down to cases and become intensified. The prisoners will be asked to explain the whys of past foreign policies in the Orient. The prisoners may fumble for lack of historical knowledge, but the interpreters and commissars will regurgitate the answers they have so well studied. The seeds of doubt and confusion will be sown. Prisoner differences in ideas will be fomented and exploited. Then, out of the confusion and conflict, the Chinese will emerge with their solutions. "You have not heard our side" they will cry. "You lack perception, just as do your leaders, who are so confused." Always the Communists will seek to disturb, to upset, to confuse, and to sow doubt. "Can you explain why your nation did this—and then that?" Pound, pound, pound; but always on issues that the Reds have studied well beforehand and have answers for. But the issues can be ones that many of the Americans have not studiously delved into. The Communists prepare their cases like lawyers going to court. Their opponents' rebuttals are weaker for lack of similar preparation.

What will be the result? It is doubtful that the Chinese Reds can ever really convert, at best, more than a small fraction; but they will succeed in confusing and misleading individual minds on subjects that they had never before analyzed. Doubt and mental confusion might smolder for a short period but would dissipate quickly upon return to lands not enslaved. In the end, the Communists would probably engender more dislike and contempt than acceptance. A possible frequent result might be a prisoner conclusion that "I don't like these devils, but let's leave them alone!"

The Red dogmas of Communism will often be dinned into the ears of prisoners. But our foe is becoming better understood as his aggressiveness grows more apparent. The Chinese Reds sincerely believe they are clever convincers. They work desperately hard to prepare rationalizations of their own case, and to indoctrinate all who will read or listen; but they are stupid enough to believe that their own vocal and paper propaganda can conceal the blood they have so wantonly spilled. Their psychological approach toward Americans is extraordinarily inept.

With shells and bullets the Chinese Communists attack the bodies of their opponents; with propaganda they attack the minds of their prisoners. But their propaganda makes little headway with Americans. The Chinese Reds are proud of a little Christmas tree which they cut and decorated in North Korea in December 1950, for it served as a pleasant little item upon which to launch a propaganda campaign. Happy over the fact that they were still alive, yet despondent over capture, 160 American soldiers were led into a decorated hall at Christmas time. The Christmas tree was only one of the decorations. The hall was hung with slogans written in English, taken from the Red propaganda mill. According to the Chinese report,[16] of rather doubtful accuracy, "A tall

---

[16] "Christmas at a P.O.W. Camp," *People's China,* 1 January 1951.

American . . . lit the red candles while several others took out their notebooks and copied down the slogans." It will be some time before the truth of this propaganda account can be ascertained, but it seems fairly clear that American prisoners are being worked on feverishly.

Communist periodicals are now claiming success in their conversion program. In February 1951, they published an article, "May We Be Heard," that purportedly had the signed endorsement of 400 American POW's. This article had all the current Communist pleas and cliches: "Let China in the UN"; "We (Americans) say, 'Pull out of Korea'"; "We (American soldiers) are ashamed"; "We can understand Chinese intervention." The signatures on the paper, I have no doubt, are genuine—but the names were probably obtained by trickery. A meal or two postponed, a false front to the paper, or any number of well-known Chinese tricks could have been resorted to in order to get such signatures.

This organized Red effort has been well documented by a returned soldier, Corporal Douglas L. Miller, USA, in his article, "They Couldn't Convert Me!" which appeared in *Parade* magazine on 27 May 1951. Corporal Miller told how he was tortured for two days, then given the silk-glove treatment of propaganda talks and lectures. "We want you to spread Communism in your army," the Reds said. One day an officer handed Miller a blank piece of paper. "You sign. We see." Corporal Miller relates that, "I signed, and that's all I know about it." The Reds released Miller to his own lines; but his signature is no doubt now prefaced by a text that could embarrass him, if it were not known that the Red propaganda injection has not "taken," and that Corporal Miller is a wiser man in the ways of the enemy because of his experience.

Prisoners can be employed as a means of exerting pressure. The Chinese know that prisoners' relatives at home are worried and anxious, and happy to believe almost any written word coming from their unfortunate loved ones. The Chinese technique is to have Red agents in the United States approach the relatives of prisoners. These agents try to sell Red propaganda.

The Chinese have only begun to use prisoners. They may later be used as hostages in political bargaining.

Prisoners Are Judged and Treated Unevenly

Perhaps it was the poor man's shoulder patch that prompted it. The Chinese in Korea knew the Indianhead insignia well. Some may have seen the countless bullet-torn Chinese bodies among many American dead who wore that particular insignia. The US 2d Division had paid a terrific price to delay the Chinese in December 1950, and it was in this phase of the Korean conflict that the Reds of China had their first real taste of American fire power and tough resistance. However, it may have been just the sadistic brutality which reveals itself at intervals wherever Chinese Communists fight.

This American soldier of the 2d Division was captured about 12 February 1951, near Hoensong. By the rules of land warfare, he should be alive today. By the rules of humanity, the Chinese never should have poured gasoline over his body; and by the laws of chance, he never should have survived the ordeal of fire, to be recaptured. This nameless American soldier died of second degree burns on 24 February, three days after he was found by UN troops.[17] This murder does not stand alone in the documentation of Chinese atrocities in Korea. There are other cases of American deaths just as unfortunate, brutal and wanton. Does this inhuman murder of prisoners represent a fixed PLA policy, or is it the result of the PLA's inability to control sadistic elements?

The current PLA prisoner of war policy was developed when the Chinese Reds were numerically inferior to their opponents in the China Civil War. It was then a policy pursued solely to win military adherents for the Chinese Communist military forces. It is dangerous to project this prisoner of war policy too far into the future, for it was tailored primarily to fit the Civil War. The motive is utterly selfish and not really humanitarian, although it is thinly camouflaged as such. In a War with foreign powers using conventional weapons, the PLA might continue this present policy;

---

[17] From the first report to the United Nations, by General Matthew B. Ridgway.

but in a struggle involving any special weapons the Chinese do not possess, the PLA is capable of replacing its present prisoner of war policy with one much more stringent—even with one as brutal as that affected by the North Koreans against their American prisoners in 1950.

For the record, however, it should be stated that, until 1951, the Chinese adhered, for the most part, to the policy of fair treatment for prisoners. But, as a commissar stated, "It should be noted that our (Red) policy of leniency did not apply to all our foes alike. Our policy of discriminating between officers and men . . . was announced in 1947. According to a manifesto issued by the PLA on October 10, severe punishment would be meted out to the people's No. 1 enemy, Chiang Kai-shek. His top accomplices were also declared national war criminals. However, we announced that those who had committed crimes against the people would be given a last chance to lighten or commute their eventual sentences by severing their relations with the reactionary regiment and rendering meritorious service to the revolutionary cause." Thus spoke Chiu Kang,[18] a member of the Political Department of the People's Revolutionary Military Council in 1950.

In the Civil War, the fundamental policy was to win over prisoners of war, "reeducate them and gradually remould their theology and behavior so as to transform them into new persons who may be of service" to Communism. "When a group of prisoners is taken we first allay their fears by our considerate treatment. They are neither searched nor forced to give up their personal belongings. Those with injuries receive medical care . . ." This may have been the intention. However, in actuality, one can expect anything. When captured, Major Collins and I were searched and we had several of our personal belongings physically torn from us before we reached the battalion command post. The Chinese Reds know the value of combat intelligence and they interrogate prisoners. One is thoroughly searched when in the division area. Medical treatment is always of questionable effectiveness if given. The Reds do not have a sufficient number of doctors

---

[18] Chiu Kang, in *People's China*, August 1950.

for their own troops. Major Collins and I lost our first-aid packets to clawing troops within the first hour. Captured officers are quickly separated from the enlisted men, and Chinese Reds search among groups for officers who might try to pass as low-ranking soldiers. They found in the Civil War that hundreds of Nationalist officers sought safety in the enlisted ranks. It is not a recommended practice. Besides, officers of UN forces are not inclined to hide. Junior officers are segregated from their seniors; they receive kindlier treatment and a different form of political reeducation, since, according to the Chinese view, they "respond to reeducation more readily than generals." With commissioned foreign officers, the Oriental view is that, being of the "upper classes" these officers cannot become revolutionaries in a short period. However, the Communists work on them at length to make them "politically neutral."

I knew one general who, captured in the April 1946 Battle of Changchun, was given the full political indoctrination treatment until late 1947. The Reds finally gave up trying to convert him and he was released to Nationalist territory. I never found out what happened to him. He may have had to take a second political course, for I believe he is still in China. One thing is certain, the higher ranking the prisoner, the more attention he will receive from the political officers. The effort in his case will not be directed toward converting him, but tricking him, to gain intelligence and for propaganda purposes. Torture will be threatened; it may also be used.

The real purpose of the fair treatment of the lower ranks was to reduce resistance and prompt surrenders. This is not working in the Korean War. The Communists may yet jettison their established policy of fair treatment.

The mob scenes in cities of China are growing in violence and number. The cry for human blood is on the lips of thousands of Chinese who, without really knowing why, are murdering men and women in the streets. Communist leaders are building up the mobs and fanning hatred ,and brutality. Foreigners in China wouldn't believe, back in 1948 (and even later), that the Communists were planning purges; yet there was evidence in Soviet history that these slaughterings were bound to come, in China. And one only had to read the Communist statements to understand that, once securely in the saddle, they were going to stamp out opposition by direct action—by slicing the heads off human necks! When Mao Tse-tung said, in his 1947 Christmas Day speech,[19] "It is necessary to reorganize and purify the ranks of the Party," the task and tone of the future were made known. If Mao thought the *Party* impure in spots he certainly had in mind elements outside the Party which were dangerous as well. The penalty for political sin in China today is "purification"; China has no "Siberia" to which to exile. It is a cut and dried matter—"purification" is death at the hands of a mob. Some victims may be honored by a formal pistol shot in the back of the head. Today's purges, conducted as they are with the help of hysterical, screaming multitudes, will be expanded. An era of wanton bloodshed has begun. Some of the Chinese people, having been fed on a diet of executions, are sure to look for more victims. There are 30 US nationals who have been imprisoned in China for an extended period,[20] not to mention our soldiers held as prisoners of war. At any time the former group may be turned over to a mob which the commissars could incite to urinate on these helpless Americans—if not to kill them outright. The fate of prisoners of war will hinge on several factors. They may be fairly treated for purposes of political indoctrination, but their fate will probably turn with the tides of the Korean War. These military prisoners are hostages. The Communists will use them to deter the United Nation's use of unconventional weapons, such as the atomic bomb.

The executions by gasoline and fire, the bayoneting of wounded, and other Chinese atrocities on the Korean battleground, are not believed to be the direct result of orders from higher Chinese authority. Red officers cannot always control the sadistic elements of their units. Higher authority probably does not, however, even discipline such murderers. Such brutal killings will occur again,

---

[19] The Present Situation and Tasks.
[20] State Department announcement, 21 May 1951.

but the real danger lies in the hysteria bred of purges extending to the PLA troops who are already involved in a sanguinary struggle. This may breed an even greater number of battlefront atrocities.

From blowing bugles and banging gongs on the front lines to the exploiting and murdering of prisoners, the PLA is making use of *all* tactics which may be expected to frighten us, individually or as a united force, into surrender. Whereas the United States is developing and perfecting new military weapons, Communist China is making full use of the ones available to it. They are not modern weapons, but they can be cruel and unorthodox ones. The Chinese Communists count heavily on their tactic of generating fear. We should not let them frighten us.

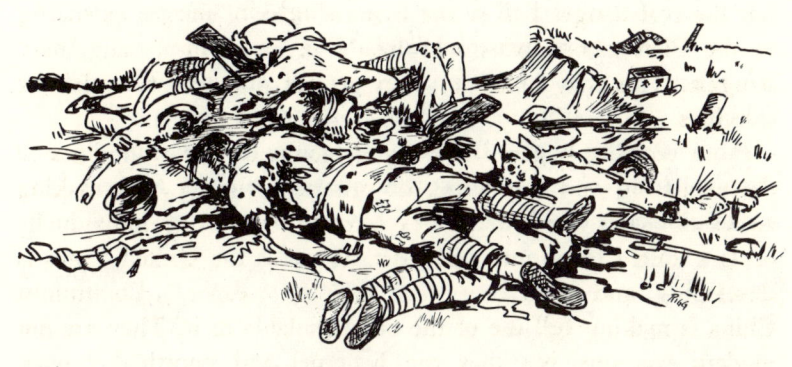

Chapter 8

FOUNDATION OF VICTORY

The PLA's "Plan to Liberate Asia"

Some may be unwilling to give credence to fact, but the PLA does plan to conquer Asia, from Japan to India. It may be argued that the Chinese cannot accomplish that objective. The answer, of course, lies in the future, but there is every indication that the Chinese Communists will try to carry out this ambitious plan. Whether or not the United Nations' military forces accomplish some form of final defeat of the Chinese and the North Korean Red Armies in Korea—or at least slow that aggression to a halt—the Chinese will continue the expansion of their armed forces and employ them in an attempt to conquer Asia.

When one thumbs ahead into the unwritten pages of history and endeavors to footnote prophecies on the blank pages, he should have a sound basis for his attempt at a prognosis. In briefest form, these are some of the indications that Red China is readying herself for further aggression—

(1) The fact that Communist world revolution is anything but dead, and that the Chinese are well fitted and well located to alter the face of Asia, leaving Europe and the Middle East to the USSR;

(2) The Army of Red China is growing[1]—in size and strength, and is gaining modern equipment;

(3) The entry of the PLA into Korea proves the willingness of Peking to use its army in aggressions on foreign soil;

(4) The efforts which Red China is making to infiltrate into and organize fifth columns and related subversive elements in neighboring Asiatic countries;

Photo by Colonel Edward T. Cowen.

WHERE THE CIVIL WAR STARTED.

From this mud-brick command post in Yenan, the Chinese Red hierarchy plotted the conquest of a nation.

Beneath their ostensible humbleness before foreign officers these Chinese leaders concealed their genuine hatred of the United States.

Left to right—General Lin Piao, General Chou En-lai, General Chu Teh, Colonel Thomas Taylor, Colonel David D. Barrett, Colonel Mason Wright, Mao Tse-tung, General Yeh Chien-ying.

On this visit to Yenan in October 1944, the United States Army officers pictured above represented the China-Burma-India Theater of Operations.

(5) The sympathy and material assistance given by the PLA to the Viet Minh forces in Indo-China;

---

[1] On 28 January 1950 the Communist sponsored *China Weekly Review* (Shanghai) said, "When the whole of China is liberated in 1950 . . . (it) will necessitate an even larger number of military administrative and educational personnel than the 7,000,000 at present on government payrolls."

(6) The many pronouncements of Mao Tse-tung, which have consistently stressed "foreign encirclement" and "the liberation of the more than a billion oppressed people of the East." [2] The Chinese have picked up the pan-Asiatic torch which the Japanese were forced to drop. The Red leaders of China feel that they are the saviors of Asia. They are gaining strength in this role because no one else has come up with a more moving formula than that of the Communists;

(7) The rapid and successful growth of the PLA has not only intoxicated the Chinese military hierarchy to a high state of aggressiveness but it has affected the rest of the Chinese Communists as well. None of them believe that their armed forces can be defeated in war.

The above indications of the PLA's ambitions justify careful evaluation. Who would have predicted, in 1945, that within four years the ragged and route-order forces of Yenan would be governing China? Today the PLA, an out of date juggernaut yet militarily effective, stands dominant over the armies of all Asia. As a national army, it is only a few years old. We know it has weaknesses, that it is in a state of organizational transition; yet it has a record of ostensibly great achievement within the compass of a few years. From a poverty-stricken military conglomeration of guerrillas it rose to conquer a larger and better equipped enemy army, between 1945 and 1949.

How did the PLA defeat the Nationalist Army? We can better see the PLA's future capabilities if we examine the circumstances and facts of its rise to dominance. I do not choose to record here a history of the China Civil War, but simply to name the more significant factors which built one army up to strength and whittled another down to defeat. The causes of Nationalist defeat in China are many, but too many of them have been oversimplified in journalistic cliches—and some have been overlooked. Here are the more significant causes.

---

[2] Mao Tse-tung, "Present Situation and Our Tasks," 25 December 1947. This is not the most recent or most direct indication; others may be found in later speeches and articles by Mao.

Manchuria Upset the Balance

If the wastelands of Mongolia extended to the Yalu River, Nanking, and not Taiwan, would still be the seat of the Nationalist Government and UN soldiers would not have fought in Korea. One cannot argue with a land mass, however.

Manchuria's richness brought the Japanese to the mainland of Asia. Of all factors in the China Civil War, that invasion vaulted the Chinese Reds to their present military dominance of Asia. When the Communists of China were still hollowing out rocks to make mines for use against the Japanese, the United States dropped atomic bombs on Nagasaki and Hiroshima.

Ragged and poor, the Red military forces of China couldn't bring any semblance of formal military power to bear against the Japanese up to 1945; but with the collapse of the Japanese Kwantung Army and the Soviet dominance in Manchuria, the future of China's Red Army was made. The reservoir of manpower, factories, farms, and arms was there for the taking. With the generous assistance of the Soviet Army, the Chinese Reds immediately obtained the arms, gradually seized regions rich in manpower, and eventually occupied all of Manchuria, freeing Lin Piao's field army to swing the balance of military power in China proper.

From 1946 on, the Chinese Nationalists were constantly pointing to the Soviet help being given to the Communists, yet they were citing incidents and facts they were unable to substantiate. Captured Soviet weapons, reports of Russian officers with Communist battalions, were offered as evidence of Soviet assistance.

In April 1946 I had a long discussion, which was in the nature of an argument, with General Shiung Shih-huei,[3] who maintained that a battalion of Soviet troops had participated in the April 1946 Battle of Changchun. Having just returned from the very midst of this battle, I remarked that I had seen not the slightest evidence of any Soviet armed participation, although I had observed Japanese manning light tanks and field artillery. General Shiung was in-

---

[3] Chief of the Generalissimo's Field Headquarters in Mukden, Manchuria. He was the senior Nationalist commander in the Northeast, but General Tu Yu-ming was in actual command of the Nationalist troops. Because of divided authority and responsibility, both commanders were in constant conflict with each other.

sistent that his intelligence sources had actually seen Soviet troops in combat; but the weight of his argument was somewhat lessened when we compared notes as to the accuracy of his agents' reports. The same spies, which reported the Soviet battalion had given Shiung a variety of inaccurate reports on my activities during and after the battle. They said that I had been arrested by the Soviets, and that later I had been taken away in a truck by the Chinese Reds and imprisoned. Although I was treated with open hostility by the few Soviets remaining in Changchun, I was not arrested. Lacking transportation, my pilot and I often flagged down Red Chinese trucks to "hitch-hike" rides about the city. We were not made prisoners, as were the five American correspondents there.

On the subject of Soviet help to the Red Chinese, the Nationalists consistently missed the forest for the trees. In the first six months of Soviet occupation the Chinese Reds gained entry to the cities, obtained arms, and secured their biggest measure of Soviet assistance. So firmly entrenched were the Chinese Reds thereafter that there was no need for the Soviets to supply any advisors on the battalion, or even the division, level. Many observers have failed to grasp these facts.

Loot and Pillage

"It was like a scene from the French Revolution," a Soviet Russian[4] in Mukden told me, "the mob lurched down the street in a 'drunken' frenzy, waving pots, pans, door knobs, light fixtures, furniture, even doors—nothing was too small or too large for this looting mob to tear from the houses. Like locusts they swept through the residences and in a matter of minutes the homes were stripped bare of all furnishings."

This was mob looting—militarily insignificant but devastatingly destructive.

There were three phases to the looting of Manchuria: The organized industrial looting by the Soviets;[5] the undisciplined

---
[4] A former emigrant Russian who had been forced to take out Soviet citizenship papers during the Soviet Army's occupation. Because he is still in Manchuria and could be subjected to punishment for his confidences, I choose to keep his name secret.
[5] The author documented this looting in its final phases and later assisted the Pauley Mission in its summary of the effects of the pillage on China's industry.

pillaging by Chinese civilian mobs; and in between, and less publicized even to this date, the organized looting by Chinese Red military units. This looting by units was a quiet take-away of cotton spindles, cloth, metals, and light machinery. While it was overshadowed in over-all significance compared to the Soviet effort and the spectacular sacking of homes by the Chinese mobs, it was none the less highly important to the economy of Lin Piao's growing field army. The Chinese Reds were careful never to inhibit their tactical mobility by carrying away heavy machinery; but they looted from Mukden, Changchun, and other cities that materiel which could directly serve their military interests or indirectly through the manufacture of shoes, clothing, and related quartermaster supplies.

There were other items the Chinese Reds also sought and gained. One day in early March 1946 a Japanese army major knocked at my door in the former Yamato Hotel in Mukden. I received him somewhat skeptically and with a measure of hostility. I knew he wanted something. Minutes could tell, and they did; for after the rough treatment received from the Soviets the Japanese were still too frightened to spend much time running about in uniform.

"He is a medical officer," remarked the interpreter who stood near the Japanese major. Defeated and cowed by the Soviets,[6] this man in uniform was still doctor and officer enough to care for his several hundred military patients. He was not afraid to appear publicly in uniform, although he was then coming into a new conqueror's realm—for the Nationalists had just assumed control of Mukden and were delighted to find any stray Japanese in military dress.

The case was simple enough; the major wanted me to see his looted military hospital—which I did a day later. Foul smelling, sickeningly unsanitary, the hospital was a collection of wards wherein ex-Kwantung Army soldiers lay dying on the cold floors.

"The major only wants some UNRRA medical supplies and food," said the interpreter; and the major nodded, with a bow.

The drama of the story was in the looting—not the request.

---

[6] The Soviet Army had evacuated Mukden a few days previously.

Dying men are not hard to recognize. There were many. The military hospital had been looted, not only of its surgical instruments and several hundred beds, but its Japanese technicians as well.

Photo by the Author.

CHINESE COMMUNISTS AND SOVIETS LOOTED THIS AIRCRAFT FACTORY, NEXT TO THE GREAT MUKDEN ARSENAL, IN 1945.
The Chinese stripped wheels from motor vehicles and airplanes and mounted them on horse carts.

Who did the looting? The Soviets? No it was principally the *Pa Lu*—the Chinese Reds. The Soviets had taken the beds, but the Chinese Communists took the technicians and the nurses. There was some doubt as to which party got the major share of the ex-ray equipment and surgical instruments.

Sewage was backing up in Mukden, due to the Communist interruption of electric power. Plague was already taking its toll. The Japanese soldiers continued to die at the rate of a dozen a day. There were other hospitals—civilian ones—in which conditions were just as poor. Lin Piao's "People's Army" had supplied itself, in a brief few days, from the people who were a few years later to cheer the army as a liberator. This was how the present Fourth

Field Army solved one of its initial logistical requirements. Its medical service was already well trained, even though foreign.[7]

The technique was applied not only to hospitals, but also to stores of materiel.

"They attacked us," the Soviet Army officer said. "We shot at them, but our guards were too few. They were overwhelmed and had to flee!" The Soviet officer in Changchun gave me this explanation of how and why the Chinese Reds took over a military depot of Kwantung Army supplies in Changchun in 1945. I found little variance to this pattern. The Soviets placed a few guards over arms depots; but they were always "attacked." I confirmed this several times over. The attacks were usually at night. Whether the Chinese were invited to attack at a given time I cannot verify, but the results were always the same. The Reds of China got the arms. "We didn't want to kill Chinese; we didn't want to favor the Communists, but what could we do?" This was the conventional cliché used by the Soviet Army men in Manchuria. The Soviets even went so far as to photograph daylight "attacks" by the Chinese Reds, so as to document the Russian case. Thus Lin Piao's men in ochre obtained the arms with which a new field army was built. There was only the question of getting men to carry these arms and the Chinese had plans made to accomplish this, too.

"Liberators" of Manchuria

Knowing that he was not strong enough to hold the lower Manchurian towns and cities, Lin Piao's initial recruiting effort was to herd together a few hundred men out of each of the smaller towns and to gather a thousand or so from each of the larger. This he did under the banner of a Chinese liberator.

Communications were not yet established with China proper. The Manchurian people knew that the Communist army had fought the Japanese and did occupy a recognized anti-Japanese position. The Civil War had not yet formally begun. What the

---

[7] Some of the Japanese medical personnel are still in Manchuria. Japanese PW's in Communist hands were estimated by Premier Shigeru Yoshida in July 1951 at 340,000 to 370,000, held in either the USSR, Red China, Outer Mongolia, or Soviet controlled territories.

Manchurians saw were uniformed Chinese, their own people in effect. The Reds proclaimed themselves to be "God-sent" liberators. The people were not overly receptive, but they had hated the Japanese and they were growing to hate the Soviets for their rape and pillage. It was logical that, under those conditions, the temper of the people ranged from a passive curiosity to a half-hearted interest in the Communists—not as Reds, but as representatives of a changed order. Some of the Japanese puppet troops, anxious to atone for their sin of past service under the red-dot flag, stripped off their collar-tabs and gladly changed allegiance. The Communists were careful about taking these men[8] under their flag. They didn't take too many at first, and when they did take more they scattered them thinly throughout the Red ranks. Selection was made not so much on a basis of guaranteed loyalty, but on that technical qualification. Red officers looked sheepishly at Japanese tanks and peered inside to view controls and switches they knew nothing about manipulating. The machines had to be moved out of Soviet Army-guarded compounds; so the drivers, most of them Japanese, went along to man them. With artillery it was much the same.

Into the Red China Maw Went Manchurians, Japanese, Koreans

Time was short. The Nationalists were moving armies northward and the Soviet occupation would not last forever. Already there were battles near the Great Wall. Towards the end of 1945, the Communists realized that it might be years before they again held the route from Chingwangtao to Mukden; so they gathered their rearguard forces to begin formal delaying action. As they fell slowly back to the north, delaying General Tu Yu-ming's armies, they recruited. (An interesting account of the situation at about this time is contained in the secret report of 5 February 1946 on Chinese Communist Activities, by an UNRRA Representative—see Appendix III.) Time did not permit lengthy po-

---

[8] Exactly how many Japanese puppet troops (i.e., Chinese and Manchurians) the PLA took over in 1945 is not known. In Manchuria, the Reds probably obtained at least 75,000 in 1945-46. The Nationalist government (according to the 1950 *China Handbook*) accepted the surrender of 650,000 puppet troops.

litical campaigning. Pressure and force were required and were used. So, out of each town and village, motley crews of reluctant men were marched, placed safely in the middle of the military columns with which they were to spend the next few years of their lives, or to die in battles to come. These were not men who marched forth to defend a new plot of Red-given land. They were sullen groups whose obedience was initially brought about by the bayonets that ringed them in. Some deserted; others were shot for trying. Some surrendered to the enemy in subsequent skirmishing; but most of them were guarded, quickly trained, handed guns and told to shoot—or be shot by the Kuomintang enemy. They were not the best soldiers, but their numbers added to the marching masses and by their presence they gave weight to the Red resistance campaign. But several things impressed them. For one, they never had heard so much talk in an army before— about a cause and about the purpose for fighting. Talk, talk, lecture, literature, slogans, songs. The commissars drummed and droned the cause of the crusade. Chinese or Japanese armies of the past had never been like this. Chang Tso-lin's and Chiang Hsueh-liang's war lord armies had molded soldiers, but never by talk. Then there was the *Pa Lu jen* (soldier) conduct that impressed the puppet "converts" and Manchurian conscripts. The discipline, the austerity, the reluctance to loot wantonly or for animal purposes; the *Pa Lu* officers, not arrogant and medal-bedecked, but watchful, alert men who cared for the needs of their soldiers. But always there was "the cause," the crusade for a new China. Whatever there was to dislike about their unsought military service, the new Manchurian soldiers had to admit that *this* army had a purpose, or at least it announced one.

What was the "enemy," the Nationalist Army, like? Would it be even better to join his forces, if military service was to be obligatory in the new era of peace? "Bloodsucking rapists who may now be tearing the clothes from your wives, sisters, and daughters! Befoulers of women, they are now occupying the territory you lived in. Fight them, so you can go back to your loved ones. Fight, so that the Red Army can return to protect your region and give you land you do not now possess!" This was the Party propaganda designed to keep Manchurians in the Red ranks.

The early Manchurian conscriptees never had a chance to see the other side. Taken away under duress, they were told that they must fight their way back and liberate their homes. There was no magic Communist formula that held tens of thousands of reluctant Manchurians in the Red ranks. It was a combination of circumstance, political indoctrination, the necessity to shoot back or get shot—and with this grew a measure of hatred for an enemy whom they did not really know. In addition to all of these factors, the Red military leaders exerted military control. Once within the military system, the Manchurian men found escape difficult and dangerous. The traditional obedience of Chinese masses to armed power was continuously in evidence.

The Chinese Reds integrated some ex-Japanese soldiers into their ranks in 1945-46. I saw them first in the 1946 Battle of Changchun, when I went up to the Red tanks which were refueling in the midst of combat. The tank crews seemed to be enjoying the battle and they grinned and waved as they crawled into their tanks to roll down the streets and shoot up Nationalist pillboxes. I had only to walk a few hundred yards to find some field artillery pieces which were being unhitched and placed in firing positions.[9]

In September 1948 a spokesman for the Survey Bureau of the Japanese Foreign Office stated to the press that an estimated 140,000 former soldiers and nurses of the Kwantung Army were either serving with the Chinese Communist Army or living in Chinese Red areas in Manchuria.

The ex-Japanese Army soldiers did not greatly increase the size of General Lin Piao's field army, but they occupied key positions in small armored and artillery units, serving also as aviation instructors, technicians, mechanics, nurses, and doctors. In 1947, the number of Japanese with Lin Piao's units in the field appeared to

---

[9] Not until I began this book did I discover that on 20 April 1946, a Japanese newspaper in Harbin, reporting on the fall of Changchun stated that "of the 60,000 Northeast Self-Government (Communist) troops, 200 were our (Japanese) countrymen; particularly, the tank unit engaged in the fierce battle of Changchun was composed entirely of Japanese military men captured by the Soviet Army." (This translation is from the *China Handbook* 1950.)

me to be noticeably less; but Communist officials in Harbin admitted to Major Collins and me that they had some Japanese members doing "auxiliary work."

Korean soldiers also were in evidence and often identified in Lin Piao's military ranks. I recall that, in 1947, there was at least one brigade, by Chinese terminology. The total number of Koreans in Lin Piao's field army by 1948 is hard to determine accurately. They may have totaled as much as 70,000; reports had them numbering as high as 100,000. General John R. Hodges' farewell statement to the South Korean Government, in 1948, charged that there were military and other connections between the North Koreans and the Chinese Communists in Manchuria. There was never any doubt about the intimate relations between the two forces, but it was hard to determine what proportion of Korean soldiers were indigenous to Manchuria (which has a large Korean population) and which were from North Korea.

The Fight for Manchuria

Originally numbering some 100,000[10] Red soldiers from Shantung and North China, Lin Piao built up this cadre to about 230,000 by April 1946. By this time he had lost the railway line, from the Great Wall to points north of Mukden in Manchuria. Lin's forces were fighting the desperate Battle of Ssupingkai (1946) after having militarily reduced the isolated Nationalist stronghold of Changchun. The great coal center of Fushun, and Anshan (the Pittsburgh of Asia) were being lost to the Nationalists, but North Korea and the Soviet territory around Dairen and Port Arthur offered sanctuaries for Lin's troops if they were pushed too far to the east and south. Later these points of refuge were used to Chinese Communist advantage, but at this time (May 1946), the bitter Lin Piao was fighting delaying actions northward to hold as many of the rich regions of Manchuria as possible.

Lin's combat units had moved in key with the pattern of the

---

[10] No accurate figures exist but this is a fair estimate. The New Fourth Army, from which many of Lin Piao's troops were drawn, numbered up to 180,000 troops. Lin Piao's initial invasion force which marched overland was believed at the time to number only about 30,000.

Soviet withdrawal. Now he had reached a point where his military actions were to be more of a deterrent to the Nationalist advances than Soviet obstructionism had been for the Soviets held only the big cities well behind him. Nationalist strength was growing. Two American-trained armies (New First and New Sixth) now added

Photo by the Author.

THESE US-TRAINED ARTILLERYMEN OF THE NATIONALISTS FOUGHT THE JAPANESE IN BURMA AND THE CHINESE REDS IN MANCHURIA.

When this picture was taken, the new First Army held a 180-mile front against General Lin Piao's field Army. The battery commander (right) was killed soon after this engagement. A few of the men of this Nationalist army became Red soldiers; but most were killed or wounded, or escaped to Taiwan. Their combat record was excellent.

their fire power and flexibility to General Tu Yu-ming's Northeast China Command. Lin's divisions had barely emerged from their old guerrilla past. Red units were padded with Manchurian manpower and studded with Japanese artillery and a few tanks, but they were neither consistent organizationally nor uniform in strength. The battles were growing larger; the weight of artillery fire had begun to have more telling effect on the outcome than maneuver. The Communists did not have a preponderance of heavier weapons and large caliber ammunition supply was critically short. Depots were scattered and the Reds were generally lacking in motor transport. Furthermore, Lin Piao's officers were having to move divisions and not battalions; they were discovering that this was a new form of warfare with which they were not too familiar.

The 1946 Battle of Ssupingkai could have been decisive. It was a toe-to-toe slugfest, with the final outcome influenced by good generalship and a preponderance of artillery. It was the first real battle (by our standards) of the Civil War campaign in Manchuria. The Communists fought well and many died. But the Communists were outnumbered. Red infantry outfought the Nationalists, but the latter's artillery out-gunned the Reds and slaughtered Communist infantry. Nationalist generalship forced Lin's hand when General Tu Yu-ming weakened his distant southern front (about 150 miles away) to bring the New Sixth Army up to outflank and outweigh the Reds. Lin Piao's good generalship was manifest in his decision to pull out of a fight that he was losing—and he withdrew with remarkable stealth and success. It was better not to fight the enemy on his own terms, Lin Piao reasoned—not until the Reds had more men. So he withdrew, abandoned hard-won Changchun, without a fight, and hesitated momentarily on the muddy shores of the Sungari River with his rugged but hastily composed army.

Then occurred one of those incidents which at the time appear to be quite simple and unimportant yet which later have in fact far-reaching and complicated effects on the war. A truce was imposed in Manchuria as of 6 June 1946. The combatants shot it out, to gain last minute advantage, and were to maneuver and skirmish later; but, insofar as the general territorial occupations were concerned, each side settled down to consolidate and make ready for the showdown of 1947. This was the turning point not only of the Manchurian campaign but of the entire Civil War; for during the period of June 1946 through February 1947 Lin Piao consolidated his rear by establishing control over the greater portion of Manchuria, dividing up farmlands, recruiting and training Manchurians —who were to build up the Northeast Democratic United Army to about a half-million men. Manchuria swung the balance of power in favor of the Chinese Communists, for it eventually gave them the weighty Fourth Field Army.

Blue Strategy Loses to Red Tactics

It became one of my tasks when flying low over Manchuria for the truce teams, to identify those towns which were held by the

---

CHINESE COMMUNIST CLAIMS FOR THE CIVIL WAR PERIOD
(From 1 July 1946 to 30 June 1950)

Personnel "Annihilated":

4,586,750	PW's taken by PLA
1,711,110	Killed or wounded
633,510	Surrendered
846,950	Revolted
293,030	Accepted reorganization in PLA
8,071,350	Total enemy troops

Material Captured:

3,161,912	Rifles and pistols
319,958	Machine guns
54,430	Artillery pieces
622	Tanks
389	Armored cars
5,527,400	Shells
507,984,800	Rounds of ammunition
200	Naval vessels
189	Military aircraft

Source: *The People's Liberation Army,* published by Foreign Language Press, Peking 1950.

Nationalists and those controlled by the Communists. The battle lines were never continuously drawn and I remember days when I couldn't even locate a fighting front, for there was considerable maneuver in the spring and early summer of 1946. However, the problem of identifying the political color of a town was not usually too difficult. In the field the troops of both sides looked almost alike from an altitude of 400 feet; the Reds, however, would potshot at your plane, and they didn't possess much motor transport. In towns, however, you could never judge by the military activity which army was the occupying power. Over both Communist and Nationalists cities waved the red and blue Chinese National flags, but the key to identity was whether or not the predominantly blue Kuomintang flag flew *with* the National flag. Gradually, as 1946 merged with the year to follow, another difference in the two territories became apparent from the air—moats and trenches. These came to signify government-held cities and railway bridges. The pattern began to appear all over China as these giant trenches slowly ringed the cities. Woven about the moats were systems of barbed wire, abatis, and pillboxes. How many new pillboxes were constructed, no one knows, but they numbered in the thousands. Then there was the inheritance of the thousands of Japanese pillboxes—solid structures of thick concrete and narrow embrasures. The Nationalists were not nearly as thorough as the Japanese in the construction of these installations of defense. The Government forces made pillboxes out of brick,[11] and even mud. One of the most ghastly masses of human flesh and splintered bones that I saw in China, was outside the Shantung city of Yenchow, where one of these brick inclosures took a direct hit from a Red artillery piece at 500 yards range.

Not only did all of these fixed defenses give a false sense of security to Government troops, but they also bred an ill-fated "pillbox psychology" among Nationalist soldiers. The Communists never built them in any significant numbers. They ditched roads, tore up railroad tracks, and blew bridges in their territories; but they seldom sat down in one place to defend anything.

This was the influence of the truce—the Nationalists built defenses to protect their gains and insure city security; the Reds recruited and trained new troops, ranging their existing forces about to harass the enemy. Whereas military aggressiveness grew

---

[11] At our house in Changchun in January 1947 we noticed that a broken part of our garden wall was disintegrating rapidly. We solved the "case of the missing bricks" when we observed them going into a new pillbox on our street corner.

Photo by the Author.

WATCHING, BUT SELDOM MARCHING.

Because he clung to his defensive positions, the Nationalist soldier was captured—and often converted into a Communist soldier.

on the Red side, a defensive sluggishness took root on the Blue side. The side of numerical and technical superiority grew morally weaker; the "have-nots" strengthened their spirit and hopes. The Blues developed their buttocks; the Reds strengthened their legs and hardened their feet. By 1947 these facts were evident to any observers traveling in China.

It gradually became the high mark of success in the Nationalist Army for a general to hold onto a city. Generals, comfortable but stagnating militarily in their city headquarters, soon began to enjoy a false sense of security, just as their men in pillboxes and trenches gained confidence that their defense works would forever protect them. In the cold winter of 1946-47, the monotonous duty of manning fixed defenses, after a long period of general inactivity, lowered the morale of Chiang's troops, whose officers became more and more content to ward off the enemy at little cost in either casualties or effort. Government soldiers hugged fires and sought the indoors, whereas the poorly-clothed Reds maintained their health by the exercise of marching. By harassing actions, the Communists confused their enemy as to their intentions.

The Blue military side was being governed by a strategy which read—hold and secure the cities and the lines of communication; the countryside can wait. And the countryside was dangerous for the Blues, for when they ranged out into it the normal Red ambush and maneuver tactics were at their best.

In these actions the Reds sought to outnumber Nationalist units in a series of small engagements, and more often than not, the force of Red arms prevailed.

The Red hierarchy held to one main theme of strategy—leave the cities alone until they rot on the vines of communication. Their's was the strategy of concentrating on tactics, pulling all their old tricks out of the bag and applying them with dash and vigor. Let the Red companies and battalions seek out their own targets and capitalize on local opportunities. Let them have the satisfaction of winning small battles, but don't overcommit them in masses to attacks we (Reds) may not win and which, if we

FOUNDATION OF VICTORY 259

don't, will lower morale. Build morale, build fighting spirit, and manufacture hope by daily indoctrination. This was the keynote of Yenan's instructions.

To the higher commanders, who were anxious to wield their growing armies in greater combat, Mao warned—be patient; time is on our side. Let inflation and other factors take full effect. Do with what you have; but above all, drain the enemy of supplies, arms, and men. Take them, even in driblets, but keep taking. Attrition isn't spectacular, but it helps win when applied against the other side.

Many Americans were reluctant to acknowledge at the time that the Nationalist strategical effort to try to take Manchuria was a *military* mistake. It was a gamble against great odds and distances, not to mention a struggle against foreign obstructionism. Later everyone could say, "Had the Generalissimo concentrated on solidifying North China and subduing the Communists there, he might have later marched, with surety and success, to Mukden and Manchuli."

One very knowledgeable and highly intelligent observer, Mr. William C. Bullitt, remarked on this strategic blunder to me in early 1947. Mr. Bullitt added that General Dwight D. Eisenhower also viewed the Nationalist effort in the Northeast as a gross over-extension of military forces. There is weight to that side of the question; but certainly the Chinese Communists, with even smaller forces (although Soviet help was to compensate greatly for this lack of numerical strength), *also* gambled strategically and over-extended their troop units, which for a long time were even *isolated* in Manchuria. The difference, of course, lies in the fact that the Chinese Reds got to Manchuria first. They marched overland and poured in by sea from Shantung to the Kwantung Peninsula. They were received with hospitality; the Nationalists with hostility. But as to whether or not it was wise for the Generalissimo to embark on the military occupation of distant Manchuria, there is this big question: Could he have afforded delaying, for long, the order that history dictated to him at Yalta? Manchuria, with all of its cross currents and complications, had been again restored to China at the conference. Could any national leader of China have hesitated long in taking possession of the prize? Should he have let the Soviets hold it in trust for the year or two it might have taken him to consolidate North China? It would seem that the Generalissimo had to *make the effort* of take-over. He failed, but not because he did not try; failure came because of faults of technique in implementing his effort.

The Communists won Manchuria because of many factors. They must be given credit for their organizational ability which whipped the apathetic and leaderless Manchurian people together. Northeast China, as it emerged out of the chaos of Soviet occupation, was crying for leadership; and the region, so long under the tramp of foreign boots, had none to offer from its own population. The simple fact is, the Chinese Reds supplied the leadership, and the leaders, for all their brutality and other shortcomings, led or drove the people. The Nationalists, in spite of all of their efforts, could not or did not implement their strategy with any great leadership or political appeal. They even lacked an announced policy toward the significant Mongol and Korean minorities.

Elsewhere in China the pattern was much the same. Everywhere the Reds capitalized on Nationalist military mistakes. The Reds didn't need any real strategy; they just let the Blues apply their own. The Reds then nibbled, cut away, and isolated their enemy, not by the application of any real strategy, but by tactics, well conceived and well carried out. By multiplying many minor successes, the Reds began to gain a slight strategical edge. There were some big battles, some Communist defeats of note, but by and large when the Government marched out with its large bodies of troops in search of a showdown, the Communists would melt away. The Reds didn't want to fight large armies in 1946 or early 1947.

The defeat of the Nationalist Government can be laid *in part* to over-extension of military forces; yet the United States abetted this over-extension by transporting the troops to Manchuria and North China by sea and air. Furthermore, within six months of the time we began this phase of airlift and transport, a truce was imposed on the conflict. When the truce wore off, the Government armies, with their relatively modern equipment, attempted to fight along conventional lines, whereas the Reds pursued a guerrilla-style warfare, gradually merging into the use of large, maneuverable, bodies of troops. Most Nationalist generals failed to grasp the significance of the Communist tactics and the Red mode of fighting; few adopted suitable countermeasures. That was a major failure. One very highly placed general complained that the Communists marched too fast for the Government troops, which just couldn't catch up with them. Another famous general, Wei Li-huang, said in 1948 that he had created a "special form" of warfare to meet the unconventional tactics of the Reds. This "special warfare" consisted mainly of putting a small unit out as "bait," so that the Communists would attack it—then the plan was to defeat the attacking Communists with other units. However, General Wei Li-huang lost his entire army; but in fairness to him it must be stated that he inherited a military cause in Manchuria that was practically lost to begin with.

During the entire war, the Government armies consistently failed to trap and annihilate sizable bodies of Communists. Too often they failed to pursue aggressively when the Communists retreated. As the war progressed, the Government officers failed to realize that mobile reserves, not fixed defenses, offered the best chance of military survival, if not victory.

In their efforts to hold cities and areas, Nationalist generals overlooked the importance of defeating the ever-growing Red field armies. For example, General Tu Yu-ming ordered the American-trained New First Army to hold a 180-mile front, and even went so far as to tell the army commander, General Sun Li-jen, that he could not move one of his divisions from a certain city. Later General Tu removed General Sun Li-jen, the army commander, for failing to hold this vast frontage with an army that was the rough equivalent of an American corps.

The Realistic Fu Tso-yi

By 1948 the military thinking of high Government officers was so warped and had so stagnated in the psychology of the defense that General Fu Tso-yi appeared to be the only field commander who thought in terms of defeating Red field forces in offensive battle. Furthermore, he believed that all Nationalist armies should abandon their heavy equipment and use no weapon larger than 76-mm artillery pieces, so as to match the Communists in mobility.

Little did anyone anticipate what was to happen to the rugged Fu Tso-yi, the symbol of anti-Communist resistance. I for one,

Photo by the Author.

GENERAL FU TSO-YI'S SOLDIERS, LIKE THOSE SHOWN AT THE RIGHT, SURRENDERED IN ORGANIZED UNITS TO THE CHINESE COMMUNISTS IN 1949.

These soldiers were immediately given political indoctrination and were integrated as units into the Chinese Red Army. Some fought in Korea in 1951. (The author and Lt. Col. Kearie L. Berry, in Inner Mongolia in 1948, about to march out under Fu Tso-yi's armed escort.)

was one of the most misled. In May 1948, I visited Fu's headquarters outside of Peking with Lt. Colonel Edward Hancock. Here we met the austere army-group commander who had so long resisted the Japanese—a man whose name was vilified weekly by the Red radio and press. Fu looked like a Communist officer, for he was dressed in the simple khaki of a soldier. He wore black slippers, but no decorations. Full of brusque, smiling confidence, he led us into his headquarters where there were intelligence maps, operational maps, air target maps and the like, plastered clear to the top of the 10-foot wall. I have never seen a Chinese headquarters which more statistically documented the enemy dispositions. General Fu showed us a wall near the door. There were pasted the faces of several dozen Red military leaders, and below each was a brief biographical sketch. "We must know those we oppose," remarked Fu.

General Fu Tso-yi was optimistic over his own ability to hold. He was doubtful that General Wei Li-huang could endure much longer in Manchuria; he thought Wei should try harder. Fu was bitter, even hostile, toward Nanking. He complained that the Generalissimo was doing little to help him, yet he said Chiang demanded the utmost. Fu had lost some of his troops, and all of his territory along the fringes of Inner Mongolia. He had a substantial portion of the Red forces in China proper facing him. In short, about 80 percent of Fu's strength was committed to the south of Peking and Tientsin, and he was peering anxiously over his shoulder toward Manchuria where the Nationalist dam threatened to break.

But it was not alone General Fu's headquarters that impressed us. Fu had torn some pages out of the Communist manual. He was fighting them at their own game and using many of their tactics. Regardless of what he later did, Fu was a great general, by Chinese standards. His campaign record, which I shall not detail, was excellent. Furthermore, he kept soldier morale in mind. Unlike other army-group commanders, he saw as best he could to the well-being of his soldiers. Knowing that soldier pay was all but worthless, he gathered his soldier families together and established the women and children in communal projects which, if nothing else, gave the dependents food and shelter.

We saw his troops demonstrate an attack on a strong point— one of the few worthwhile demonstrations I ever saw given by Chinese. The use of explosives and live ammunition was so extensive and so daringly applied that Fu's troops were in almost as much danger during this exercise as they would have been in combat. I left the field believing some troops had been seriously wounded or killed, but perhaps they were not. In any event, here was a good general with excellent troops, both with combat records to prove their merit. Yet the bulk of these troops surrendered easily, and many thousands are now in the PLA.

The Nationalist dam in Manchuria broke, to the surprise of no one, in 1948, and General Lin Piao's hordes poured down from the Northeast to stab Fu Tso-yi in the back. There was no real strategical envelopment of Fu's forces. Lin Piao's tired soldiers simply knocked at the Peking gates in a tactical fashion, after having demonstrated, with the help of other Reds, at Tientsin, what would happen to a defender of any city. General Fu had lost troops in Tientsin, and rather than trying to escape with his army or run away, Fu accepted the "silver bullet" the Reds offered him. What was his fate? He is now, in title at least, Minister of Water Conservancy and chief of a war zone. He even writes non-military articles for the Communist press.

The Chinese Civil War became the graveyard of many Nationalist military reputations because too many generals were afraid to take the risks of offensive action or aggressiveness. Some, of course, could not count on the loyalty of their troops.

The Weakness of Chiang Kai-shek

Generalissimo Chiang Kai-shek's career paralleled Napoleon's in one respect. The Generalissimo suffered from the ambition and selfishness of many of his lieutenants, men he had helped raise to power. Many of his subordinates were dishonest. They padded troop strength lists beyond reality, gave up too easily in battle, or most commonly of all, underrated the Communists; and they engaged in local and national intrigues. The Generalissimo was a badly informed national leader who, despite his own mistakes, did seek the truth. In my one and only conference with the Generalissimo, I was impressed by the earnestness with which he sought the truth.

Chiang Kai-shek has been widely criticized, but some of the criticism regarding his military ability has been undeserved

However, he made military mistakes. One of the least excusable was the usurpation of the command responsibilities of his subordinate generals.

Arriving on the scene, or telephoning from Nanking, the Generalissimo would assume personal command of a battle or campaign. He would often issue orders in the midst of a campaign that would upset the plan of the general in command. Even worse, he has sent a personal representative to a front with orders which by-passed army and army group commanders. On all major fronts there was a "President's Headquarters," alongside and separate from those of the commanders of the army groups. This produced dual responsibility and authority without properly defining either.

There was inherent in this general situation violation of sound principles of command. This interference by the Generalissimo was often justified, but the manner was not. His practice of dual headquarters usually resulted in personality clashes, brought on through a misunderstanding of responsibility. Generals Tu Yuming and Shiung Shih-hui in Manchuria make a case in point; there was continual friction between them. In general, these malpractices only served to confuse the commanders and make them "lose face"; and it damaged their initiative and morale. Even though the Generalissimo's strategy may have been better than that of his subordinates at times, it was poorly or resentfully carried out when Chiang suddenly imposed his will and authority on an army group commander. Why Changchun, isolated, foodless, and under siege, should ever have been held in 1948 is more than anyone could understand; yet this was the order from Nanking—and it was carried out to the point at which the full and final defeat of the Blue forces involved was accomplished. Here was an example of strategy that, for whatever purpose it was designed, couldn't have been better calculated to mesh with Communist tactics, and with their plans for victory.

Factors in the Nationalists' Defeat

The Communists did a lot more running and waiting than they did fighting. They also did a lot of propagandizing and broadcasting, magnifying beyond proper proportion certain Nationalist ills, one of which was corruption. Foreigners often fell victims to this cliche.

Corruption had its place in the disintegration of Chiang's military structure, but in a nation where the practice of "squeeze" is endemic, the term "corruption" was too often used to define inefficiency. The term corruption proved to be a convenient handle for foreign critics who have exaggerated it insofar as the Nationalist military is concerned. Inflation spurred a good bit of the corruption among the officers, some of whom could not support their families without entering into some extra-curricular business. It must be remembered that foreigners, especially Americans, paid even their chauffeurs more than the wages of Nationalist field grade officers. The entire army was inadequately paid.

However, if we examine the reasons why the Reds won, or the Nationalists lost, we cannot rate corruption as high among the reasons as we can rate some other factors. The effect of money "squeezed" out of military payrolls, cannot compare with the effect of China's monetary inflation on the troops. Inflation caused wide fluctuation in a soldier's pay—one month it would be worth a dollar in US currency and the next month had a value of 20 cents. If he didn't get his pay at all, it might have been due to corruption; but the soldiers did not go consistently without their pay, however small. When they lacked food, or decent food, which they often did, it was because the currency wouldn't buy as much rice as it once did, rather than because of a light-fingered quartermaster or commander. Six months of inflation had a more devastating influence on Nationalist troop morale than did one year of corruption among the military.

No; the reasons for Communist victory, if they could be found in the realm of non-military factors, lay beyond corruption within the Nationalist ranks. Corruption existed, but as a cause of military victory or defeat it was only secondary, at best. What then, were the other causes?

Nationalist troops were already tired of war in 1945, and with just reason. The absence of rotation or any real personnel policy,[12] discouraged them. There was no real hope of discharge except by death or wounds. The pay was low, so the soldiers stole from the farmers in order to have an occasional decent meal. The men resented the comparatively luxurious living of the higher officers. Above all, inflation and potential death destroyed their hope. Thus, the soldier, the one essential weapon of battle, was neglected by the Nationalists. Surrender and desertion became more common as the war neared its climax.

What were the Communists doing, during this period, that could give them a combat edge? The Reds caught the backwash of inflation, but they guarded their soldiers from its impact. Noticing that even their currency trailed, to some extent, the spiraling of deflated Nationalist dollars, the Reds were clever enough not to pay their troops in cash that might show a visible depreciation. Red army units bought the food and small luxuries and issued them to the troops. There were usually sufficient supplies to give the Communist soldiers a feeling of consistent support. They did not know that their unit funds were often inadequate, that even in Red territory certain prices doubled— they simply saw consistency of food, under most conditions (except certain days of combat), and they gained the impression that their leaders had a firm hold on the situation. The Communist key lay in not letting the soldiers fumble with currency "lettuce". As the Reds learned from reading Lawrence's *"Seven Pillars of Wisdom,"*[13] soldiers' money is meant for frivolous items if the troops are at all well cared for.

The Communists kept attacking and kept their troops moving. Above all they kept their soldiers away from the towns and cities where money could have been spent if it had been available. Nationalist soldiers, on the other hand, lived in or passed through the populated centers where money could buy the delicacies and

---

[12] The US Military Advisory Group applied our own personnel policy to a brigade in a rear area in the winter of 1947-48. Soldier and officer morale showed an immediate improvement in that unit. Unfortunately the lessons of this experiment were not copied by Chinese Government forces elsewhere.

[13] In the early days of their struggle, the Chinese Communists looked upon this vivid account of Lawrence's struggle as a virtual tactical manual.

pleasures. Thus the Government trooper came to contrast his position with the wealth he saw in the cities; while the Red soldier saw little contrast between his status and that of the farmers and villagers, where wealth was little in evidence. Each environment had its own impact on soldier morale.

But the war was also influenced by other factors as well. The absence of a proper logistical concept was inherent in too many of Chiang's generals. As the armies grew to unwieldy size, it became more important that planning should be on a logistical, not merely tactical, plane.

An example of defeat by logistics occurred in Manchuria in mid-1948 when General Wei Li-huang had a maximum effective combat force of about 250,000 men, yet his total strength amounted to approximately 700,000. Thus, G-3 could only count on the effective help of one-third the number that G-4 was obliged to feed and support. This problem was even more acute because the entire army group was at that time cut off from the rest of China and the Nationalists were trying to supply it by air. General Wei had taken over an almost unsupportable mass of troops and his line of overland communication with North China was severed. However, he failed[14] to reopen this line, or successfully fight his way out. His troops at Mukden, Fushun, and Changchun eventually surrendered without any real fight.

Logistical problems on the Communist side were never this complex, because their forces were trimmed down to effective combat units. The Reds were careful to maintain in any locality only the number of troops they could effectively support there.

American arms and equipment, requiring special calibers of ammunition and tons of fuel, presented a serious problem to the Nationalists, over and above the requirements of food and clothing.

The two main bases of Government military supply were in the Nanking-Shanghai and Kunming-Chungking areas. At best, these were quite distant from the fighting fronts in the north.

---

[14] General Wei, before US Army advisors, actually refused to try to reopen a corridor.

The bulk of supplies for Manchuria and North China had to go there by a long sea route. Too often local commanders in the North intercepted supply ships, returned them empty, or dispatched them to other ports on their own unauthorized orders.

This misuse of transportation was even more evident with the railways, where critical rolling stock was held up so as to provide troop barracks, or unnecessarily delayed in unloading. Trains were often commandeered and used by local Nationalist commanders without authority. The entire transport system was hampered by this warlord-type of interference.

All American surplus equipment in the Kunming-Chungking region had to be sent a long and arduous river route, by the Yangtze, to reach even the nearest fronts, which were in Central China. The tonnage that could be transported monthly was not only limited by the few river steamers and other river transport available, but such shipments were further complicated by the necessity of three or more trans-shipments in order to reach the combat units. Only a fraction of the tonnage in that southern region came out, because the logistical organization was inefficient.

It was axiomatic that all supplies suffered attrition losses while en route to the various fronts. A part of the pilferage was by civilians, but the serious losses resulted from intermediate military units taking supplies that were not consigned to them. This was a disciplinary problem which the Nationalists were never able to solve. To curb the practice, discipline would have had to be exercised on the generals themselves. All this helped the Communists, who watched and waited for favorable opportunities. When they learned that a large amount of railway rolling stock was on the tracks at Tsinan (Chinan), they isolated that Shantung city and destroyed the railway lines adjacent to it. That was a big blow at the Nationalist military effort, one so effective that the Government conceived and carried out a later campaign to reopen the lines to the city, *solely* for the purpose of reclaiming bottled up freight cars.

Like the civil war in Russia, the Chinese conflict ranged largely around rail lines. The Chinese Communists showed great ability in destroying these ribbons of communication. They not only blew up the bridges and burned the ties but also they carried away the rails—and in places obliterated all traces of the very rights of way. The Government had its share of railroad troubles without Red interruptions. Railways were under a Nationalist ministry separate from that of Defense, but the military commandeered trains and trackage when it chose to do so. This was not done on a coordinated level or in accordance with recognized priorities, but was hit or miss, in the best tradition of warlord-ism.

This misuse of transportation by the military was not only costly, wasteful, and grossly inefficient; in one instance, it was also murderous. In 1947 a military commander at Kaifeng demanded a train in order to move his troops westward. The station master told the military authorities that an eastbound train was traveling the single track toward Kaifeng and that they would have to wait until it arrived. The military brushed aside the local civilian rail officials and made up their own train, dispatching it westward. The result was a head-on collision, and on a critically important bridge, which was destroyed. The loss of life sustained in this unnecessary mishap was estimated to be at least 150.

As the Government armies showed less and less ability to stem the Red tide, they often found their elements floundering in tactical isolation, as a result of Communist encirclements. The Chinese Air Force, which had had so little effect on the Civil War, was called upon to make an increasing number of air drops to beleaguered units. This is a difficult and costly technique. The Chinese never mastered air drops. I have stood inside Communist lines and watched the Red soldiers cheer Nationalist parachute drops, then open up the remains of poorly packaged supplies that had been intended for suffering and needy Nationalist troops several thousand yards distant.

As the rail lines became more and more completely severed, armies and even army groups, called on the Government for air supply. There existed among the Chinese a naive belief that aircraft tonnage could match railway tonnage.

In mid-1948, all the aircraft in China were insufficient to carry the tonnage needed by Nationalist armies, which at that time were cut off or isolated by the Chinese Reds. The well-regimented, and fairly well-organized Mukden airlift (of 1948) was capable of transporting only one-third the daily tonnage needed by General Wei Li-huang's army group there.

Except for the transport of men and supplies, the Chinese Air Force was rarely effective in sustaining the war against the Communists. Fighter and bomber planes were frequently used against unprofitable targets, at great expense to the Government. There was always the problem of air-ground cooperation. Ground force generals, for the most part, did not make proper use of aircraft, even when they were able to bring the planes under their direct or indirect control. Only Fu Tso-yi seemed to apply his aircraft properly, but air strength was placed at his disposal much too late in the war.

The Chinese Nationalist Air Force lacked the proper night flares, the training, and the equipment to do night bombing. The Communists moved large bodies of troops at night, for the most part. In actual combat, the cost of maintaining fighters and bombers was completely out of proportion to the results achieved, and it was money which might better have been spent on the infantry.

In final analysis, the Nationalist Army became an unwieldy instrument of the Government. The army was so large and so dispersed that it could not be successfully supplied, administered, or maintained for effective combat by the staffs that existed. The Nationalist Army was burdened with excessive overhead in personnel, and too many of its commanders, and even staffs, lacked an adequate understanding of the importance of logistics in war.

In 1945, the Government armies held the military advantages of numerical strength and of better arms and equipment. Morale on both sides was about equal, but the Nationalist soldiers never really understood the significance and importance of their cause, because the Government failed to impress it upon them. But as the Communists increased in power, the Nationalist military structure grew successively weaker and the Reds accurately sensed every crack of the timbers. Commanders, from Chu Teh on down, anticipated a long war in 1947; but, with Nationalist weaknesses apparent and growing, they were tempted to take bolder action than had been planned for that date. The Reds parlayed their military moves and couldn't stop winning—not because they were so strong, but because the enemy was growing so weak. Yenan's military clique took a big gamble in their campaign for Hsuchou. They won. From there on, the war was a series of marches. Final victory came easier than any Communist official had expected.

How did it all happen so quickly?

The primary cause of the defeat of the Chinese Nationalist Army was the military aggressiveness of the Chinese Communist forces, and sound tactics, which were based on the military capabilities and limitations of the Red military. Communist victory was achieved without the extensive use of modern, large-caliber weapons, motor transport, or aircraft, but by sound, aggressive tactics on the ground.

The second contributing factor in the defeat of Government armies was their own poor leadership, which too often resulted in the application to a given situation of wrong tactics and bad strategy.

Soviet assistance to the Chinese Reds in Manchuria contributed measurably to the eventual defeat of the Nationalists. This aid not only entrenched the Communists in the vital area of Manchuria, but also armed them and permitted their early and rapid growth.

A very important factor was the low morale of Government troops. This grew during the truce era of 1946-7 and was accelerated by rising inflation and military inefficiency. Low morale was the greatest single factor in final defeat. These things created the now formidable People's Liberation Army of Red China.

How the PLA Absorbed the Defeated Nationalists

The mass surrender of Nationalist divisions, armies, and army groups, in 1948-49, became so rapid that it took the Communists by surprise. The Reds, therefore adopted the solution—one not entirely to their taste from the political and security points of view, of integrating entire Nationalist units into their ranks.

THE PLA'S CLAIMS OF LOSSES INFLICTED ON THE NATIONALIST FORCES DURING FOUR YEARS OF CIVIL WAR

These cannot be accepted at face value, but the proportion of killed versus captured has some degree of accuracy.

```
  966,200  Killed and wounded
1,630,000  Captured
─────────
2,596,200  Total (July 1946-June 1947)*

  540,200  Killed or wounded
  953,000  Captured
   28,200  Other
─────────
1,521,400  Total (July 1947-June 1948)*

   31,410  Killed and wounded
  881,010  Captured
  661,380  Other casualties
─────────
1,573,800  Total (July 1948-June 1949)

  173,300  Killed
1,122,740  Captured
  390,730  Surrendered
  671,150  Revolted
   22,030  Accepted reorganization
─────────
2,379,950  Total (July 1949-June 1950)
```

TOTAL: 8,071,350 Nationalist troops.

* *China Digest,* 10 August 1948.

How does one incorporate enemy units into one's own military establishment? In the China Civil War the PLA had to solve this problem—from necessity rather than desire. The PLA took so many Nationalist units intact that it could not afford to keep them in PW camps nor could it afford to turn the prisoners loose. One of the largest masses of enemy troops which surrendered to the PLA almost intact was the force commanded by General

---

CHINESE COMMUNIST ADMITTED LOSSES IN THE CHINA CIVIL WAR

335,000 Killed or wounded*
19,500 Missing in action
2,500 Captured
357,000 Total lost, from July 1946 to June 1947

82,300 Killed
325,000 Wounded**
40,000 Missing in action
5,300 Captured
452,600 Total lost, from July 1947 to June 1948**

533,300 total lost from July 1948 to June 1949 (no breakdown of figures available).

19,600 Killed
59,200 Wounded
3,300 Captured
7,500 Missing
89,600 Total lost from July 1949 to 30 June 1950

GRAND TOTAL: 1,432,500 Communist casualties.

* PLA claims 200,000 of the wounded were returned to duty.
** PLA claims three-quarters of wounded were returned to duty, thus making the effective losses for the year only 212,900.

Fu Tso-yi. The Red avalanche from the north was anxious to retain its momentum and move on to Central China, so a quick decision was necessary. In mid-February 1949, General Lin Piao, Commissar Lo Jung-huan, Political Directors Tan Cheng and Tao Chu, and Lin's Chief of Staff, General Liu Ya-lou presided over a meeting with Fu Tso-yi's officers in Peking to announce the plan to use Fu's troops. The plan which was quickly implemented, contained the following provisions—

(1) The following three grades of command of the former KMT troops—the North China 'Bandit Suppression' Headquarters, the two army group headquarters of the Fourth and Ninth Army Groups, and the Eighth Army Headquarters— shall all be liquidated. All personnel of these headquarters, and all their attached corps troops, are to be incorporated into the People's Liberation Army Peiping-Tientsin Front Headquarters, its various army group headquarters and army headquarters. The 25 divisions under these three grades of former KMT command are to be reorganized into independent divisions of the People's Liberation Army. The special units of these three grades of command are to be merged with the special units of the People's Liberation Army.

(2) The political personnel of these KMT troops who wish to remain and work in the Liberation Army must undergo training before they can be employed.

(3) All grades of officers of the former KMT troops, who accept the work of the Liberation Army, are to receive, together with their families, the same treatment as that of officers of all grades of the Liberation Army and their families.

(4) Officers of the former KMT troops who wish to further their studies, are to be organized into classes for studies according to their posts and capacities. Their treatment, during their period of study, is to be the same as that of the cadres who are at their posts.

(5) KMT officers who wish to go home will be treated as follows:

(a) All officers returning home are, without exception, to be paid for three months at their original pay.

(b) These KMT officers (including their families) will be given passenger tickets by the Peiping-Tientsin Front Headquarters and will be provided with food and lodging while traveling in the liberated areas.

(c) They may take with them all personal belongings, but not arms and public properties.

(d) KMT officers returning home may, at (their) discretion, be accompanied by one or two guards, in accordance with their posts and needs.

(e) All KMT officers with homes in the liberated areas may be allotted their due share of land. In the case of their landlord families, their land and properties, regardless of whether they have been distributed or not, are to be disposed of according to Article Eight of the Basic Program of the Agrarian Law. So long as the officer abides by the laws of the Democratic Government, he will not be taken to task for his conduct toward the peasants in the past.

(f) All KMT troops returning home will be issued "certificates of participation in the peaceful liberation of Peiping." They will still be welcomed if they later wish to return and work for the People's Liberation Army.[15]

**JAPANESE ARMS AND EQUIPMENT
LEFT IN CHINA***

The following materiel was taken over by the Nationalist Government up to 15 April 1946. Later the materiel was either destroyed in the Civil War or captured by the Chinese Communist military forces—

685,897 Rifles
29,822 Light and heavy machine guns
12,446 Artillery pieces
15,785 Trucks
74,159 Horses
  383 Tanks
  151 Armored cars and trucks

* According to the *China Handbook*, 1950.

With considerable amount of handwaving and rhetorical emphasis, Lin Piao made it clear that all former Nationalists would require "a thorough transformation in their political nature and style of thinking." General Lo Jung-huan followed Lin on the platform, to announce that the reorganization was "not merely a simple military reorganization or merely a change of designation . . . but was a political reorganization." In traditional Communist style the evening wound up with "entertainment, including songs and plays extolling the glorious traditions of the PLA."

But this was only an interim measure, taken at a time when the PLA still had battles to occupy it. Since the night of plays the former Nationalist officers have, for the most part, been eased

[15] *New China News Agency*, North Shensi, 1 March 1949.

out of their positions with their troops, either by transfer to other units, by dismissal from the Red Army—or by gunshot purge! The higher officers have almost all retired to civilian life, or have

> ## JAPANESE ARMS AND EQUIPMENT TAKEN BY THE SOVIET ARMY
>
> This materiel, according to the Chinese Nationalist Government, was taken over by the Soviets between 9 August and 9 September 1945. Large portions of this materiel went into the hands of General Lin Piao's field army, which it equipped—
>
> - 300,000 Rifles
> - 17,197 Horses and mules
> - 4,836 Machine-guns
> - 2,300 Motor vehicles
> - 1,226 Artillery pieces
> - 925 Airplanes
> - 369 Tanks
> - 133 Radio sets
> - 125 Tractors
> - 35 Armored cars
> - 742 Depots with munitions and military supplies
>
> In addition, at the time of its surrender, the Japanese Kwantung Army had in its hands (according to Nationalists) the following—
>
> - 104,777 Horses
> - 21,084 Supply cars
> - 8,989 Machine guns
> - 11,052 Mortars
> - 1,436 Artillery pieces
> - 815 Special vehicles
> - 287 Command cars
>
> (Source: the *China Handbook*, 1950)

gone to prison. What has been the fate of the living, since 1950? Their past lives have been examined in detail by Red intelligence personnel, to determine whether they ever mistreated Red prisoners, owned any appreciable amount of land, or committed any one of the many "crimes against Communism." There are no official records to list the dead officers—but many are now dead of a current malady called "public purge." Most of the troops incorporated into the PLA, under this February 1949 plan, still remain in the PLA—except for those buried in Korea.

Sino-Korean Conflicts and Cooperation

When the small columns passed each other in the darkness there was no trouble. In daylight hostile stares were exchanged and often the North Korean soldiers listened to swear words from combat weary Red Chinese. Sometimes there was shoving, with rifle butts and bayonets jabbed to lend weight to hate and bitterness. Fists were rarely used for orientals ordinarily do not fight that way, but there were some minor conflicts between the North Koreans and the Red Chinese in the winter of 1950-51. There was a language barrier. The Chinese were on foreign soil against a fire power that shredded their ranks and they looked with jealousy and resentment on certain groups of Red Korean soldiery that had not shared their combat lot. On the surface it appeared that there might be serious friction growing between the two Communist allies, but the commissars' grapevine channeled reports of the clashes on up to men of both sides who had a common purpose. Both sides issued orders: Strengthen discipline, punish severely, segregate where necessary, balance the rations, and keep everyone fighting—the enemy. Authority had its effect and the resentful Chinese soldiers curbed their anger in the face of severe penalties. The crack between the Red allies never really developed. Military cooperation on a high level has long been good between the North Koreans and the Red Chinese, because the officers see eye to eye on most problems. It would be difficult to drive a sure wedge between these two allies and produce serious or significant military cracks. And here is the reason.

Red Chinese and North Korean cooperation is good because of a common purpose and a smooth beginning in Manchuria. The foundation of present day cooperative efforts was established when (on orders from Yenan) General Lin Piao incorporated

Korean elements in his field army in Manchuria after World War II. Some of his first Korean soldiers came from Soviet occupied Korea in 1946, but the majority originated from Manchuria's significant Korean minority. Some were ready-made Communists like those in the "Dare to Die Corps"—others were made Communists by the Chinese commissars. Prominent in the establishment of Lin Piao's Korean Communist Volunteer Forces were Poh Siao-shan and Chiang Hsin-tai, both Korean Reds and the former an individual well wined and dined in Yenan during World War II. Some time in 1947 Li Li-san (now Chinese Minister of Labor) visited North Korea and signed a mutual assistance pact with the Red Koreans, providing for the more formal exchange of Manchurian foodstuffs in return for Korean military assistance. According to the intelligence files of the Chinese Nationalist Government this agreement resulted in the entry of 100,000 North Koreans into Lin Piao's field army. It is probable that this figure is somewhat exaggerated, but the exchange was actual. In December 1947 another agreement was concluded in which the Red Chinese recognized the North Korean People's Committee as the political power of the Korean nation. In 1948 a Soviet Korean-Chinese joint military committee was established in Pyongyang to coordinate certain military activities of the three Communist parties. The Manchurian-Korean border was constantly being crossed by Chinese and Korean Reds in this era, and cooperation extended into many endeavors, but the military was foremost at the time because of the growing military power of the Chinese Reds in the China Civil War. American observers in Manchuria at the time had ample evidence of the high degree of Sino-Korean cooperation and mutual assistance. General John R. Hodge in his farewell statement to South Korea made the newspaper headlines when he charged the existence of definite connections between the two Communist parties. Late in the China Civil War there was an "Iron Corps" with the PLA forces that invaded the island of Hainan. This corps contained numerous Koreans. Even the Peking regime has admitted that many Koreans were in its military forces during the Civil War, although it claims all of them were from China. The fact remains that Communist Koreans aided the Red Chinese when they badly needed help. Peking has now repaid that debt, but the Red Chinese can and will cooperate well with any nation that seeks to destroy United States military forces.

Chapter 9

SHOESTRING LOGISTICS

Rifles and Rice; Mud and Sweat

To view this army from the rear is awe-inspiring. The regimentation of disciplined men in uniform is one thing, but the obedience, efficiency, and amount of traction generated by columns of horses, carts, trucks, wagons, and farmers—all gathered from the local region—give witness to an organizational capacity that, for all its appearance of antiquity, is unique and, to a degree, efficient.

But a modern quality is lacking. The early morning fog finds these exotic supply columns moving rapidly to make shelter, before the sun and enemy aircraft can seek out the vehicles that clog the roads. Silent civilians, their mask-like faces uncleansed for days, trudge with their empty stretchers toward the front. Shut in, surrounded, and drawn along by the men in uniform, the gloom on the faces of these civilians portends the seriousness of their tasks of tomorrow. Whenever the trucks or the horse carts slow or stall on the muddy, slippery roads, these silent men, the PLA's main evacuation service, keep moving on, gaining a slight bit of ground on the rough shoulders of the road. Here and there a body of soldiers will talk kindly with these men, offering them a few quick words on the latest rumors and exchanging knowing glances at each other's cigarette supply. The bond is evident; the soldiers know that, on some tomorrow, their body survival may depend on the lean legs of these black-gowned men, whose very large numbers always seem to portend larger casualty lists than a few modern ambulances ever would.

Like the effect on American troops passing a newly laid-out field of white crosses, the hundreds of stretcher bearers are a sight the Chinese soldiers could do without. I have seen its depressing effect, the wonderment in soldier faces as to whether the high command had conscripted *too many* civilians, and whether it knew that all their canvas pallets were to be filled. The ungainly caravans of motor vehicles, horses, carts, and sometimes even camels, move at varying paces, carrying loads of different weights. The sacks of grain and rice, the boxes of shells and explosives, the conglomeration of other supplies and equipment carried, give visual evidence that logistical standardization is lacking. But, like a spring uncoiling, the power of the movement is characterized by the harnessed energy of great masses of labor. Whatever its deficiencies, the PLA compensates in good part for its logistical weakness by utilizing the labor and sweat of millions.

The Chinese can skillfully extemporize but, by tradition and environment, they seem to lack a proper concept of military logistics. The biggest problem facing the leaders of the People's Liberation Army today is the solution of logistics problems—for what they hope will be a modern military force.

The old concept of "take from the enemy"—the parasite philosophy of Chinese logistics—is now obsolete, and they know it.

Keeping Manpower and Logistics in Balance

The Chinese Communists have made a good start. They recognized long ago that a Chinese soldier, reasonably well fed and clothed, was worth several of his number maintained by the old haphazard standards. It is a matter of record, known by many American officers in China during World War II, that thousands of Chinese Nationalist soldiers were weakened by hunger as they marched and fought the Japanese. There were simply too many men under arms for the low level of logistical organization that served their giant numbers.

The Chinese Communists knew this and learned from it. They were realists, who put their soldiers to work in the fields so that they could be fed. The Yenan leaders built their army on a very narrow margin of supplies and money. It was never an easy struggle. Where they were hard-pressed, they sallied out to capture the needed supplies. They built their army up from the bottom, with a low military overhead; but they held to a basic tenet that each soldier must be fed and clothed. The soldier himself had two legs; he could transport himself. It must be remembered that the Red Army of China never had to bother about trucks, airplanes, oil, gasoline, and heavy tonnages of ammunition until about 1948. It never had the logistical problems to cope with that the Central Government's military had.

Winning the Civil War sooner than it had anticipated, the PLA's numbers grew to great proportions in 1948 and 1949, as it captured and integrated thousands. Here was presented, not only a political problem, but an economic and military one. Part of the reason the PLA is as large as it is today, lies in the fact that it inherited too many men in uniform. To release them quickly to civil life would have caused a serious unemployment problem in China. The source of bandits and guerrillas in China is the unemployed and the hungry, especially those who once carried rifles. So the Red regime of Peking told its military leaders to retain, for the time being, the extra hundreds of thousands in uniform.

The Red Chinese army officers do not want a clumsy, unwieldy military machine, but they have one. The Red generals know China's military history quite well, and they have grown to military prominence by their ability to lead relatively small, compact forces to victory. But there are economic, political, and military reasons for keeping a giant force under arms. General Chu Teh and his officers solved yesterday's problems without too much difficulty. But tomorrow's logistical problem is even bigger, since the army is to be modernized. The PLA possesses a greater variety of types and makes of weapons than any other military force. These weapons are old, and the ammunition supply for these castoffs is difficult at best. Today's weapons and materiel must gradually be discarded in favor of new and standardized equipment of Russian design. The Chinese Reds may brag about their quantities of captured American weapons, but actually they don't want them.

One sound logistical factor has been paramount in this Communist army up to 1950. Its leaders have not allowed the regular army to grow larger in troop strength than could be supported by the economy of the areas they controlled. This was an important factor in the army's success, for its hordes were never too hungry too long, and a decent level of morale was maintained. When the number of men exceeded the number of guns, the Reds simply placed the surplus personnel in the ranks of the militia and gave them spears.

Now the army has entered its expensive era. No longer can hand labor alone supply this army with its needs. The PLA requires planes, oil, tanks, trucks, and heavier equipment, which must be bought from the USSR—at considerable monetary expense. At its present strength, the army is a burden to the nation; but it is still established on a financial and economic base that can support it, because Mao Tse-tung is putting all of China's wealth into the armed forces. However, were the PLA to expand its ranks several fold, it would run into the dangers that so weakened the Nationalist army.

There have been some sharp disagreements and considerable friction behind the Iron and Bamboo Curtains. Mao Tse-tung's men find the Soviets consistently demanding food, cash, and controls in return for Soviet arms and material. It took the Chinese trade delegation four difficult months to negotiate the 1951 agreements for barter and the supply of Russian materiel under the 300 million credit program. This was only the beginning. The Red Chinese are unhappy over Soviet figured prices. A Russian bomber costs the Chinese almost one quarter of a million dollars. A propeller-driven fighter plane costs $67,000, while a T-34 tank lists at $111,000. These are actually bargain prices (tanks in the US cost almost $250,000 each) but not to Chinese economy. The rub is China's unbalanced national budget and serious inflation. It is far harder for the Chinese to raise $40,000 for a Soviet artillery piece than it is for the US to pay $75,000 for a similar item. This is why the Peking regime is forcing the people to contribute funds to the direct purchase of planes, guns, and tanks. (Between the spring of 1951 and 31 August 1951 the Chinese people had purchased 203 planes for the Red Air Force through public subscription campaigns.)

The Soviets want cash for many items, but foodstuffs are also included in these complicated exchanges. Between September 1949 and September 1950 Red China is reported to have sent 15 million tons of food to the USSR in return for Soviet military aid. Deliveries are currently slow from the USSR and this irks the Chinese, who have many trucks idle for lack of oil, spare parts, and tires. Soviet demands for more controls within China constitute the biggest worry for the Peking war lords. They see the Russians already dominating in Sinkiang and Manchuria. So, to modernize the PLA, the Red Chinese militarists are having to pay through the nose *for everything!*

The Peasant-Powered Army

"Find out if the women are making slippers in great numbers." This was one way you could, in the past, determine if a Red offensive was in the offing. For the Communists would regiment the country-side, employing women in piece-work projects for the manufacture of shoes and slippers. The soldiers wore out their slippers fast under any conditions, but the army always tried to supply them all with new footgear before a large campaign.

Portions of the countryside were different. In Manchuria, in the early autumn of 1948, no one seemed to be working except the women. The horses were gone; the farm yards were quiet. From the railway city of Tsitsihar to the muddy banks of the

Sungari River, rural life seemed momentarily suspended. General Lin Piao was moving elements of his field army into an offensive, and to do so he assembled about 300,000 Manchurian peasants, 460,000 horses, and 120,000 horse-carts and wagons. In anticipation of the many wounded his forces never suffered, Lin Piao had conscripted about 170,000 stretcher bearers from among the laborers and farmers of the northeast. This was the typical civilian mass that regularly supported field armies.

I witnessed the same army in earlier campaigns, and there always appeared to be a very high ratio of civilians to the men in uniform. The horse carts were unusually numerous, heavily loaded, often mired down in mud or snow, but always carrying a significant tonnage of food, ammunition, forage, clothing, and explosives. If one paused to examine the old reports of US military observers in the Russo-Japanese war of 1905, one would find that the present-day horse-carts are no different from the ones used in 1905. Each cart carries about a ton. Thus some 30 of these carts, which require no heavy drums of fuel, equal twelve 6x6 trucks in tonnage transported.

Speed is not a primary concern with the PLA; that is, speed in motorized terms. It is an infantry army that marches on its own feet at rates of two and one-half to four miles an hour. The two-wheel horse-cart averages three to five miles per hour. Roads in China are notoriously bad. In Manchuria, for example, I averaged at best 18 miles an hour in a jeep, and the usual average was 10 to 12 miles an hour. Thus there was not the contrast between horse and motor speeds that one would expect. Trucks never gave the Nationalists any real military advantage, for on long hauls the railways were best suited. Archaic and out-dated, horse-carts are still favored by the PLA; and they are effective transport for that army, even though it is now using thousands of motor vehicles.

When Mukden fell in November 1948 and Lin Piao was victorious in Manchuria, he swung his army columns southwest, and marched through the gates of the Great Wall of China. Lin Piao's columns, marching 600 miles in 22 days, included trucks as well as horses and carts. The route traversed was mountainous, the roads rougher than the trucks could take. Bridges were out and the ice was too thin to support men and animals; so the infantry forded the rivers. But the newly-captured trucks lagged behind the wagons, and distant reconnaissance revealed some stretches of road as almost impassable. This mobile army, which, almost overnight, had invested its cargo weight in American trucks (taken in Mukden), was on the verge of losing its famed mobility because of poor roads and broken bridges. Lacking organized engineer units with which to repair these, the local manpower was regimented to come to the aid of the army. Thus, in peopled-China, the army could resort to the eternal solution of that land, the labor of coolies. The Communist army gathered about 50,000 peasants and, with only hand tools, these freezing laborers worked in the snow to restore 180 miles of road to truck-passable condition. It was reported that only 36 hours of labor were required to complete the project. General Lin Piao's columns marched south, to fight briefly and then parade these trucks in Peiping.

This was General Lin Piao's first real experience with motorized columns. No one in Peking realized what a time he had had with this equipment, or how many more vehicles might have been paraded had they not broken down en route. General Lin could conscript peasants to build bridges, but he lacked motor mechanics and spare parts.

But when Lin Piao's troubled truck columns were moving down from Manchuria, elements of two other field armies were engaged in the greatest campaign of the China Civil War. The Huaihai campaign was the PLA's greatest combat effort of the Civil War. One can get some idea of the PLA's approach to battlefield logistics from its preparations for this campaign. The Chinese Reds committed 550,000[1] men, comprising 19 armies and three independent brigades, against about the same number of Nationalist troops, initially organized into about 55 divisions. The PLA was on the offensive, so it took its time—several months

---

[1] *China Handbook*, 1950.

—in preparing for the campaign. By its own claims, the PLA used in its rear millions of "civilian aides" to grind the grain, cook for the army, construct defenses and bring up supplies.[2] (The Huaihai campaign lasted from 7 November 1948 to 10 January 1949. The campaign swirled around Hsuchou from 9 November 1948 to 4 December 1948.)

Generals Liu Po-cheng and Chen Yi already had at their disposal several hundred thousand conscripted farmers who had repaired roads, built bridges, and carried ammunition and wounded, in the 7-day Battle of Tsinan (Chinan) which had ended in September 1948. They put 80,000 of the civilian laborers to work near the front (on about 27 December 1948), while 100,000 more were ordered to work on roads and bridges.[3] On the 3 December, 37,000 more farmers and laborers were ordered to the front to give direct assistance of the combat units, for transport of food and ammunition and the evacuation of wounded. Marching and countermarching, the Communist armies confused, blocked, attacked, and overran the Nationalists in large numbers. The Red columns made the utmost use of their vaunted mobility and the Nationalists couldn't match them. But Communist soldiers were finding that their supply tails were lagging. At one unidentified portion of the mixed front supplies were badly needed. Again, no reason to call a quartermaster! The Red command quickly conscripted from Huaian and nearby districts 23,000 *hand* carts,[3] had them loaded with grain, and ordered the civilians to march! They did, for two days. The Red troops were fed. There was no advance staff planning; just orders to the people. Few regions in China have ever been so militarily mobilized as this one was. The magic of it all was that the supply effort meshed well with the fluidity of military movements, which were rapid. The farmers had to march as fast, and often longer (in days) than some of the soldiers. For example, the "East Kiangsu peasants sent 40,-000,000 catties of grain (a catty equals 1 1/3 pounds) to the front at a speed of 30 to 35 miles a day."

---

[2] "The Battle of Huaihai," *People's China*, 1 August 1950.
[3] Communist Hsin Hua (Radio) Station, N. Shensi, 1948.

Everybody moved. If they were not driving or wheeling carts they were carrying individual loads. Some civilians averaged (according to Red claims) 35 to 40 kilometers a night with 90-pound loads. Others carried artillery shells in baskets at the ends of Chinese shoulder-poles. These "war service workers" suffered some casualties, but their several million backs were what the PLA relied upon logistically, for the army lacked a large scale organic service of supply to support its numbers. The Communists long beforehand enlisted the services of thousands of peasant women to sew extra strong shoes "with the slogan 'For Victory' embroidered on their toes."

This campaign was barely over when the PLA dispatched 12,000 cadres to Northern Kiangsu to organize another million people for the drive across the Yangtze. Portions of this million of peasants built 969 bridges and are reported to have repaired over 1,000 miles of road.[4] The remainder helped assemble the thousands of small boats the Communists were to use in the Yangtze River crossings. They assisted in the organization of nearly a hundred supply stations in hidden places along the Yangtze. Others were sent out, under staff officers, to villages where they chalk-marked the doors of the future billets for the onrushing Red hordes. Some 60,000 of the Shantung peasants were sent home in March 1949, as the PLA regimented manpower closer to the scene of activity for the new campaign. It was always the practice not to carry the regimented peasants too far from their homes if they could pick up new groups.

One of the reasons why the PLA gained combat dominance over the Nationalists was that the PLA placed a larger proportion of men (per unit) in the firing lines than the Government armies were able to do. This was possible because the PLA used civilians to evacuate their wounded and transport the great bulk of their supplies. A Nationalist force of 10,000 soldiers, on the other hand, included many who were formally organized in service of supply elements.

This was the pattern of logistical support in the Civil War.

---

[4] *New China News Agency*, 1949.

It is essentially the same in the PLA today, except that the Communist Army has a greater number of trucks. These are under military control in organized units. Motor transport is centralized under field-army and group-army control. By our standards, lower units still lack an adequate supply of motor vehicles. The Red logistical effort in combat is still to "organize on the spot," using the resources and manpower of the region. In Korea the Chinese are employing Manchurian horse-cart drivers (who own their vehicles and animals) and stretcher bearers. They also employ some Korean civilians, but the "peoples support" comes mainly from home. The Chinese press is praising these civilian "volunteers." The Chinese Communists pay these men so little they might almost be termed volunteers—except for the guns in their backs that make them serve.

The Wounded Die Needlessly Because Medical Service Is Poor

As his wounds ooze blood or dirty bandages start smelly infection, the Chinese soldier may be conscious enough to curse the PLA's lack of doctors and medical service. The soldier doesn't know it, but Red China has one doctor for every 33,000 persons.[5] If this one doctor visited just half of these potential patients for five minutes each, it would take him almost 8 months—providing they were all within reach. This is the reason why the PLA has such poor medical service and why the army's wounded die in large numbers.

In 1946, the registered doctors in China totalled 13,447,[6] and the registered dentists numbered 371. Of these 13,447 doctors, the US Army Surgeon General's office estimated that only about 8,000 practicing doctors could in any way meet US military standards. Even if all these 8,000 doctors were directly serving the 2,720,000-man armed forces of Red China, there would be only one doctor for about 340 men in uniform. This is a hypothetical high. No figures are available as to the number of medical officers in the PLA, but it is doubtful that the Red Chinese field armies in

---

[5] Based on the 1949 population figure of 463,493,418 persons.
[6] *China Handbook*, 1950, page 688.

combat are served by more than one medical officer for 3,000 men.

After World War II, the Chinese Nationalist Army had 1,922 qualified doctors, 18 dentists, 384 nurses, and 438 technical personnel. This was all the medical personnel the military could procure, yet it was estimated that 10,500 doctors were required per 1,500,000 men—or one for every 143 men.

How many doctors fled the Red regime's onrushing armies during the Civil War is unknown, but it is probable that the figure amounted to a thousand or two at least. The Chinese Communists have been complaining of the fact that China urgently needs more hospitals, medical colleges, and above all, doctors.[7] The Reds estimate that 100 million Chinese people need medical attention each year and that throughout China there are only 2,000 hospitals with a total of 90,000 beds.[8] By present day Communist figures, Chinese education has in the past 40 years given China only 18,000 to 20,000 doctors, 300 dentists, 2,000 pharmacists, 13,000 nurses, and 10,000 mid-wives.[8] Excluding military medical-teaching institutions, the Reds say China, in 1950, had some 38 medical schools, 12 colleges of pharmacy, and 6 dental schools, with a combined total of 14,000 students. They say China needs five million hospital beds and half a million doctors with three to four million auxiliary medical workers.

It is doubtful that the PLA, today, has more than six medical-teaching institutions, or more than 1,200 military students undergoing training for military hospitals and other medical installations. The Chinese five-year plan calls for 30,000 doctors, public health officers, and pharmacists. The army will get a portion of these and it plans to produce a few of its own.

As regards medical equipment, supplies, and mobile field hospitals, the situation is stringent in the Red army of China. By 1947, with US and Japanese medical supplies exhausted, even the Nationalist army was depending on native sources for two-

---

[7] They also claim they inherited a wealth of filth in the cities they captured. Peking they said, had 201,638 tons of garbage and refuse which required 73,000 workers, 35,407 carts, and 800 trucks to clean up.

[8] Li Teh-chuan, "Health Work in New China," *People's China,* 1 October 1950.

thirds of its requirements. At that time the Communist army was even more short than the Nationalists of medical supplies and doctors. The Communist military forces were using UNRRA supplies which had been given for use with the civilian population.

In early March 1947, Major Collins and I talked with Doctor Lo,[9] a Swiss "doctor of fortune" serving in the field with General Lin Piao's army, on the Sungari Front in Manchuria. Doctor Lo explained in considerable detail the "awful shortages" of drugs and other medical supplies that the Northeast Democratic United Army (now the Fourth Field Army) was experiencing. The winter had been extremely cold and Major Collins had a frost-bitten foot, so Doctor Lo treated it with vaseline and a new bandage. This gave us a chance to ask him how badly the Communist soldiers were suffering from frostbite. He said that Lin Piao's army had had a considerable number of cases, and would have had more had not the unit commanders kept their troops marching and maneuvering. "We have found," Doctor Lo said, "that the Manchurian farmer's crude leather shoe, stuffed with straw, is the best foot gear for the region." (At this time the Nationalists were using American army shoes and shoe-packs and were experiencing considerable difficulty with frozen feet. However, the Nationalists manned fixed defenses and did little marching, hence were more susceptible to frostbite.) Doctor Lo said it was the policy of the PLA to billet troops in farm houses and villages, where possible, and march them out to the front each day. He and his officers worried over the plague,[10] also.

By Western standards, Chinese Red soldiers in Korea are anything but well cared for medically. About half of the Chinese prisoners captured by United Nation's Forces in the winter of 1950-51 were acute sufferers from severe frostbite. They were prone to remark that they had received little or no medical orientation on the care of their feet in extreme temperatures;

---

[9] Dr. Lo would never give his full name, but his first words were, "I'll bet you think I am a Russian?" He was in charge of a military field hospital and ranked high on Lin Piao's medical staff, having served with the Chinese Reds for 7 years.

[10] In Manchuria, the Communists estimate there are 30,000 cases a year. In 1949 they conducted a special campaign against it, reportedly killing 2,189 tons of rats in the process.

or that they had received only the poorest, if any, treatment once they were frostbitten.

The Peking regime is making great claims for its inoculation campaign,[11] but it has done no more than jab the needle into some key personnel, such as high government officials, generals, Party officials.

The Red soldiers of China are not as yet inoculated against disease under any real organized system. Here again the army lacks

U. S. Army Photo.

THE CHINESE RED ARMY IS LOUSE-RIDDEN.
A United States Army medical team dusts Communist captives with DDT; Korea, March 1951.

modernity. Despite the immunity that many of its soldiers may possess against diseases endemic to regions of China, the PLA *is* wide open to plague and many other diseases. It has reportedly suffered sickness casualties in Korea equal to its combat losses.

---

[11] Claims for January to June 1950: 36,000,000 small pox vaccinations; 200,000 BCG inoculations; 6,800,000 injections against cholera; 4,701,000 against plague; 336,000 against typhoid; 5,056,000 (combined vaccine) against typhoid and cholera.

The PLA is louse-ridden. I have sat for hours amid dozens of Red Chinese soldiers who undid their clothing down to the skin and flicked off the lice.

The PLA's medical service is makeshift. Even the system of stretcher-bearer evacuation is makeshift. The Chinese Red soldiers who lie on the ground and clutch their bloody wounds usually lack first aid kits. They are in serious trouble. Evacuation at best is uncertain; real medical treatment doubtful. The odds are that the majority of seriously wounded Chinese will die.

Fighters Who Farm

One of the few armies of the world that works its soldiers in civilian enterprises is the PLA. China may not be able to afford the luxury of a large army, but she is determined to try. The army is now being made to defray some of its expenses, and contribute to the national wealth, by hard labor on farms and in factories.

Columns of hungry, ragged refugees roamed China's roads during and after the Civil War. Their thousands never were counted with accuracy as they filtered southward—pausing sometimes to bury their dead, or to seek shelter for the pregnant mothers who were bearing new unfortunates. Finally these columns would reach a milepost of despair, to find that a sea barred their way to freedom. There was no more escape as the PLA swept south, so China's masses of displaced persons turned around, to filter back in the direction of their homes. The refugees typified the disrupted state of China's economy and the issues the Communists had to face when they inherited the new provinces. The nation's economy had been badly disrupted by the Civil War.

The PLA, with its military tasks growing less in 1949, was the Communist's only real, organized instrument with which to begin economic restoration. But the army was becoming an expensive luxury. So, on 23 September 1949, in its Common Program, the Chinese People's Consultative Conference stipulated that—

"The armed forces of the People's Republic of China, shall, during peace time, systematically take part in agricultural and industrial production in order to assist in national construction work, provided that their military duties are not thereby hampered." [12]

On 5 December 1949, Mao Tse-tung issued a directive that integrated the army into the reconstruction program, so as to speed up economic recovery. By his carefully written directive, Mao turned a portion of his soldiery away from their rifles and cannon toward the fish nets of lakes, the implements of the farm, and the tools of the factories. Troop units were given orders to apply their brawn and skill to agriculture, stock raising, fishing, irrigation works, construction works, certain industrial and transportation enterprises, and even some handicrafts.[12] However, commercial transactions were prohibited, and are today.

According to Communist claims, 40 percent of the production proceeds go to the soldiers engaged in the work; the remaining 60 percent is evenly divided among reinvestment, the army's daily expenses, and payment of taxes.

The Chinese Reds publicly claim that "a part of General Lin Piao's Fourth Field Army was called back from Central-South China" in the spring of 1950 for production purposes in Manchuria.[13] The particular reason for the movement is open to some question, but large elements of the PLA are today flexing their backs in non-military labor.

Few Americans really saw the empty miles of tie-less railway road-beds in China, where even the embankments had been leveled by the Communist Army in its war against the Nationalist government. Today, the political power that completely destroyed hundreds of miles of railways is having to repair and reconstruct the destroyed trackage. Under Mao's directive, the People's Liberation Army has undertaken the reconstruction of several railway lines. New railway construction also is in progress. On 16 June 1950, PLA troopers lifted picks, shovels, and saws to begin the construction of the 530 kilometer Chengtu-Chungking Railroad; other military units began the 540 kilometer construction of the Tienshui-Lanchow Railway in Kansu Province.

---

[12] "The PLA in Production" by Cheng Lien-tuan, *People's China*, 1 August 1950.
[13] *People's China*, 1 August 1950.

It is an old tradition of the Communist Army to put the soldiers to work in this fashion; so most of their claims on the subject today can be accepted. Here is a typical case.

In 1950, the Chinese military in the remote territory of Sinkiang was reported engaged in operating the following enterprises—

85 flour mills	3 weaving mills
37 coal pits	3 paper mills
15 oil presses	2 gold mines
8 soap factories	

—and they were reported to be herding 5,000 cows and 70,000 sheep; and raising 14,000 hogs and 50,000 chickens! Supposedly they planted 200,000 trees.

The Red leaders further claim that, up to July 1950, the army had contributed 4,650,000 man-days of work to various water conservancy projects in North China. The PLA has under its direct control 70 small scale industrial establishments manned by men in uniform, and 357 "handicraft shops," most of which are actually beancurd mills providing the army with food.

The significant item about all these reported figures is that the PLA is actively engaged in China's reconstruction and economic program and is helping to support its own multi-millioned numbers in uniform. For many years to come this will be the character of the army—an army that is a financial burden to the nation under Peking's Red rule.

Munitions Production Is Insignificant

China has no munitions industry. The nation has never manufactured its own artillery shells and big guns, although the sprawling Mukden arsenals are capable of a very limited manufacture of light artillery—and possibly by this time, can produce some large shells. Thus the supplies of munitions that the Chinese Red army requires must come from the USSR. That will be the source of supply for at least the next ten years, and it will cost the Chinese money and food; for the expenses are high for munitions transported across the lengthy Trans-Siberian Railway. This is a new problem for the Reds of China, who seek to place their military forces on a modern level, and it is causing much worry.

Some evidence of China's dependence on foreign nations for military supplies is indicated in the figures given by the 1950 *China Handbook*—

"China's production of light arms in middle of 1947, met only 70 to 90 percent of her demands. She manufactured no heavy weapons. As for ammunition, she produced only 3 percent of the bullets and 20 percent of the shells she needed."

During the Civil War the Nationalist arsenals were so busy filling monthly needs that no improvements were made. The Communists, on the other hand, gradually built up a number of small arsenals which manufactured rifle bullets, hand grenades, mines, and mortar ammunition. There were probably about 70 of these small arsenals scattered through Communist-controlled regions by the end of 1948; and trickling though their production was, they did produce about one-half of the PLA's needs for small arms ammunition.

During the Civil War, the PLA was often short of munitions and, as a result, a good portion of its tactics was directed at the capture of Nationalist supplies. The big windfall that sustained the Communists in the early portion of this war was the tremendous quantity of Kwantung Army stocks they secured.

General Chu Teh's army is unique in that it has only one large arsenal worthy of a real bombing effort by an enemy. This is the Mukden Arsenal, built by war-lord Chang Tso-lin and enlarged by the Japanese during their occupation of Manchuria. The United States bombed this munitions plant during World War II but made only a few isolated hits, with the result that the AA gun production was cut from about twelve weapons a month to six. A few miles northeast of Mukden, the Japanese built the Second Mukden Arsenal, which we never hit. It appeared as a "factory area" on our bombing maps, but, as it was wartime-constructed, we never knew until after the war just what it manufactured. I saw both arsenals during the Soviet occupation of Manchuria. They were looted of about 60 percent of their machinery. The Soviets took the main portion, but Chinese Communist military forces carried off some small items of machinery. It was in May 1948 that I last saw the No. 1 Mukden Arsenal; and the city itself was completely surrounded by Lin Piao's troops. This arsenal had made a surprising recovery in Nationalist hands. From out of the wreck of rusty lathes, missing drop-forges and general ruin, they restored this giant installation to the production of small arms and mortar ammunition, hand grenades, 37-mm shells, rifles, machine guns, tommy guns; and they were nearing a steady but limited production of light artillery. In 1948, both arsenals, relatively undamaged, fell into Chinese Communist hands. Their production today is estimated to be sufficient to maintain six to 10 Chinese Communist divisions in combat action.

The next largest arsenal is at Taiyuan, in Shansi Province. All during the Civil War it was under Marshal Yen Hsi-shan and had a sufficient output to provide several Nationalist divisions with small arms and mortar ammunition. It is an antique arsenal, by American or European standards.

Bombing Chinese Communist arsenals *in China* is unprofitable —for the effort, risk, and expense involved. The two Mukden arsenals, producing about 65 percent of Red China's light munitions, might be considered profitable targets.

Bottlenecks Limit and Inhibit Military Massing

Consisting of millions, the PLA can commit hundreds of thousands of men in one region, as in Korea; but this army, like any other in the world, cannot long ignore the laws of logistics.

There is a tendency to view this Chinese Army as one massive whole, of frightening proportions. This is wrong. The PLA must be considered from the viewpoint of "how many men can it place in actual combat in a given area." This is the view General Douglas MacArthur took of the Chinese in Korea when he said, "Chinese superiority in numbers will be nullified by Chinese problems of supply. Our strategy now is based, in the face of the great Chinese hordes, on forcing the enemy to lengthen his supply line in areas where we can attack it. Somewhere, when his line is extended, the enemy's available equipped and supplied forces should be about even to ours." General James A. Van Fleet, on 10 June 1951, voiced a similar analysis in these words, "The enemy is not capable of bringing in enough Chinese to drive us out of Korea."

No Red Chinese general has ever achieved fame or prominence in China's wars because he was a successful G-4, quartermaster, or logistician. There are, on the other hand, generals who enjoy great reputations because they managed to operate on logistical shoestrings, or drove their ill-assorted supply staffs to regiment the public and rape the countryside for transport and foodstuffs. Chinese Communist generals do not find among their number any who are talented or educated engineers. Here is where the PLA differs widely from the other major armies of the world. Up to 1949, it succeeded on China's one logistical reserve—massed labor. As the PLA says, it must rely on the people; but project this army out of China in a region where its fifth columns have not had a chance to align the people, and it flounders logistically.

However, the PLA is not without a few important logistical strengths. Considering its technical backwardness, the PLA has done exceedingly well to keep its troops fighting in Korea; but no army can successfully maintain its supply lines against enemy air superiority. It is only a matter of time until the Red Army's truck columns in Korea will dwindle.

China's greatest logistical strength is its people. Its major logistical strength lies in the following factors—

(1) Under the regimentation of Communist rule, millions of people can be required to serve the army directly for transportation of supplies and evacuation of casualties;

(2) There are Soviet military advisors, qualified in higher staff duties, who can assist and train Chinese officers in logistics;

(3) The Chinese soldier, with his lower standard of living, does not require as many pounds of supplies monthly as does a European or American soldier; and needs less ammunition;

(4) Because the PLA lacks motor vehicles, and marches in-

fantry on its feet, its divisions do not have to cope with too great fuel supply problems;

(5) The officers and men are able to improvise and possess endless ability to forage for themselves and to endure.

Out-balancing the strengths, however, are these logistical weaknesses—

(1) There is an insufficient number of staff officers with either the training or experience to qualify them properly for the tasks of modern logistics;

(2) The PLA has not completed the organization or the training of a large service of supply;

(3) There is no effective military air transport service, capable of air lifting any appreciable tonnage. The armed forces also lack modern water transport and landing craft for extensive amphibious and over-water operations;

(4) China must obtain the greater portion of her gasoline from sources beyond her borders. Oil must be imported;[14]

(5) The railway network in China is limited in mileage and efficiency. The roads and highways are poor;

(6) The medical service is woefully weak and inadequate;

(7) In terms of modern combat, the PLA itself is too large for its existing services of supply support.

The Chinese might commit one million, or even two million, men to the peninsula of Korea at one time, but that is unlikely because of the logistical limitations. The PLA does not have the modern organized supply system to support such numbers in one large package. Red commanders are realists. They may be willing to waste men in actual combat, but they are not deliberately going to overconcentrate masses which they cannot feed and cannot supply adequately with ammunition. Thus there will be a limit to the number of troops they will place in a given area, such as Korea, at one time. There are only so many roads and so many

---

[14] There are two synthetic oil plants in Manchuria, at Fushun and Chinchow. They were built by the Japanese because oil was not indigenous to Manchuria. By an intricate German process, they produce oil from coal shale, but their combined production is insufficient to maintain more than one field army with motor fuel, under peace time conditions.

trucks available, and even those are in poor condition. The Chinese Armed Forces do not yet include an air force large enough to dominate the sky; so they must reckon with an enemy who does. In June 1951, the Chinese reached about the maximum number of troops they could adequately support within Korea. If they concentrate more, they begin to offer larger targets for hostile aircraft. The real danger of Chinese numbers lies in their being fed into a theater or campaign in a steady replacement flow.

In January 1951, General MacArthur estimated that the Chinese could "supply around 1,500,000 troops at the Yalu River" from Manchurian bases. "But they lose 50 percent of their equipped frontline strength by the time they cross the 38th Parallel. They . . . lose another 10 percent 50 miles south." These difficulties multiply by "geometric progression."

The PLA is all of 35 years behind the US Army in logistical organization and concepts. But the future holds the promise that the PLA and its regional logistical facilities will improve. The Soviets have between 20,000 and 50,000 technicians and "advisors" in China today. The impact of this foreign assistance is already evident in the work being done on airfields, railways, and roads. The Soviets are giving splendid direction to the establishment of a sounder logistical base for China and its army. Today's assistance is probably more energetic and efficient than that the Soviets gave China between 1924 and 1927.

Chapter 10

MAO TSE-TUNG'S CARPETS OF DEAD

The Soviets Arrive

Within four weeks after the signing of the Sino-Soviet Pact, on 14 February 1950, over 3,000 Russian officers and advisors were unpacking their cheap suitcases in the hotels of Mukden, Peking, Shanghai and other Chinese cities. Here was implementation! The United States, which had about 3,000 officers and men in its Military Advisor Group (MAGIC), never implemented a training mission or a military pact as rapidly.

Imagination is being demonstrated by the Soviet officers who are training and helping to reorganize the PLA today. These Soviet officers, professionals at combat, are giving the needed injection of modernism to the PLA and are getting to the roots of the problems that exist. Chinese divisions are being reorganized along Soviet lines; which means that they are being increased in soldier strength to around 11,000 and given a higher ratio of fire power. It also means that the total number of divisions eventually will be reduced. Training is realistic under Soviet guidance, and the Russians are applying more modern training methods and aids,

Weapons new to the Chinese are being supplied, or are scheduled for future delivery, and Chinese soldiers are being schooled in their use. Artillery techniques are especially emphasized. The Soviets are endeavoring to correct the imbalance of the PLA, and to bring the armed forces qualitatively up to a modern level.

The question arose in 1951 as to why the Chinese forces in Korea hadn't been equipped with the Soviet arms and equipment that were common to the Red Korean Army in 1950. There is no mystery about it. Between the signing of the Sino-Soviet Pact and the launching of Chinese aggression in Korea, less than a year lapsed. Soviet tanks, artillery pieces, and such, must travel the lengthy Trans-Siberian Railway to reach China. It has required time to get any substantial tonnage of the heavier weapons into the PLA's hands and additional time to train the Chinese in their use. The Soviets have not wanted to see Russian arms and equipment thrown away because of improper use. Artillery divisions cannot be organized and trained overnight. The time is approaching when the effect of Soviet training and arms will be felt.

Some of our own military evaluations of Nationalist China's army are a guide to the present Soviet views of the PLA. Before the US China Theater closed up, it made a careful evaluation of the weakness of the sprawling Nationalist Army. Lieutenant General Albert C. Wedemeyer and his staff visualized an eventual 60 Chinese Nationalist divisions organized along US lines. (By the end of 1945, Nationalist China had about 252 divisions of varying strengths, with an army of 3,800,000.[1]) However, this US Army vision was a distant one and the "Alpha" program was aimed at 39 divisions, of which only 12 were realized before the exodus of the Nationalists from the mainland.

The Soviets do not visualize the PLA in terms of exactly 60 divisions of 11,000 each,[2] *but* they obviously see in that army the

---

[1] The *China Handbook* 1937-45, compiled by the Chinese Ministry of Information, published by the MacMillan Co., New York, 1947, page 764.
[2] The new type of Soviet Rifle Division has a strength of 11,000 men. The mechanized division is 12,500 in strength; the tank division, 10,500. These are the most reliable current figures and are from Colonel Ely's *"The Red Army Today,"* The Military Service Publishing Company, Harrisburg, Pa.

traditional Chinese excess of small divisions and not enough larger ones. Artillery divisions, antiaircraft divisions, and a modicum of armor will be added to the field and group armies. The Soviet influence is already evident in the Red Chinese Air Force, which is growing rapidly. Now the Soviets are apparently restraining its combat action so that, when it does fight, it will do so in strength and yet with a fair measure of combat know-how.

The Soviet Military Mission to Red China must be visualized in terms of what a similar Russian mission did in North Korea. The Soviet advisors did not take long (just over a year) to shape the North Korean Army into an effective satellite military force. In 1950 the North Korean Army shouted "Banzai" and charged with utter recklessness into attack; but it was both fronted by well-manned Soviet tanks and backed up by Soviet-trained artillerists. The Red Koreans did not attack as a horde of ill-armed orientals but as a force as modern, in general organization and arms, as the Soviet satellite army of Czechoslovakia. The Red Koreans attacked using the most modern European tactics. Their armor daringly led them forward and hesitated at nothing.

In June 1950 the North Koreans had a *modern* military force, even though it lacked a few refinements. The PLA can likewise be projected!

Until September 1951 the PLA had not demonstrated any real modern quality, organizationally or tactically. The PLA lacked the dash of the 1950 Red Koreans and did not have a modern trick in its tactical or strategical bag. But this will change—not suddenly, but steadily under Soviet tutelage. The Chinese and their Soviet advisors are studying lessons learned in Korean combat.

Within this text the quantitative whole of the PLA has, in some degree, been examined. The PLA has been shown to be in a state of military transition while at the same time fighting a war of its own choosing. This war in Korea—to which the PLA has sent "volunteers"—has interrupted, but has not postponed, the creation of a modern element in the Red Army of China.

On the training grounds and firing ranges of Manchuria and North China, modern combat elements of the PLA are being created under Soviet supervision. Whether these newly-organized combat units ever appear in Korea as separate divisions and regiments or under the title of a larger "volunteer" force is hard to determine. Certain PLA units could even be combined with foreign volunteers, to form an international army matching the UN Forces in variety of languages spoken. However, there is a certainty that improved enemy units will appear on the battlefield if the Korean war extends into 1952. In any event, by that year the PLA will have improved the combat quality of certain of its armies.

But the Red Army of China has other missions than the Korean. There is Taiwan, that it promises to invade. How successful will it be in this venture? Then there is Tibet, which it falsely claims to have invaded before May 1951.

The Phony Invasion of Tibet

The Red Chinese army that tried to invade the wind-howling passes of Tibet got licked! Three thousand PLA troops disappeared into a mountainous space, and months later they still hadn't been heard of.

The invasion proper began on 7 October.[3] Eight months later the invasion forces were still not in Lhasa, the capital of the "Roof of the World." The assault against this remote region was one of the costliest military failures of the Chinese Communists. Politically, the venture had full success, for it forced the Dalai Lama to flee immediately and later (23 May 1951) to conclude a settlement relinquishing Tibet to the Chinese. In early 1951 the Peking Reds shouted "victory" to the world, but even by July 1951 they hadn't yet achieved military possession of that mountainous land.

The over-confident Reds attacked Tibet as winter began—a foolish mistake bred of logistical miscalculation. The invasion was planned for the summer of 1950, but the reconstruction of roads

---

[3] There is a difference of opinion as to the exact date, depending on the point from which the invasion was said to have started. The magazine, "East Europe and Soviet Russia," reported, on 6 November 1950, that the Reds issued the order on 25 October 1950. Colonel C. H. Lanza reported the date to be 7 October 1950. *People's China* confirmed the latter date, on 16 November 1950.

and the erection of bridges, some of them of steel, was slower than anticipated and delayed the starting date of the assault. Overconfidence bred the effort to attack in the face of the coming snows. The PLA has never conceded that a piece of terrain has been a serious barrier to its movements.

It was a big military mistake to begin the invasion on the date finally selected. But perhaps the Chinese Politburo felt that the risks were worth the world publicity—and the international "prestige" gained by this attack against the most remote populated territory left on earth.[4]

Violent weather and precipitous terrain defeated the Chinese in their invasion effort. The Red militarists banked too much on the toughness of their troops and not enough on the logistical, medical, and meteorological aspects of this ambitious assault.

What happened? First of all, the invading army (of about 35,000) decided to take along trucks instead of camels and horses, although they had some of the latter. Trucks require roads and bridges. These had to be built and repaired in the *Chinese* provinces of Szechuan and Sikang, in order to get the army as far as the city of Chamdo. Yet Chamdo is almost 200 road miles from the recognized boundary of Tibet and about 385 air miles from Lhasa itself. This engineering project got under way in the spring of 1950, months before the invasion began. Roaring rivers, muddy swamps, deep valleys and precipitous, winding passes over snowy mountains, gave the Red engineers and other military units innumerable and almost unimaginable troubles.[5]

With accelerators down to the floor boards and gears meshed in low, the columns of trucks, loaded with gasoline and other supplies, roared off. The infantry marched on foot, as it always does in China. The trucks were needed to carry ponton bridge equipment for rivers yet unspanned.[6] The columns found it difficult

---

[4] The invasion of Taiwan had been postponed. Perhaps the Politburo figured that it needed a military victory to crow over. They think in such terms. Invasion of Tibet was logical in this concept.

[5] "Red Drive in Tibet Held a Costly One," by Henry R. Lieberman, New York *Times* correspondent, 23 March 1951.

[6] Official Chinese Communist photographs show that some US Army pontoon equipment was used.

and often impossible to maintain the old marching momentum. By late November the Chinese press carried great claims of success[7] to the reading public; but in between the lines one could read that the PLA forces were having their difficulties.

The first trouble that developed, other than terrain difficulties, was a shortage of gasoline. Uphill climbs and rocky, rutted roads kept the vehicles in low gear, and fuel consumption was beyond the original staff estimates. Furthermore, in the region of Sikang, there were no available fuel stocks. All the petrol had to be carried in by truck. This cut down the pay load that could be carried. Adding to these difficulties was the fact that, in the high altitudes, the infantry was tiring—to the extent that its commanders sought vehicles upon which their men could ride. The vehicles to fulfill these demands were not available.

There were two columns to the invasion. The main one, originating in Szechuan and marching west, consisted of five divisions of the Second Field Army. The second column, of about two divisions (from the First Field Army), advanced south and southwest from Chinghai (Tsinghai) Province. Both these invasion forces had about 700 miles to go to reach Lhasa.

Not only were the lines of communication poor, but the regions themselves were barren of food and sparsely populated. The food problem was serious. It was estimated that it cost six catties (about eight pounds) of rice to transport one catty just from the city of Chengtu to the town of Tachienlu (Tatsienlu). This was about 175 road miles.

The Red army crossed a barren land which had no people; the army could not take food from the inhabitants, in its usual parasite fashion, for there was none. The army had to increase its transport facilities. The Red columns did engage in labor all the civilians they could muster. At the Kinsha and Yalung rivers a great many people were pressed into labor, not only to build bridges and transport food but also to construct boats for the river crossings.[8] However, the main military body made progress and

---

[7] Yu Shah, "The 'Sun of Happiness' Rising Over Tibet," *People's China*, 1 December 1950.
[8] *People's China*, 16 November 1950.

by 19 October its advance elements reached the outskirts of Chamdo (Changtu), where they arranged a display of fireworks for the enemy. The Chamdo garrison was frightened away without any real combat. However, the Red army is reported[9] to have had about 10,000 casualties, or approximately one-third of its strength. According to the report, about 2,000 Chinese soldiers froze or starved to death; 3,000 were seriously stricken with a fever beyond the knowledge of the doctors; 2,000 were killed in hostile action; and "3,000 disappeared when they were ordered to cut off the Tibetans behind Changtu." An old Sikang folk song describes the weather conditions at the time of the "invasion"—

> During the first three months the snow
> > buries the mountains.
> During the next three, the rain
> > knocks your head off.
> During the third three you can get
> > through by climbing like a dog.
> During the last three months,
> > you had better stay home.

The "Roof of the World" was never militarily invaded before Tibet capitulated in fear in May 1951. The PLA's attempt was a military failure and in addition one which was financially very costly. Even the peaceful occupation by army forces was slow and behind schedule. Seldom in history has a mountainous nation been conquered by the fear of an army poised *outside* its actual borders!

The Amphibious Technique Is Terrible

The Korean War was not the only deterrent to the Red invasion of Taiwan. The Chinese Communists discovered, after a few trials, that their amphibious techniques were uncertain, and certainly unmodern. This gave pause to a portion of their plans for invasion. There were, however, larger factors in the postponement—the interposition of the US Seventh Fleet, and the need that developed

---

[9] This report and the figures which follow were obtained by Henry R. Lieberman in Hong Kong, from a Chinese engineer who participated in the Yangtze River crossing and who, at the time of the Tibetan invasion, was in the southwest China region.

Official Chinese Communist Photo.

AMPHIBIOUS TRAINING.

Launching the amphibious assault on the Choushan (Islands) south of Shanghai.

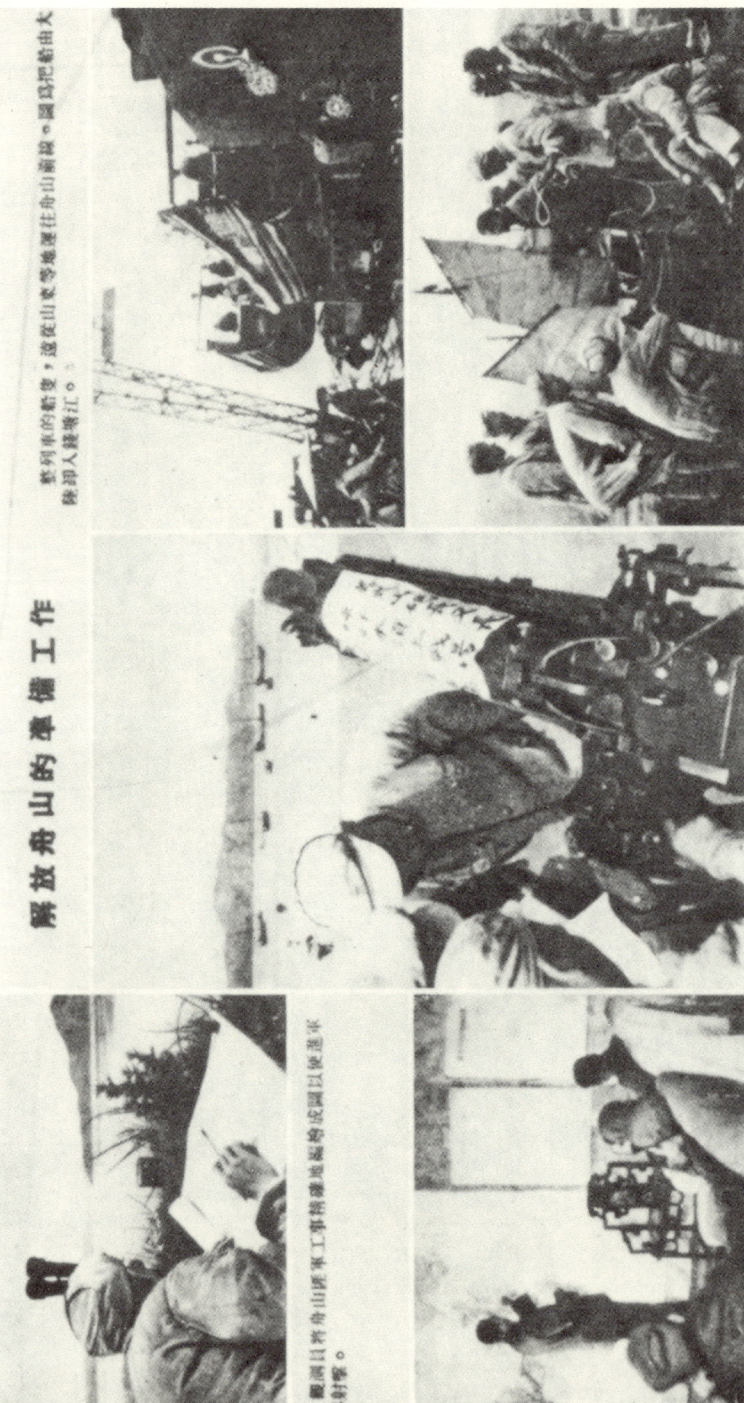

解放舟山的準備工作

Official Chinese Communist Photo.

At the top left, a military surveyor is shown charting the beaches; while (below left) General Wang Chien-an, one of the Army commanders, plans his part in the operation. In the center, a Red machine gunner learns to use a US machine gun. The placard on the gun reads "American guns are long and strong. Learn to use this well for combat." At the right, soldiers learn details of their amphibious craft from a model of a junk.

(as judged by the Sino-Soviet conference which reportedly took place in Peking in August 1950) to move PLA troops to Manchuria, and subsequently into Korea. But the initial pause resulted from the Red discovery that they lacked proficiency in amphibious operations. The PLA is still training in this type of specialized operation, but none of its elements are skilled in it. Publicly the Communists claim mastery of amphibious warfare; inwardly they know they are weak in this technique.

Cocky and confident after their "over-water" crossing of the Yangtze River in the spring of 1949, the Red Chinese swept the mainland areas almost clean of Government troops; then undertook island invasion. The PLA, not at all navy-wise, approached what it considered to be a not too difficult problem. "Get the ships and get the army men on them—then get everyone onto the islands." This was the view of most Red military commanders.

Fishermen and traders were rounded up in the steamy ports of South China, and told to strip down their junks and other vessels or use by the PLA. As the Red staff officers compiled lists of vessels and made up loading tables, they began to sense that here was a type of operation with complexities. Who, for instance, was going to navigate the swarms of troop-laden junks? The PLA checked its ranks, but found almost no men or officers with proper sea experience. So the fishermen who knew the sea, were relied upon for navigation; but to insure their loyalty, they were given brief political indoctrination.

What of water speeds? How constant, how variable, and how fast? The vessels varied greatly in speed because of differences in types. The PLA staffs did not like this, but they gave orders for small invasions. However, in the end, it was the non-military, the non-naval sailors and skippers of the junks, who bore the real burden of responsibility, once the little invasion forces put out to sea. Division and army commanders had earlier compared notes and decided that for the moment this would have to do. But the army was not happy about relying on a corps of miscellaneous ship owners and sailors for its assaults by sea. The PLA felt uncertain and insecure in its first invasions.

The army has been accustomed to relying on civilian masses for help, but to place the safety of military units in the hands of a few civilians for precarious cross-water assault was embarrassing. Red officers sensed the inefficiency in this system. They feared sabotage and they could not fully trust the motley crews of the junks to deliver their men to a given beach at a given time.

The army left familiar ground when it began amphibious operations. Momentarily it laid aside war plans to devote time, study, and training to amphibious techniques. Today, certain United States Army field manuals on this subject are being studied by the Chinese Reds. For years Yenan's widespread military intelligence has been collecting U.S. military manuals, magazines, and books. After World War II, when it was contemplated that Red units would be integrated into the Nationalist Army, several U.S. Army field manuals were turned over to the Communists. The Reds have all of the U.S. tactical, technical, and operational data on amphibious doctrine they can translate and digest. They need only improved organization, more practice, and a measure of combat experience to bring them up to an efficient level. It is in the conduct of amphibious assault that the PLA will borrow doctrine and devices more from the United States than from the Soviets.

The Red Chinese Navy is essentially made up of a miscellaneous collection of several hundred vessels captured from the Nationalists. There are at least 45 LST's in good condition and manned by crews which were for the most part Nationalist trained. The cruiser *Chungking* and more than a half a dozen destroyer type vessels are now in the Red Fleet, which includes numerous US landing craft. Most of the vessels that the fleeing Nationalists scuttled have since been raised and repaired. Red China's armed forces do not include, however, sufficient modern landing craft for the number of troops they plan to use in the invasion of Taiwan, so motorized junks and other native craft will be greatly relied upon. There have been reports to the effect that the USSR is giving Red China some submarines.

Photographs from inside the Bamboo Curtain show groups of soldiers crowding around intricate models of junks. Quite obviously the instructors are training their men in matters such as loading and stowage. This demonstrative training is being given in a large number of class rooms with an ample number of models—for model-making is an established trade in China, where thousands of exact copies of the multiple forms of junks were formerly offered for sale to tourists.

During the amphibious assaults on Chou-shan and the other islands, drownings apparently caused as many if not more casualties than Nationalist gunfire. Here again was manifest the PLA's official disregard for human life. In short-distance, inter-island assaults, hundreds of soldiers were issued the triangular bamboo frames, and the companies and battalions were told to "shove off and make for the next island." Individually afloat in these crude life rafts, the Red soldiers were expected to battle their way across hundreds of yards of choppy water against the currents of wind and tides—not to mention enemy fire from hostile shores. Did all these luckless Chinese soldiers know how to swim? No; but they were obedient to orders. Afraid? Yes; but the commissars had reassured them that it was purely a matter of floating with a favorable current to the hostile shore. One cannot record the poignant emotions of these luckless, simple soldiers, naive in their faith in their officers and political commissars—who were fumbling at a new technique; but one can sense that there was poor morale in a unit of floating soldiers.

The documented record shows that hundreds of Red soldiers were literally lashed together by ropes, in these bamboo life-takers, and were towed between junks and sampans toward the assault beaches.

In early 1949, the "hill-billies" of Generals Chen Yi and Su Yu were fearful of the Yangtze River waters. General Chen Yi and his staff were quick to sense this soldier fear, so they rapidly improvised some modified amphibious training on the lakes of North China. This was in preparation for the Yangtze crossing. The training had one simple objective—to eliminate fear. The Reds already had gathered hundreds of river junks, launches, and sampans from the miles of inland waterways near the Yangtze, but rehearsals were conducted nevertheless. Even the width of the training lakes frightened the young soldiers.

The training revealed some remarkable contrasts in efficiency. One division got its men across a lake in a matter of hours, while another division, on the same lake, was three days in closing all of its units on the far shore. In the final crossing of the swirling and dirty Yangtze, some of the soldiers were equipped with the triangular bamboo life rafts while others had peasant-woven straw "life rings." The latter were made of some 17 pounds of straw and would keep a man afloat for a brief period. It was just prior to this crossing that General Chen Yi stripped down and waded knee-deep in muck and mire to shovel free a portion of an obstructed canal. Chinese Communist generals know when their troops need the encouragement supplied by personal example. Red soldiers certainly needed such reassurances in 1949.

The Yangtze River crossing was accomplished at four major points and many smaller ones. It was a large undertaking for the Chinese Communists.

One American writer and observer[10] credits the crossing as one of the "military greats" of the Civil War, and a monument to Chinese ingenuity. However, the Reds did not have to assault shores which were strongly defended. Some of the later waterborne attacks educated the Reds in the grim realism of amphibious assault.

As an example of how costly island real estate was to the Red Chinese, consider Chinmen Island in October 1949. There, according to Irving Short, an American observer of the battle, the Communists lost 7,000 men as prisoners to the Nationalists, and in addition some 13,000 were drowned or killed. But bloated and floating Chinese bodies do not warrant tears and sympathy among the PLA officers. The bodies which were swept onto the beaches simply made the commissars curse and shout for more daring and more efficiency. The failure was obvious to many officers who could not safely reveal their inner thoughts to the commissars.

The PLA needed more than training and daring, it needed

---

[10] Harrison Forman.

proper shipping. China was combed for DUKWS (amphibious trucks), LCI's (landing craft, infantry), and other vessels which were placed under centralized control. A better fleet was gradually created in late 1949 and early 1950.

Two of the Chinese field armies have undergone specialized training in amphibious warfare. They are the Fourth Field Army, elements of which made a few amphibious landings and "liberated" Hainan; and the Third Field Army, many units of which have studied the lessons of the Fourth. The units which attacked the Chou-san Islands were from the Third Field Army. Present day PLA doctrine calls for the use of the so-called "model troops" to spearhead combat assaults.

Red officers have been worried over their chances of success in the proposed invasion of Taiwan. However, to compensate for the PLA's lack of amphibious excellence, the officers are planning a giant operation, wherein sheer numbers and volume are expected to insure success. General Su Yu, Vice Commander of the Third Field Army, has this to say about the coming invasion of Taiwan[11]—

It is an extremely big problem, and will involve the biggest campaign in history of modern Chinese warfare.

General Su Yu who has participated in some of the biggest campaigns of the China Civil War estimates[14] that the Nationalists have 230,000 regulars on Taiwan—or 44 divisions, which constitute 71 percent of the total 340,000 (or 61 divisions). Without specifying Communist numbers, General Su Yu broadly hints that Red attack forces will be at least double, and possibly triple, the Nationalist defensive strength. This latter proportion should be expected. General Su Yu's analysis of enemy numbers preceded the Chinese Communist entry into the Korean war and must be viewed in the light of subsequent history, now recorded. The fact remains however, that the Third Field Army has been officially chosen for the "liberation." As in Hainan, where Red General Feng Pai-chu led[12] the local people in armed rebellion, a fifth

---

[11] "Liberation of Taiwan in Sight," by General Su Yu, *People's China*, 16 February 1950.

[12] *People's China*: 1 May 1950; 16 May 1950.

column must be expected in Taiwan when the Red attack is launched.

What are the chances of Communist success when they try to invade Taiwan? Without detailing the multiple factors, one fact stands dominant—the Reds must be beaten at sea when they are in transit. Once they get within a few hundred yards of the beach their multiple masses will roll beachward with weighty impetus. If any sizable beachheads are established, the defenders will be in serious trouble. Cut off Red supplies? This can be done by hostile air in daytime; but the Reds supply and move by night—and they are rarely stopped after dark. Like the Soviet Army in river crossings, the Chinese will swarm ashore on Taiwan, to establish many bridgeheads, exploiting those which stick and ignoring those which fail.

Once the Communists get their invasion feet on the island, Taiwan is likely to fall. If the Reds are defeated, it will be when they are still afloat.

How the Supreme Commander of Taiwan Evaluates the PLA

Lieutenant General Sun Li-jen, Commander in Chief of Chinese Ground Forces and the Nationalist general charged with the defense of Taiwan, has never retreated before the Chinese Communists. He fought them to a standstill in Manchuria before he was selected, in 1947, to head a new training command on Taiwan. He has been on the island since 1947. At any time he may face a devastating onslaught by the Chinese Communists—the enemy which General Sun, in his own words, describes below—

RED TACTICS AND TECHNIQUE

Lack of air cover and shortage of heavy weapons and equipment taught the Chinese Reds the necessity of concealment, camouflage, and night marches, and the desirability of closing with their opponents as soon as possible, before the fire of (enemy) heavy weapons could be fully developed. Such concepts not only helped to develop consummate skill . . . in camouflage and night operations, but also . . . led to a firm conviction that they could surprise their opponents. The principles of security and surprise were . . . learned, and their military (operations) are . . . characterized by surprise attacks, night operations, ruses, and ambushes.

Their ideology has taught them ruthlessness. Their favorite tactic—the 'human sea' attack—is used either as a means to effect a rupture . . . or as a decisive stroke when victory hangs in the balance.

RED PRE-BATTLE PREPARATIONS

They very carefully drew plans to "prepare" the anticipated theater of war for, combat.

The usual procedure was infiltration of political commissars, followed by floods of propaganda exploiting discontent, fomenting unrest, and fraternizing with the local populace with the double object of gaining sympathy, thus facilitating food supply and gaining invaluable information about the enemy. It was a clever way of casting an invisible net of intelligence over the area of operations. This proved to be of immense value to their armies. The Chinese Reds prepared their troops before . . . battle. They raised (morale) to a high pitch by intensive indoctrination and propaganda which, alone, has won them spectacular successes . . . Numerous meetings . . . of little groups of officers and men took place . . . before and after a campaign; discussions . . . of the problems were encouraged and comments and criticisms were freely given. In this way the soldiers not only got more acquainted with the mission before them but had . . . a feeling of self-importance.

THE SOLDIERS

Fodder of cannon . . . recruited by persuasion, propaganda or coercion . . . morale high . . . in some cases fanatic; . . . their enthusiasm . . . kept up by ruthless propaganda . . . and by fabricated stories. (The soldiers') incredible endurance, spirit of sacrifice and a philosophic belief in fatalism . . . makes them formidable. . . . The overwhelming majority of privates lack . . . education . . .

THE OFFICERS

They can be grouped in three categories: . . . the diehard . . . Communists, who form a small percentage; . . . the opportunists . . . defectionists from the Nationalist camp . . . who form a fairly high percentage; finally the indifferent or reluctant, who form the majority.

Two decades of almost incessant fighting and moving about, and the terrible conditions under which they lived, has given them neither the time nor the opportunity to study . . . modern warfare or indulge in deeper reflections on the military art. The majority . . . possess a good knowledge of the teachings of Sun Tzu . . . but only very superficial military education in the modern sense. The intoxicating effect of repeated victories is exercising a gripping and fatal influence on the mentality of the majority . . . resulting in self-satisfaction, arrogance, and ignorance.

TRAINED PERSONNEL

For lack of experienced and trained personnel . . . military technology and scientific appliances . . . the Chinese Red Army (is) still in its primitive stage, and (the Red) 'know how' technique . . . on guerrilla scales, has clearly failed to cope with . . . modern warfare . . . on problems of supply and administration.

The administrative personnel . . . are mostly youngsters with unbounded enthusiasm and courage, but with little education or training. How badly they are in need of trained personnel can be seen in their absurd system of admitting school boys, who have not finished their elementary or lower-middle schooling, into military colleges or universities.

THE HIGH LEADERS

Despite their varied experiences, they still belong to that class of warriors "who wage war without understanding it." When confronted by a modern force . . . the myth of their invincibility will be exploded; and the world will be amazed by the rate of disintegration.

IN SUMMARY

The Chinese Red Army will learn . . . that success in battle cannot be won by morale alone, but also requires material, tactical excellence of troops, high standards of professional competence and skill among . . . officers, and adherence to sound strategical principles.

The time will come when the . . . Communists will realize that . . . 'human sea' tactics are no match against modern science and organization . . . Until then the Chinese Red Army is, at best, an unbalanced force which will crack up the moment it is pitched against a modern army.

—SUN LI-JEN
Lieutenant General

Taiwan, 20 May 1951

The Future Pattern in Indo-China

The French are in for more trouble! Indo-China will likely be the next significant pressure point of Chinese Communist military aggression, but the Chinese moves will probably be subtle in comparison with the outright entry of their "volunteer" armies into

Korea. Red Chinese military efforts to aid the Viet Minh forces will continue to be clandestine in nature because the Chinese do not want their hand called, initially at least. Up to mid-1951, evidence of the extent of Chinese military aid to the Viet Minh has not been made public to a degree which would fully warrant a formal accusation of aggression on an international level, but the French Government was not disclosing all of its carefully collected secrets. The French were militarily capable of coping with the rebel forces existing during 1951. The French doubtless have refrained from making accusations on minor issues, awaiting the day when increased Chinese military assistance to the rebels will force the French to disclose more detailed information, and appeal for United Nations' assistance.

The PLA has trained and equipped some 24,000 troops in South China for the Viet Minh, and in addition it has loaned military advisors and technicians to that insurgent army. French military officials reported in mid-1951 that two more divisions were being equipped by the PLA. Thus the indications are that the Communists of China intend even greater assistance in the future. The Reds of Peking have gone so far as to begin rationalization of their position: in December 1950 the Peking regime charged 120 French air intrusions over Chinese territory between 1 September 1950 and 31 October 1950.

The heavy demands of a war in Korea did not permit the PLA to divert very much effort in support of the rebels in Indo-China. However, as the PLA gains more Soviet war materiel, and if the demands in Korea lessen, the PLA will give its poorer Communist brothers its military surpluses of weapons and equipment. The railway from Nanning to the Indo-Chinese border is complete, or nearly so. This link was constructed solely for military purposes, one of which is the supply of arms and equipment to the Viet Minh. The PLA does not have to pour many "volunteers" into Indo-China. It needs only to arm and train the regimented Viet Minh forces at secret bases, direct the officers toward more tactical skill, and then wait patiently for the French forces to exhaust themselves in the festering paddies and jungles. Oriental patience is the great weapon in that struggle—the patience of sloe-eyed guerrillas who were born into the region of heat, jungle and flies, against the patience of Westerners who were not. The strategical concept is not all "hustle and get this over with"—it is: "wear the enemy down." Chinese Communist military timetables are not designed for speed, but for certainty.

Until August 1951 no regular PLA units were identified as fighting with the Viet Minh rebels, but individual Chinese "volunteers" were known. In the future it is probable that Red Chinese soldiers will be scattered through the Viet Minh ranks rather than employed in Chinese units. This pattern will prevail only if the Viet Minh is not effectively defeated. If the rebels are effectively beaten, Red China is likely to repeat her pattern of open intervention as she did in Korea.

Air Force—the Reluctant Dragon

We face some bloody and flesh-shredding carnage if the Red Chinese and their allies ever get bold enough to launch an air force at us in Korea. We, not they, are the most vulnerable to air attack, for we have the preponderance of motorization and the more extensive logistical installations in Korea. Our logistical "tail" lies mostly on the Korean peninsula; whereas the Chinese supply route extends into the sanctuary of Manchuria. Thus the Chinese, or any other hostile air force, has available to it more profitable targets, proportionately, than are open to us.

Why hasn't the Chinese air force attacked us? Mao Tse-tung has dressed his fly-boys in snappy new uniforms, Soviet advisers have given the young pilots training that has set their brains awhirl, and the Chinese have some flashy aircraft on their airfields. But these slant-eyed pilots, as a group, have been uncertain about their ability to tangle seriously with hostile aircraft. The Chinese hierarchy hasn't wanted to lose all their pretty planes in one fell swoop. The Soviets apparently advised them to be careful and to learn the fly-trade gradually. Fortunately for us, we have not seen the Chinese attempt to dominate the Korean skies; but we are in for serious trouble, at least for a brief period, when they do.

The Chinese Communist Air Force (CCAF) had its origin in 1946, when Lin Piao's men took over the airplane scrap heaps that were left on Japanese airfields in Manchuria. From acres of Japanese military and civil aircraft, the Chinese Reds salvaged a dozen or so planes. (Most of the aircraft, left on the ground, had been demolished by the Soviets earlier.) General Lin's staff scraped up some Japanese pilots who were ordered to train a few Chinese Reds to fly. This was the original "air force." At that time the Reds simply wanted something in the way of air transport for key army officers. General Chou Pao-chung, in addition to his other positions, was then chief of the "Reorganization Section of the Northeast Aviation Headquarters." He was a driving force behind the effort to equip the Communist military with aircraft. But from 1946 to 1949, the Reds in Manchuria could muster only a few planes. Since the Nationalist Air Force dominated the skies, the Reds centered their air activity at distant Chiamussu and at hidden airfields in northern Manchuria. The aircraft the Reds possessed did not, in any way, constitute an air force, or even an air division.

Russia wasn't ready to give Lin Piao any fighter or bomber craft; but aid came in another form. The Soviets helped train Chinese pilots in the USSR. The extent of this activity was hard to discover at the time, but numerous reports added up to the significant fact that such air training was going on. Then, in 1948, the Chinese Consul General in Khabarovsk reported that, on 23 June 1948, a group of some 50 Chinese, wearing Communist Air Force uniforms, were seen on Marx Street in Khabarovsk. On 28 September 1948, Kato Matsudaira, Chief of the Survey Bureau of the Japanese Foreign Office, told the press that thirty Japanese pilots had returned from the USSR where they had been training Chinese pilots. The planes could be given to China at any propitious moment and they could be used immediately, providing there were pilots. This was apparently the Soviet view of the moment.

Soviet help had readied the pilots who were on hand when the PLA won the Civil War. The Chinese Reds persuaded a few

Nationalist pilots to bring their planes into Red areas, but there was no large scale defection of Nationalist Air Force personnel to the Red side. However, as the Civil War swept the Nationalists toward South China, the Reds captured and gathered up aircraft, pilots, mechanics, and ground crew personnel.[13] It was with this acquisition of old US C-47 and C-46 transports, P-51 fighters, and B-25 bombers that the CCAF took on real substance. By the time of the establishment of the Red Regime in Peking (1949), General Chu Teh could hear his own planes roar overhead. Soviet aircraft were introduced shortly thereafter.

Who are the mysterious pilots of the MIG's that fly out from the airfields near Antung, Manchuria? "All of us would like to know . . ." stated Captain James Jabara, the first jet ace in history, who concluded that "the consensus is that the enemy has two teams. The first team, a lot of people think, is made up of highly trained European Communist and ex-*Luftwaffe* pilots. The second stringers are Chinese and possibly North Koreans."[14]

Red China has not had time to develop and train a large group of Chinese pilots—especially jet flyers. About 200 ex-Nationalist pilots, many with American training, are now in Communist China. They are a valuable nucleus and by now probably well enough indoctrinated for the Reds to permit them to fly near the borders of China. It is not probable, however, that any of these pilots are flying jets.

There are already reports that, to bolster its backward air force, Red China has imported pilots and crewmen from Russia, East Germany, Poland, Rumania, Czechoslovakia, Hungary, Bulgaria, Albania, Lithuania, India, and even Burma, to form an international volunteer air force.[15] It is probable that the Chinese have gathered several hundred good pilots from the World War II reservoirs of such personnel. The bonds between Communists of different nations are known, and it is entirely likely that the

---

[13] The Communists claimed, in 1950, that 2,000 former Nationalist pilots, mechanics, and technicians worked for them in their Air Force.
[14] Captain James Jabara, "We Fly MIG Alley," *Air Force,* June 1951.
[15] According to the *China News* of Taiwan (from a Hong Kong dispatch of 7 May 1951), such a force is in being and is commanded by a Soviet Air Force general.

governments of the more technically advanced Red-controlled nations have sent help to the aviation-backward regime in China. Soviet Russia, seldom caught at overt assistance of this sort, undoubtedly ordered her satellites to provide this help.

However, the cards gradually are being turned face upward; Soviet advisory help in aviation is now an established fact, so that the presence of Soviet pilots on a "lend-lease" or volunteer basis in Red China may soon be acknowledged.

"MIG Alley" in North Korea is a combat training ground for Chinese pilots who are learning to bring their flying skill up to the excellence of the Soviet aircraft they fly. The embryo Chinese air force is growing stronger with this experience and is learning the tactical ways of American military aviation. Certainly every experience is being recorded in writing and carefully studied. There may be no flashiness in oriental pilotage and tactics, but one can be certain that there will be studied thoroughness in the emerging techniques. One morning we may wake up to some devastating air attacks.

What is the combat strength of this Red Air Force about which

---

RED AIR LOSSES IN KOREA
(June 1950 through 9 May 1951)*

Communist Losses

149 Red planes destroyed.
27 Red planes probably destroyed.
167 Red planes damaged.

Of these, 53 MIG-15 fighters were destroyed in air combat, with 17 others probably destroyed and 103 damaged in air-to-air fighting.

Total number of United Nations planes lost to enemy action— 212.

* (According to Lt. General O. P. Weyland, Deputy Commander, Tactical Air Force, 12 May 51)

> **THE MIG-15 IN USE FOR RED CHINA IS A RUGGED JET**
>
> Soviet designed and manufactured, the MIG-15 superficially modernizes Red China's Armed Forces. It is a sturdy jet that has great resistance to combat damage, but it appears to be devoid of creature comforts and deficient in the instruments and radio equipment that, taken together, appear to give the US Sabre (F-86A) a slight edge. The poor Red gunnery may result, in part, from pilot fatigue and the lack of refinement in interior design and equipment. However, the MIG is a rugged instrument of destruction with these known characteristics:*
>
> | | |
> |---|---|
> | *Armament* | 1 x 37-mm cannon (on right)
2 x 20-mm cannon (on left) |
> | *Weight* | 10,850 lbs. (normal gross) |
> | *Power Plant* | Centrifugal-flow type "Rolls-Royce, Nene," Modified Static Thrust, 5,000 lbs. Military power, 4,800 lbs. |
> | *Speed* | 615 mph at 25,000 ft. |
> | *Rate of Climb* | 8,800 feet a minute at 25,000 feet |
> | *Service Ceiling* | 45,000 ft. |
> | *Normal Range* | About 700-800 miles with wing tanks |
>
> *Source: *Air Force* Magazine, June 1951.

we know so little? Estimates range from 1,000 to 3,000 aircraft, but reliable sources hold to a mean of about 850 combat aircraft, with transport planes adding another 300. Of the 850 combat planes, only about 180 are jets and 600 are conventional propeller-driven fighters. The number of bombers is reputed to be about 70. The remainder, or 200 planes, are training and reconnaissance craft. The total is 1,350 military aircraft of all types directly available to the CCAF.

The disposition of military aircraft in early 1951 was not all in the direction of Manchuria and Korea, although a considerable traffic of planes from the USSR, was reported in Manchuria. The Chinese had at least one-half their combat air force in Central and South China, apparently defensively disposed against any attacks from Taiwan. Nanking, Shanghai, and Hankow are the most active military air centers outside of Manchuria.

The presence of speedy jets with the Red Chinese armed forces does not necessarily make the forces modern. The Red Chinese armed forces have some ultra-modern aircraft, but they lack such in between necessities as a tactical air force, an adequate number of mechanics and technicians, artillery spotting aircraft, helicopters, and other essential types. The concentration of the moment is on fighter pilots and planes—a defensive medium the Peking military men feel is necessary to protect China's cities and coastline. Bombers appear to have second priority and, curiously enough for a ground army of the PLA's character, there is no visible emphasis on tactical aviation.

Both the Red Chinese Air Force and Navy were, up to August 1951, defensive in character and in primary role. Mao's military men seemed to feel that they could not risk committing their air arm; that it had to be saved and built up, even if the ground forces took terrific losses in the interim. However, we must watch out for a foreign "volunteer air force" which may appear—already trained, organized, and equipped.[16]

The Chinese Red Air Force is now strong enough to produce momentary havoc in Korea or elsewhere!

---

[16] On 21 May 1951, the *United Press* reported from Washington:

"Russia has tipped the balance of air power in the Far East in her favor by stationing one-fourth of her total combat planes in that area, military intelligence officials estimated today.

"The Russian operational air fleet was estimated by these officials to be 20,000 first-line combat planes. They said indications were that Red Air Force strength in the Orient totaled 5,000 planes.

"In addition to the Far Eastern air arm, the officials estimated that the Reds have deployed 7,000 planes along the Iron Curtain in Western Europe and about 8,000 in the Soviet Union itself.

"The exact numerical strength of American air power in the Far East is veiled in secrecy. But officials admitted that the US planes were far outnumbered in the area. They also said that the United States has as much air power based in the Far East as it feels it can spare now."

Korea Shows Up Red Deficiencies

The Chinese Reds have waged war in Korea just the way their tactical concepts up to 1950 had been written. They have repeatedly struck out in "one main direction," in keeping with Mao Tse-tung's teachings. The PLA has demonstrated obedience to its ten principles of war. It attacked us initially when we were moving. Later it attacked our weakest military elements, the South Korean units. In between its own giant offensives the PLA has generally avoided battle. Lin Piao's military hand and concepts were also evident in the tactics applied. The use of Red aircraft was the only modern touch up to mid-1951.

The Chinese Reds made their greatest strategic mistake in 1950—their failure to destroy the US X Corps in December 1950. Mobile on foot but with mechanization missing, the Chinese arrived too late, with too little, at the beachheads of Hungnam—Hamhung. They missed their one great strategic opportunity.

Mao Tse-tung and his generals have shown that they are willing

Photo by the Author.

PATHWAY TO POWER.
The Chinese Red leaders are determined to follow their program of aggression—even though it leads over carpets of dead.

to lay down veritable carpets of dead to achieve their aggressive aims. The PLA and the people are docile instruments in the hands of this fanatical hierarchy. The mainland Chinese will obey the Red regime and there is visible on the horizon at this time no hope of any successful revolution against its rule.

Since 1937 at least four million Chinese soldiers have become casualties while serving under General Chu Teh's red colors. Against the Japanese the Chinese Communist military sustained at least two million casualties. In the China Civil War the Reds admit to one and one-half million losses. Up until the truce arguments began, the PLA had sustained over 550,000 casualties in Korea. At least four times (1944, 1945, 1947-48 and 1948-49) in its history the PLA has suffered the loss of just over or just under a half-million men in one single year of combat and conflict! One would think that the Red leaders would hesitate in the face of such bloodshed, but they do not. Often they are more concerned over materiel losses than human losses. It is costly in all aspects to an enemy of the Red Chinese to shoot them up on a machine-gun and artillery basis, for this is the way the Red Chinese want us to fight them—their way. To defeat the PLA in any region, it is necessary to resort to the unconventional weapons which should be combined with a concentrated campaign of psychological warfare. Soldier fear must be generated. The object should be to induce wholesale surrenders. In the long run it is unprofitable to try and shoot every Communist soldier. PLA armies *can* be put to panic if the right methods are used. Imagination is necessary. For example, eerie, luminous paint could be sprayed over road intersections in the Red rear areas while announcements warn the Chinese against the consequences of crossing such "poisonous" areas—devices like these, combined with new and powerful weapons which do have deadly effect, can demoralize large segments of the PLA. The emphasis must be on generating *fear, confusion,* and *doubt.* Capital must be made of the inherent Chinese fear of death by lightning or electrocution. To effectively win a war against the PLA, an opponent should develop a trunkful of tricks and ruses designed to play on Chinese soldier minds. Potent weapons, combined with imaginative psychological warfare methods, can disintegrate the morale of the PLA's masses. Chinese, or any other men, fear the unknown. The Red soldiers of the Peoples' Liberation Army are well acquainted with conventional weapons. Atomic weapons used against them would of course produce utter havoc.

The Chinese Communist Army has, I hope, been described in this volume in fair degree. There remains but one fact to repeat and one opinion to express:

Mao Tse-tung does not fear long wars, or atomic bombs. His army can be defeated!

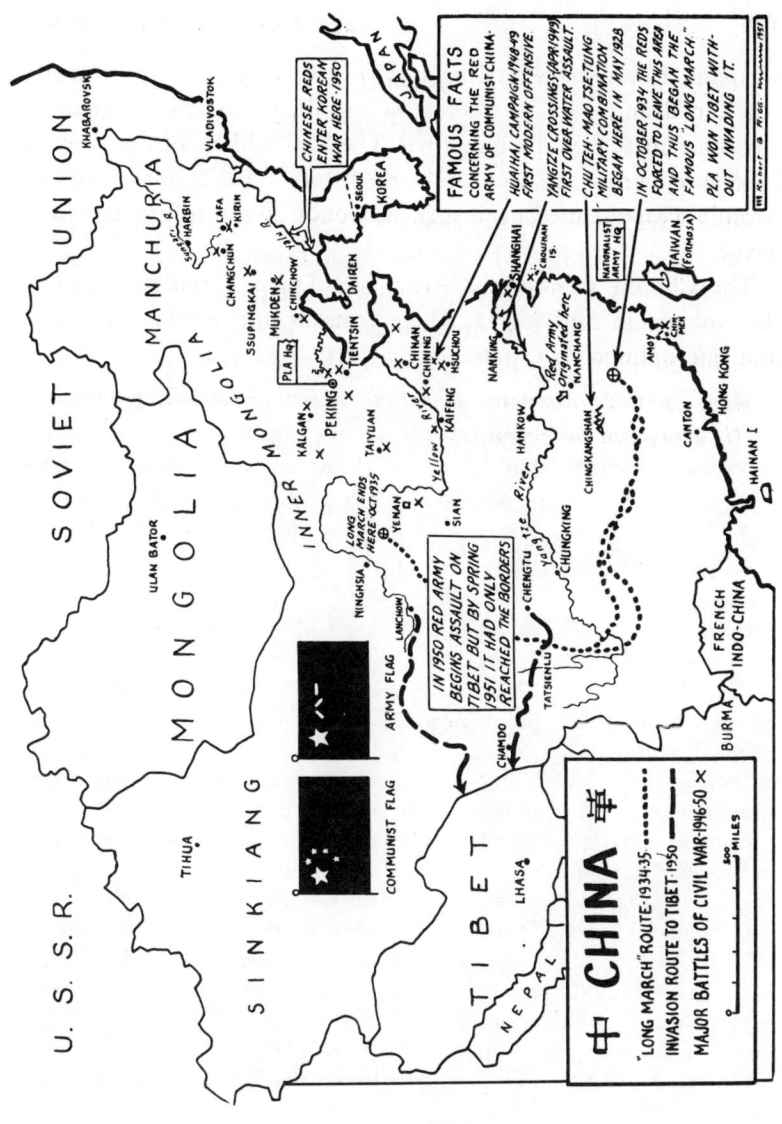

Appendix I
MAP OF CHINA—AND FAMOUS FACTS ABOUT THE ARMY OF COMMUNIST CHINA

Appendix II
THE MORE PROMINENT GENERALS OF THE CHINESE RED ARMY

There are more than a thousand general officers in the PLA. Listed here are 181 Red Chinese generals who are prominent today. Obviously this list is not complete and there are a few whose exact military titles are uncertain. This is not a "Who's Who," but simply a list of high officers with their last known title or position given for purposes of quick and easy identification. Names of a few of the old-time leaders do not appear here because they have not recently been identified. Most of these general officers occupy several civilian posts as well, but only their military assignments are here listed.

General CHANG Chen, a member of headquarters of Fourth Field Army in 1949.

General CHANG, Chi-ch'un, Deputy Chief of the General Political Section of the PLA in 1951.

General CHANG Chih-chung, former Nationalist officer who deserted during 1949 peace negotiations. Chairman of National Research Section of the People's Revolutionary Military Council in 1950.

General CHANG Ching-wu, Director of a bureau in the PLA's headquarters, and negotiator with the Tibetans in 1951.

General CHANG Chung, a Yunnanese Communist who went south in advance of the main armies and organized fifth columns in 1947 and 1948. Engaged in work mainly outside the PLA in 1950.

General CHANG Hsueh-ssu, member of the General Staff of the PLA in 1949. He was reported to have been purged in 1951.

General CHANG Keh-hsia, a former Nationalist Army Commander who defected to the Communist and still retained his original command under the Communists as late as 1949.

General CHANG Nan-sheng, in headquarters of the Second Field Army in 1949.

General CHANG Ting-cheng, Deputy Commander of the Third Field Army in 1951.

General CHANG Tsai-feng, reported as the commander of a Ninth Army in North China in early 1949.

General CHANG Tse-chang, Chief of Staff of a Red military command in North China in 1947.

APPENDIX 331

General CHANG Tsung-hsun, Acting Commander of the First Field Army in 1951.

General CHANG Wen, member of the Central and South China Military-Political Affairs Committee in 1950.

General CHANG Yun-i, member of the headquarters of South China Liberation Army in 1949. Believed to be a Deputy Commander of the Third Field Army in 1950. Commander of the Kwangsi War Zone in 1951.

General CHAO Erh-lu, Chief of Staff of the Fourth Field Army, 1951.

General CHAO Kuang-hsing, ex-Nationalist officer and defector who commanded the Communist 104th Division (35th Army) late in 1948.

General CHAO Li-huai, Commander of 49th Army of Fourth Field Army, 1951.

General CHAO Shou-shan, Second Deputy Commander of the First Field Army in 1951.

General CHEN Hai-han, Chief of Staff of the First Field Army in 1950.

General CHEN Jui-ting, Commander of the Third (Mecz) Army in the Nanking area in 1951; a so-called "armor expert."

General CHEN Keng, Deputy Commander of the Second Field Army, Deputy Commander of the South China Military Area and Commander of the Yunnan War Zone in 1951.

General CHEN Man-yuan, Chief of Staff of the Shansi-Suiyuan Anti-Japanese Base under General Lu Cheng-tsao in 1945. Known to have been on the Staff of the South China Liberation Army in 1949 and believed to have been its Chief of Staff.

General CHEN Min-jen, Deputy Commander of the Hunan Provincial Military Zone in 1949.

General CHEN Po, in headquarters of the First Field Army in 1949.

Admiral CHEN Shao-kuan, former Nationalist naval officer now serving the Communists.

General CHEN Shih-chu, Chief of Staff of the Third Field Army in 1951.

General CHEN Ta-nan, reported as the Commander of a "Seventh Army" in North China in late 1948.

General CHEN Yi, Commander of the Third Field Army in 1951.

General CHENG Chien, the most successful Nationalist defector, Cheng is one of the five Vice-Chairmen of the Revolutionary Military Council (1951).

General CHENG Tzu-hua, Commander, as well as Political Commissioner, of the Shansi War Zone 1950.

General CHENG Shih-chu, Chief of Staff of the Third Field Army in 1950.

General CHIANG Wei-ch'ing, in the headquarters of the Third Field Army in 1949.

General CHIEN Hsin-chung, in the headquarters of the Second Field Army in 1949.

General CHOU Pao-chung, Deputy Commander-in-Chief of the Fourth Field Army in 1951.

General CHOU Shih-ti, Deputy Commander of the Southwest China Military Area.

General CHOU Sze-ti, nominated to be Red China's chief delegate to the Allied Council in Japan in 1950.

General CHU Chia-pi, Commander of the Yunnan People's First Column in 1948.

General CHU Kuang, a commissar in an unspecified army, 1950.

General CHU Teh, Commander-in-Chief of the People's Liberation Army in 1951.

General CHUANG Tien, Commander of the Kwangsi-Yunnan-Kweichow Column in 1950.

General CHUNG Chih-ping, in the headquarters of Fourth Field Army in 1949.

General FANG Fang, Commander of Fukien-Kwangtung Column. Also a member of the Central and South China Military and Political Affairs Committee and the Canton Military Control Commission.

General FENG Mai-ch'ao, in the headquarters of the South China Liberation Army in 1949.

General FENG Pai-chu, Commander of the Hainan Column of the Fourth Field Army in 1949. The fifth columnist who led uprisings on Hainan.

General FU Chung, a member of the PLA's General Staff in 1949.

General FU Tso-Yi, ex-warlord and Nationalist general who turned over his troops to PLA in 1949. Has since become a member of the People's Revolutionary Military Council, Minister of Water Conservancy. In 1951 was Commander of the Suiyuan War Zone.

General HAN Hsien-chu, Deputy Commander of the Hunan Provincial Military Zone in 1949. Also served with the Fourth Field Army.

General HO Chi-li, in the headquarters of the Third Field Army in 1949.

General HO Chi-feng, former army commander of the Nationalist forces who defected to the Communists in 1948.

APPENDIX   333

General HO Chih-pin, ex-Nationalist and defector who commanded the Red 105th Division (35th Army) in late 1948.

General HO Lung, Commander of the Northwest China Military Area in 1951.

General HSI Chung-hsun, Political Commissioner of PLA's North West Military Headquarters after 1948. Political commissar with the First Field Army in 1951.

General HSIAO Ching-kuang, Commander of the Hunan (Provincial Military) War Zone and Deputy Commander of the Fourth Field Army in 1951.

General HSIAO Hua, Commander of Liaotung Military Region under Lin Piao in 1947. In the Soviet Union in 1948. Active in occupation of Peking. Visited Europe in 1949.

General HSIAO Keh, Chief of Staff of the Fourth Field Army in 1950. Believed to have been killed in Korea, 1951.

General HSIEH Fang (alias SENG Wang), one of the 1951 negotiators in the Korean truce talks. He is reportedly a graduate of a Moscow university.

General HSIEH Fu-chih, a high ranking officer believed to be with the Second Field Army in 1951.

General HSIEH Sheng-k'un, in the headquarters of the Third Field Army in 1949.

General HSU Hsiang-chien, Deputy Commander of the North China Military Headquarters in 1948. Named Army Chief of Staff under the People's Revolutionary Army Committee of the CCP in October 1949.

General HSU Kuan-ta, a group army commander in the First Field Army in 1951.

General HSU Shih-yu, Commander of the Shantung War Zone in 1951. Has been closely associated with Chen Yi's Third Field Army.

General HU Ch'i-tsai, in the headquarters of the Fourth Field Army in 1949.

General HUANG Chen, Chinese Ambassador to Hungary in 1950.

General HUANG Yi-feng, prosecutor and "Judge Advocate General" in Lin Piao's field army up to 1949.

General HUANG Ko-cheng, an army commander in Lin Piao's field army, 1949.

General HUANG Ta-hsuan, in the headquarters of the Fourth Field Army in 1949.

General HUANG Yu, in the headquarters of the South China Liberation Army in 1949.

General HUANG Yuan, a commander with General Chen Yi's forc in 1948.

General JAO Shu-shih, Political Commissioner of the Third Field Army in 1951.

General JEN Pai-ke, in the headquarters of the First Field Army in 1949.

General JEN Pi-shih, the Chief Political Commissar of the PLA in 1951.

General KAO Kang, Political Commissar in the Fourth Field Army in 1948. By 1950 his work had carried him partially away from the PLA into diplomacy, but he retained control of troops in Manchuria up to 1951.

General KAO Shu-hsun, in the headquarters of the Second Field Army in 1949.

General KENG Piao, Chinese Ambassador to Sweden in 1950.

General KUNG Chung-chow, reported as a division commander in 1949.

General K'UNG Tseng-shou, Commander of the Ninth Army in 1950.

General KU Ta-t'sun, in the headquarters of the South China Liberation Army in 1949.

General LAI Chuan-chu, an officer of fairly high position in Fourth Field Army in 1950.

General LAI Shao-chi, in the headquarters of Third Field Army in 1949.

General LEI Jeng-tien, Commissar of the Kwangtung-Kwangsi Column about 1948.

General LIANG Chun, Chief of "Operations" for General Liu Po-cheng's forces operating north of the Lunghai Railway in 1947.

General LIAO Yun-chou, in the headquarters of the Second Field Army in 1949.

General LI Chin-chieh, in the headquarters of the South China Liberation Army in 1949.

General LI Ching-chuan, Deputy Political Commissar of the Southwest China Military Area in 1950.

General LI Ching-yu, a commissar with one of the field armies in 1948.

General LI Fu-chun, Deputy Chief Political Commissar of the PLA in 1949.

General LI Hai-tao, a division commander in Lin Piao's field army in 1946.

General LI Kuo-ying, member of the PLA's General Staff in 1949.

General LI Lan-t'ing, in the headquarters of the Third Field Army in 1949.

APPENDIX 335

General LI Hsien-nien, Deputy Commander under Liu Po-cheng in 1949. Chairman of the Hupei Provincial People's Government; and Commander of the Hupei War Zone, 1951.

General LI Shih-ying, Chief of the Public Security Department of the East China Military-Political Commission in 1950.

General LI Ta, Chief of Staff of the Second Field Army about 1949.

General LI T'ao. As a member of the General Staff of the PLA in 1949, he negotiated with the Red shelled *Amethyst* for a British apology. Headed a mission of officers to the North Korean Army in 1951.

General LI T'ien-yu, in the headquarters of Fourth Field Army in 1949.

General LI Tsing-chuan, one of the more senior political commissars with the People's Liberation Army.

General LI Yun-chang, reported as a commander of an Eighth Army in the North China Area in 1948. Was a highly placed officer in the Third Field Army in 1949.

General LIN Piao, Commander of the Fourth Field Army in 1951.

General LIN Ping, former Political Commissar of the East River Column. Commander of the Kwangtung-Kiangsi-Hunan Column.

General LIU Chen-tsao, Army Commander in the Fourth Field Army in 1950.

General LIU Chai-jen, a division commander in General Lin Piao's forces in Manchuria, 1946.

General LIU Chuan-tien, a brigade or division commander in Lin Piao's field army in 1946.

General LIU pai-yu, in the headquarters of the Fourth Field Army in 1949.

General LIU Po-cheng, Commander of the Second Field Army in 1951.

General LIU Shan-pen, a member of the PLA's General Staff in 1949.

General LIU Ya-lou, Chief of Staff of the Fourth Field Army in 1949.

General LIU Yu-kang, Chief of the Political Department of the Second Field Army in 1948.

General LIU Yung-shen, Commander of the Fukien-Kwangtung-Kiangsi Column in 1950.

General LO Fan-ch'un, in the headquarters of the South China Liberation Army in 1949.

General LO Jui-ching, Political Commissioner of the First Field Army in 1949.

General LO Jung-huan, Political Commissioner of the Fourth Field Army in 1951.

General LU Cheng-tsao, Vice Director of the Railway Department of the People's Revolutionary Military Council, 1950, and a member of the PLA's General Staff.

General LUNG Yun, escaped from Nationalist arrest in 1948 to join the Communists and become a member of the People's Revolutionary Military Council in 1950.

General MA Ning, in the headquarters of the Second Field Army in 1949.

General MA Pai-shan, Vice Commander of the Hainan Column in 1950.

General NIEH Jung-chen, Vice Chief of Staff of the People's Revolutionary Military Council and commander of troops in North China in 1951.

General NI Chih-liang, Ambassador to the North Korean Government in 1950.

General PENG Ming-chih, Red Chinese Ambassador to Poland in 1950.

General PENG Te-huai, Commander of the First Field Army; also Deputy Commander-in-Chief of the PLA and Vice-Chairman of Revolutionary Military Council (1951).

General PIEN Chang-wu, Red Chinese Military Attaché to Moscow in 1950.

General POH Siao-shan, "Yenan-raised" Korean Communist leader who went to Manchuria after World War II and helped organize the "Korean Communist Volunteer Army."

General PO Yi-po, Commissar of General Liu Po-cheng's field army in 1947. Political Director of Suiyuan War Zone, 1951.

General PU K'e, in the headquarters of the Second Field Army in 1949.

General SU Ching-kuan, Deputy Chief of Sanitation of the People's Revolutionary Military Council, about 1949. Has long been Chief Medical Officer for the Communist armies.

General SU Yu, Deputy Commander of the Third Field Army in 1951.

General SUN Chen, served under command of General Chou Pao-chung in Manchuria in 1946.

General SUN Chih-yuan, in the headquarters of First Field Army in 1949.

APPENDIX

General SUNG Shih-lun, Commander of a group army in the Third Field Army in 1950.

General TAI Ching-yuan, member of the PLA's General Staff in 1949.

General TAN Cheng, Chief of the General Political Section of the PLA in 1949.

General TAN Chen-lin, Deputy Commander of the Third Field Army in 1951.

General TAN Hsi-lin, Red Chinese Ambassador to Czechoslovakia in 1950.

Commander TANG Cheng-kuo, a female Commander of Communist Amazons in the Women's Self-Defense Corps in 1945. May now have general officer status.

General TANG Kuo-tung, in the headquarters of the Third Field Army in 1949.

General TANG Yen-shih, Chief of Staff of the North China Military Area in 1950.

General TAO Chih-yueh, ex-Nationalist and defector (1949), who commanded his former troops in Sinkiang under the new designation of Communist 22d Group Army up to 1950.

General TAO Chu, was Assistant Director of the Political Department of General Lin Piao's field army in 1948.

General TAO Yung, Commander of the 7th Column Northern Kiangsu in 1946.

General TENG Hsiao-ping, a political commissar of the Central Plains Liberation Area in 1948, Commissar of the Second Field Army in 1949, Political Commissioner of the South Military Area in 1950.

General TENG Hua, Commander of a group army in the Fourth Field Army in 1950. Peace negotiator in Korea in 1951.

General TENG Tai-yuan, representative of the Second Field Army in 1949, subsequently becoming Minister of Railways in that year.

General TENG Tzu-hui, Director of the Political Department on the Staff of the Fourth Field Army in 1951.

General TING Chih-hui, in the headquarters of the Fourth Field Army in 1949. Has since turned his talents to diplomacy, helping Chou En-lai negotiate the Sino-Soviet Pact in 1950.

General TSAI Shu-fan, in the headquarters of the Second Field Army in 1949.

General TSANG Sheng, Commander of the Kwangtung-Kwangsi Column, about 1948.

General TS'AO Li-wei (TS'AO Li-huai), Commander of the 49th Army of the Fourth Field Army in 1950.

General TSENG K'e, in the headquarters of the Second Field Army in 1949.

General TSENG Chi-tsai, former subordinate of General Chang Chung's; organizer of "Fifth Column" activity in South China 1947-1948.

General TSENG Sheng, Commander of the Kwangtung-Kwangsi Column in 1951.

General TSENG Tse-cheng, Commander of the 50th Army of the Fourth Field Army in 1950.

General TSO Hsieh-chung, in the headquarters of the First Field Army in 1949.

General TU Chang-fu, in the headquarters of the Third Field Army in 1949.

General TU Kuan-jen, in the headquarters of the First Field Army in 1949.

General WAN Yi, Commander of Kirin Provincial Units in 1947 and a group army commander under Lin Piao in 1950.

General WANG Chang-chiang, Commander of the 8th Sub-Region of the Shansi-Suiyuan Anti-Japanese Base in 1945. Position unknown in 1951.

General WANG Chao, in the headquarters of the First Field Army in 1949.

General WANG Chen, a column commander in the Northwest PLA in 1949. Became Commander of the 22d Group Army (ex-KMT Troops) in Sinkiang in January 1950.

General WANG Cheng, member of the General Staff of the PLA in 1949.

General WANG Ch'ien-an, an army commander with the Third Field Army in 1949. Commander of Chekiang War Zone, 1950.

General WANG Chia-hsiang, ambassador to the USSR, 1950.

General WANG Ching-hsiu, a group army commander in the Fourth Field Army in 1950.

General WANG Chi-ming, high ranking officer in the Second Field Army, where he may be Chief of Staff (1951).

General WANG Pei-huan, director of the Peiping Military Tribunal in 1951.

General WANG Shih-tai, in the headquarters of the First Field Army in 1949.

General WANG Tsai-tien, Deputy Commander of the Inner Mongolian War Zone under Yun Tse in 1951.

General WANG Wei-chou, Deputy Commander of Northwest Military Area in 1949.

APPENDIX 339

General WANG Yu-ping, Red Chinese ambassador to Rumania in 1950.

General WEI Hsiao-t'ang, in the headquarters of the Second Field Army in 1949.

General WEI Lai-kuo, in the headquarters of the Third Field Army in 1949.

General WU Ch'i-wei, in the headquarters of the South China Liberation Army in 1949.

General WU Hsiu-chuan, Chinese Red representative who visited the United Nations Headquarters in 1950.

General WU Hua-wen, former Commander of the Nationalist 84th Reorganized Division, which Wu brought over to the Communists. He was designated Commander of the 35th Army (his original division), reorganized in October 1948.

General YANG Cheng-wu, member of the PLA's General Staff in 1949. Reported to be Deputy Commander of the North China Military Area and also a group army commander under Lin Piao in 1950.

General YANG Ch'i-ing, a member of the PLA's General Staff in 1949 and Vice Minister of Public Security.

General YANG Kuo-fu, Commander of a 3d Brigade (New 4th Army) in the Shantung Area in 1945. Was in Manchuria in 1947.

General YANG Li-san, in the headquarters of the Second Field Army during 1949.

General YANG Te-chih, Deputy Commander of an army in 1945. A group army commander in the First Field Army in 1951.

General YANG Yu-po, ex-Nationalist and defector who commanded the Red 103d Division (35th Army) in late 1948.

General YAO Che, Commander of the Suiyuan-Mongolian War Zone in 1951.

General YEH Chien-ying, Chairman of the Kwangtung Provincial Government and Commander of the Kwangtung War Zone in 1951.

General YEH Fei, former Commander of 10th Group Army. In 1950, Commander of Fukien (Provincial Military District) War Zone.

General YUAN Chung-hsien, Red Chinese ambassador to India in 1950.

General YUN Tse, (alias WU Lan-fu) Commander of the Inner Mongolian People's Defense Army and President of the Inner Mongolia Autonomous Region in 1951.

Appendix III

REPORT ON CHINESE COMMUNIST ACTIVITIES, 5 FEBRUARY 1946

By an UNRRA Representative in Manchuria

In order that the China (UNRRA) Office may be conversant with current political events and the general situation, a weekly conference has been arranged with General Chao Chia-shiang, Chief of Staff to Northeast (Nationalist) Military Command.

At the first of these conferences, held on Tuesday, 5 February 1946, the General gave the following information.

To preserve continuity, the General divided his material into two sections—(1) general summary of events since the surrender, and (2) current events and developments to be continued each week.

(1) **General Summary.** During the Manchoukuo regime there was no organized partisan or Communist activity in the Northeast. Shortly after 15 August 1945, Communist forces, under Li Yun-chang (nephew of Li Ta-chao) and Tseng Ko-lin (both natives of Changli), entered Shanhaikwan and advanced unopposed up the coast to Chinhsien. This was accomplished by buying the services of certain White Russians at Pei-Tai-Ho Beach—to masquerade as Soviet representatives sent to accept the Japanese surrender and begin disarming Japanese forces.

Between Shanhaikwan and Chinhsien (Chinchow) these forces, numbering not more than a few thousand, were reinforced by Soviet forces coming in from the west. They advanced together to Chinhsien city. They were joined by a further Communist detachment, under Lu Cheng-tsao, from Hopei Province. After entering Chinhsien, they augmented their forces by local recruitment, sometimes under pressure; and with arms secured from the Japanese, they deployed throughout the Northeast.

Further reinforcements were shipped from Yentai (Chefoo) by ship to Yingkow and Dairen and sent on to Changchun and Harbin, together with armed Japanese who volunteered for service.

Another detachment under Lin Piao entered the Northeast from Jehol. This detachment was also reinforced by ex-puppet officials, opportunists, and dissatisfied elements, and proceeded to occupy Liaoning Province.

The policy of all these forces was—
(a) To secure ex-Japanese arms and equipment.
(b) Recruit and arm local people and Japanese technicians.
(c) Set up Sino-Soviet friendship cells as propaganda agencies.
(d) Secure further re-inforcements from Shantung.

In all these activities they were aided and abetted by Soviet forces.

On the advance of the National Army, the Communist forces withdrew. Their main forces are now located in the area between Changchun and Mukden and are under the supreme command of Lin Piao. Estimated strength (5 February) is 200,000—armed principally with Japanese equipment.

Soviet armored cars and tanks operated with Communists at the battles of Yingkow and Anshanchang. These areas are vital to both Communists and Soviets. They control the Railway from Dairen to Mukden, and the entry via Yingkow of sea-borne reinforcements from Shantung.

In reply to a protest from the National Government, the Soviet Commander stated that Soviet Troops operating in that area were probably from the Korean-occupation Army and had entered via Antung Province, an area outside his control.

Antung Province is the only area which the Soviet Government has directly refused to hand over to the Chinese National Government. The reason given is that the area is necessary to the Soviet "for security reasons." Antung is the corridor from Korea to Port Arthur.

(Chinese) Communist activities to date have been characterized by—

(a) Destruction of communication facilities—including telegraph lines and bridges—except those of use to Communists and Soviets jointly.

(b) Organized terror-tactics, under Soviet control.

(c) Disruption of rural economy by—

(1) Compulsory circulation of military currency (at the rate of 10 yen for one Communist dollar).

(2) Looting of draught animals.

(3) Levying of food.

(4) Conscription.

Evidence of these activities is given in damage to the railway between Shanhaikwan and Chinhsien, as follows—

54 instances of track dislocations.
16 bridges destroyed or damaged.
1% of telegraph communications destroyed.
6 water towers and tunnels destroyed.

Furthermore, 2,700,000 head of livestock and draught animals were looted by Communists and Soviets jointly.

USSR forces in Northeast are estimated at 100,000. They are deployed generally along railway lines and at strategic industrial centers, as follows—

Changchun, 6th Army;
Dairen & Port Arthur, 5th Army;
Mukden, 6th Mechanized Division.

Approximately 40,000 Japanese forces have evaded disarming and constitute a menace to security.

(2) **Current Events and Developments.** Asked to give authoritative information on certain reports (outlined), the General stated—

(a) Estimated food *surplus* in the hands of farmers in Chinchow province is 200,000 metric tons. The Tientsin newspaper report, that food had been shipped from Tientsin to the Northeast, is not in accordance with facts.

(b) Most urgent need is draught animals for farms.

(c) General Tu (Yu-ming), as a result of our recent conversation and recommendation, has advised Chungking that the establishment of a bank to negotiate loans to farmers for spring planting is an urgent necessity.

(d) The railway line from Dairen to Mukden is in process of change to broad (Russian) gauge, or has already been changed.

(e) Relations between China and USSR have reached a stalemate. USSR has demanded unconditional economic cooperation in the Northeast. This demand is tantamount to a request for USSR economic domination. USSR states that industrial resources and potential in the Northeast are vital to Soviet security. Acceptance of this demand would mean loss of the Northeast to China and disruption of China's relations with Allies, to whom China intends to observe her obligations.

Next conference will take place at 3:00 p.m. Tuesday, 12 February 1946.

Appendix IV
BASIS FOR ESTABLISHMENT OF THE ARMED FORCES OF RED CHINA

(From the Text of the Common Program of the Chinese People's Political Consultative Conference (29 September 1949) As It Relates to the Armed Forces.)

Article 10. The Armed Forces of the People's Republic of China—that is, the People's Liberation Army—the people's public security forces and people s police, are armed forces belonging to the people. Their tasks are to defend the independence, integrity of territory and sovereignty of China, and the revolutionary fruits and all legitimate rights and interests of the Chinese people . . .

Chapter Three—Military System.

Article 20. The People's Republic of China shall build up a unified army; that is, the People's Liberation Army and the people's public security forces, which shall be under the command of the People's Revolutionary Military Council of the Central People's Government, and which shall institute a unified command, unified system, unified formation and unified discipline.

Article 21. The People's Liberation Army and the people's public security forces shall, in accordance with the principle of unity between the officers and rank and file, and unity between the army and the people, set up a political work system and educate the commanders and fighters of these troops in the revolutionary and patriotic spirit.

Article 22. The People's Republic of China shall strengthen the modernized land force and establish an air force and a navy to consolidate national defense.

Article 23. The People's Republic of China shall enforce the system of people's militia to maintain local order, lay the foundation for national mobilization, and prepare for the enforcement of an obligatory military service system at the appropriate moment.

Article 24. The armed forces of the People's Republic of China shall, during peace time, systematically take part in agricultural and industrial production, to assist in national construction work, on the condition of not hindering military tasks.

Article 25. Dependents of revolutionary martyrs and revolutionary servicemen who suffer from privation, shall receive preferential treatment from the state and from the society. The People's Government shall appropriately provide the means of livelihood and settling down for disabled servicemen and retired servicemen who have participated in the revolutionary war.

Appendix V
CHINESE COMMUNIST GUERRILLA UNIT TABLES OF ORGANIZATION AND EQUIPMENT

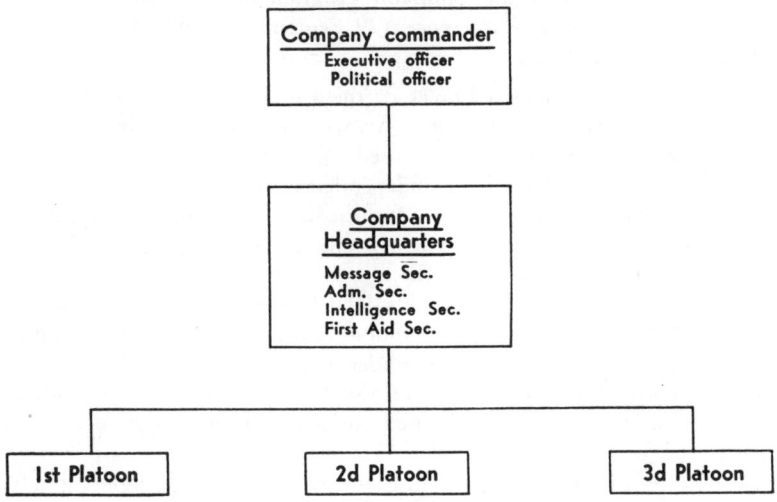

Each platoon of three squads each.
Squads are eight men each plus squad leaders.

TYPICAL ORGANIZATION OF AN INDEPENDENT GUERRILLA COMPANY

(From Mao Tse-tung's "Yu Chi Chan")

Personnel Strength

Line Units
3 platoon leaders
9 squad leaders
72 men in squads

Headquarters
3 officers
1 message section chief
1 signal man
1 administrative section chief
3 public relations men
1 barber
10 cooks
1 medical section chief
9 intelligence men
2 duty personnel

Total: 122 men; 99 rifles and 3 pistols
Note: 20 men ordinarily are not armed.

APPENDIX

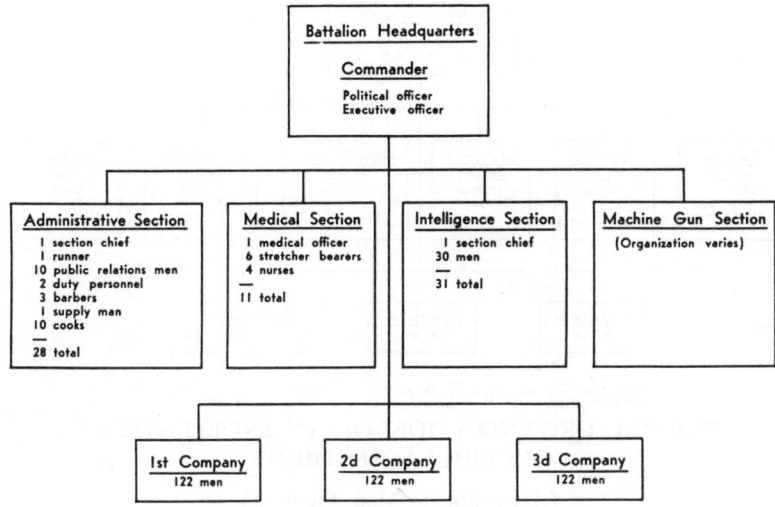

TYPICAL ORGANIZATION OF AN INDEPENDENT GUERRILLA BATTALION

(According to Mao Tse-tung)

Comments—

(1) The intelligence section is organized in two to four squads, at least one of which consists of plain clothes men. Where horses are available, one squad will be needed.

(2) If men are not available as stretcher bearers, cooks are used. Non-partisans may also be employed.

Total Strength: 441 men; 43 pistols or revolvers; 300 rifles.

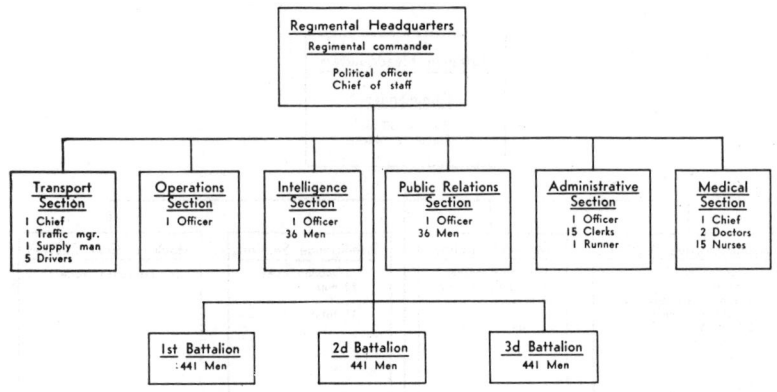

TYPICAL ORGANIZATION OF AN INDEPENDENT GUERRILLA REGIMENT

(According to Mao Tse-tung)

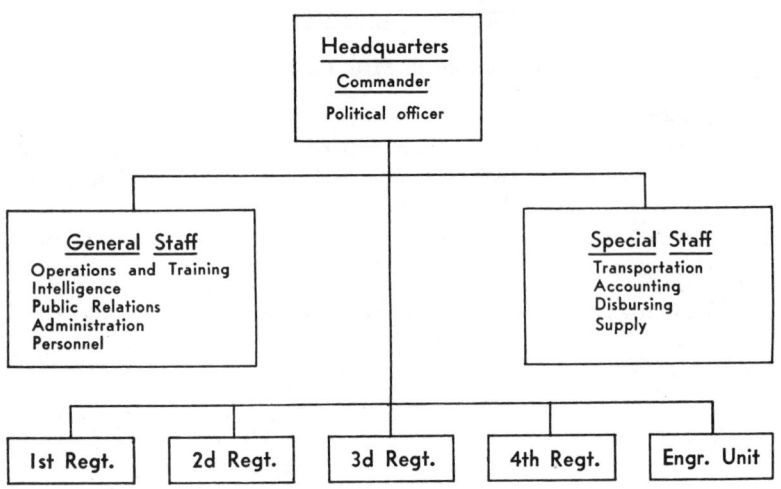

TYPICAL ORGANIZATION OF AN INDEPENDENT GUERRILLA BRIGADE (OR DIVISION)

(According to Mao Tse-tung)

INDEX

(NOTE: The names of Mao Tse-tung, Chu Teh, Lin Piao and other Chinese Communist generals whose characteristics are described in the chapter, "The Hierarchy in the Palace," thread so continuously through the text that incidental mention of them is omitted in the Index.

A complete list of Chinese Communist generals is given in Appendix II.)

A

Administration (General Affairs) Section, General Staff	73
Age, average:	
Of generals	59
Of soldiers	123
Airborne troops:	
Chief of	74
Chou Pao-chung's interest in	37, 321
Lack of experience with	21
Training of	101, 102
Aircraft:	
Backwardness in	150
Looting of factory	247
Air Force, Chinese Communist:	
As a component of the PLA	69
Evaluation of	320
Deficiencies in	325
Defensive character of	325
Future of	323
History of	321, 322
Interest in, by Chou Pao-chung	37, 321
International character of	322
Lack of experience with	22
Losses in Korea	323
Personnel priorities for	151
Soviet influence on	304
Soviet aircraft in	322
Strategy of withholding	325
Strength of	64, 301, 324
Tactical disposition of	325
Women in the	132
Air Force, Nationalist	191, 192, 270, 271
Ambassadors, Chinese Communist	20
Ambush:	
Tactics of	2, 176
Against U. S. Marines	176, 177
In Korea	176
America, attitude of Chou Pao-cheng toward	37, 47
America, hatred of	137, 280
Ammunition, shortage of	153
Amphibious training and operations:	
At Chinmen Island	314
Casualties in	314
Current training in	312-314
In crossing Yangtze River	311-313

    Lack of experience in 22
    Liver fluke contracted during 6
    "Model troops" in 112
    Of Third Field Army 89
    On Chou-San Islands 313
    Training, for crossing Yangtze 313, 314
    Training pictures of 309, 310
    Variety of craft used in 311
    Weaknesses in 308, 311, 312
Annihilation, war of 189
Anping Incident 44
Antiaircraft:
    Chief of 74
    Future of 304
    Lack of experience with 21
    Strength of 21
    Units at Tientsin **95**
Anti-Japanese Military and Political College 29
Antitank defense, interest of Ho Lung in 43
Armed forces, basis for establishment of 343
Armor:
    Contempt for 43
    Future of 304
    Increase in 98
    Lack of experience with 21
    Of North Korean Army 304
    Quality of 100
    Strength in 100
    Training in 151
    Training, by Soviets 208
    T-34 tank 3, 11
    Under direct control of GHQ 74
Arms, standardization of 73
Army, strength of an 63
"Army" war 55
Arsenals 17, 73, 155, 296-298
Artillery:
    Emphasis on, in Korea 152
    Future of 304
    Lack of experience with 21
    Of North Korean Army 304
    Organization of 102
    Quality of 102
    Strength of 103
    Su Yu's skill in handling 33
    Under direct control of GHQ 74, 102
    Soviet training in 208, 303
Asia, plans for "liberation" of 2, 54, 241-243
Asiatic air pilots, in Chinese Communist Air Force 322
Athlete's foot 6

INDEX   349

Atom bomb, lack of fear of 9, 21, 48
Atrocities (See Sadism)
Attack the tail tactics 216
Attrition, strategy of 260
Attrition, war of 41
Awards and decorations 110-112

B

Background, of soldier 124
Balu-jen (Eighth Army men, Communist) 130
Barrett, Colonel David D. .... 47, 57, 165, 242 (picture)
Battalion, strength of a:
    Regular army 63, 65
    Guerrilla 345
T/O and E (Table of organization and equipment):
    Division 63
    Regiment 63, 65
    Battalion, guerrilla 345
    Brigade (or division), guerrilla 346
Battle:
    Methods of 202
    Situations and instructions 202
Bayonets:
    Fear of 9
    Torture with 105
Beheading 105
Berry, Lt. Col. Kearie L. 262
Billeting, by peasants 289
Birthplaces, of generals 58
Bivouac, technique of 174
Bleucher, General (Soviet) 45
Bodyguards 14
Bombing, by U. S. in Manchuria 297
Briefing, of subordinate commanders 177
Brown, Col. Rothwell H. 190
Brutality (see Sadism)
Budget, military 17
Budyenny, Marshal 27
Bugles:
    In combat 213
    In communications 214
Bullitt, William C. 259
Byroade, Brig. Gen. Henry A. 190

C

Cadres, of loyal soldiers 108
Calculated risk engagements 204
Camouflage, use of 185
Capture, of author 154, 176, 230, 237
Captured equipment and materiel (See Equipment and materiel, captured)
Carlson, Colonel Evans F. 27, 52
Carpets of dead 1, 199, 200, 327

Casualties, PLA:
    Total since 1937 327
    In Korea 92, 179, 327
Cavalry:
    In First Field Army 82
    In Fourth Field Army 91
    In Korea 186
    In Mongolian Army 97, 98
    Under direct control of GHQ 74
Censorship, organizational position of 73
Central Committee, Chinese Communist Party 25, 31, 35, 38, 40, 46, 70
Central Kwangtung (or Yueh-ching) Column 78
Central People's Government Council 25, 31, 35, 38, 40, 46
Central Plains Liberation Army 83
Central Shensi Liberation Army 160
Central-South Military Area 94
Chamdo (Changtu), Tibet 308
Chang Chen, General (picture) 90
Chang Chen-tung, General 89
Chang Hsueh-liang, General (Nationalist) 47, 250
Chang Hsueh-ssu, General (picture) 68
Changchun, Battle of 37, 100, 244
Chang Ling, General (Nationalist) 34
Chang Nan-sheng, General (picture) 83
Chang Tso-lin, General (Nationalist) 250, 297
Chang Tsung-hsun, General 82
Chang Yun-i, General .... 77 (picture), 94
Chao Erh-lu, General 93
Chao Li-huai, General 94
Chao Shou-shan, General .... 77 (picture), 82
Chekiang Area 89
Chen Chi-han, General 94
Chengtu Officers' School 59
Cheng Tzu-hua, General 95
Chen Hai-han, General 82
Chen Hsi-lien, General 85
Chen Jui-ting, General 89
Chen Keng, General 59, 89
Chen Man-yuan, General (picture) 77
Chen Po, General (picture) 79
Chen Shih-chu, General 88
Chen Tsai-tao, General 94
Chen Yi, General, characteristics of 38
Chen Yun, Commissar 93
Chiang-Han Area 85
Chiang Kai-shek, Generalissimo:
    Release of, after Sian 47
    Weaknesses of 264, 265
Chiang Wei-ch'ing, General (picture) 86

INDEX 351

Chien Hsin-chung, General (picture) 83
China:
    Map of 329
    Modern aspects of 10
    Population of 7
    Problems of invading 183, 223
"China's Patton" (Liu Po-cheng) 33
Chinchow, Battle of 125
Chin Chi, General 82
Chinese Communist Activities, Report on 340
Chinese Communist Party (CCP):
    As first consideration in army 124
    As producer of military leaders 20
    Flag of 329
    Growth of 171
    Organization of 66-70
    Paris and Berlin branches of 45
    PLA generals, dates of joining 60
    Representation in armed forces 69
    Strength of 21
Chinese Nationalists (see Nationalists)
Chiu Kang 237
Chongjin 2
Chou En-lai, General:
    Characteristics of 45
    Picture of 46, 54, 242
Chou Pao-chung, General, characteristics of 36
Chou Shih-ti, General 85
Chu Hsi, philosopher 52
Chu Jui, General 103
Chung Chih-ping, General (picture) 90
Chuang Tien, General 78
Chu Chia-pi, General 78
Chu Teh:
    Characteristics of 25, 26
    Control of generals by 24
    Military education of 59
    Picture of 26, 47, 68, 242
    Position of, in hierarchy 66
Cigarettes 116
Civilian Aides, in logistics 288
Civilian bureaucrats 16
Civilian control, of army 68, 69
Civil officials, shortage of 21
Civil War, Chinese:
    Effect on health of leaders 19
    Ending sooner than expected 10
    Principal factors in 243
    Statistics of 255
Classified Materials Section, General Staff 73
Clubb, O. Edmund 228

352   INDEX

Collins, Major John W. ..14, 29, 44, 105, 154, 219, 288 (picture), 230, 237, 292
Combat-calloused soldiers 106
Combat efficiency 5
Combat Heroes 110
Combat pictorials 114
Comfort Mission 17
Comintern 53
Command and General Staff College (US) 157
Commanders and commissars, dual capacity 21
Command decision, Soviet principles of 208
Command post, description of a 3, 4
Command, principles of 203
Command, rotation of 68
Commemoration Badge of the Chinese Communist Republic 111
Commissars:
    As correctors of "bad habits" 14
    Influence of 23, 24
    Control by 108-115
    Position of in hierarchy 67, 70-73
Committee to Resist the US and Air Korea 17
Common Program, The 110, 150, 294, 343
Communications:
    As factor in Nationalist defeat 269-271
    Inadequacy of 177, 195
    In the field, typical example 4
Communications Section, General Staff 73
Concepts, basic military 182, 187
"Confessions" by prisoners of war 232
Conscriptions (see Recruiting)
Control:
    Web and tenacles of 70
    In combat 178
Corruptions:
    In Nationalist Army 264, 266
    In PLA 118
Cossacks, Russian 96
Coughing and spitting, in headquarters 4, 19, 158
Counter-revolution, hope of 327
Courts, People's, brutalities committed by 220
Cowen, Colonel Edward T. .... 54 (picture), 288
Criticism, by soldiers 109, 123
Cross ditching, roads and railways 29

D

Daily life, of the soldier 116-118, 123
Dare to Die Corps 279
Decision, war of quick 188
Dead:
    Carpets of 1, 199, 200, 327
    Decoys of 212
Defection:
    Of Japanese puppet troops 249

INDEX

Of Nationalists	35, 47, 81, 107, 108, 228, 272
Of Nationalist pilots	322
Possible, by Chen Yi	39
Possible, by troops in Korea	171

Defense:
    Capability of 186
    Fixed, contempt for 37
    Psychology of Nationalists 256-258
Delegate to the National Congress, Badge for 111
Democratic Youth League, New 141
Denchfield, Major Robert D. and Lt. Raymond C. 3
den Ouden, Lt. Col. M. P. A. 210
Disappear, ability of PLA to 191-193
Discharge 109, 123, 134
Discipline, in the army:
    Basis of 121-123
    Control through 134
    In Korea 16
    Lack of, by Nationalists 269
    Of Manchurian recruits 250
Discontent 15, 106, 108
Disloyalty 6
Division, strength of a 63
Division slice:
    In PLA 16, 64, 289
    In Soviet Army 64
    In US Army 64
"Division" war 55
Doctors, shortage of 165, 290, 291
Dope, taking of 105
Drafting (see Recruiting)
Dragon Lantern 104
Drill, training in 153
Drunkenness 106

E

Eastern Laborers' University (Soviet) 35, 59
East Military Area 89
Economic committees 120
Education (see also Illiteracy):
    Elementary character of 145, 146
    Level of 145
    Of generals 55, 58, 59
    Of junior officers 160
    Political, of soldiers 40
    Program 145
    Purpose of 147
Eisenhower, General of the Army Dwight D. 259
Ekval, Major Robert 44
Ely, Col. Louis B. 179
Engineers:
    Quality and equipment of 102

Chief of 74
Entertainment 116
Equipment, of the soldier 119-121, 173
Equipment and materiel, captured:
    Artillery pieces 102
    Attitude toward US 284
    Competition for 32
    Distributed to First Field Army 81
    Inability to operate 11
    Japanese 92, 101, 321
    Nationalist, problems created by 10
    Obsolete concept of 282
    Scope of 6
    US aircraft 322
    US, as factor in Nationalist defeat 268
    US vehicles 98, 99
European flyers in Chinese Communist Air Force 322
Ex-Nationalists:
    As critical manpower 124
    In Chinese Communist Air Force 322
    Motivation of 115
    Treatment of, when wounded 125
    Unreliability of 124

F

Fair treatment, of soldiers 122
Fang Fang, General 78
Farming, by soldiers 14
Fear:
    As means of control 116
    Of bayonets 9
    Of enemy 187
Feet, care of 157
Feng Mai-cha'o, General (picture) 77
Feng Pai-chu, General 78
Field armies:
    As type of military organization 69
    Geographical origin of 77
    Organization of 75, 76
    Regional character of 76
    Size of one 5
    Strength of each 62
    Variation in strength of 149
Field army commanders 23, 24
Field force, Chinese Communist Army 62, 63
Field manuals, US 312
Fifth Field Army:
    Commander of (picture) 35
    Description of 94
    Strength of 62
Fiftieth Army, PLA 91
Fifty-second Army (Nationalist) 130

INDEX 355

Fighter's Companion, The 145
Financial problems of PLA 12, 16, 17
Fire power of UN faced by PLA 196
First Cavalry Division, US 185
First Army (Nationalist) 175, 252, 261
First Field Army:
    Commander of (picture) 40
    Description of 79
    General Staff of (picture) 79
    Strength of 62
Flag, of PLA 13
Fleas and lice 87
Food, of the soldier:
    Fighting for 216
    Kinds and quality of 116-118, 123
    On the march 174
    Supplied despite inflation 267
Footwear, characteristics of 157
Foreign minister (Chou En-lai) 45, 46
Formosa (see Taiwan)
Fourth Field Army:
    Amphibious training of 315
    As labor force 295
    Beginning of 130, 255
    Commander of (picture) 28
    Description of 89
    General Staff of (picture) 90
    Looting by, in Manchuria 247
Fu Chung, General (picture) 68
Fukien-Kwangtung Column 78
Fukien-Kwangtung-Kiangsi (or Min Yueh Kan Border) Column 78
Fukien Area 89
Funds, drive for 17
Furloughs, limitation on 14
Fu Tso-yi, General (Nationalist) 2, 90, 95, 98, 261-264

G

Gardens, unit 118
General Affairs Section, General Staff 73
Generals:
    As amateurs in modern war 56
    Background, education, Party status of 56-61
    Characteristics of 13, 56-61
    Roster of 330
Generalship, modern 13, 21
General Staff:
    Description of 71
    Organization of 73
    Picture of 68
Genghis Khan 96
Gimo rifle 153

Gobi Desert March 80
Gongs, in combat 213
Grenades:
    Proficiency with 154
    Training in 153
Grenoble, University of 59
Griffith, Colonel Samuel B. 49
Group-army, organization of 76
Guerrilla(s):
    Basic concept of 188
    Columns, modernized 77
    Compared to virgins, rabbits, gnats 226
    Leaders 21
    Mao's views on 51
    Operations, by Chou Pao-chung 37
    Operations by Ho Lung 43
    Operations by Nieh Jung-chen 36
    Prevalence of 131
    Tables of organization and equipment 344
    Tactics studied by Japanese 35
    Uprising 11
    Use of, at Kiangsu 88
    War against Japanese 55
Guerrilla warfare:
    Anti-Red 227
    Basic characteristics of 226
    Conditions favorable to 222
    In other Asiatic countries 223
    In relation to land space 223, 224
    In World War II 227
    Principles of 225
    Situations which could produce 222, 223
    Strategy of 224
    Supporting treacherous action 211
    Types of bases used in 225

H

Hainan (or Chiung-yen) Column 78, 91
Hainan, amphibious invasion of 279, 315
Hancock, Lt. Col. Edward 262
Hand carts 288
Han Hsien-chu, General (picture) 90
Hankow Military Academy 59
Han soldiers 81
Harbin 14, 44
Hate, indoctrination by 9
Headquarters, General, of PLA:
    Description of 71
    Organization chart of 72
    Need for reorganization of 74

INDEX

Headquarters, in field 3
Health:
    Education in 146
    Geographical aspects of 157
    Of leaders 19
    Of officers and men 56, 87
    Problems of 157
Health Department, Rear Services 73
Hierarchy, military:
    Description of 17
    In relation to atom bomb 21
Hodge, General John R. 252, 279
Ho Chi-li, General (picture) 86
Ho Lung, General:
    As commander, Northwest Military Area 82
    Characteristics of 43
    Picture of 42, 79
Homesickness, of soldier 126
Honan Area 94
Hopei Area 95
Ho Ping-yen, General 82
Horse carts, requisitioning of 286
Horse cart torture 105
Hospitals, lack of 291
Hsi Chun-hsun, General 82
Hsiao Ching-kung, General 93, 94
Hsiao Hua, General 190
Hsieh, Fu-chin, General 85
Hsu Kuan-ta, General 82
Hsieh Sheng-k'un, General (picture) 86
Hsu Kuo-chen, General 82
Hsu Shih-you, General 89
Hsuchou Campaign 33, 88, 215
Hu Ch'i-tsai, General 90
Huaihai campaign:
    Logistics of 287
    As classic 164
Huang Chen, General 20
Huang Sun-chien, Vice Commander 78
Huang Ta-hsuan, General (picture) 90
Huang Yi-feng, General, characteristics of 44
Huang Yu, General (picture) 77
Huan-nan (Southern Anhwei) Area 85
Human waves, technique of 197, 198
Hunan Military Academy 59
Hunan Area 94
Hunhuzes (Red Beards) 128
Hupei Area 94

I

I-ko-chao-meng (Skh-cho Mongol League) Area 97

Illiteracy:
    In the PLA 2, 5, 6, 143, 144
    In China 143, 144
Improvisation, skill in 151
Indo-China:
    As object of Chinese Communist aggression 52, 318-320
    Aid given to Viet Minh by PLA 319
    Aid given to Ho Chi-minh 33
    Inrelation to Korean campaign 319
    PLA strategy in 319, 320
Indoctrination:
    About Korea 168, 169
    Anti-American 137
    As part of daily routine 117
    At military academies 161, 163
    Contents of program of 167-169
    Control through 134
    Influence of victory on 168
    Lack of, in Nationalist army 271
    Methods of 166
    Of Manchurian recruits 250
    Of Nationalists 11, 276
    Psychology of 167-170
    Strength of, in PLA 166
    Typical pattern of session 167
Induction (see Recruiting)
Industrialization, backwardness in 150, 295, 296
Infantry:
    Commanders 21
    In Korea 177, 195
    Plans to modernize 223
    Power in 22
Inflation, as factor in Nationalist defeat 266
Inner Mongolia 91, 96, 97
Inner Mongolian Autonomous Region 97
Inner Mongolian People's Defense Army 97
International army, possibility of 305
International Volunteer Corps 91
Insignia, officers' 3
Instructors, military:
    Noncoms as 155
    Technicians as 155
Intelligence Section, General Staff 73
Internationalist clique 37
Iron Corps (North Korean) 279

J

Jabara, Captain James 322
Jao Shu-shih, General 88
Japanese (personnel):
    As technicians 251

INDEX 359

    As trainers of pilots 321
    In Chinese Communist Army 2
    In Manchuria 251
    Medical officer, case of 246
    Still prisoners of war 248
Japanese, tactics against 211, 215, 216
Japanese, arms and equipment:
    Left in China (statistical) 276
    Taken by Soviet Army (Statistical) 277
Japanese Foreign Office 251, 321
Japanese Infantry School 59
Japanese Military Cadet Academy 59
Jen Pai-ke, General (picture) 79
Jen Pi-shih, General 73
JMP (Jen Min Piao) 116
Jointed worm tactics 214
Junior officers:
    Casualty rate of 161
    Education and leadership of 160
    New generation of 160, 165
    Political reliability of 161
    Potential capabilities of 160

K

K'ang K'e-ching, General (picture) 68
Kansu Area 82
Kao Ko-min, General 98
Kao Kang, General 190
Kao Shu-hsun, General (picture) 83
Kazakh soldiers 81
Khirgiz soldiers 81
Kiangsu 88
Komsomol (Soviet) 141
Koo Fen-Wei, Major (Nationalist) 125
Korea:
    Ambush of UN troops in 176
    Application of Ten Military Principles in 182
    As primary worry 15
    Bugle and gong technique in 212, 213
    Chance of mass surrender in 8
    Chance of PLA crumbling in 138
    Chinese Communist air losses in 323
    Chou En-lai's influence on strategy in 48
    Combat tricks in 211
    Comparison of tactics in 178, 179, 185
    Estimate of air situation in 323
    Fourth Field Army in 91, 92
    Guerrilla tactics in 214
    In relation to future plans of PLA 241
    In relation to guerrilla warfare 222, 223
    Lack of Soviet equipment in 303

Lin Piao in 30
Logistical limitations in 298-300
Mao's strategy in 51, 52
Medical care in 292
Possible modernization of PLA in 305
PLA strategy in 129
PLA tactics in 27, 194-196
Problems in, general 12
Problems of fuel and motor vehicles in 74
Reported opposition to invasion of 45
Safe Conduct Pass used in 136, 137
Stratetical disadvantages of UN in 320
Transfer of reserve to 95
Truce in 229
Korean Communist Volunteer Forces 279
Korean soldiers in Manchurian army 252, 279
Ku Ta-T'sun, General (picture) 77
Kwangsi Military Academy 59
Kwangsi Area 94
Kwangsi-Yunnan-Kweichow (or Kuei Tien Chien Border) Column 78
Kwantung Army 90, 92, 251
Kwangtung-Kwangsi (or Liang-Kuang) Column 78
Kwangtung-Kiangsi-Hunan (or Yueh Kan Hsiang Border) Column 78
Kwangtung-Kwangsi (or Yueh Kuein Border) Column 78, 79
Kwantung Military School 59
Kwantung Area 94

L

Labor, by soldiers 2
Labor emulation campaigns 17
Labor gangs, as source of recruiting 128
Labor Heroes 110
Lai Shao-chi, General (picture) 86
Land:
    Distribution in recruiting 128-131
    Given to war veterans 128
    Limitations on 131
Land space 11, 12, 33, 51, 183, 185, 196, 223
Language:
    As problem in modernizing army 148
    Influence on organization of army 148
    Instruction in, at military academies 164
    Problems of 147
    Reform of, Chinese 148
Latham, Lt. Willard 185
Leadership:
    By generals 21
    In PLA (Estimate by Formosa commander) 318
    Injury to, by Chang Kai-shek 265
Lenin, study of 85
Liaison Group, U. S. Army 29
Liang, General, comment on wounded 125

INDEX 361

Liang Kuang, General 78
Liao Cheng-chih, ... 17
Liao Yun-chou, General (picture) 83
Liayuan, Battle of 194
"Liberators of Tibet" 83
"Liberators" of Manchuria 248
Li Chen, General (picture) 79
Li Chin-chieh, General (picture) 77
Lieberman, Henry R. 308
Li Hsien-nien, General 94
Li Jen-lin, General 85
Li Kuo-ying, General (picture) 68
Li Lan-t'ing, General (picture of) 86
Li Li-san 44, 45
Li Ta, General 85
Li T'ao, General (picture) 68
Li Tien-yu, General (picture) 90
Li Yun-chang, General (picture) 86
Li Yun-chang, General 89
Lin Feng, Communist Governor 128
Lin Piao, General:
    Characteristics of 27
    Picture of 28, 242
    Tactical concepts of 201
Lin Ping, General 78
Lippa, Dr. Ernest M. 105, 220
Liu Chen-tsao, General 94
Liu Chih-yuan, Commander 95
Liu Chuan-tien, General 190
Liu Jui-ching, General 60
Liu Mei-ts'un, General (picture) 90
Liu Pai-yu, General (picture) 90
Liu Po-cheng, General:
    Characteristics of 31
    Picture of 31, 83
Liu Shan'pen, General (picture) 68
Liu Ya-lou, General 274
Liu Yu-Kang, General 85
Liu Yung-sheng, General 78
Liver fluke 6
Lo, Doctor 292
Lo Fan-Ch'un, General (picture) 77
Logistics:
    As factor in defeat of Nationalists 268, 270, 288, 289
    As morale factor 282
    Basic concept of 189
    Background of 283
    Bottlenecks in 298
    Future problems of 284, 301
    In balance with manpower 282-284
    In Battle of Tsinan 288

In Fourth Field Army	93
In Huaihai campaign	287
In Second Field Army	84
Inadequacy of, in Nationalist army	283
Lack of understanding of	282
Medical shortages	290-294
Of Tibetan invasion	306, 307
Pen Te-huai's interest in	41
Shoestring aspects of	281, 282
Speed of movement	286, 287
Strengths of PLA in	299
Supply column, typical scene	281
Lo Jung-huan, General	90 (picture), 93, 274, 276
Lo Jui-ch'ing, General (picture)	79

Long March:

As drain on health	19
Description of	22
In teaching history	146
Map of	329
Number of generals in	60
Long Struggle	146

Looting:

By Soviets	298
Technique of	248
Control of	218
Of supply depots	248
Of Manchuria	245-248
Of military hospitals	246, 247
Loud speakers, in Korea	143
Love Thy Feet, Poem	114
Loyalty, of soldiers	106, 108
Lu Ch'eng-ts'ao, General (picture)	68

M

Manchuria:

Campaign in	252-255
Characteristics of opposing armies in	255-258
Characteristics of peasants of	93
Chinese Communists as "liberators" of	248
Japanese occupation of	244
Lin Piao's recruiting policy in	129-131
Looting in	245-248
Preparations for campaign, 1948	285
Recruiting in	248-250
Soviet dominance in	244
Strategy in	255-261
Strength of PLA in	252
Transfer of reserve to	95
Truce in	254, 256
Maneuver, war of	188
Ma Ning, General (picture)	83

INDEX 363

Manpower:
- In relation to logistics 284
- Political reasons for retaining 283
- Surfeit of, after Civil War 283

Manuals, US, Field and Technical 156, 159

Mao Tse-tung, General:
- Ambitions of 54
- Characteristics of 48
- Opinion, of Nationalist troops 125
- Picture of 47, 242
- Position, in hierarchy 66, 71

Ma Pai-shan, General .... 77 (picture), 78
Ma Yen-Kang, General 98
MacArthur, General of the Army Douglas 298, 301

Map(s):
- Combat, description of 4, 174, 175
- Of China 329

March(ing):
- Ability to 6
- At night 175
- Characteristics of a 3
- In winter 172
- Length of 175
- Technique of 173
- Training in 153

March column newspapers 113
March radio stations 115
Marines, United States 44, 112, 176, 177, 196, 230
Marksmanship, of soldier 2, 135, 153, 154
Marriages, limitation on 12, 109
Marshall, General of the Army George C. 44, 229
Marx, study of 85
Massacre Valley 176
Matsudaira, Kato (Japanese) 321
Mauser rifle 108, 134
McGunical, Sergeant Donald L. 213
McNair, Major Joel N. 129
Mechanization 6, 98, 112

Medical service:
- Inadequacy of 15, 123, 290-294
- Shortage of equipment 291, 292
- Shortage of medical supplies 292
- Shortage of personnel 87, 290, 291
- Training 165, 291

Mei-yo-fatze philosophy 168
Mengliao, Battle of 34
Mennonite Mission 105
Mess committees 119
Mess, kinds of 123
MIG-15, Soviet jet plane, statistics of 324

Military academies:
  Austerity of life at 162
  Content of courses 162, 163
  Entrance requirements of 161
  Lack of 11
  Length of courses 160-163
  Location of 161
  Political aspects of 160-164
  Teaching medicine at 165
Military and Administrative (Political Committees) 69
Military Areas 69
Military concepts, of Mao Tse-tung 187
Military Hero's Decoration 110, 111
Military Principles, Ten:
  As applied in Korea 182, 194-196
  Description of 178-182
Military School Political Committee Member's Badge 111
Military science, at academies 164
Military training (See Training)
Militia, People's:
  As component of People's Security Forces 69
  As pool of surplus manpower 284
  Purges in 16
  Strength of 5, 63, 64
Militia Cadres, Conference of 63
Miller, Corporal Douglas L. 235
Mines (and booby traps):
  Mass production of 155
  Tactical use of 186
  Types of 155
Mobile Warfare, principles of 205
Mobility 4, 172, 173
Model Anti-US Fighter 112
Multiple-Point Attack 206
Munitions:
  Cost of 285
  Production of, in Manchuria 296, 297
Model Troops 110
Model Worker's Medal 111
Modernization, of PLA:
  Dependence on technical personnel 150, 196, 197
  Lack of 3, 10-12, 281, 302, 304
  Of infantry 223
Mongol Army 96
Mongol Soldiers 81
Morale:
  In PLA 7-9, 12-15, 135
  In Nationalist Army 272
Moslem soldiers 81
Motivation, of soldier 133

INDEX

Motorization:
Backwardness in 150
Dependence on Soviet in 98
First experience in 287
Ignorance of 112
Mutual help (coach and pupil) system, in instruction 156

N

Na Chin-shuang-ho-erh, General 98
Napalm bolmbs 9
Nationalists: (see also Ex-Nationalists)
Artillerymen, US trained 253
At Battle of Ssupingkai 130
Causes of defeat of 243, 260, 261
Combat characteristics of 139
Estimated strength of, on Taiwan 315
Evaluation of, by General Wedemeyer 303
Excluded from land division 131
Fate of captured officers 277
Given "opportunity" to prove worth 131
Integration of, into PLA 273-278
Lack of leadership of 260
Logistical factors in defeat of 289
Losses during Civil War (Statistical) 273
Morale of 8
Strength of, army 303
Navy, Chinese Communist:
Amphibious vessels in 312, 315
As component of PLA 69
Lack of experience with 22
Strength of 64
Submarines in 312
New generation of soldiers 140
Nga Ben, General (Tibetan) 213
Ni Chih-liang, General 20
Nieh Jung-chen, General:
Characteristics of 35
Picture of 35, 68
Nie-meng (Inner Mongolian) Area 98
Night Attack, Principles of 206
Noncommissioned officers:
As instructors 155, 156
Characteristics of 135
Renouncing families by 140
North China Reserve Army 94
North Korea:
Cooperation of Chinese Red soldiers with troops of 278
Common purpose with Chinese Communists 278
Incorporation of troops of, in Manchurian army 279
Pact signed with, by Chinese Red 279

North Korean army:
  Modern character of 304
  Similarity of PLA to 138
  Soviet influence on 304
North Military Area 95
Northeast Aviation Headquarters 321
Northeast China Command 76, 253
Northeast Military Academy 59
Northeast Military Area 103
Northwest China PLA 79
Northwest Military Area 82

O

Obedience:
  In amphibious operations 313
  Ingrained character of 137, 138
Occupation, of cities:
  Control by police 219
  Control of installations 219
  Levying taxes 218
  Looting 218
  Orders issued for control 217
Officer, characteristics of, estimate by Commander of Formosa 317
Officer-enlisted relationship 164, 165
"One-eyed Dragon" (see Liu Po-cheng)
Operations Section, General Staff 73
Orders, combat, technique of 177
Ordnance Department, Rear Services 73
Outer Mongolia 80
Overhead, excessive (see Division slice)

P

Padding payrolls 14
Palace Guard 36, 94
Paoting Military Academy 59
Paper work 5
Parachutists, Nationalist 270
Paratroops 101, 102
Paris, University of 59
Pauley mission 245
Pay:
  Of officers 15
  Of soldiers 110, 116, 123, 267
Peasants:
  As "volunteers" 290
  Conscription of 286-290
  In Tibetan campaign 307
  Use of, in logistics 285-290
Peking 95
Peng Chen, Mayor of Peking 220
Peng Ming-chih, General 20, 94

INDEX 367

Peng Te-huai, General:
    Characteristics of (picture) 40
    Maxim of 9
People's Consultative Conference 294
People's Democratic Dictatorship 53
People's Liberation Army (PLA):
    Ability to disappear 191-193
    As a rabble 5
    Assets of 13
    Attitude toward populace 135
    Birth of 5
    Captured equipment and materiel ....
    ....6, 10, 11, 32, 81, 92, 98, 99, 101, 102, 268, 282, 284, 321, 322
    Casualties in Civil War (statistics) 274
    Casualties, in Korea 92, 179, 327
    Casualties, since 1937 327
    Chances of the crumbling of 138
    Characteristics of 139
    Composition of 90
    Daily life in 116-118
    Danger in further expansion of 284
    Defensive capability of 186
    Discipline in 16, 121, 123, 134, 250
    Division strength 63, 302, 303
    Education program in 144-147
    Esprit de corps in 134, 135
    Estimate of, by commander of Taiwan 316
    Financial problems of 12, 16, 17
    Firmness of structure of 126
    Flag of 13, 329
    Future character of 171
    Future possibilities of 304
    Generalship in 13, 21
    Growth of 10, 11, 13
    Heterogeneous character of 23
    History of 13
    How it can be defeated 327
    Illiteracy in 2, 5, 6, 143, 144
    Impression on populace 127, 130
    In invasion of Tibet 11, 33, 86, 213, 305-308
    Liabilities of 13
    Logistics of 41, 84, 93, 189, 268, 270, 281-294, 298, 299, 301, 306, 307
    Mechanization of 6, 98, 112
    Mobility of 4, 172, 173
    Modern aspects of 3, 10-12, 150, 196, 197, 223, 281, 302-304
    Morale 7-9, 12-15, 135
    On foreign soil 138
    Organization of 5, 62, 63, 67
    Plan to "liberate" Asia 241-243
    Possibility of defection, in Korea 171
    Problems at close of Civil War 10, 149

Quality of men in 134
Reorganization of 6, 16, 149
Rise to power of 243
Strength of 5, 63, 65
Tactics ...157, 164, 173, 176-178, 191-198, 213-216, 221, 256-258, 316, 326
Training 5, 123, 129, 149, 152-159, 163, 309-314, 318, 319
Unbalanced strength of 22
Variety of weapons of 5
Vigor and drive of 138
Wars fought by 13
People's Police 69
People's Political Consultative Conference 343
People's Public Security Forces 69
People's Revolutionary Military Council:
    Organization of 66, 67
    Position in Chinese Communist Party 70
People's Self-Defense Army, Manchurian 37
Period of service 123
Personnel policy:
    Lack of, by Nationalists 266
    Soundness of PLA's 267
Personnel (Unit Affairs) Section, General Staff 73
Pill box psychology 256
Pingyuan Area 95
Pioneer Youth Corps 141
PLA (see People's Liberation Army):
Plague, threat of 293
PMD anti-personnel mines 155
PMZ-40, dual purpose mine 155
Po I-po, General 98
Police, Communist, control by 133
Politburo, organizational position of 66
Political Affairs Bureau, GHQ staff 71
Political Bureau, General 69, 71, 72
Political control, by military 66, 67
Political education stations 113
Political status, of generals 60
Pond, Sergeant Clayton 190
Populace:
    Cooperation with, by Fu Tso-yi 263
    Dependence on 12
    Impression on, by PLA 127, 130
    Leadership of, in Manchuria 260
    Participation by, in money campaigns 285
    Reliance on, in Korea 183
Popular Movement's Department 72
Pratt, Fletcher 178
Premier (Chou En-lai) 45, 46
Principles of combat 201-206
Prisoners of war:
    Absorption of, Nationalist, into PLA 275-277

INDEX

    Author as a 105, 106
    As financial burdens 16
    Brutal treatment of 2, 44
    Fair treatment of 39
Prisoners of war, Chinese Communist:
    Possible defection of 138
    Return of, to PLA, recommended 170
    Typical captives (picture) 170
    Typical example of 129
Prisoners of war (US, UN):
    Attempts to indoctrinate 229, 231-234
    "Confessions" of 232
    Considerate treatment of 232, 237
    Court trial of 230
    History of policy toward 236, 237
    Interrogation of 231
    Possible fate of some 239
    Pressure on relatives 235
    Reading matter given to 233
    Segregation of officers 238
    "Signed indorsements" of 232, 235
    Production costs 17
Propaganda:
    As used by General Su Yu 34
    By women in army 132
    Extensive use of 135
    Films 163
    Use of in PLA, as estimated by commander of Taiwan 317
Propaganda Department 71
Promotion 124
Psychological warfare, Chinese Communist 228-236
Psychological warfare, US-UN:
    As surest weapon in defeating PLA 327
    In Korea (see also Safe Conduct Pass, Surrender Leaflet, Loud Speakers)
    Return of PLA prisoners as factor in 170
Psychology:
    As most effective weapon in defeating PLA 327
    Of Chinese Communists 229, 230
    Of Nationalists 256-258
    Pillbox 256
    Western, failure to understand 238
Public confession meetings 115
Pu K'e, General (picture) 83
Punishment 134
Purge:
    Ho Lung, as leader of 45
    Of militia 64
    Of Nationalists 108
    Of officers and men 6
    Scope of current purges 16, 30, 58, 142
Pusan 129

R

Radar 103, 151
Railways, reconstruction of 295
Rations, limitation of 14
Rear Services:
    Headquarters 73
    Of Second Army 84
    Organization of 72
Reconstruction, after Civil War 295, 296
Recruiting (induction, conscription):
    Attitude toward 127
    Distribution of land in 128
    In Manchuria 248, 249
    In other areas 128
    In Second Field Army 84
    In Third Field Army 88
    Of "volunteers" 127, 128
    System of 123, 127-129
    Verbatim account of, by soldier 129
Red Star, Citation Badge of the 111
Refuges, after Civil War 294
Regiment:
    Guerrilla, T/O&E 346
    Organization chart of 65
    Strength of a 63, 65
Revolutionary Military Council, People's:
    Generals serving on 61
    Organization chart of 67
    Position and authority of 66, 69
Revolutionary Soldier Committees 124
Rice patrols 216
Rifle:
    Care of, by soldier 112
    Training with 152
"Rifle-barrel" poems 114
Rifleman, uniform and equipment of 119-122
Rommel, General (German) 29, 30

S

Sadism 2, 3, 19, 43, 104, 136, 137, 220, 221, 236, 238, 239
Safe conduct pass 136, 143
Sanitation, problems of 291
Second Division, US 129, 176, 236
Second Field Army:
    Commander of (picture) 31
    Description of 83
    Strength of 62
Secret Police 69
Self-propelled weapons (see SU-76)
Seven Pillars of Wisdom, Lawrence 267
Seventh Infantry Division, US 3, 177, 196

INDEX

Seventy-fourth Army (Nationalist)	34
Shansi Area	95
Shantung Area	89
Shih-ch'u, General (picture)	86
Shiung Shih-hui, General (Nationalist)	244
Shoe (slipper)-making:	
As sign of military action	285
By civilian women	74
With "For Victory" on toes	289
Short Attack, treatise on	29, 201, 205
Sian Incident	47
Sibo soldiers	81
Sickness, in PLA	293
Sinkiang:	
Area	82
"Liberation" of	81
National People's Army	81
Sino-Soviet Treaty of Alliance	53
Sixth Field Army, PLA (projected)	95
Sixth Field Army (Nationalist)	253
Sixtieth Army (Nationalist)	91
Slippers (see Shoes)	
Slogans, use of	117
Snipers	110, 115
Soldier, Chinese Communist:	
Age average	123
As laborer	2, 117, 146, 149, 294-296
Background of	124, 125
Callousness of	106
Characteristics of	139
Chinese, as soldier material	126
Description of	106
Dissatisfaction of	106, 108
Education of	6, 140
Evaluation of, by Taiwan commander	317
Human side of	106
Lack of mechanical knowledge of	112
Indoctrination, early and late	166
Lack of sophistication of	109
Louse-ridden condition of	293
Loyalty of	106, 108
Marching ability of	139
Morale of	139
Motivation of	133
Pride in self-restraint of	135
Privileges of	123
Quality of	134
Relations with women by	113
Self-criticism by	109, 115
Stupidities of	112
Sustained by a cause	8

INDEX

Training of 134
Transfer because of language 148
Sophistication, of Nationalists 109
Soule, Major General Robert H. 183, 184, 196, 214, 228
South China, effect of PLA on 11
South China Liberation Army, staff of (picture) 77
South Military Area 85
Soviet Army, in China 82
Soviet assistance:
   Antiaircraft 103
   Arsenals 17
   Cost of 18, 285
   Equipment provided 285, 303
   Food 285
   Future influence of 304
   General 6, 37
   Heavy equipment 284
   In Manchuria 244, 245, 259
   Limitations on 152
   Motorization, mechanization 98, 103
   Munitions 296
   Providing training manuals 55
   Providing pilots in Korea 323
   Staff organization aid 74
   Submarines reported 312
   Tanks, artillery, airplanes 11, 285
   To Fourth Field Army 91
   To Fifth Field Army 95
   Training, general 207-209
   Training air pilots 321, 323
   Training officers provided 302
   Technician training 151
Soviet combat divisions, strength of 303
Soviet domination, fear of 285
Soviet Military Mission 302, 304
Soviet training manuals 159
Sparrow Tactics 214
Special Staff, PLA 74
Special Troops, PLA 76
Springfield rifle 153
Squad leader 109
Ssupingkai, Battle of 37, 97, 130, 191, 192, 254
Staff operations, on marches 174
Staff organization:
   Description of 271-276
   Inadequacy of 24
Standardization of weapons 153
State Administrative Council 68, 70
Stilwell, General Joseph 126
Strategic Problems of China's Revolutionary War 187

INDEX 373

Strategy (Strategists):
    Against Nationalists 255-261
    Chou En-lai as a 45
    Failure of, in Korea 15, 16
    Greatest mistake in 326
    Guerrilla 221-223
    Lack of 24, 25
    Mao Tse-tung as a 48-54
    Of counter-offensive 188
    Of Nationalists 255-261
    Of withdrawal 184
    With reference to US-UN 54
Strength, personnel:
    Chinese Communist Army 63
    Group army 63
    Field army 63
    Army 63
    Division 63
    Regiment 63-65
    Soviet division 63
Strength report 15
Stretcher bearers 281, 282, 286, 290
Strong points, attack on 197
Students, left-wing 21
Su Ching, General (picture) 90
SU-76, self-propelled gun 11, 102
Su Yu, General:
    Characteristics of 33
    Estimate of Nationalist strength by 315
    Picture of 86
Success, in battle, effect of 6
Sui-meng (Suiyuan-Mongolia) Area 98
Suiyan Area 98
Sun Chih-yuan, General (picture) 79
Sun Li-jen, General (Nationalist):
    Evaluation of PLA by 175, 316
    Relief of 261
Sun Tzu, principles of 49, 50, 52, 177, 184
Sun Yi, General 95
Sunday, duties on 14
Sung Shih-lun, General 89
Su-pei (North Kiangsu) Area 89
Supervisory personnel (indoctrination) 116
Supply 15
Supply Department, Rear Services 73, 74
Supply depots, looting of 248
Surrender:
    In mass 8
    Leaflets 143
    Passes 231
    Psychology of 7, 143

T

Tactics:
- Ambush 176
- Against strong points 197
- Attack the tail 216
- Based on small arms 178
- Breaking contact 194
- Bugle and gong 213
- Differences between Nationalist and PLA 256-258
- Disappearing 191-193
- Estimate of PLA, by Taiwan commander 316
- Feinting attack 192
- Flexibility of 185
- Infiltration 193
- In Korea, summary of 326
- Japanese 192
- Jointed worm 214
- Of General Fu Tso-yi 261-264
- Of the mass 198
- Of marching 173
- Of the future 186
- On wide frontage 177
- Rice patrols 216
- Small unit 178, 198
- Soviet 185, 186, 207, 208
- Sparrow 214
- Tunnel 215
- US, at military academies 164
- US, in training PLA 157
- Use of refugees in 221
- When encircled 194

Tai Ching-yuan, General (picture) 68

Taiwan (Formosa):
- PLA chances in invasion of 316
- Plans to invade 6, 11, 34, 305
- Problems connected with 15, 39, 305-308

Tan Cheng, General 12, 14, 15, 147, 274
Tan Chen-lin, General 88
Tan Hsi-lin, General 20
Tang Kuo-tung, General (picture) 86
Tanks (see Armor)
Tao Chih-Yueh, General (Nationalist) 81
Tao Chu, General 274
Tapestry Chair 105
Tapieh Mountains 33
Tartar soldiers 81
Taxes levying 218
Taylor, Col. Thomas (picture) 242

Technicians:
- Lack of 125, 150
- Training of 150

INDEX   375

Teng Hau, General 94, 190
Teng Hsiao-ping, General 85
Teng Tai-yuan, General (picture) 83
Teng Tzu-hui, General 93
Texts, military 11, 55-57
Third Division, US 183, 196
Third Field Army:
    Amphibious training of 315
    Commander of 38
    Description of 86
    Strength of 62
Third (Mechanized) Army 89
Third (Mechanized) Group Army 100
Thought control 115
Three Rules and Eight Remarks 117
Tibet, invasion of:
    By Second Field Army 33, 86
    Casualties in 308
    Combat strength of PLA in 306
    Combat tricks used in 213
    Logistics of 306, 307
    Miscalculations of 306
    Preparing for 11
    Timing of 305
Tieh Chien, General 78
Tientsin 87, 95
Ting Chih-hui, General (picture) 90
TM-38 anti-vehicular mine 155
T/O & E (Tables of organization and equipment):
    Battalion, independent guerrilla 345
    Brigade, independent guerrilla 346
    Company, independent guerrilla 344
    Division, independent guerrilla 346
    Regiment, regular forces 65
Toilets 86, 109
Tommy gunner, uniform and equipment of 120
Torture (see Sadism)
Tourtillot, Col. George P. 190
Training:
    By demonstration groups 156
    By ear 158, 159
    By films 163
    By visual aids 158
    Conventional pattern of 158
    Emphasis on infantry 152
    Evaluation of PLA, by Taiwan commander 318
    For combat 153
    In amphibious operations 309-314
    In guerrilla warfare 159
    In lower units 152
    In marksmanship 153

    Lack of 5
    Mutual help system 155
    Overconfidence in 149
    Program content of 152, 153
    Recruits 129
    Regularity of 158
    Schedules 152
    Summary of 123
    Troops for Indo-China campaign 319
Training and Military Schools Section, General Staff 73
Training films 163
Transfer, of soldiers, because of language 148
Transportation and Fuel Supply Department, Rear Services 74
Transportation:
    As factor in Nationalist defeat 269
    Present status of, motor 290
Treachery:
    Disguised as refugees 211, 212
    Disguised as women 211
    In invasion of Tibet 213
    Trojan horse technique 210
    Use of enemy dead 212
    Wearing enemy uniforms 210, 211
Trench hand bills 115
Truce group (team):
    In Manchuria 190, 193
    Chinese Communist members of 229
T'sai Shu-fan, General (picture) 83
Tseng-K'e, General (picture) 83
Tseng Sheng, General 78
Tseng Tse-cheng, General .... 90 (picture), 93
Tsinan (Chinan), Battle of 34, 269, 288
Tsinghai Area 82
Tsining, Battle of 1, 199, 200, 201
Tso Hsieh-chung, General (picture) 79
Tu Chung-fu, General (picture) 86
Tu Kuan-jen, General (picture) 79
Tunnel tactics 215
Turkish Army 9
Tu Yu-ming, General (Nationalist) 76, 92, 191, 253, 254, 261
Twenty-fourth Division, USA 7
Twenty-fifth Division, USA 170

U

Uniform, of Chinese Communist soldier 119-123
Unit Affairs Section, General Staff 73
United Nations:
    Chinese Communist representative at 20
    Forces, ambushed 176
    Mao's strategy concerning 54

Propaganda against 169
Strategy in Korea 195-197
Troops resisting bugle and gong technique 213

UNRRA:
    Report by representative in Manchuria 340
    Supplies furnished by 246
United States Army:
    Communist guerrilla transported by 78
    Firepower envied by PLA 9
United States Military Advisory Group 267
United States policy in Manchuria 260
United States Seventh Fleet 308
Unit funds 116, 119
Unit TO&E, guerrilla 344
Université de Travail 35, 59
Urination Corps 104

V

Van Fleet, General James A. 299
Veterans, serving in PLA 124
Victory, basic methods of achieving 204
Victory of the Chinese People (film) 163
Vigor and drive of PLA 138
Visual aids, in training 158

W

Waders of the Yangtze 83
Wan Yi, General 94
Wang Chao, General (picture) 79
Wang Chen, General 82, 193
Wang Cheng, General (picture) 68
Wang Ch'ien-an, General .... 86 (picture), 89, 309
Wang Chi-ming, General 85
Wang Ching-hsiu, General 94
Wang Pei-huan, General 220
Wang Shang-hsieh, General 82
Wang Shih-t'ai, General (picture) 79
Wang Tsai-tien, General 98
Wang Yueh-feng, General 98
Wang Yu-ping, General 20
"War of Liberation" 88
War service workers, in logistics 289
Weapons:
    Cost of 285
    Variety of 284
Wedemeyer, Lt. Gen. Albert C. 303
Wei Hsiao-t'ang, General (picture) 83
Wei Lai-kuo, General (picture) 86
Wei Lai-kuo, super-sniper 115
Wei Li-huang, General (Nationalist) 261, 263, 271
Whampoa Military Academy 59

Women in the army:
  Appearance of 131
  As walking blood banks 132
  In the Air Force 132
  Jobs performed by 132
  Morals of 133
  Personnel strength of 133
  "Special Services" activities 132
  Uniform of 132
Women, soldier's relations with 113
Women, peasant, working for army 285
Worden, William L. 221
Wright, Col. Mason (picture) 242
Wu Chí-wei, General (picture) 77
Wu Hsiu-chuan, General 20
Wu Yu-heng, General 78
Wutai Mountains 36

Y

YaM-5 anti-tank mine 155
Yang Cheng-wu, General .... (picture) 68, 94
Yang Ch'i-ch'ing, General (picture) 68
Yang Li-san, General (picture) 83
Yang Shang-kun 54
Yang Te-chih, General 82
Yang Yung, General 85
Yangtze River, amphibious crossing of 311
Yao Che, General 98
Year of the Tiger 12
Yeh Chien-ying, General .... 57 (picture), 94, 96, (picture) 242
Yeh Fei, General 89
Yen Hsi-shan, Marshall (Nationalist) 124, 159
Yenan, Caves of .... 16, 22, 47, 80, 161, (picture) 242
Yuan Chung-hsien, General 20
Yun Tse, General 97, 98
Yunnan Military Academy 59
Yunnan Area 85